PRAISE FOR
THE VALUE OF EVERYTHING

Winner of the 2018 Leontief Prize for Advancing
the Frontiers of Economic Thought

Shortlisted for the *FT* and McKinsey Business
Book of the Year 2018

'Offers a fundamental re-think of what constitutes
real value in the economy' *Forbes*

'A restless thinker . . . Mazzucato's mission is to overturn the
now dominant neoclassical theory of value . . . Mazzucato is
seeking to recreate the dynamic public-private interaction – and
the spirit of adventure – that led to triumphs such
as the moon landings' *New Statesman*

'The normally iron-clad security of shareholder value is
challenged as a material motivator, a theme further explored by
Mariana Mazzucato in The Value of Everything, who argues
that we urgently need to rethink where wealth comes
from to heal a sick system' *Management Today*

'Essential reading' *FT Magazine*

'Mazzucato calls for nothing less than a
complete reconsideration of our system of
economic values' *New Statesman*

'Her target is the conventional wisdom that so-called wealth
creators deserve to accumulate massive riches. Mazzucato
sides with the actual makers, those who struggle in an
economy tilted in favour of the ultrawealthy . . . She is
especially eloquent when commenting on arrogant
tech-giant billionaires' *Kirkus Reviews*

'She excoriates the global financial industry. We need to
rethink our ideas on value, and how financialisation
has turned us away from value creation to
value extraction' *Business Live*

'Mazzucato notes that the rise of entrepreneurship, along
with the past deregulation of financial industries, is
fueling the fire of economic inequality and an
economy without value' *Booklist*

The Value of
EVERYTHING

MAKING *and* TAKING
in the GLOBAL ECONOMY

MARIANA MAZZUCATO

PUBLICAFFAIRS
New York

PublicAffairs
Hachette Book Group
1290 Avenue of the Americas, New York, NY 10104
www.publicaffairsbooks.com
@Public_Affairs

First published in Great Britain in 2018 by Allen Lane, an imprint of Penguin Random House UK.

First US Edition: September 2018
First Trade Paperback Edition: May 2020

Published by PublicAffairs, an imprint of Perseus Books, LLC, a subsidiary of Hachette Book Group, Inc. The PublicAffairs name and logo is a trademark of the Hachette Book Group.

The Hachette Speakers Bureau provides a wide range of authors for speaking events. To find out more, go to www.hachettespeakersbureau.com or call (866) 376-6591.

The publisher is not responsible for websites (or their content) that are not owned by the publisher.

The illustration on p. 230 is by Jon Berkeley for The Economist. Reproduced by permission.

Typeset Sabon LT Std by Jouve (UK), Milton Keynes

Library of Congress Control Number: 2018950683

ISBNs: 978-1-61039-674-5 (hardcover), 978-1-5471-5824-7 (paperback), 978-1-61039-675-2 (ebook)

10 9 8 7 6 5 4 3 2 1

For Leon, Micol, Luce and Sofia

Contents

Acknowledgements	xi
Preface: Stories About Wealth Creation	xiii
Introduction: Making versus Taking	1
Common Critiques of Value Extraction	4
What is Value?	6
Meet the Production Boundary	8
Why Value Theory Matters	11
The Structure of the Book	15
1. A Brief History of Value	21
The Mercantilists: Trade and Treasure	22
The Physiocrats: The Answer Lies in the Soil	28
Classical Economics: Value in Labour	33
2. Value in the Eye of the Beholder: The Rise of the Marginalists	57
New Times, New Theory	58
The Eclipse of the Classicals	59
From Objective to Subjective: A New Theory of Value Based on Preferences	60
The Rise of the 'Neoclassicals'	62
The Disappearance of Rent and Why it Matters	71
3. Measuring the Wealth of Nations	75
GDP: A Social Convention	76
The System of National Accounts Comes into Being	83

Measuring Government Value Added in GDP 85

Something Odd About the National Accounts: GDP Facit Saltus! 90

Patching Up the National Accounts isn't Enough 98

4. Finance: A Colossus is Born 101

Banks and Financial Markets Become Allies 103

The Banking Problem 104

Deregulation and the Seeds of the Crash 110

The Lords of (Money) Creation 115

Finance and the 'Real' Economy 117

From Claims on Profit to Claims on Claims 122

A Debt in the Family 127

5. The Rise of Casino Capitalism 135

Prometheus (with a Pilot's Licence) Unbound 137

New Actors in the Economy 142

How Finance Extracts Value 146

6. Financialization of the Real Economy 161

The Buy-back Blowback 162

Maximizing Shareholder Value 165

The Retreat of 'Patient' Capital 171

Short-Termism and Unproductive Investment 174

Financialization and Inequality 177

From Maximizing Shareholder Value to Stakeholder Value 183

7. Extracting Value through the Innovation Economy 189

Stories about Value Creation 189

Where Does Innovation Come From? 191

Financing Innovation 195

CONTENTS

Patented Value Extraction   202

Unproductive Entrepreneurship   206

Pricing Pharmaceuticals   207

Network Effects and First-mover Advantages   213

Creating and Extracting Digital Value   219

Sharing Risks and Rewards   222

8. Undervaluing the Public Sector   229

The Myths of Austerity   233

Government Value in the History of Economic Thought   239

Keynes and Counter-cyclical Government   241

Government in the National Accounts   245

Public Choice Theory: Rationalizing
    Privatization and Outsourcing   249

Regaining Confidence and Setting Missions   259

Public and Private Just Deserts   263

From Public Goods to Public Value   264

9. The Economics of Hope   270

Markets as Outcomes   274

Take the Economy on a Mission   277

A Better Future for All   279

Bibliography   281

Notes   297

Index   331

Acknowledgements

In 2013 I wrote a book called *The Entrepreneurial State*. In it I debunked how myths about lone entrepreneurs and start-ups have captured the theory and practice of innovation, ignoring one of the key actors that has been an investor of first resort: the state. Innovation is a collective process, with different types of public institutions playing a pivotal role. That role is ignored, so our theory of value creation is flawed. And this is a major reason for wealth often being distributed in dysfunctional ways.

The book you have in your hand is a direct consequence of this early reasoning. We cannot understand economic growth if we do not go back to the beginning: what is wealth and where does value come from? Are we sure that much of what is passing for value creation is not just value extraction in disguise?

To write the book I needed to delve into the last 300 years of thinking about value. No easy task! Many people very kindly helped me achieve this daunting task – from the deep dive into theory to swimming in the richness of industrial stories.

I would like to thank Gregor Semieniuk, who like me received a PhD from the Graduate Faculty of the New School in New York – a rare place that still teaches alternative theories of economic thought. He generously shared his extraordinary knowledge about value theory, from the physiocrats to the classicals. Gregor was a tremendous support in helping me document, in a 'user-friendly' way, the debates between the Physiocrats, Smith and Ricardo – and the strange fact that even Marx had no real theory of the way in which the state can contribute to value.

Michael Prest provided expert and endlessly patient editorial assistance, using his magic pen to make the often too dense material flow much better. He cheerfully cycled to our meetings on even the hottest days of the year and was not just a friendly editor but also a great companion, bringing calm to what often felt like hectic months trying to finish a book while I was raising a large family and starting up a new department at UCL. Our weekly meetings in the Lord Stanley pub in Camden to pore over the material often trailed off into a stream of consciousness dwelling on the ills of modern capitalism – and were nothing but pure joy. With the occasional pint (or two) to keep us going.

Other critical friends include Carlota Perez, who provided me with her wise insights not only on content but also on style, and the following people, who looked at particular chapters in the book and double checked it for errors in its final stages, selflessly offering their wisdom and care: (in alphabetical order) Matteo Deleidi, Lukas Fuchs Tommaso Gabellini, Simone Gasperin, Edward Hadas, Andrea Laplane, Alain Rizk, and Josh Ryan Collins. Of course, any errors, or strongly opinionated statements, can be attributed only to me.

My editor Tom Penn at Penguin was a great sounding board during our endless coffee-filled meetings at the British Library – having the rare qualities of a meticulous proofreader while also retaining a deep engagement with the content, both economic and philosophical.

I also want to thank the excellent administrative assistance I have had over the last four years, first at SPRU in the University of Sussex and now in a new institute that I have founded at UCL, the Institute for Innovation and Public Purpose IIPP). Gemma Smith in particular has helped me always try to get messages across – whether on the 10 o'clock news or in a policy brief – that could be understood by the general public. With the new team at IIPP, I hope the book's message about the need for revived debate about key questions around value can be linked with the IIPP's ambition to redefine ways of conceptualizing public value in particular: how to create it, nurture it and evaluate it.

Lastly, I want to thank Carlo, Leon, Micol, Luce and Sofia for putting up with the many long nights and weekends that the book entailed – letting me climb up the stairs and plop myself down to the most happy and conversive dinner table a wife and mother can ask for – putting life back at the centre, where it should be.

Preface: Stories About Wealth Creation

Between 1975 and 2017 real US GDP – the size of the economy adjusted for inflation – roughly tripled, from $5.49 trillion to $17.29 trillion.[1] During this period, productivity grew by about 60 per cent. Yet from 1979 onwards, real hourly wages for the great majority of American workers have stagnated or even fallen.[2] In other words, for almost four decades a tiny elite has captured nearly all the gains from an expanding economy. Is this because they are particularly productive members of society?

The Greek philosopher Plato once argued that storytellers rule the world. His great work *The Republic* was in part a guide to educating the leader of his ideal state, the Guardian. This book questions the stories we are being told about who the wealth creators are in modern-day capitalism, stories about which activities are productive as opposed to unproductive, and thus where value creation comes from. It questions the effect these stories are having on the ability of the few to extract more from the economy in the name of wealth creation.

These stories are everywhere. The contexts may differ – finance, big pharma or big tech – but the self-descriptions are similar: I am a particularly productive member of the economy, my activities create wealth, I take big 'risks', and so I deserve a higher income than people who simply benefit from the spillovers of this activity. But what if, in the end, these descriptions are simply just stories? Narratives created in order to justify inequalities of wealth and income, massively rewarding the few who are able to convince governments and society that they deserve high rewards, while the rest make do with the leftovers. Consider some of these stories, first in the financial sector.

In 2009 Lloyd Blankfein, CEO of Goldman Sachs, claimed that

'The people of Goldman Sachs are among the most productive in the world.'[3] Yet, just the year before, Goldman had been a major contributor to the worst financial and economic crisis since the 1930s. US taxpayers had to stump up $125 billion to bail it out. In light of the terrible performance of the investment bank just a year before, such a bullish statement by the CEO was extraordinary. The bank laid off 3,000 employees between November 2007 and December 2009, and profits plunged.[4] The bank and some its competitors were fined, although the amounts were small relative to later profits: fines of $550 million for Goldman and $297 million for J. P. Morgan, for example.[5] Despite everything, Goldman – along with other banks and hedge funds – proceeded to bet against the very instruments which they had created and which had led to such turmoil.

Although there was much talk about punishing those banks that had contributed to the crisis, no banker was jailed, and the changes hardly dented the banks' ability to continue making money from speculation: between 2009 and 2016 Goldman achieved net earnings of $63 billion on net revenues of $250 billion.[6] In 2009 alone they had record earnings of $13.4 billion.[7] And although the US government saved the banking system with taxpayers' money, the government did not have the confidence to demand a fee from the banks for such high-risk activity. It was simply happy, in the end, to get its money back.

Financial crises, of course, are not new. Yet Blankfein's exuberant confidence in his bank would have been less common half a century ago. Until the 1960s, finance was not widely considered a 'productive' part of the economy. It was viewed as important for transferring existing wealth, not creating new wealth. Indeed, economists were so convinced about the purely facilitating role of finance that they did not even include most of the services that banks performed, such as taking in deposits and giving out loans, in their calculations of how many goods and services are produced by the economy. Finance sneaked into their measurements of Gross Domestic Product (GDP) only as an 'intermediate input' – a service contributing to the functioning of other industries that were the real value creators.

In around 1970, however, things started to change. The national accounts – which provide a statistical picture of the size, composition and direction of an economy – began to include the financial sector in their calculations of GDP, the total value of the goods and services produced by the economy in question.[8] This change in accounting coincided with the deregulation of the financial sector which, among other things, relaxed controls on how much banks could lend, the interest rates they could charge and the products they could sell. Together, these changes fundamentally altered how the financial sector behaved, and increased its influence on the 'real' economy. No longer was finance seen as a staid career. Instead, it became a fast track for smart people to make a great deal of money. Indeed, after the Berlin Wall fell in 1989, some of the cleverest scientists in Eastern Europe ended up going to work for Wall Street. The industry expanded, grew more confident. It openly lobbied to advance its interests, claiming that finance was critical for wealth creation.

Today the issue is not just the size of the financial sector, and how it has outpaced the growth of the non-financial economy (e.g. industry), but its effect on the behaviour of the rest of the economy, large parts of which have been 'financialized'. Financial operations and the mentality they breed pervade industry, as can be seen when managers choose to spend a greater proportion of profits on share buy-backs – which in turn boost stock prices, stock options and the pay of top executives – than on investing in the long-term future of the business. They call it value creation but, as in the financial sector itself, the reality is often the opposite: value extraction.

But these stories of value creation are not limited to finance. In 2014 the pharmaceutical giant Gilead priced its new treatment for the life-threatening hepatitis C virus, Harvoni, at $94,500 for a three-month course. Gilead justified charging this price by insisting that it represented 'value' to health systems. John LaMattina, former President of R&D at the drugs company Pfizer, argued that the high price of speciality drugs is justified by how beneficial they are for patients and for society in general. In practice, this means relating the price of a drug to the costs that the disease would cause to society if not treated, or if treated with the second-best therapy available. The industry calls this 'value-based pricing'. It's an argument refuted by critics, who cite case studies that show no correlation between the price of cancer drugs and the benefits they provide.[9] One interactive calculator (www.drugabacus.org), which enables you to establish the 'correct' price of a cancer drug on the basis of its valuable character-istics (the increase in life expectancy it provides to patients, its side effects, and so on), shows that for most drugs this value-based price is lower than the current market price.[10]

Yet drug prices are not falling. It seems that the industry's value creation arguments have successfully neutralized criticism. Indeed, a high proportion of health care costs in the Western world has nothing to do with health care: these costs are simply the value the pharma-ceutical industry extracts.

Or consider the stories in the tech industry. In the name of favour-ing entrepreneurship and innovation, companies in the IT industry have often lobbied for less regulation and advantageous tax treat-ments. With 'innovation' as the new force in modern capitalism, Silicon Valley has successfully projected itself as the entrepreneurial force behind wealth creation – unleashing the 'creative destruction' from which the jobs of the future come.

This seductive story of value creation has lead to lower rates of capital gains tax for the venture capitalists funding the tech compa-nies, and questionable tax policies like the 'patent box', which reduces tax on profits from the sale of products whose inputs are patented, supposedly to incentivize innovation by rewarding the generation of intellectual property. It's a policy that makes little sense, as patents are already instruments that allow monopoly profits for twenty years, thus earning high returns. Policymakers' objectives should not be to increase the profits from monopolies, but to favour the reinvestment of those profits in areas like research.

Many of the so-called wealth creators in the tech industry, like the co-founder of Pay Pal, Peter Thiel, often lambast government as a pure impediment to wealth creation.[11] Thiel went so far as to set up a 'seces-sionist movement' in California so that the wealth creators could be as independent as possible from the heavy hand of government. And Eric Schmidt, CEO of Google, has repeatedly claimed that citizens' data is safer with Google than with government. This stance feeds a modern-day banality: entrepreneurs good, government bad – or inept.

Yet in presenting themselves as modern-day heroes, and justifying their record profits and cash mountains, Apple and other companies conveniently ignore the pioneering role of government in new technologies. Apple has unashamedly declared that its contribution to society should not be sought through tax but through recognition of its great gizmos. But where did the smart tech behind those gizmos come from? Public funds. The Internet, GPS, touchscreen, SIRI and the algorithm behind Google – all were funded by public institutions. Shouldn't the taxpayer thus get something back, beyond a series of undoubtedly brilliant gadgets? Simply to pose this question, however, underlines how we need a radically different type of narrative as to who created the wealth in the first place – and who has subsequently extracted it.

And yet – where does government fit into these stories of wealth creation. If there are so many wealth creators in industry, the inevitable conclusion is that at the opposite side of the spectrum featuring fleet-footed bankers, science-based pharmaceuticals and entrepreneurial geeks are the inert, value-extracting civil servants and bureaucrats in government. In this view, if private enterprise is the fast cheetah bringing innovation to the world, government is a plodding tortoise impeding progress – or, to invoke a different metaphor, a Kafkaesque bureaucrat, buried under papers, cumbersome and inefficient. Government is depicted as a drain on society, funded by obligatory taxes on long-suffering citizens. In this story, there is always only one conclusion: that we need more market and less state. The slimmer, trimmer and more efficient the state machine the better.

In all these cases, from finance to pharmaceuticals and IT, governments bend over backwards to attract these supposedly value-creating individuals and companies, dangling before them tax reductions and exemptions from the red tape that is believed to constrict their wealth-creating energies. The media heap wealth creators with praise, politicians court them, and for many people they are high-status figures to be admired and emulated. But who decided that they are creating value? What definition of value is used to distinguish value creation from value extraction, or even from value destruction?

Why have we so readily believed this narrative of good versus bad? How is the value produced by the public sector measured, and why is it more often than not treated simply as a more inefficient version of the private sector? What if there was actually no evidence for this story at all? What if it stemmed purely from a set of deeply ingrained ideas? What new stories might we tell?

Plato recognized that stories form character, culture and behaviour: 'Our first business is to supervise the production of stories, and chose only those we think suitable, and reject the rest. We shall persuade mothers and nurses to tell our chosen stories to their children, and by means of them to mould their minds and characters rather than their bodies. The greater part of the stories current today we shall have to reject.'[12]

Plato disliked myths about ill-behaved gods. This book looks at a more modern myth, about value creation in the economy. Such myth-making, I argue, has allowed an immense amount of value extraction, enabling some individuals to become very rich and draining societal wealth in the process.

The purpose of this book is to change this state of things, and to do so by reinvigorating the debate about value that used to be – and, I argue, should still be – at the core of economic thinking. If value is defined by price – set by the supposed forces of supply and demand – then as long as an activity fetches a price, it is seen as creating value. So if you earn a lot you must be a value creator. I will argue that the way the word 'value' is used in modern economics has made it easier for value-extracting activities to masquerade as value-creating activities. And in the process rents (unearned income) get confused with profits (earned income); inequality rises, and investment in the real economy falls. What's more, if we cannot differentiate value creation from value extraction, it becomes nearly impossible to reward the former over the latter. If the goal is to produce growth that is more innovation-led (smart growth), more inclusive and more sustainable, we need a better understanding of value to steer us.

In other words, this is not an abstract debate but one with far-reaching consequences – social and political as well as economic – for everyone. How we discuss value affects the way all of us, from giant corporations to the most modest shopper, behave as actors in the economy and in turn feeds back into the economy, and how we measure its performance. This is what philosophers call 'performativity':

how we talk about things affects behaviour, and in turn how we theorize things. In other words, it is a self-fulfilling prophecy.

Oscar Wilde famously captured the value problem when he said that a cynic is one who knows the price of everything but the *value of nothing*. He was right – and indeed economics is known as the cynical science. But it is exactly for this reason that change in our economic system must be underpinned by bringing value back to the centre of our thinking – we need a revived ability to contest the way the word value is used, keeping alive the debate, and not allowing simple stories to affect who we think is productive and who is unproductive. Where do those stories come from – in whose interests are they told? If we cannot define what we mean by value, we cannot be sure to produce it, nor to share it fairly, nor to sustain economic growth. The understanding of value, then, is critical to all the other conversations we need to have about where our economy is going and how to change its course. And only then can economics go from being a cynical science to a hopeful one.

Introduction:
Making versus Taking

The barbarous gold barons – they did not find the gold, they did not mine the gold, they did not mill the gold, but by some weird alchemy all the gold belonged to them.

Big Bill Haywood, founder of the
Unites States' first industrial union, 1929[1]

Bill Haywood expressed his puzzlement eloquently. He represented men and women in the US mining industry at the start of the twentieth century and during the Great Depression of the 1930s. He was steeped in the industry. But even Haywood could not answer the question: why did the owners of capital, who did little but buy and sell gold on the market, make so much money, while workers who expended their mental and physical energy to find it, mine it and mill it, make so little? Why were the *takers* making so much money at the expense of the *makers*?

Similar questions are still being asked today. In 2016 the British high-street retailer BHS collapsed. It had been founded in 1928 and in 2004 was bought by Sir Philip Green, a well-known retail entrepreneur, for £200 million. In 2015 Sir Philip sold the business for £1 to a group of investors headed by the British businessman Dominic Chappell. While it was under his control, Sir Philip and his family extracted from BHS an estimated £580 million in dividends, rental payments and interest on loans they had made to the company. The collapse of BHS threw 11,000 people out of work and left its pension fund with a £571 million deficit, even though the fund had been in surplus when Sir Philip acquired it.[2] A report on the BHS disaster by the House of Commons Work and Pensions Select Committee accused Sir Philip, Mr Chappell and their 'hangers-on' of 'systematic plunder'. For BHS workers and pensioners who depended on the company for a decent living for their families, this was value extraction – the appropriation of gains vastly out of proportion to economic contribution – on an epic scale. For Sir Philip and others who controlled the business, it was value creation.

While Sir Philip's activities could be viewed as an aberration, the excesses of an individual, his way of thinking is hardly unusual: today, many giant corporations are also guilty of confusing value creation with value extraction. In August 2016, for instance, the European Commission, the European Union's (EU) executive arm, sparked an international row between the EU and the US when it ordered Apple to pay €13 billion in back taxes to Ireland.[3]

Apple is the world's biggest company by stock market value. In 2015 it held a mountain of cash and securities outside the US worth $187 billion[4] – about the same size as the Czech Republic's economy that year[5] – to avoid paying the US taxes that would be due on the profits if they were repatriated. Under a deal with Ireland dating back to 1991, two Irish subsidiaries of Apple received very generous tax treatment. The subsidiaries were Apple Sales International (ASI), which recorded all the profits earned on sales of iPhones and other Apple devices in Europe, the Middle East, Africa and India; and Apple Operations Europe, which made computers. Apple transferred development rights of its products to ASI for a nominal amount, thereby depriving the US taxpayer of revenues from technologies, embodied in Apple products, whose early development the taxpayer had funded. The European Commission alleged that the maximum rate payable on those profits booked through Ireland which were liable for tax was 1 per cent, but that in 2014 Apple paid tax at 0.005 per cent. The usual rate of corporation tax in Ireland is 12.5 per cent.

What is more, these 'Irish' subsidiaries of Apple are in fact not resident for tax purposes anywhere. This is because they have exploited discrepancies between the Irish and US definitions of residence. Almost all the profits earned by the subsidiaries were allocated to their 'head offices', which existed only on paper. The Commission ordered Apple to pay the back taxes on the grounds that Ireland's deal with Apple constituted illegal state aid (government support that gives a company an advantage over its competitors); Ireland had not offered other companies similar terms. Ireland, the Commission alleged, had offered Apple ultra-low taxes in return for the creation of jobs in other Apple businesses there. Apple and Ireland rejected the Commission's demand – and of course Apple is not the only major corporation to have constructed exotic tax structures.

But Apple's value extraction cycle is not limited to its international tax operations – it is also much closer to home. Not only did Apple extract value from Irish taxpayers, but the Irish government has extracted value from the US taxpayer. Why so? Apple created its intellectual property in California, where its headquarters are based. Indeed, as I argued in my previous book, *The Entrepreneurial State,*[6] and discuss briefly here in Chapter 7, all the technology that makes the smartphone smart was publicly funded. But in 2006 Apple formed a subsidiary in Reno, Nevada, where there is no corporate income or capital gains tax, in order to avoid state taxes in California. Creatively naming it Braeburn Capital, Apple channelled a portion of its US profits to the Nevada subsidiary instead of reporting it in California. Between 2006 and 2012, Apple earned $2.5 billion in interest and dividends reported in Nevada to avoid Californian tax. California's infamously large debt would be significantly reduced if Apple fully and accurately reported its US revenues in that state, where a major portion of its value (architecture, design, sales, marketing and so on) originated. Value extraction thus pits US states against each other, as well as the US against other countries.

It is clear that Apple's highly complex tax arrangements were principally designed to extract the maximum value from its business by avoiding paying substantial taxes which would have benefited the societies in which the company operated. Apple certainly creates value, of that there is no doubt: but to ignore the support taxpayers have given it, and then to pit states and countries against each other, is surely not the way to build an innovative economy or achieve growth that is inclusive, that benefits a wide section of the population, not only those best able to 'game' the system.

There is yet another dimension to Apple's value extraction. Many such corporations use their profits to boost share prices in the short term instead of reinvesting them in production for the long term. The main way they do this is by using cash reserves to buy back shares from investors, arguing that this is to maximize shareholder 'value' (the income earned by shareholders in the company, based on the valuation of the company's stock price). But it is no accident that among the primary beneficiaries of share buy-backs are managers with generous share option schemes as part of their remuneration packages – the same managers who implement the share buy-back programmes. In 2012, for example, Apple announced a share buy-back programme of up to a staggering $100 billion, partly to ward off 'activist' shareholders demanding that the company return cash to them to 'unlock shareholder value'.[7] Rather than reinvest in the business, Apple preferred to transfer cash to shareholders.

The alchemy of the takers versus the makers that Big Bill Haywood referred to back in the 1920s continues today.

COMMON CRITIQUES OF VALUE EXTRACTION

The vital but often muddled distinction between value extraction and value creation has consequences far beyond the fate of companies and their workers, or even of whole societies. The social, economic and political impacts of value extraction are huge. Prior to the 2007 financial crisis, the income share of the top 1 per cent in the US expanded from 9.4 per cent in 1980 to a staggering 22.6 per cent in 2007. And things are only getting worse. Since 2009 inequality has been increasing even more rapidly than before the 2008 financial crash. In 2015 the combined wealth of the planet's sixty-two richest individuals was estimated to be about the same as that of the bottom half of the world's population – 3.5 billion people.[8]

So how does the alchemy continue to happen? A common critique of contemporary capitalism is that it rewards 'rent seekers' over true 'wealth creators'. 'Rent-seeking' here refers to the attempt to generate income, not by producing anything new but by overcharging above the 'competitive price', and undercutting competition by exploiting particular advantages (including labour), or, in the case of an industry with large firms, their ability to block other companies from entering that industry, thereby retaining a monopoly advantage. Rent-seeking activity is often described in other ways: the 'takers' winning out over the 'makers', and 'predatory' capitalism winning over 'productive' capitalism. It's seen as a key way – perhaps *the* key way – in which the 1 per cent have risen to power over the 99 per cent.[9] The usual targets of such criticism are the banks and other financial institutions. They are seen as profiting from speculative activities based on little more than buying low and selling high, or buying and then stripping productive assets simply to sell them on again with no real value added.

More sophisticated analyses have linked rising inequality to the particular way in which the 'takers' have increased their wealth. The French economist Thomas Piketty's influential book *Capital in the Twenty-First Century* focuses on the inequality created by a predatory financial industry that is taxed insufficiently, and by ways in which wealth is inherited across generations, which gives the richest a head start in getting even richer. Piketty's analysis is key to understanding why the rate of return on financial assets (which he calls capital) has been higher than that on growth, and calls for higher taxes on the resultant wealth and inheritance to stop the vicious circle. Ideally, from his point of view, taxes of this sort should be global, so as to avoid one country undercutting another.

Another leading thinker, the US economist Joseph Stiglitz, has explored how weak regulation and monopolistic practices have allowed what economists call 'rent extraction', which he sees as the main impetus behind the rise of the 1 per cent in the US.[10] For Stiglitz, this rent is the income obtained by creating impediments to other businesses, such as barriers to prevent new companies from entering a sector, or deregulation that has allowed finance to become disproportionately large in relation to the rest of the economy. The assumption is that, with fewer impediments to the functioning of economic competition, there will be a more equal distribution of income.[11]

I think we can go even further with these 'makers' versus 'takers' analyses of why our economy, with its glaring inequalities of income and wealth, has gone so wrong. To understand how some are perceived as 'extracting value', siphoning wealth away from national economies, while others are 'wealth creators' but do not benefit from that wealth, it is not enough to look at impediments to an idealized form of perfect competition. Yet mainstream ideas about rent do not fundamentally challenge how value extraction occurs – which is why it persists.

In order to tackle these issues at root, we need to examine where *value* comes from in the first place. What exactly is it that is being extracted? What social, economic and organizational conditions are needed for value to be produced? Even Stiglitz's and Piketty's use of the term 'rent' to analyse inequality will be influenced by their idea of what value is and what it represents. Is rent simply an impediment to 'free-market' exchange? Or is it due to their positions of power that some can earn 'unearned income' – that is, income derived from moving existing assets around rather than creating new ones?[12] This is a key question we will look at in Chapter 2.

WHAT IS VALUE?

Value can be defined in different ways, but at its heart it is the production of new goods and services. How these outputs are produced (production), how they are shared across the economy (distribution) and what is done with the earnings that are created from their production (reinvestment) are key questions in defining economic value. Also crucial is whether what it is that is being created is useful: are the products and services being created increasing or decreasing the resilience of the productive system? For example, it might be that a new factory is produced that is valuable economically, but if it pollutes so much to destroy the system around it, it could be seen as not valuable.

By 'value creation' I mean the ways in which different types of resources (human, physical and intangible) are established and interact to produce new goods and services. By 'value extraction' I mean activities focused on moving around existing resources and outputs, and gaining disproportionately from the ensuing trade.

A note of caution is important. In the book I use the words 'wealth' and 'value' almost interchangeably. Some might argue against this, seeing wealth as a more monetary and value as potentially a more social concept, involving not only *value* but *values*. I want to be clear on how these two words are used. I use 'value' in terms of the 'process' by which wealth is created – it is a flow. This flow of course results in actual things, whether tangible (a loaf of bread) or intangible (new knowledge). 'Wealth' instead is regarded as a cumulative stock of the value already created. The book focuses on value and what forces produce it – the process. But it also looks at the claims around this process, which are often phrased in terms of 'who' the wealth creators are. In this sense the words are used interchangeably.

For a long time the idea of value was at the heart of debates about the economy, production and the distribution of the resulting income, and there were healthy disagreements over what value actually resided in. For some economic schools of thought, the price of products resulted from supply and demand, but the value of those products derived from the amount of work that was needed to produce things, the ways in which technological and organizational changes were affecting work, and the relations between capital and labour. Later, this emphasis on 'objective' conditions of production, technology and power relationships was replaced by concepts of scarcity and the 'preferences' of economic actors: the amount of work supplied is determined by workers' preference for leisure over earning a higher amount of money. Value, in other words, became *subjective*.

Until the mid-nineteenth century, too, almost all economists assumed that in order to understand the prices of goods and services it was first necessary to have an objective theory of value, a theory tied to the conditions in which those goods and services were produced, including the time needed to produce them, the quality of the labour employed; and the determinants of 'value' actually shaped the price of goods and services. Then, this thinking began to go into reverse. Many economists came to believe that the value of things was determined by the price paid on the 'market' – or, in other words, what the consumer was prepared to pay. All of a sudden, value was in the eye of the beholder. Any goods or services being sold at an agreed market price were by definition value-creating.

The swing from value determining price to price determining value coincided with major social changes at the end of the nineteenth century. One was the rise of socialism, which partly based its demands for reforms on the claim that labour was not being rewarded fairly for the value it created, and the ensuing consolidation of a capitalist class of producers. The latter group was, unsurprisingly, keen on the alternative theory, that price determined value, a story which allowed them to defend their appropriation of a larger share of output, with labour increasingly being left behind.

In the intellectual world, economists wanted to make their discipline seem 'scientific' – more like physics and less like sociology – with the result that they dispensed with its earlier political and social connotations. While Adam Smith's writings were full of politics and philosophy, as well as early thinking about how the economy works, by the early twentieth century the field which for 200 years had been 'political economy' emerged cleansed as simply 'economics'. And economics told a very different story.

Eventually the debate about different theories of value and the dynamics of value creation virtually vanished from economics departments, only showing up in business schools in a very new form: 'shareholder value',[13] 'shared value',[14] 'value chains',[15] 'value for money', 'valuation', 'adding value' and the like. So while economics students used to get a rich and varied education in the idea of value, learning what different schools of economic thought had to say about it, today they are taught only that value is determined by the dynamics of price, due to scarcity and preferences. This is not presented as a particular theory of value – just as Economics 101, the introduction to the subject. An intellectually impoverished idea of value is just taken as read, assumed simply to be true. And the disappearance of the concept of value, this book argues, has paradoxically made it much easier for this crucial term 'value' – a concept that lies at the heart of economic thought – to be used and abused in whatever way one might find useful.

MEET THE PRODUCTION BOUNDARY

To understand how different theories of value have evolved over the centuries, it is useful to consider why and how some activities in the economy have been called 'productive' and some 'unproductive', and how this distinction has influenced ideas about which economic actors deserve what – how the spoils of value creation are distributed.

For centuries, economists and policymakers – people who set a plan for an organization such as government or a business – have divided activities according to whether they produce value or not; that is, whether they are productive or unproductive. This has essentially created a boundary – the fence in Figure 1 below – thereby establishing a conceptual boundary – sometimes referred to as a 'production boundary' – between these activities.[16] Inside the boundary are the wealth creators. Outside are the beneficiaries of that wealth, who benefit either because they can extract it through rent-seeking activities, as in the case of a monopoly, or because wealth created in the productive area is redistributed to them, for example through modern welfare policies. Rents, as understood by the classical economists, were *unearned* income and fell squarely outside the production boundary. Profits were instead the returns earned for productive activity inside the boundary.

Historically, the boundary fence has not been fixed. Its shape and size have shifted with social and economic forces. These changes in the boundary between makers and takers can be seen just as clearly in the past as in the modern era. In the eighteenth century there was an outcry when the physiocrats, an early school of economists, called landlords 'unproductive'. This was an attack on the ruling class of a mainly rural Europe. The politically explosive question was whether

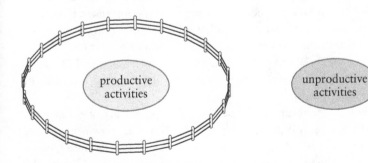

Figure 1. Production boundary around the value-producing activities of the economy

landlords were just abusing their power to extract part of the wealth created by their tenant farmers, or whether their contribution of land was essential to the way in which farmers created value.

A variation of this debate about where to draw the production boundary continues today with the financial sector. After the 2008 financial crisis, there were calls from many quarters for a revival of industrial policy to boost the 'makers' in industry, who were seen to be pitted against the 'takers' in finance. It was argued that rebalancing was needed to shrink the size of the financial sector (falling into the dark grey circle of unproductive activities above) by taxation, for example a tax on financial transactions such as foreign exchange dealing or securities trading, and by industrial policies to nurture growth in industries that actually made things instead of just exchanging them (falling into the light grey circle of productive activities above).

But things are not so simple. The point is not to blame some as takers and to label others as makers. The activities of people outside the boundary may be needed to facilitate production – without their work, productive activities may not be so valuable. Merchants are necessary to ensure the goods arrive at the marketplace and are exchanged efficiently. The financial sector is critical for buyers and sellers to do business with each other. How these activities can be shaped to actually serve their purpose of producing value is the real question.

And, most important of all, what about government? On which side of the production boundary does it lie? Is government inherently unproductive, as is often claimed, its only earnings being compulsory transfers in the form of taxes from the productive part of the economy? If so, how can government make the economy grow? Or can it at best only set the rules of the game, so that the value creators can operate efficiently?

Indeed, the recurring debate about the optimal size of government and the supposed perils of high public debt boils down to whether government spending helps the economy to grow – because government can be productive and add value – or whether it holds back the economy because it is unproductive or even destroys value. The issue is politically loaded and deeply colours current debates, ranging from whether the UK can afford Trident nuclear weapons to whether there is a 'magic number' for the size of government, defined as government spending as a proportion of national output, beyond which an economy will inevitably do less well than it might have done if government spending had been lower. As we will explore in Chapter 8, this question is more tainted by political views and ideological positions than informed by deep scientific proofs. Indeed, it is important to remember that economics is at heart a social science, and the 'natural' size of government will depend on one's theory of (or simply 'position' on) the purpose of government. If it is seen as useless, or at best a fixer of occasional problems, its optimum size will inevitably be notionally smaller than if it is viewed as a key engine of growth needed to steer and invest in the value creation process.

Over time, this conceptual production boundary was expanded to encompass much more of the economy than before, and more varied economic activities. As economists, and wider society, came to determine value by supply and demand – what is bought has value – activities such as financial transactions were redefined as productive, whereas previously they had usually been classed as unproductive. Significantly, the only major part of the economy which is now considered largely to lie outside the production boundary – and thus to be 'unproductive' – remains government. It is also true that many other services that people provide throughout society go unpaid, such as care given by parents to children or by the healthy to the unwell, and are not well accounted for. Fortunately, issues such as factoring care into the way we measure national output (GDP) are increasingly coming to the fore. But besides adding new concepts to GDP – such as care, or the sustainability of the planet – it is fundamental to understand why we hold the assumptions about value that we do. And this is impossible if value is not scrutinized.

WHY VALUE THEORY MATTERS

First, the disappearance of value from the economic debate hides what should be alive, public and actively contested.[17] If the assumption that value is in the eye of the beholder is not questioned, some activities will be deemed to be value-creating and others will not, simply because someone – usually someone with a vested interest – says so, perhaps more eloquently than others. Activities can hop from one side of the production boundary to the other with a click of the mouse and hardly anyone notices. If bankers, estate agents and bookmakers claim to create value rather than extract it, mainstream economics offers no basis on which to challenge them, even though the public might view their claims with scepticism. Who can gainsay Lloyd Blankfein when he declares that Goldman Sachs employees are among the most productive in the world? Or when pharmaceutical companies argue that the exorbitantly high price of one of their drugs is due to the *value* it produces? Government officials can become convinced (or 'captured') by stories about wealth creation, as was recently evidenced by the US government's approval of a leukemia drug treatment at half a million dollars, precisely using the 'value-based pricing' model pitched by the industry – even when the taxpayer contributed $200 million dollars towards its discovery.[18]

Second, the lack of analysis of value has massive implications for one particular area: the distribution of income between different members of society. When value is determined by price (rather than vice versa), the level and distribution of income seem justified as long as there is a market for the goods and services which, when bought and sold, generate that income. All income, according to this logic, is earned income: gone is any analysis of activities in terms of whether they are productive or unproductive.

Yet this reasoning is circular, a closed loop. Incomes are justified by the production of something that is of value. But how do we measure value? By whether it earns income. You earn income because you are productive and you are productive because you earn income. So with a wave of a wand, the concept of *unearned income* vanishes. If income means that we are productive, and we deserve income whenever we are productive, how can income possibly be unearned? As we shall see in Chapter 3, this circular reasoning is reflected in how national accounts – which track and measure production and wealth in the economy – are drawn up. In theory, no income may be judged too high, because in a market economy competition prevents anyone from earning more than he or she deserves. In practice, markets are what economists call imperfect, so prices and wages are often set by the powerful and paid by the weak.

In the prevailing view, prices are set by supply and demand, and any deviation from what is considered the competitive price (based on marginal revenues) must be due to some imperfection which, if removed, will produce the correct distribution of income between actors. The possibility that some activities perpetually earn rent because they are perceived as valuable, while actually blocking the creation of value and/or destroying existing value, is hardly discussed.

Indeed, for economists there is no longer any story other than that of the subjective theory of value, with the market driven by supply and demand. Once impediments to competition are removed, the outcome should benefit everyone. How different notions of value might affect the distribution of revenues between workers, public agencies, managers and shareholders at, say, Google, General Electric or BAE Systems, goes unquestioned.

Third, in trying to steer the economy in particular directions, policymakers are – whether they recognize it or not – inevitably influenced by ideas about value. The rate of GDP growth is obviously important in a world where billions of people still live in dire poverty. But some of the most important economic questions today are about how to achieve a particular type of growth. Today, there is a lot of talk about the need to make growth 'smarter' (led by investments in innovation), more sustainable (greener) and more inclusive (producing less inequality).[19]

Contrary to the widespread assumption that policy should be directionless, simply removing barriers and focusing on 'levelling the playing field' for businesses, an immense amount of policymaking is needed to reach these particular objectives. Growth will not somehow go in this direction by itself. Different types of policy are needed to tilt the playing field in the direction deemed desirable. This is very different from the usual assumption that policy should be directionless, simply removing barriers so that businesses can get on with smooth production.

Deciding which activities are more important than others is critical in setting a direction for the economy: put simply, those activities thought to be more important in achieving particular objectives have to be increased and less important ones reduced. We already do this. Certain types of tax credits, for, say, R&D, try to stimulate more investment in innovation. We subsidize education and training for students because as a society we want more young people to go to university or enter the workforce with better skills. Behind such policies may be economic models that show how investment in 'human capital' – people's knowledge and capabilities – benefits a country's growth by increasing its productive capacity. Similarly, today's deepening concern that the financial sector in some countries is too large – compared, for example, to manufacturing – might be informed by theories of what kind of economy we want to be living in and the size and role of finance within it.

But the distinction between productive and unproductive activities has rarely been the result of 'scientific' measurement. Rather, ascribing value, or the lack of it, has always involved malleable socio-economic arguments which derive from a particular political perspective – which is sometimes explicit, sometimes not. The definition of value is always as much about politics, and about particular views on how society ought to be constructed, as it is about narrowly defined economics. Measurements are not neutral: they affect behaviour and vice versa (this is the concept of performativity which we encountered in the Preface).

So the point is not to create a stark divide, labelling some activities as productive and categorizing others as unproductive rent-seeking. I believe we must instead be more forthright in linking our understanding of value creation to the way in which activities (whether in the financial sector or the real economy) should be structured, and how this is connected to the distribution of the rewards generated. Only in this way will the current narrative about value creation be subject to greater scrutiny, and statements such as 'I am a wealth creator' measured against credible ideas about where that wealth comes from. A pharmaceutical company's *value-based pricing* might then be scrutinized with a more collective value-creation process in mind, one in which public money funds a large portion of pharmaceutical research – from which that company benefits – in the highest-risk stage. Similarly, the 20 per cent share that venture capitalists usually get when a high-tech small company goes public on the stock market may be seen as excessive in light of the actual, not mythological, risk they have taken in investing in the company's development. And if an investment bank makes an enormous profit from the exchange rate instability that affects a country, that profit can be seen as what it really is: rent.

In order to arrive at this understanding of value creation, however, we need to go beyond seemingly scientific categorizations of activities and look at the socio-economic and political conflicts that underlie them. Indeed, claims about value creation have always been linked to assertions about the relative productiveness of certain elements of society, often related to fundamental shifts in the underlying economy: from agricultural to industrial, or from a mass-production-based economy to one based on digital technology.

THE STRUCTURE OF THE BOOK

In Chapters 1 and 2 I look at how economists from the seventeenth century onwards have thought about steering growth by increasing productive activities and reducing unproductive ones, something they conceptualized by means of a theoretical production boundary. The production boundary debate, and its close relationship to ideas of value, has influenced government measures of economic growth for centuries; the boundary, too, has changed, influenced by fluctuating social, economic and political conditions. Chapter 2 delves into the biggest shift of all. From the second half of the nineteenth century onwards, value went from being an objective category to a more subjective one tied to individual preferences. The implications of this revolution were seismic. The production boundary itself was blurred, because almost anything that could get a price or could successfully claim to create value – for example, finance – suddenly became productive. This opened the way to increased inequality, driven by particular agents in the economy being able to brag about their extraordinary 'productivity'.

As we will see in Chapter 3, which explores the development of national accounts, the idea of the production boundary continues to influence the concept of output. There is, however, a fundamental distinction between this new boundary and its predecessors. Today, decisions about what constitutes value in the national accounts are made by blending different elements: anything that can be priced and exchanged legally; politically pragmatic decisions, such as accommodating technological change in the computer industry or the embarrassingly large size of the financial sector; and the practical necessity of keeping the accounting manageable in very big and complex modern economies. This is all very well, but the fact that the production boundary debate is no longer explicit, nor linked openly to ideas about value, means that economic actors can – through sustained lobbying – quietly place themselves within the boundary. Their value-extracting activities are then counted in GDP – and very few notice.

Chapters 4, 5 and 6 examine the phenomenon of financialization: the growth of the financial sector and the spread of financial practices and attitudes into the real economy. In Chapter 4 I look at the emergence of finance as a major economic sector and its transition from being considered largely unproductive to becoming accepted as largely productive. As late as the 1960s, national accountants viewed financial activity not as generating value but as simply transferring existing value, which placed it outside the production boundary. Today, this view has changed fundamentally. In its current incarnation, finance is seen as earning profits from services reclassified as productive. I look at how and why this extraordinary redefinition took place, and ask if financial intermediation really has undergone a transformation into an inherently productive activity.

In Chapter 5 I explore the development of 'asset manager capitalism': how the financial sector expanded beyond the banks to incorporate an increasingly large number of intermediaries dedicated to managing funds (the asset management industry), and ask whether the role of these intermediaries, and the actual risks they take on, justify the rewards they earn. In doing so, I question the extent to which fund management and private equity have actually contributed to the productive economy. I ask, too, whether financial reform can be tackled today without a serious debate over whether activities in the financial sector are properly classified – are they what should be seen as rents,

rather than profits? – and how we can go about making this distinction. If our national accounting systems are really rewarding value
extraction as though it is value creation, maybe this can help us
understand the dynamics of value destruction that characterized the
financial crisis.

Building on this acceptance of finance as a productive activity,
Chapter 6 examines the financialization of the whole economy. In
seeking a quick return, short-term finance has affected industry:
companies are run in the name of maximizing shareholder value
(MSV). MSV arose in the 1970s as an attempt to revitalize corporate
performance by invoking what was claimed to be the main purpose
of the company: creating value for shareholders. I will argue, however, that MSV has been detrimental to sustained economic growth,
not least because it encourages short-term gain for shareholders at the
expense of long-term gains for the company – a development closely
linked to the increasing influence of fund managers seeking returns
for their clients and for themselves. Underlying MSV is the notion of
shareholders as the biggest risk takers, meriting the large rewards
they often obtain.

Risk-taking is often the justification for the rewards investors reap,
and Chapter 7 continues to look at other types of value extraction
carried out in its name. Here I consider the kind of risk-taking
required for radical technological innovation to occur. Innovation is
without doubt one of the most risky and uncertain activities in capitalism: most attempts fail. But who takes it on? And what sort of
incentives must be created? I explore the biased view of the current
innovation narrative: how public-sector risk-taking is ignored, the
state being seen as merely facilitating and 'de-risking' the private sector. The result has been policies, including reforms to the intellectual
property rights (IPR) system, which have strengthened the power
of incumbents, limiting innovation and creating 'unproductive
entrepreneurship'.[20] Building on my previous book *The Entrepreneurial State*, I will show how entrepreneurs and venture capitalists
have been hyped up to represent the most dynamic part of modern
capitalism – innovation – and have presented themselves as 'wealth
creators'. I will unpick the wealth-creating narrative to show how,
ultimately, it is false. Claiming value in innovation, most recently

with the concept of 'platforms' and the related notion of the sharing economy, is less about genuine innovation and more to do with facilitating value extraction through the capture of rents.

Picking up on the false innovation narrative, Chapter 8 will ask why the public sector is always described as slow, boring, bureaucratic and unproductive. Where did this depiction come from and who is benefiting from it? I will argue that, in the same way and at the same time that finance was made productive, the public sector has been made to appear unproductive. Modern economic thought has relegated government to just fixing market failures rather than actively creating and shaping markets. The value-creating role of the public sector, I contend, has been underestimated. The dominant view, which originated in the backlash against government in the 1980s, fundamentally affects how government sees itself: hesitant, cautious, careful not to overstep in case it should be accused of crowding out innovation, or accused of favouritism, 'picking winners'. In questioning why public-sector activities are ignored in GDP accounting, I ask why this should matter, and outline what a different view of public value might look like.

It is, I conclude in Chapter 9, only through an open debate about value – its sources and the conditions that foster it – that we can help steer our economies in a direction that will produce more genuine innovation and less inequality, and which will also transform the financial sector into one that is truly focused on nurturing value creation in the real economy. It is not enough to critique speculation and short-term value extraction, and to argue for a more progressive tax system that targets wealth. We must ground those critiques in a different conversation about value creation, otherwise programmes for reform will continue to have little effect and will be easily lobbied against by the so-called 'wealth creators'.

This book does not try to argue for one correct theory of value. Rather, it aims to bring back value theory as a hotly debated area, relevant to the turbulent economic times in which we find ourselves. Value is not a given thing, unmistakably either inside or outside the production boundary; it is shaped and created. In my view, today finance nurtures not the industries for which it is meant to 'grease' the wheels of commerce, but rather other parts of the financial sector itself. It thus lies outside the boundary, even though it is formally counted as being inside. But this does not have to be the case: we can shape financial markets so that they do indeed belong inside the boundary. This would include both new financial institutions dedicated to lending to those organizations interested in long-term high-risk investments that can help foster a more innovative economy, as well as changing measures in the tax code that reward long-term investments over short-term ones. Similarly, as I discuss in Chapter 7, changes to the current unhelpful use of patents could help them stimulate innovation rather than stifle it.

To create a fairer economy, one where prosperity is more broadly shared and is therefore more sustainable, we need to reinvigorate a serious discussion about the nature and origin of value. We must reconsider the stories we are telling about who the value creators are, and what that says to us about how we define activities as economically productive and unproductive. We cannot limit progressive politics to taxing wealth, but require a new understanding of and debate about wealth creation so that it is more fiercely and openly contested. Words matter: we need a new vocabulary for policymaking. Policy is not just about 'intervening'. It is about shaping a different future: co-creating markets and value, not just 'fixing' markets or redistributing value. It's about taking risks, not only 'de-risking'. And it must not be about levelling the playing field but about tilting it towards the kind of economy we want.

This idea that we can shape markets has important consequences. We can create a better economy by understanding that markets are outcomes of decisions that are made – in business, in public organizations and in civil society. The eight-hour working day has formed markets – and that was the result of a fight held in labour organizations. And perhaps the reason there is so much despair across the globe – despair now leading to populist politics – is that the economy is presented to us simply as 'made' by trade rules, technocrats and neoliberal forces. Indeed, as the book will show, 'value' theory itself is presented as a sort of objective force determined by supply and demand, rather than deeply embedded in particular ways of seeing the world. The economy can indeed be made and shaped – but it can be done either in fear or in hope.

The specific challenge I pose here is to move beyond Oscar Wilde's cynic, who knows the price of everything but the value of nothing, towards an economics of hope, where we are better empowered to question the assumptions of economic theory and how they are presented to us. And to choose a different path among the many that are available.

I

A Brief History of Value

There is one sort of labour which adds to the value of the
subject upon which it is bestowed: there is another which has
no such effect. The former, as it produces a value, may be
called productive; the latter, unproductive labour.

Adam Smith, *The Wealth of Nations* (1776)

Today we take increasing prosperity for granted. We assume that by
and large the next generation will be better off than the last. But it was
not always so. For most of human history people had no such expectations and, partly because living standards improved at best very
slowly, few thinkers devoted much time to asking why some economies grow and others do not. In the early modern period, the pace
of change quickened. Previously static economies became dynamic.
Movement was in the air. The rise of the nation state in Europe, the
need to finance war, colonization, machinery, factories and coal, combined with expanding populations to stimulate new thinking across
many fields. Governments and people of all stations in life wanted to
know what was causing unprecedented movement and how it could be
managed. What taxes can we raise? Why are my wages so low compared with the profits of capitalists? How sure can one be of the future
when investing now? What creates value?

Understanding the nature of production is key to answering such
questions. Once productive activities have been identified, economic
policy can try to steer an economy, devoting a greater share of capital
and effort to productive activities which propel and sustain economic
growth. But the distinction between what is or is not productive has

varied depending on economic, social and political forces. Ever since economists began to explore the changing conditions of production some 300 years ago they have struggled to provide a rationale for labelling some activities productive and others unproductive. After all, economists are creatures of their time like everyone else; in terms of understanding value, what's important is to distinguish durable principles from transitory ones – and also, as we will see, the way that ideological positions develop.

This chapter explores how theories of value evolved from roughly the mid-seventeenth century to the mid-nineteenth century. The thinkers of the seventeenth century focused on how to calculate growth according to the needs of the time: fighting wars, or increasing competitiveness relative to another country – for example, England against its commercial and naval rival, Holland. The *mercantilists* focus on trade and the needs of merchants (selling things). From the mid-eighteenth to the late nineteenth century, economists saw value as arising from the amount of labour that went into production, at first farm labour (the *physiocrats*) and then industrial labour (the *classicals*). This value, they believed, therefore determined the price of what was finally sold. Their theories of value – of how wealth was created – were dynamic, reflecting a world being transformed socially and politically as well as economically. These economists focused on objective forces: the effects of changes in technology and the division of labour on how production and distribution are organized. Later, as we will see in the next chapter, they were superseded by another perspective – that of the *neoclassicals* – focused less on objective forces of production and more on the subjective nature of the 'preferences' of different actors in the economy.

THE MERCANTILISTS: TRADE
AND TREASURE

Since ancient times, humanity has divided its economic activity into two types: productive and unproductive, virtuous and vile, industrious and lazy. The touchstone was generally what kind of activity was thought to further the common good. In the fourth century BC,

Aristotle distinguished a variety of more or less virtuous jobs, depending on the class (citizen or slave) of the ancient Greek *polis* dweller.[1] In the New Testament, the apostle Matthew reported that Jesus said it was 'easier for a camel to go through the eye of a needle than for a rich man to enter into the Kingdom of God'.[2] During the Middle Ages, the Church disparaged and even denounced moneylenders and merchants who 'bought cheap and sold dear';[3] while they may not have been lazy, they were considered unproductive and vile.

Pre-modern definitions of what work was or was not useful were never clear-cut. With the onset of colonialism in the sixteenth century these definitions became even more blurred. European colonial conquest and the protection of trade routes with newly annexed lands were expensive. Governments had to find the money for armies, bureaucracies and the purchase of exotic merchandise. But help seemed to be at hand: extraordinary amounts of gold and silver were discovered in the Americas, and a vast treasure poured into Europe. As these precious metals represented wealth and prosperity, it seemed that whoever bought, owned and controlled the supply of them and the currencies minted from them was engaged in productive activities.

Scholars and politicians of the time who argued that accumulating precious metals was the route to national power and prosperity are called mercantilists (from *mercator*, the Latin word for merchant), because they espoused protectionist trade policies and positive trade balances to stimulate the inflow, and prevent the outflow, of gold and silver. The best-known English advocate of mercantilism was a merchant and director of the East India Company called Sir Thomas Mun (1571–1641). In his influential book *England's Treasure by Forraign Trade*, Mun summed up the mercantilist doctrine: we must, he said, 'sell more to strangers yearly than wee consume of theirs in value'.[4]

Mercantilists also defended the growth of national government as necessary to fund wars and expeditions to keep trade routes open and to control colonial markets. In England, Holland and France, mercantilists advocated shipping Acts, such as England's Navigation Act of 1651, which forced their countries' and colonies' trade exclusively into ships flying the national flag.

As mercantilist thinking developed, and people started to conceive of wealth production in national terms, the first estimates of national income – the total amount everyone in the country earned – started to appear. Seventeenth-century Britain saw two groundbreaking attempts to quantify national income. One was by Sir William Petty (1623–87), an adventurer, anatomist, physician and Member of Parliament, who was a tax administrator in Ireland under Oliver Cromwell's Commonwealth government.[5] The other was by the herald Gregory King (1648–1712), a genealogist, engraver and statistician whose work on enacting a new tax on marriages, births and burials provoked his interest in national accounting.

Petty and King were ingenious in their use of incomplete and messy data to generate surprisingly detailed income estimates. They had to work with rudimentary government tax figures, estimates of population and patchy statistics on the consumption of basic commodities such as corn, wheat and beer. What their estimates lacked, however, was a clear value theory: Petty and King were concerned only with calculating the nation's output, not with how that output came about. Nevertheless, their attempts at national accounting were unprecedented and laid the foundations for modern national accounts.

In the 1660s, as Petty worked on his income studies, England was emerging from its experiment with republicanism, and was struggling with Holland and France for supremacy at sea. Petty wanted to find out whether England had the resources to survive these threats to its security: as he put it, to 'prove mathematically that the [English] State could raise a much larger revenue from taxes to finance its peace and wartime needs',[6] because he believed the country was richer than commonly thought.

Petty made a decisive breakthrough. He realized that income and expenditure at the national level should be the same. He understood that, if you treat a country as a closed system, each pound one person spends in it is another person's income of one pound. It was the first time anyone had grasped and worked with this fundamental insight. To make up for the lack of available statistics, Petty worked on the assumption that a nation's income is equal to its expenditure (omitting savings in good times, although he was aware of the potential discrepancy).[7] That meant he could use expenditure per person, multiplied by population, to arrive at the nation's income. In so doing he started, implicitly, to impose a production boundary, including within it only money spent on the production of 'Food, Housing, Cloaths, and all other necessaries'.[8] All other 'unnecessary expenses', as defined by Petty, were omitted.

In this way, by extension, Petty came to see any branch of the economy that did not produce those necessities as unproductive, adding nothing to national income. As he worked, his idea of the production boundary began to crystallize further, with 'Husbandmen, Seamen, Soldiers, Artizans and Merchants . . . the very Pillars of any Common-Wealth' on one side; and 'all the other great Professions' which 'do rise out of the infirmities and miscarriages of these' on the other.[9] By 'great professions' Petty meant lawyers, clergymen, civil servants, lords and the like. In other words, for Petty some 'great professions' were merely a necessary evil – needed simply for facilitating production and for maintaining the status quo – but not really essential to production or exchange. Although Petty did not believe that policy should be focused on controlling imports and exports, the mercantilists influenced him heavily. 'Merchandise', he argued, was more productive than manufacture and husbandry; the Dutch, he noted approvingly, outsourced their husbandry to Poland and Denmark, enabling them to focus on more productive 'Trades and curious Arts'.[10] England, he concluded, would also benefit if more husbandmen became merchants.[11]

In the late 1690s, after the first publication of Petty's work *Political Arithmetick*, Gregory King made more detailed estimates of England's income. Like Petty, King was concerned with England's war-making potential and compared the country's income with those of France and Holland. Drawing on a wide variety of sources, he meticulously calculated the income and expenditure of some twenty different occupation groups in the country, from the aristocracy to lawyers, merchants to paupers. He even made forecasts, for example of population, predating the arrival of the forecasting 'science' some 250 years later, and estimated the crop yield of important agricultural items.

As in Petty's work, an implicit production boundary began to emerge when King assessed productivity, which he defined as income being greater than expenditure. King thought merchant traders were the most productive group, their income being a quarter more than their expenditure, followed by the 'temporal and spiritual lords', then by a variety of prestigious professions. On the boundary were farmers, who earned almost no more than they spent. Firmly on the 'unproductive' side were seamen, labourers, servants, cottagers, paupers and 'common soldiers'.[12] In King's view, the unproductive masses, representing slightly more than half the total population, were leeches on the public wealth because they consumed more than they produced.

Figure 2 shows that there were discrepancies between the 'productive' professions Petty and King identified. Almost all the professions Petty deemed unproductive King later saw as productive, while several of those producing value for Petty – seamen, soldiers and unskilled labourers – did not make the cut in King's analysis. Their different views may have stemmed from their backgrounds. A man of humble origins and republican instincts, Petty started out serving Oliver Cromwell; moving in aristocratic and court circles, King was perhaps less inclined to think that Petty's 'great professions' were unproductive. Both, however, classed 'vagrants' as unproductive, an analysis that has parallels today with people receiving welfare from governments financed by taxes on the productive sectors.

Some of Petty's and King's ideas have proved remarkably durable.[13] Perhaps most importantly, in what they both called 'Political Arithmetick' they laid the basis for what we today call the 'national accounts' to calculate GDP, the compass by which countries attempt to steer their national economic ships.

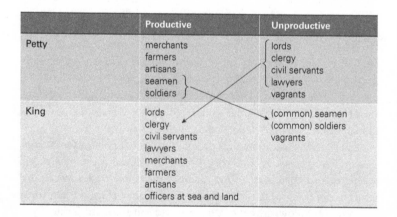

Figure 2. The production boundary in the 1600s

Mercantilist ideas still resonate in current economic practices. Modern 'management' of exchange rates by governments, trying to steal a competitive advantage for exports and accumulate foreign exchange reserves, harks back to mercantilist notions of boosting exports to accumulate gold and silver. Tariffs, import quotas and other measures to control trade and support domestic enterprises are also reminiscent of these early ideas about how value is created. There is basically nothing new in the calls to protect Western steel producers from Chinese imports or to subsidize domestic low-carbon energy generation to substitute for imports of oil, gas and coal. The emphasis by populist politicians on the negative effect of free trade, and the need to put up different types of walls to prevent the free movement of goods and labour, also gestures back to the mercantilist era, with emphasis more on getting the prices right (including exchange rates and wages) than on making the investments needed to create long-run growth and higher per capita income.

Petty and King were seminal figures in these early forays into the question of how and where value is created. Yet, ultimately, both could label productive and unproductive occupations however they chose. Their work was purely descriptive. It did not attempt to quantify or model relations between different groups and individuals in the economy,[14] or to quantify how the system reproduced itself and maintained the conditions for future production. In short, their work was not linked to an underlying theory of what constitutes wealth and where it comes from: a value theory. Any policy for economic growth was therefore idiosyncratic because it was unclear what generated it. But during the following century, this would start to change.

As the study of economics developed during the course of the eighteenth century, thinkers became increasingly concerned with finding a theory to explain why some nations grew and prospered while others declined. Although the economists of the time did not use the term 'production boundary', the idea was at the heart of their work. Their search for the source of value led them to locate it in production, first in land – understandably so, in predominantly agrarian societies – and then, as economies became more industrialized, in labour. The labour theory of value reached its apogee with Karl Marx in the mid-nineteenth century, when the Industrial Revolution was in full swing.

THE PHYSIOCRATS: THE ANSWER LIES IN THE SOIL

The first efforts to find a formal theory of value came in the mid-eighteenth century from the court of Louis XV of France, in the twilight – so it turned out – of that country's absolute monarchy. There, François Quesnay (1694–1774), often described as the 'father of economics', was the king's physician and adviser. He used his medical training to understand the economy as a 'metabolic' system. Crucially, in metabolism, everything must come from somewhere and go somewhere – and that, for Quesnay, included wealth. Quesnay's approach led him to formulate the first systematic theory of value that classified who is and is not productive in an economy, and to model how the entire economy could reproduce itself from the value generated by a small group of its members. In his seminal work *Tableau Économique*, published in 1758, he constructed an 'economic table' which showed how new value was created and circulated in the economy. In it he continued the metabolic analogy: pumps were drawn to signify the ways in which new value was introduced, and outgoing tubes illustrated how value left the system.

At the time Quesnay wrote, French society was already facing the problems that would lead to the French Revolution fifteen years after his death. French agriculture was in a bad state. Farmers were choked by high taxes, imposed by their usually noble landlords to fund their lavish lifestyles and by central government to finance war and trade. Adding to this burden, the French government's mercantilist policy, faced with a now aggressively expanding Britain, kept the prices of agricultural produce low to provide cheap subsistence to domestic manufactures, which could in turn be cheaply made and exported in exchange for the highly coveted gold, still generally believed to be a measure of national wealth. Faced with this situation, Quesnay and his followers built a powerful argument in favour of the farmers and against the mercantilists. Though they came to be known as the physiocrats, after one of Quesnay's publications, they called themselves something else: 'Les Économistes'.

Contrasting sharply with the prevailing mercantilist thinking that gave gold a privileged place, Quesnay believed that land was the source of all value. Figure 3 illustrates how for him, in the end, everything that nourished humans came from the earth. He pointed out that, unlike humans, Nature actually produced new things: grain out of small seeds for food, trees out of saplings and mineral ores from the earth from which houses and ships and machinery were built. By contrast, humans could not produce value. They could only transform it: bread from seeds, timber from wood, steel from iron. Since agriculture, husbandry, fishing, hunting and mining (all in the darker blob in Figure 3) bring Nature's bounty to society, Quesnay called them the 'productive class'. By contrast, he thought that nearly all other sectors of the economy – households, government, services and even industry, lumped together in the lighter blob – were unproductive.

Quesnay's classification was revolutionary. Breaking away from the mercantilists, who placed exchange and what was gained from it – gold – at the centre of value creation, he now linked value creation inextricably with production. Developing his classification of productive and unproductive work, Quesnay grouped society into three classes. First came farmers and related occupations working on the land and water; according to Quesnay, this was the only productive class. Next

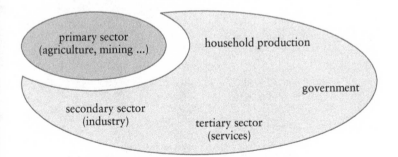

Figure 3. The production boundary in the 1700s

were manufacturers, artisans and related workers who transform the materials they receive from the productive class: wood and stone for furniture and houses, sheep's wool for clothing and metals from the mines for tools.[15] Yet, argued Quesnay, this class did not add value; rather, their work merely recirculated existing value. The third class was the unproductive 'proprietor', 'distributive' or 'sterile' class, which was made up of landlords, nobility and clergy. Here, 'distributive' was meant pejoratively: this class redistributes value, but only to itself, for the sole reason that it owns the land and does not give anything in return.[16]

In Quesnay's table, the productive part of the system is entirely based on the farmers, but others also have a useful role in ensuring that the system reproduces itself. Figure 4 shows in detail the

	Productive class		Proprietors		Sterile class	
Steps	Money	Products	Money	Products	Money	Products
			Circulation			
0 (start)	0	4 food 1 raw material	2	nothing	0	2 goods
1	1	3 food 1 raw material	1	1 food	0	2 goods
2	1	2 food 1 raw material	0	1 food 1 goods	1	1 goods
3	2	2 food 1 raw material	0	1 food 1 goods	0	1 goods 1 food
4	1	2 food 1 raw material 1 goods	0	1 food 1 goods	1	1 food
5	2	2 food 1 goods	0	1 food 1 goods	0	1 food 1 raw material
6	0	2 food 1 goods	2	1 food 1 goods	0	1 food 1 raw material
			Production			
		2 food + 1 goods consumed produce: 4 food 1 raw material		1 food + 1 goods consumed produce: nothing		1 food and 1 raw material consumed product: 2 goods
		New circulation → start at the top				

Figure 4. Example of the *Tableau Économique*

process of production, income and consumption of each class or economic sector, and how they interact. Perhaps the world's first spreadsheet, it is also the first consistent abstract model of economic growth.

A Numerical Example for the *Tableau Économique*

The logic of Quesnay's model is illustrated in Figure 4. The most important thing is where the initial wealth comes from, how it is circulated, and what percentage is reinvested into production (in nature) in the next round, creating more value – the latter being the essence of the growth process. In the simplest case of a non-expanding economy, the productive class has an initial amount of 'products of the earth' (translated from 'produits de la terre'), valued here for the sake of argument as 5 billion livres' worth. These are divided 4/5 food (for the farmers to subsist on) and 1/5 in material for the sterile class. The proprietors hold 2 billion in cash that they have collected in taxes from the productive class, and the sterile class has an inventory of 2 billion livres' worth of tools and other manufactured goods.

From this, a process of circulation takes place, each step of which corresponds to a move from one row to the next. In every step, an equal amount of value changes hands, to prepare for the next round of production. But no new value is created. An exception is the step from period 5 to 6 in the circulation process, at which a transfer rather than exchange of 2 billion livres takes place. Only money flows, not products.[17] At the end, production takes place, with 2 billion surplus products in the productive sector, while 2 billion have been unproductively consumed in the proprietor class, starting a new round of circulation. Obviously, if the surplus is bigger than consumption, the economy will grow from round to round.

(All units are in billions of French livres; solid arrows indicate product flows, dashed arrows indicate money flows.)[18]

Most significant is how the table neatly shows, from row to row, that as long as what is produced is greater than what is consumed, an amount will be left over at the end to be reinvested, thereby allowing the economy to continue reproducing itself. If any of the unproductive members of society take too much, reducing the amount the farmer can reinvest in production, the economy will grind to a halt. In other words, if value extraction by the unproductive members exceeds value creation by the productive members, growth stops.

Though he himself did not use the term, Quesnay's theory of value incorporates a very clear production boundary, the first to be drawn with such precision, which makes it clear that the surplus the 'productive' sectors generate enables everyone else to live.

Other economists quickly weighed in with analysis and criticism of Quesnay's classification. Their attack centred on Quesnay's labelling of artisans and workers as 'sterile': a term that served Quesnay's political ends of defending the existing agrarian social order, but contradicted the everyday experience of a great number of people. Refining Quesnay's thinking, his contemporary A. R. J. Turgot retained the notion that all value came from the land, but noted the important role of artisans in keeping society afloat. He also recognized that there were other 'general needs' that some people had to fulfil – such as judges to administer justice – and that these functions were essential for value creation. Accordingly, he re-labelled Quesnay's 'sterile' class as the 'stipendiary', or waged, class. And, since rich landowners could decide whether to carry out work themselves or hire others to do so using revenues from the land, Turgot labelled them the 'disposable class'. He also added the refinement that some farmers or artisans would employ others and make a profit. As farmers move from tilling the land to employing others, he argued, they remain productive and receive profits on their enterprise. It is only when they give up on overseeing farming altogether and simply live on their rent that they become 'disposable' rent collectors. Turgot's more refined analysis therefore placed emphasis on the character of the work being done, rather than the category of work itself.

Turgot's refinements were highly significant. In them, we see the emergent categories of wages, profits and rents: an explicit reference to the distribution of wealth and income that would become one of the cornerstones of economic thought in the centuries to come, and which is still used in national income accounting today. Yet, for Turgot, land remained the source of value: those who did not work it could not be included in the production boundary.[19]

Quesnay and Turgot's almost complete identification of productivity with the agricultural sector had an overriding aim. Their restrictive production boundary gave the landed aristocracy ammunition to use against mercantilism, which favoured the merchant class, and fitted an agricultural society better than an industrial one. Given the physiocrats' disregard for industry, it is hardly surprising that the most significant critique of their ideas came from the nation where it was already clear that value was not just produced in agriculture, but in other emerging sectors: a rapidly industrializing Britain. The most influential critic of all was Quesnay's contemporary, a man who had travelled in France and talked at length with him: Adam Smith.

CLASSICAL ECONOMICS: VALUE IN LABOUR

As industry developed rapidly through the eighteenth and nineteenth centuries, so too did the ideas of a succession of outstanding thinkers like Adam Smith (1723–90), David Ricardo (1772–1823) and Karl Marx (1818–83), a German who did much of his greatest work in England. Economists started to measure the market value of a product in terms of the amount of work, or labour, that had gone into its production. Accordingly, they paid close attention to how labour and working conditions were changing and to the adoption of new technologies and ways of organizing production.

In *The Wealth of Nations*, first published in 1776 and widely regarded as the founding work of economics, Smith's famous description of the division of labour in pin factories showed his understanding of how changes in the organization of work could affect productivity and therefore economic growth and wealth. Another enormously influential book, Ricardo's *On the Principles of Political Economy and Taxation*, first published in 1817, contained a famous chapter called 'On Machinery', in which he argued that mechanization was reducing demand for skilled labour and would depress wages. And in Marx's *Capital*, Volume 1 of which was first published in 1867, the chapter called 'The Working Day', which dealt with the development of the English Factory Acts governing working conditions, showed his fascination with production as the field on which the battle for workers' rights, higher wages and better conditions was being fought.

Smith, Ricardo and others of the time became known as the 'classical' economists. Marx, a late outrider, stands somewhat apart from this collective description. The word 'classical' was a conscious echo of the status given to writers and thinkers of the ancient Greek and Roman worlds, whose works were still the bedrock of education when the term 'classical economics' began to be used in the later nineteenth century. The classical economists redrew the production boundary in a way that made more sense for the period they lived in: one which saw the artisan-craft production of the guilds still prominent in Smith's time give way to the large-scale industry with huge numbers of urban workers – the proletariat – that Marx wrote about in the third quarter of the nineteenth century. Not for nothing was their emerging discipline called 'political economy'. It did not seem odd to contemporaries that economics was intimately part of studying society: they would have found odd the idea, widespread today, that economics is a neutral technical discipline which can be pursued in isolation of the prevailing social and political context. Although their theories differed in many respects, the classical economists shared two basic ideas: that value derived from the costs of production, principally labour; and that therefore activity subsequent to value created by labour, such as finance, did not in itself create value. Marx, we will see, was more subtle in his understanding of this distinction.

Adam Smith: The Birth of the Labour Theory of Value

Born in 1723 into a family of customs officials in Kirkcaldy, in the county of Fife, Scotland, Adam Smith became Professor of Moral Philosophy at the University of Glasgow before turning his mind to what we now call economic questions, although at the time such questions were deeply influenced by philosophy and political thought.

With Britain well on the path to industrial capitalism, Smith's *The Wealth of Nations* highlighted the role of the division of labour in manufacturing. His account of pin-manufacturing continues to be cited today as one of the first examples of organizational and technological change at the centre of the economic growth process. Explaining the immense increase in productivity that occurred when one worker was no longer responsible for producing an entire pin, but only for a small part of it, Smith related how the division of labour allowed an increase in specialization and hence productivity:

> I have seen a small manufactory of this kind where ten men only were employed, and where some of them consequently performed two or three distinct operations. But though they were very poor, and therefore but indifferently accommodated with the necessary machinery, they could, when they exerted themselves, make among them about twelve pounds of pins in a day. There are in a pound upwards of four thousand pins of a middling size. Those ten persons, therefore, could make among them upwards of forty-eight thousand pins in a day. Each person, therefore, making a tenth part of forty-eight thousand pins, might be considered as making four thousand eight hundred pins in a day. But if they had all wrought separately and independently, and without any of them having been educated to this peculiar business, they certainly could not each of them have made twenty, perhaps not one pin in a day; that is, certainly, not the two hundred and fortieth, perhaps not the four thousand eight hundredth part of what they are at present capable of performing, in consequence of a proper division and combination of their different operations.[20]

These insights were original and profound. Smith was writing while the Industrial Revolution introduced machines into factories on a large scale. When harnessed to the division of labour, mechanization would radically increase productivity – the principal engine of economic growth. But even the simple reorganization of labour, without machinery, by which each worker specialized and developed skills in a specific area, enabled Smith to make this critical point.

Equally significant was Smith's analysis of how the 'market' determines the way in which consumers and producers interact. Such interaction, he contended, was not down to 'benevolence' or central planning.[21] Rather, it was due to the 'invisible hand' of the market:

> Every individual is continually exerting himself to find out the most advantageous employment for whatever capital he can command. It is his own advantage, indeed, and not that of the society which he has in view. But the study of his own advantage naturally, or rather necessarily, leads him to prefer that employment which is most advantageous to society ... He intends only his own gain, and he is in this, as in many other cases, led by an invisible hand to promote an end which was not part of his intention.[22]

Like Quesnay, Smith launched a more general attack on mercantilist policies which, he argued, restricted competition and trade. He also argued strongly for policies that would increase savings, and hence the amount of capital available for investment rather than unproductive consumption (say, on luxuries). But for Smith, industrial workers – not, as for Quesnay, farmers – were at the heart of the productive economy. Manufacturing labour, not land, was the source of value.[23] The labour theory of value was born.

Smith has become the figurehead of much modern economic theory because of his ideas about how capitalism is founded on supposedly immutable human behaviour, notably self-interest, and competition in a market economy. His metaphor of the 'invisible hand' has been cited *ad nauseam* to support the current orthodoxy that markets, left to themselves, may lead to a socially optimal outcome – indeed, more beneficial than if the state intervenes.

Smith's book is actually a collection of recipes for politicians and policymakers. Far from leaving everything to the market, he thinks of himself as giving guidance to 'statesmen' on how to act to 'enrich both the people and the sovereign'[24] – how to increase the wealth of nations. This is where Smith's value theory enters the picture. He was convinced that growth depended on increasing the relative share of 'manufactures' – factories employing formerly independent artisans or agricultural workers as dependent wage labourers – in the overall make-up of industry and believed that free trade was essential to bring this about. He felt that the enemies of growth were, first, the protectionist policies of mercantilists; second, the guilds protecting artisans' privileges; and third, a nobility that squandered its money on unproductive labour and lavish consumption. For Smith (as for Quesnay), employing an overly large portion of labour for unproductive purposes – such as the hoarding of cash, a practice that still afflicts our modern economies – prevents a nation from accumulating wealth.

Value, Smith believed, was proportional to the time spent by workers on production. For the purposes of his theory, Smith assumed a worker of average speed. Figure 5 shows how he drew a clear line (the production boundary) between productive and unproductive labour. For him, the boundary lay between material production – agriculture, manufacturing, mining in the figure's darker blob – and immaterial production in the lighter blob. The latter included all types of services (lawyers, carters, officials and so on) that were useful to manufactures, but were not actually involved in production itself. Smith said as much: labour, he suggested, is productive when it is 'realized' in a permanent object.[25] His positioning of government on the 'unproductive' side of the boundary set the tone for much subsequent analysis and is a recurring theme in today's debates about government's role in the economy, epitomized by the Thatcher–Reagan reassertion in the 1980s of the primacy of markets in solving economic and social issues.

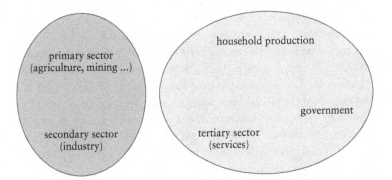

Figure 5. The production boundary according to Adam Smith

In Smith's view, 'how honourable, how useful, or how necessary soever' a service may be, it simply does not reproduce the value used in maintaining (feeding, clothing, housing) unproductive labourers. Smith finds that even 'the sovereign', together with 'all the officers both of justice and war who serve under him, the whole army and navy, are unproductive labourers'.[26] Priests, lawyers, doctors and performing artists are all lumped together as unproductive too.

What informs Smith's classification is his conviction that some types of labour do not 'reproduce' the value needed to keep those workers alive at a subsistence level. In other words, if all the subsistence that was needed to keep a person alive was a certain amount of grain, then anyone who does not produce as much value as that amount of grain is by definition unproductive.

How, then, are those that do not produce this unit of value kept alive?

Smith's answer lay in the concept of a 'surplus'. Many productive workers produce the equivalent of more grain than they need to feed themselves to survive. A manufacturer makes things that, when exchanged, will yield more grain than needed to keep the productive workers alive. The surplus then sustains unproductive labourers, including the entourages of aristocrats, who kept 'a profuse and sumptuous table' with 'a great number of menial servants, and a multitude of dogs and horses'.

This is where Smith addressed head-on how the wealth of nations could grow. It was in effect his policy advice. Instead of 'wasting' the surplus on paying for unproductive labour, he argued, it should be saved and invested in more production so that the whole nation could become richer.[27] Smith was not criticizing the wealthy per se. But he was criticizing those who wasted their wealth on lavish consumption – 'collecting books, statues, pictures', or 'more frivolous, jewels, baubles, ingenious trinkets' – instead of productive investment. (This, after all, was the age of the Grand Tour, when young aristocrats travelled to the Continent to improve their education and returned laden with ancient artefacts.) Smith was particularly attracted to the prospect of investment in machines, then just beginning to be used in factories, because they improved workers' productivity.

His emphasis on investment linked directly to his ideas about rent. Smith believed that there were three kinds of income: wages for labour in capitalist enterprises; profits for capitalists who owned the means of production; and rents from ownership of land. When these three sources of income are paid at their competitive level, together they determine what he called the 'competitive price'.[28] Since land was necessary, rent from land was a 'natural' part of the economy. But that did not mean rent was productive: 'the landlords, like all other men, love to reap where they never sowed and demand a rent [from the earth] even for its natural produce'.[29] Indeed, Smith asserted, the principle of rent from land could be extended to other monopolies, such as the right to import a particular commodity or the right to plead at the bar. Smith was well aware of the damage monopolies could do. In the seventeenth century, a government desperate for revenue had granted – often to well-placed courtiers – an extraordinary range of monopolies, from daily necessities such as beer and salt to mousetraps and spectacles. In 1621 there were said to be 700 monopolies, and by the late 1630s they were bringing in £100,000 a year to the Exchequer.[30] But this epidemic of rent-seeking was deeply unpopular and was choking the economy: more than that, it was one of the proximate causes of the Civil War, which led to the execution of Charles I. Many Englishmen understood what Smith meant when he said that a free market was one free of rent.

Smith's penetrating analysis of how advanced capitalist economies functioned won him many followers. Equally, his staunch advocacy of free trade, in an era in which mercantilist policies were beginning to be seen as old-fashioned (Smith, indeed, believed that merchants were unproductive because they only provided the ephemeral service of moving goods around, rather than producing anything of value), made his book a hit among the 'free traders' who eventually overturned England's Corn Laws, which imposed heavy tariffs on imported corn to protect domestic landowners, and other protectionist measures. Armed with Smith's ideas, free traders showed that nations could get richer even if there was no trade surplus and no gold accumulation. Amassing gold was unnecessary and insufficient for growth. Huge amounts of gold flowed to Spain from its colonies, but the kingdom did not become more productive.

The victory of the free traders over the mercantilists is better understood in terms of their rival conceptions of value. Mercantilists thought gold had inherent worth and that everything else could be valued in terms of how much gold it was exchanged for. Following Smith, free traders could trace value to labour, and the logic of value was thereby inverted. Gold, like all other things, was valued by how much labour it took to produce.[31]

Smith's theory was not immune to criticism. He had actually put forward at least two theories of value, which created confusion about both the production boundary and precisely who was productive – in particular, whether the provision of services in themselves created value.[32]

In essence, Smith was confused about the distinction between material and immaterial production. For Smith, as we have seen, a servant 'adds' no value that could be used by the master on something other than, literally, keeping the servant alive. But he also argued that if a manufacturing worker earns £1 in turning a quantity of cotton, whose other inputs also cost £1, into a piece of cloth that sells for £3, then the worker will have repaid his service and the master has made a profit of £1. Here a definition of productivity, irrespective of whether what is produced is a solid product or a service, emerges. Adding value in any branch of production is productive; not adding value is unproductive. Following this definition, services such as cleaning or vehicle repair can be productive – thereby invalidating Smith's own material–immaterial division of the production boundary. The debates about Smith's theories of value rumbled on for centuries. Other of Smith's ideas, such as free trade and the unproductive nature of government, have also left an enduring legacy.

But he is often misconstrued. His understanding of politics and philosophy was never sidelined in his economic reasoning. His *Theory of Moral Sentiments* and *The Wealth of Nations* were not contradictory but part of his deep analysis of what drives human behaviour and how societies organize themselves, and why some societies might grow in wealth more than others. Smith's analysis of 'free markets' was closely tied to his understanding of production, and the need to limit rent-seeking behaviour.

David Ricardo: Grounding Smith's Value Theory

In the 1810s, another towering figure of the English classical economic school used the labour theory of value and productiveness to explain how society maintains the conditions which enable it to reproduce itself. David Ricardo came from a Sephardic Jewish family which originated in Portugal and moved to Holland before settling in England. Ricardo followed his father as a London stockbroker, although he was later estranged from his family after becoming a Unitarian. He grew fabulously rich from his speculative activities, most notoriously by profiting from inaccurate information that was circulating on the Battle of Waterloo in 1815. He was said to have made £1 million (in 1815 value) from holding on to bonds while everyone else was selling (due to the false rumours that Wellington was losing against Napoleon), an almost unimaginable sum at the time, after which he promptly and wisely retired to the country, well away from London.

Ricardo was drawn to economics by reading Smith's *The Wealth of Nations*, but was concerned with something that he felt was glaringly absent from Smith's theory of value: how that value was distributed throughout society – or what we would today call income distribution. It need hardly be said that, in today's world of growing inequality of income and wealth, this question remains profoundly relevant.

Smith had observed that the value produced by labour, when sold, is redistributed as wages, profits and rent; he had also seen that labour's exact share of this value – wages – would vary.[33] However, Smith had no coherent explanation for the way in which wages were apportioned, or why they differed between professions and countries or over time.[34] Ricardo, by contrast, felt that the distribution of wages was, as he stressed in his magnum opus *On the Principles of Political Economy and Taxation*, the 'principle problem' in economics and ultimately regulates the growth and wealth of a nation.

Ricardo actually believed in the labour theory of value, and, unlike Smith, was at pains to point out that the value of a commodity was strictly proportional to the amount of labour time needed to produce it. Ricardo emphasized agriculture for a different reason from Quesnay. He wanted to explain the distribution of income, and for him productivity in agriculture was the hinge upon which that distribution turned. Workers, Ricardo believed, were paid a subsistence wage: in essence, they earned enough to pay for food and shelter. But food comes from agriculture, so the price of food regulates wages: a low price of food (or 'corn', as Ricardo wrote in the language of the day) will permit lower wages and therefore higher profits and incentives to invest in future production (for example in manufacturing) and promote economic growth. A high wage due to low productivity in agriculture will mean lower profits, and hence little investment in future production, which in turn leads to slower economic growth.

Ricardo inherited this 'dismal theory' of wages from his contemporary Thomas Malthus (1766–1834), another English writer on political economy, who proposed that whenever real wages are above subsistence level, the population will grow until it is so large that the demand for food will push up food prices enough to bring wages back to subsistence level.[35]

In Ricardo's view, then, wages depended heavily on the productivity of agriculture: if productivity rose and food became cheaper, wages would fall. And in manufacturing and the other branches of the economy, whatever did not have to be paid to the worker would flow to the capitalist as profit. Profits are the residual from the value that workers produce and do not need to consume for their own 'maintenance', as Ricardo put it, 'to subsist and perpetuate their race'.[36]

This in turn leads to Ricardo's theory of growth and accumulation – increasing the stock of capital or wealth to help fuel subsequent further increases in wealth. As profits grow, so capitalists invest and expand production, which in turn creates more jobs and raises wages, thereby increasing the population, whose wages finally go back to subsistence level, and so on. The economy is a perpetual growth machine, with more and more people earning the subsistence wage.

But Ricardo's theoretical genius really came to the fore in tackling his third class of society: landlords. Production in agriculture depends on two types of input: goods and services needed for production. One type can be scaled – increased in proportion to requirements. It includes labour, machinery, seeds and water. The other type cannot be scaled: good arable land. As Mark Twain is supposed to have said, 'Buy land, they're not making it any more.'

Since the population will grow thanks to investment and rising wages, and more and more food will need to be produced to feed everyone, at some point all the best land for corn production will be spoken for. Less fertile or productive land will then be cultivated.

However, since all the corn is sold at one price to the workers, who are on subsistence wages, the more productive land already in use yields a higher profit than the less productive land. Here Ricardo developed his celebrated theory of rent.

Ricardo defined rent as a transfer of profit to landlords simply because they had a monopoly of a scarce asset. There was no assumption, as in modern neoclassical theory (reviewed in Chapter 2), that these rents would be competed away. They remained due to power relationships inherent in the capitalist system. In Ricardo's time much of the arable land was owned by aristocrats and landed gentry but worked by tenant farmers or labourers. Ricardo proposed that the rent from more productive land always goes to the landlord because of competition between tenants. If the capitalist farmer – the tenant – wants to hang on to the largest possible profit by paying less rent, the landlord can give the lease to a competing farmer who will pay a higher rent and therefore be willing to work the land for only the standard profit. As this process goes on, land of increasingly poor quality will be brought into production, and a greater portion of the income will go to the landlords. Ricardo predicted that rents would rise.

More significantly, rising rents were the flipside of rising food prices, caused by lack of good-quality agricultural land. More costly food increased the wages workers needed for subsistence. This growing wage share, Ricardo believed, put a squeeze on profits in other sectors such as manufacturing. As economic development proceeded, the profit rate – basically the manufacturing capitalist's return on capital – would fall. The profit share – the part of the national income going to capitalists – would also fall. Correspondingly, the wage share going to manufacturing workers would rise. But the extra wages would have to be spent on food, which was more expensive because landlords were charging higher rents. As a result, much of the nation's income would ultimately go to landlords. This would halt further economic growth and investment in, say, manufacturing because the low returns would not justify the risks.[37]

By highlighting the different types of incomes earned, such as rent, profits and wages, Ricardo drew attention to an important question. When goods are sold, how are the proceeds of that sale divided? Does everyone involved get their 'just share' for the amount of effort they put into production? Ricardo's answer was an emphatic 'No'.

If some input into production – such as good arable land – is scarce, the cost of producing the same output – a given quantity of corn – will vary according to availability of the input. The cost is likely to be lower with good land, higher with inferior land. Profits, instead, are likely to be higher with good land and lower with inferior land. The owner of good land will pocket the difference in profit between the good land and inferior land simply because he or she has a monopoly of that asset.[38] Ricardo's theory was so convincing that it is, in essence, still used today in economics to explain how rents work.[39] Rents in this sense could mean a patent on a drug, control of a rare mineral such as diamonds, or rents in the everyday sense of what you pay a landlord to live in a flat. In the modern world, oil producers like those of the Organization of Petroleum Exporting Countries (OPEC) collect rents from their control of an essential resource.

Ricardo's gloomy picture of economic stagnation is relevant to a modern debate: how the rise of the financial sector in recent decades and the massive rents it earned from speculative activity have created disincentives for industrial production. Some heterodox economists today argue that growth will fall if finance becomes too big relative to the rest of the economy (industry) because real profits come from the production of new goods and services rather than from simple transfers of money earned from those goods and services.[40] To 'rebalance' the economy, the argument runs, we must allow genuine profits from production to win over rents – which, as we can see here, is exactly the argument Ricardo made 200 years ago, and John Maynard Keynes was to make 100 years later.[41]

Indeed, as is also argued today, Ricardo believed that the pool of (mainly unskilled) workers held the losing ticket. In Ricardo's day, agricultural labour flocked to the fast-growing cities and the supply of unskilled labour exceeded demand for it. Without bargaining power, these workers were paid a meagre subsistence wage. Ricardo's portrayal of rents dominating production also had a political impact. It helped to persuade Britain to abolish the Corn Laws in 1846 and embrace free trade, which diminished the power of big vested interests and allowed production costs, rather than embedded monopoly and the privileges that went with it, to govern production. The ensuing decades saw Britain become the 'workshop of the world'. But the abolition of the Corn Laws brought about a political transformation as well as an economic one: it tipped the balance of power away from aristocratic landlords and towards manufacturing as the nineteenth century wore on. Value theory influenced political behaviour, and vice versa – the performativity referred to in the Preface.

Other lessons about the sources of value and who generates it can be drawn from Ricardo's model of accumulation. Like Smith, Ricardo was concerned with understanding how the economy reproduces itself. Like Smith, he focused on the difference between investment in durable capital and consumption: 'When the annual productions of a country more than replace its annual consumption, it is said to increase its capital; when its annual consumption is not at least replaced by its annual production, it is said to diminish its capital.'[42] Ricardo hastened to add, though, that all goods produced – from clothes to carts – must be consumed or used; otherwise they would depreciate just like inventory.

Here Ricardo made a fundamental point about consumption, by which he means consumption by capitalists, not just households. As with production, consumption can be productive or unproductive. The productive kind might be a capitalist who 'consumes' his capital to buy labour, which in turn reproduces that capital and turns a profit. The alternative – unproductive consumption – is capital spent on luxuries that do not lead to reproduction of that capital expenditure. On this matter, Ricardo is absolutely clear: 'It makes the greatest difference imaginable whether they are consumed by those who reproduce, or by those who do not reproduce another value.'[43]

So Ricardo's heroes are the industrial capitalists, 'those who reproduce', who can ensure that workers subsist and generate a surplus that is free for the capitalist to use as he or she sees fit. His villains are those 'who do not reproduce' – the landed nobility, the owners of scarce land who charge very high rents and appropriate the surplus.[44] For Ricardo, capitalists would put that surplus to productive use, but landlords – including the nobility – would waste it on lavish lifestyles. Ricardo echoes Smith here. Both had seen with their own eyes the extravagance of the aristocracy, a class which often seemed better at spending money than making it and was addicted to that ultimate unproductive activity – gambling. But Ricardo parted company from Smith because he was not concerned about whether production activities were 'material' (making cloth) or 'immaterial' (selling cloth). To Ricardo, it was more important that, if a surplus was produced, it was spent productively.

Significantly for our discussion, Ricardo singled out government as the ultimate example of unproductive consumption. Government, in his view, is a dangerous leech on the surplus. Most of government spending comes from taxes, and if it consumes – by spending on armies, for example – too large a share of the national income, 'the resources of the people and the state will fall away with increasing rapidity, and distress and ruin will follow'.[45] Ricardo believed that government is by nature unproductive.

At the time Ricardo was writing, such issues were uppermost. Only a few years earlier, the British government had had to raise unprecedented amounts of money from taxes and issuing bonds to wage the war against Napoleon, from which the nation emerged heavily in debt. Could it afford the immense military expenditure which Ricardo's theory deemed unproductive? He found to his relief that the increase in value production by private companies more than compensated for the increase in unproductive government consumption. Unlike Smith, Ricardo did not write about that part of government expenditure which creates the conditions for productivity in the first place: infrastructure (bridges, roads, ports and so on), national defence and the rule of law. By omitting to discuss the role of government in productivity, he paved the way for generations of economists to be equally oblivious – with hugely significant consequences that we will look at in Chapter 8.

In essence, Ricardo's theory of value and growth led to a production boundary that does not depend on a job or profession itself (manufacturer, farmer or vicar) or on whether the activity is material or immaterial. He believed that industrial production in general leads to surpluses, but for him the real question is how those surpluses are used. If the surpluses finance productive spending, they are productive; if not, they are unproductive.

Ricardo focused on the 'plight' of capitalists and their struggle against landlords. However, he never addressed the awkward fact that labour creates value but the capitalists get the spoils – the surplus over and above the subsistence wages paid to labourers. In the course of the nineteenth century, as England industrialized, inequalities and injustices multiplied. The labour theory of value was to interpret production in a way that cast capitalists in a much less favourable light.

Karl Marx on 'Production' Labour

Ricardo's appreciation of the dynamism of capitalism compared with past eras prefigures the emphasis Marx placed a generation later on the system's unprecedented power to transform societies. Born in 1818, Marx grew up in the German city of Trier, one of nine children of Jewish parents, both lawyers. In his own legal studies at university, Marx was drawn to a critical version of Hegel's philosophy of dialectics, propounded by Hegel's disciples, which set out how intellectual thought proceeds via negation and contradiction, through a thesis, its antithesis, and then a synthesis. Marx was particularly interested in how history is shaped by contradictions between material forces – such as capital and labour – and by the resolution or synthesis of those contradictions. After being barred from taking a professorship at the University of Jena because of his radical political leanings, he became editor of a progressive newspaper, *Rheinische Zeitung*. Then in 1843 he moved to Paris, where he met Friedrich Engels, his future co-author and collaborator. Two years later Marx was expelled from France because of his socialist political activities and settled in Brussels. There in 1848 he published with Engels the *Communist Manifesto*. Marx wrote voluminously on politics for the rest of his life but it is remarkable that, despite being opposed to capitalism, he analysed it objectively in order to understand where it was taking humankind and what the alternatives might be.

Marx developed his own version of the labour theory of value. He emphasized how definitions of 'productive' activity depend on historical circumstances – the society of any given time. He also focused on the nature of productive activity within the capitalist system. Under capitalism, firms produce commodities – a general term for anything from nuts and bolts to complete machines. If commodities are exchanged – sold – they are said to have an exchange value. If you produce a commodity which you consume yourself it does not have an exchange value. Exchange value crystallizes the value inherent in commodities.

The source of that inherent value is the one special commodity workers own: their labour power, or – put another way – their capacity to work. Capitalists buy labour power with their capital. In exchange, they pay workers a wage. Workers' wages buy the commodities such as food and housing needed to restore a worker's strength to work. In this way, wages express the value of the goods that restore labour power.

This description of the source of value largely followed Ricardo. But Ricardo had tried unsuccessfully to find an external commodity that could serve as an 'invariable standard of value' by which the value of all other products could be determined. Marx solved this problem by locating this invariable measure in workers themselves. He was careful to distinguish labour expended in production from labour power, which is the *capacity* to work. Workers expend labour, not labour power. And in this distinction lies the secret of Marx's theory of value. Humans can create more value than they need to restore their labour power. For instance, if a worker has to work five hours to produce the value needed to restore labour power per day, the labour power's value is equivalent to the five hours of work. However, if the working day lasts ten hours, the additional five hours' work will create value over and above that needed to restore labour power. Labour power creates surplus value.

The ingenuity of capitalism, according to Marx, is that it can organize production to make workers generate unprecedented amounts of this surplus value. In early societies of hunter-gatherers and subsistence farmers, people worked enough to create the value that would allow them to survive, but no surplus over and above that. Later, under feudalism, they could be forced to produce enough surplus to satisfy the (unproductive) consumption of the feudal lord, which, as Smith and Ricardo knew, could be substantial. But after the means of production were taken away from independent producers – mostly by violence and expropriation through property rights legislation, such as enclosures of common land in England by big landowners – they became workers, 'free' and without property.

Capitalists were able to purchase the workers' labour power because workers lost their independent means of subsistence and needed a wage to survive. The trick is to get them to work longer than needed to produce value (wages) that they spend on their subsistence needs – again, food and housing.[46] Workers, in other words, are *exploited* because capitalists pocket the surplus value workers produce over and above their subsistence requirements. And, unlike the feudal lords, capitalists will not squander all of the surplus on consumption, but will have incentives to reinvest part of it in expanding production to make yet more profits. However, Marx noted that there was a contradiction in the system. The drive to increase productivity would increase mechanization, which, in displacing labour (machines taking over human work), would then eventually reduce the key source of profits: labour power. He also foresaw the problem of growing financialization, which could potentially undermine industrial production. Throughout his analysis, his focus was on change, and the effects of change on the creation of value.

Indeed, the extraordinary aspect of Marx's theory is his fundamental insight that capitalism is dynamic and constantly changing. But it was not just economically dynamic. Marx was struck by the social upheavals he could see all around him, such as the mass movement of rural workers into cities, which created an urban proletariat. He saw that capitalist *society*, not just the capitalist economy, was utterly different from preceding societies and was in permanent flux – a very evident phenomenon today as we struggle to come to terms with the massive changes brought by digital, nano, biological and other technologies.

Economists had previously thought of 'capital' as purely physical – machinery and buildings, for example – and surplus as solely positive, helping the economy to reproduce itself and grow. But Marx gives capital a social dimension and surplus a negative connotation. Labour produces surplus value, which fuels capital accumulation and economic growth. But capital accumulation is not just due to productive labour. It is also deeply social. Because workers do not own the means of production they are 'alienated' from their work. The surplus they produce is taken away from them. Work is necessary for earning the wages they receive to buy the food, shelter and clothes they need to survive.[47] Moreover, in a capitalist market society, relations between people are mediated by commodity exchange. In a specialized society with division of labour, humans produce the social product – net national income – together and depend on other humans. But precisely because the division of labour, which Smith extolled, left most workers overly specializing in discrete aspects of the production process, he believed that social relations became relations between commodities (things).[48]

Marx was so fascinated by the dynamics of capitalism that he produced his own theory of value to explain how it works. Unlike earlier economists, who tended to define production by sector or occupation (agriculture or manufacturing, merchant or clergyman), Marx defined the production boundary in terms of *how* profits are made. Marx asked how, by owning the means of production, the capitalist could appropriate surplus value while the workers who provided the labour received barely enough to live on – exactly the question Big Bill Heywood posed. By placing this distinction at the heart of value theory, Marx generated a new and unprecedented production boundary. Marx's value theory changed economics – at least for a time.

Marx argued that workers are productive if they create surplus value which the capitalist class then retains. For Marx, while workers in capitalist production are productive, the key questions when drawing his production boundary are: who participates in capitalist production? And who receives the surplus that is produced?

Figure 6 gives a graphical answer to these questions. The production sphere, the light grey blob, includes three basic sectors: primary, comprising essential materials such as food and minerals (the only source of value for Quesnay); secondary, which is industry, the basis of value creation in Smith and Ricardo; and tertiary, the services considered by Smith to be 'immaterial'. The darker blob within, called the 'circulation sphere', reflects Marx's analysis, which we will discuss later, that some aspects of finance are essential to production and deserve to be placed on that side of the production boundary. On the other side of the boundary, Marx followed Smith and Ricardo in regarding government and households as unproductive.

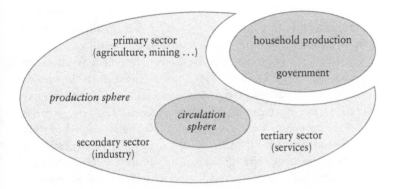

Figure 6. The production boundary according to Karl Marx

At any moment in a capitalist economy, there is a ratio of surplus value to value used for workers' subsistence – what Marx calls simply the rate of surplus value. It determines what share of the economic product can potentially be used for accumulation and growth. Marx referred to capital that is used to hire labour as 'variable' capital: the workers produce more capital than is invested in them, so the capital that hires them 'varies' in relation to the capitalist's total capital. Capital not used to hire workers is invested in other means of production that are 'constant' capital – including machinery, land, buildings and raw materials – whose value is preserved but not increased during production.[49]

The value used for workers' subsistence, the 'wage share', could not be less than was needed to restore labour power or workers would perish, leaving the capitalist unable to produce surplus value. Historically, the wages of the poor had tended to be at subsistence level. But here Marx introduces a powerful new idea which has informed thinking ever since: class struggle. Workers' wages were set by class struggle. The side with more power could force through a wage rate favourable to itself. Which class had more power was related to what we would call today the tightness of the labour market. If wages increased because workers had a lot of bargaining power in a tight labour market, capitalists would substitute more machines for labour, creating more unemployment and competition among workers for jobs. Marx thought that capitalists would try to keep a 'reserve army' of the unemployed to hold down wages and maintain or increase their own share of the value workers created.

The value of labour power is expressed to workers as wages, to capitalists as profits. The rate of profit for an enterprise is the surplus value divided by variable and constant capital – roughly what today we call the rate of return on a company's assets. The average profit rate of the economy as a whole is total surplus value divided by total variable and constant capital. But the size of the average profit rate depends on the composition of capital (how much variable and constant capital) and on class struggle – effectively, the size of workers' wages relative to value produced. The average profit rate is also affected by economies of scale as the productivity of workers rises with a growing market and the increasing specialization of workers.[50] In particular, Marx believed that increasing agricultural production would not lead to Ricardo's stationary, food-constrained world.[51] He was right: broadly speaking, food production has kept pace with population increase. Marx was also acute in his understanding of the capacity of technology to transform society. He would not have been surprised by the extent to which automation has replaced people, nor perhaps by the possibility of machines more intelligent than their human creators.

Marx's analysis of who got what in capitalism did not stop there. He also distinguished between different functions of various capitalist actors in the economy. In doing so he used his value theory shrewdly to identify those who produce value and those who do not.

Like economists before him, Marx believed that competition would tend to equalize rates of profits across the economy.[52] But at this point Marx introduced a distinction that is critically important for his and for subsequent theories of value: the way in which different kinds of capitalists came by their profits. The first two categories Marx identified were production (or industrial) capital and commercial capital. The first produces commodities; the second circulates commodities by selling them, making the money received available to production capital for buying the means of production (the dark grey sphere in the lighter blob in Figure 6). As Marx explained, the first creates surplus value, the second 'realizes' it. Any unsold commodity will therefore be of no use to a capitalist, regardless of how much he or she exploits his or her workers, because no surplus value is realized. Commercial capital, Marx noted, had existed for millennia: international merchants such as the Phoenicians and the Hanse bought cheap and sold dear. What they did not do was to add value by capitalist production. Under capitalism, the commercial capitalists realize the value produced by the production capitalists. To apply Marx's theory to a modern-world example, Amazon is a commercial capitalist because it is a means by which production capitalists sell their goods and realize surplus value. Banks' money transfer services are also an example of commercial capital.[53]

Marx suggested that, initially, production enterprises might also carry out commercial capital activities. As production expands, however, separate capitalist enterprises will probably emerge to carry out these functions as commodity or money capitalists. Crucially, these capitalists and the labour they employ are purely concerned with the 'circulation' of capital; they do not produce commodities which generate surplus value and therefore they are unproductive.[54] However, because they are also capitalist firms, they require the same rate of profit as does production capital. Consequently, some surplus value is diverted to become their income, diminishing the average profit rate in the economy.[55] Although labour in firms engaged in the circulation of capital does not create surplus value, it is seen by the commercial capitalist as productive because it secures the capitalist's share in existing surplus value and becomes a profit.[56] The emergence of distinct commercial capital enterprises alters the structure of the whole economy and the amount of surplus value available to production capitalists.

Marx then identified 'interest-bearing' capital – capitalists such as banks who earned interest on loans that production capitalists took out to expand production. The generation of interest is possible because, in capitalism, money represents not just purchasing power – buying commodities for consumption – but also the potential to generate more profit in the future through investment as capital.[57] The interest is deducted from the production capitalist's profit rate. Interest-bearing capital, unlike commercial capital, does not lower the general rate of profit; it just subdivides it between recipients of interest and earners of profit.

The relationship between these two types of capital has distinct advantages. It can increase the scale and speed of capitalist production by making it easier to obtain capital and reduce the turnover time (the time it takes for capital to produce, sell and buy new means of production – one 'period' of production). Interest-bearing capital and the credit system it supplies also reduce the importance of commercial capital, for example by shortening the time the production capitalist has to wait for the merchant to return with the proceeds from sales. However, since interest-bearing capital does not produce any surplus value, it is not directly productive.[58]

Finally, in addition to these types of capitalists, Marx identified another: owners of scarce things like land, coal, a patent, a licence to practise law, and so on. Such scarce things can improve productivity above the general productivity level – the same product can be produced in less labour time or with fewer means of production. That in turn creates 'surplus profits' – what Smith and Ricardo might have thought of as 'rent' – for capitalists, or landlords and proprietors, who can exploit these advantageous production conditions. Marx thus outlined a theory of 'monopoly' gain.

The key, in Marx's view, is that labour is productive if – and only if – it produces a surplus value for production capital, the engine of the capitalist system; that is, value above and beyond the value of labour power. For Marx, then, the production boundary is defined not by sectors or occupations but by how profits are generated – more specifically, whether an occupation is carried out in a capitalist production context. Only the capitalist enterprise will accumulate the surplus value that can lead to an expansion of production. In this way, the capitalist economy reproduces itself.

Participating in 'circulation' or earning interest is not a judgement on such activities' 'usefulness'. It was simply necessary, Marx argued, for capital to transform itself from commodity form into money form and back again.[59] In fact, Marx thought that a well-functioning sphere of circulation could raise the profit rate by reducing turnover time for capital. If the 'circulation sphere' was not functioning properly – for example, the system of credit that fuelled it was inefficient – it risked absorbing too large a chunk of the surplus value that capitalists hoped to generate by selling their goods and as a result impeding growth.

Marx refined Adam Smith's distinction between productive (industry) and unproductive (services) sectors into something much more subtle. As can be seen in Figure 6, in Marx's theory of value every privately organized enterprise that falls within the sphere of *production* is productive, whether it is a service or anything else. Here, Marx's achievement was to move beyond the simple categorization of occupations and map them onto the landscape of capitalist reproduction.[60] Marx's production boundary now runs between goods and services production on one side and all those functions of capital that were not creating additional surplus value, such as interest charged by moneylenders or speculative trading in shares and bonds, on the other. Functions lying outside the production boundary take a chunk of surplus value in exchange for circulating capital, providing money or making possible surplus (monopoly) profits.

What is more, in distinguishing between different types of capitalist activity – production, circulation, interest-bearing capital and rent – Marx offers the economist an additional diagnostic tool with which to examine the state of the economy. Is the sphere of circulation working well enough? Is there enough capacity to bring capital to the market, so that it can be exchanged and realize its value and be reinvested in production? What proportion of profits pays for interest, and is it the same for all capitalists? Do scarce resources, such as 'intellectual' ones like patents on inventions, create advantageous conditions for producers with access to them and generate 'surplus profits' or rents for those producers?

Ricardo and Marx refined the theory of rent to make it clear that rent is income from *redistributing* value and not from creating it. Landlords do not create the soil but they can generate income from their right to exclude from the land others (capitalists) who might use it to produce value. Rent of any kind is basically a claim on the total of social surplus value and therefore lowers productive capitalists' profits. As we will see in the next chapter, neoclassical (mainstream) economics has fundamentally changed this idea of rent into one of imperfections and impediments – which can be competed away.

All these issues have come to the fore again since the 2008 financial crisis. At their heart is how finance has been self-serving, and not actually serving what the American economist Hyman Minsky (1919–96) called the 'capital development of the economy'.[61] In other words, instead of facilitating industrial production, finance has simply degenerated into a casino, aiming to appropriate as much of the existing surplus as possible for itself.[62] But whether that casino is seen as a mere imperfection or as a stable source of unearned income (whereby activities that are not creating value are somehow allowed to be presented as such) makes all the difference in policies that aim to reform the system.

Marx's attempt to define the production boundary was more rigorous than those of Smith and Ricardo and was certainly a long way from those of Petty and King. He introduced the idea of labour power as an objective and invariable standard of value, building on the essential premise shared by earlier economists that value derived from labour. He also shared with them the belief that government was unproductive. The early and classical economists left a legacy of ideas about value – on currencies and protection, free trade, rent, government and technology – which have reverberated down the centuries and remain alive today.

The next chapter explores how, even as the ink was drying on Marx's writing in the British Museum Reading Room, the intellectual world of the classical economists was about to be turned upside down.

2

Value in the Eye of the Beholder:
The Rise of the Marginalists

*... the distribution of the income of society is controlled by
a natural law ... this law, if it worked without friction,
would give to every agent of production the amount of
wealth which that agent creates.*

J. B. Clark, *The Distribution of Wealth:
A Theory of Wages, Interest and Profits* (1965)[1]

In Marx's hands, value theory became a powerful tool for analysing society. While Smith had praised the merits of individual pursuit of happiness and profit, and Ricardo had made the capitalist entrepreneur the hero of the economy, Marx was much more critical of both. As the Industrial Revolution progressed and threw masses of labourers in Europe into urban poverty, his labour theory of value was not just a set of abstract ideas, but an active critique of the system that he saw developing around him. If labour produced value, why was labour continuing to live in poverty and misery? If financiers did not create value, how did they become so rich?

However, the labour theory of value's days were numbered. This chapter is about the emergence of a new set of ideas that inverted the earlier argument that value was nested in objective conditions of production, and that all other economic categories, such as the price of goods and services, were subsumed to it. The classical economists lost their crown to a new dynasty, the neoclassicals.

NEW TIMES, NEW THEORY

Socialist critiques of value theory were multiplying even before Marx wrote *Capital*. A group called the 'Ricardian socialists' used Ricardo's labour theory of value to demand that workers get better wages. They included the Irishman William Thompson (1775–1833), Thomas Hodgskin (1787–1869) and John Gray (1799–1883), both British, and John Bray (1809–97), who was born in the US but worked for part of his life in Britain. Together, they made the obvious argument that if the value of commodities derives from labour, the revenue from their sale should go to workers. This idea underlay the co-operativism of the textile manufacturer Robert Owen (1771–1858), for whom the solution was that workers should also participate in ownership, of both factories and publicly created infrastructure. Marx and Engels were friendly with some of these groups, but very unfriendly towards others whom they thought had no proper analysis of why things were going wrong. The pair collaborated with the groups to whom they were well disposed to produce critiques of capitalism.

Intellectual opposition to capitalism had its practical counterpart in a growing array of radical and socialist political organizations which connected the often dire conditions of working people with programmes of action to remedy them. In Britain, the Chartists (1837–54) demanded reforms to the political system. Trade unionism began to gain a significant following. The Amalgamated Society of Engineers was formed in 1851 and the Trades Union Congress in 1868. During the recession of the 1880s, socialism became more widespread, culminating in the founding of the Labour Party in 1900. Here, Britain was a relative latecomer: the Socialist Workers' Party of Germany was founded in 1875 and the Federation of the Socialist Workers of France four years later.

Faced with these threats to the status quo, the powers that be needed a new theory of value that cast them in a more favourable light. Other influences also encouraged the search for a new analysis of how capitalism works and the troubling question of where value comes from. Malthus's pessimism about the dangers of population growth was an affront to the later-nineteenth-century belief in progress – and the facts did not appear to support him, because the food shortages he predicted had not materialized. Non-conformism offered a moral basis on which to argue that the immiseration of the masses that Marx and others feared was neither inevitable nor desirable. The development of natural sciences and mathematics encouraged attempts to place economics on a similar 'scientific' footing, as opposed to what was becoming seen as the more 'literary' endeavours of the political economists. Above all, perhaps, the rising power of capitalists in a society long dominated by aristocratic landowners and local gentry meant that a new analysis of capitalism was required to justify their standing.

THE ECLIPSE OF THE CLASSICALS

A series of thinkers and economists who were roughly contemporaneous with Marx began to lay the foundations for what has become modern mainstream economics. Landlords were defended as productive by Lord Lauderdale (1784–1860), a Scottish earl, and profits by Nassau Senior (1790–1864), an English lawyer and economist, as a reward for abstaining from consumption. Linking profits to a notion of sacrifice allowed a useful moral justification for the large income inequality between capitalists and workers.[2] Furthermore, as scarce capital could be either invested or saved, profits were no longer linked to theories of exploitation but came to be seen as simply a return for saving and not consuming.

But to put the classicals to bed properly, a new theory of value had to be invented. Two of the principal architects of what became known as neoclassical economics were Léon Walras (1834–1910) and William Stanley Jevons (1835–82). Walras was a professor of economics in Lausanne, Switzerland. For him, 'the characteristic of a science properly speaking is the complete indifference to any consequences, advantageous or undesirable, of its attachment to the pursuit of pure truth'.[3] Walras was keen to show that economics was a real science, less fuzzy than sociology or philosophy, so set out to discover 'pure truths' in the science of theoretical economics rather than focus on applications. Jevons, a Professor of Political Economy at University

College, London, began his 1871 *The Theory of Political Economy* with the assertion that economics, 'if it is to be a science at all, must be a mathematical science'. He justified this statement by stating that economics deals with quantities: there were, he continued, 'laws' in economics, which could become like other 'exact' sciences if sufficient commercial statistics were available. Jevons called his economic theory 'the mechanics of utility and self-interest'.

Another economist who linked value to utility was Carl Menger (1840–1921), one of the founders of the 'Austrian school' of economics. As we shall see later, utility is a broad concept, combining ideas about a product's efficiency – is the car reliable? – with vaguer notions of satisfaction and even happiness – does the new car impress the neighbours? For Menger, the value arising from utility set the cost of production; the cost of production, including the cost of labour, did not determine value. Although original, Menger's ideas did not fit comfortably into the new narrative that economics had to be much more abstract, expressed neatly in mathematical equations based on Newtonian physics.

FROM OBJECTIVE TO SUBJECTIVE: A NEW THEORY OF VALUE BASED ON PREFERENCES

Walras, Jevons and Menger provided a positive and 'scientific' view of reproduction, exchange and income distribution. They used the construct which later came to be called 'marginal utility', and their propagation of a new view on value theory is now referred to as a 'marginal revolution'[4] – it was, however, a slow one.

The marginal utility theory of value states that all income is reward for a productive undertaking. Given the large investments being made in factories and the edifices of the Industrial Revolution, it suited the changing circumstances of the second half of the nineteenth century. But it did not come out of nowhere; indeed, it has a long history. In medieval times, thinkers argued that 'just prices' were those that reflected an object's utility. In his *Summa Theologica*, the thirteenth century philosopher-theologian Thomas Aquinas discussed the concept of the just price in a section of the book called 'Of Cheating, Which Is Committed in Buying and Selling'. Just price was a normative concept, against what was seen as the wrong price resulting from morally evil greed. The medieval Church inveighed against the sin of greed and avarice, which broadly meant profiteering by middlemen and moneylenders. In Dante's *Inferno*, usurers are consigned to the hottest part of hell (circle 7) because they are making money not from the productive sources, which for Dante were Nature or Art, but from speculation and differences in interest rates. Indeed, he is so disgusted by usury that he puts usurers just below the circle of hell housing the sodomites.

This normative and moral view of price, linked to cheating or criminal behaviour, began to fade after the seventeenth century – the time of Petty and King – but lingered on until firmly supplanted by the concept of individual utility, which held that it was not about good or bad but how common goals could be reached through each individual trying to maximize the benefit to him- or herself. In 1776 – the year that Adam Smith published *The Wealth of Nations* – the Englishman Jeremy Bentham argued that 'the greatest happiness of the greatest number' should be the 'measure of right and wrong'.[5] In other words, an action should be evaluated according to its consequences in a particular context: killing may be justified if it prevents more killing. This 'utilitarian' theory of ethics spilled over into ideas about production. In France, Jean-Baptiste Say (1767–1832), Smith's contemporary and a hostile critic of Quesnay, argued in his 1803 book *Treatise on Political Economy* that the value of a commodity resides in its utility to a buyer and, therefore, that productive labour is labour which produces utility. In Say's view, labour in services – which classical economists thought fell squarely into the 'unproductive' category, because they failed to produce 'things' – could in fact be reclassified as productive, so long as those services fetched a price and labour got paid a wage.[6]

The most influential person in developing utility theory was the late-nineteenth-/early-twentieth-century British economist Alfred Marshall (1842–1924), Professor of Political Economy (as it was still called) at Cambridge. Significantly, he was trained as a mathematician. Marshall's 1890 *Principles of Economics* diffused the new ideas to generations of students. The economics library in Cambridge is known simply as the Marshall Library; introductory economics textbooks still include diagrams he developed in the nineteenth century.

In many respects Marshall was a natural heir to the classical tradition. He accepted that the cost of production was important in determining a commodity's value. But he and his followers shifted thinking about value from the study of broad quantities of capital, labour and technology inputs and their returns to that of small incremental quantities. Using mathematical calculus, they focused on how a small – or 'marginal' – change in one variable causes a change in another: for instance, how a small change in price affects the quantity of product demanded or supplied.

So what was the new value theory, marginalism, about? First, it is based on the notions of utility and scarcity and is subjective: the value of things is measured by their usefulness to the consumer. There is, therefore, no 'objective' standard of value, since utility may vary between individuals and at different times. Second, this utility decreases as the amount of a thing that is held or consumed increases. The first Mars Bar you eat in a day may provide a lot of utility or satisfaction and even happiness. It is enjoyable and maybe staves off hunger pangs. But as you go on eating Mars Bars they cease to be so enjoyable and may even make you feel ill. At some point the utility gained from eating them will decrease.[7] In this way, the utility of the last bar is less, possibly much less, than that of earlier bars. This is 'marginal utility' – in the case of a Mars Bar, worth less to you than the previous one, 'decreasing marginal utility'. By the same token, the scarcer a thing is, the more utility it gives you – 'increasing marginal utility'. One Mars Bar on a desert island can give you more happiness than any number of bars bought from your corner shop.

THE RISE OF THE 'NEOCLASSICALS'

Prices, then, reflect the utility that buyers get from things. The scarcer they are – the higher their marginal utility – the more consumers will be willing to pay for them. These changes in the marginal utility of a product came to be known as consumer 'preference'. The same principle applies to producers. 'Marginal productivity' is the effect that an extra unit of produced goods would have on the costs of production. The marginal cost of each extra Mars Bar that rolls off the production line is lower than the cost of the previous one.

This concept of marginalism lies at the heart of what is known today as 'neoclassical' theory – the set of ideas that followed the classical theory developed by Smith and Ricardo and was extended by Marx. The term *neo*classical reflected how the new theorists stood on the shoulders of giants but then took the theory in new directions. Microeconomic theory, the theory of how firms, workers and consumers make choices, is based on the neoclassical theory of production and consumption which rests on the maximization of profits (firms), and utility (consumers and workers).

As a mathematician, Marshall used mathematical calculus, borrowed from Newtonian physics, to develop his theory of how an economy worked. In his model, the point at which a consumer's money is worth more to him or her than the additional (marginal) unit of a commodity (that next Mars Bar) that their money would purchase, is where the system is in 'equilibrium', an idea reminiscent of Newton's description of how gravity held the universe together. The smooth, continuous curves of these equilibrating and evolutionary forces depict a system that is peaceful and potentially 'optimal'. The inclusion of concepts like equilibria in the neoclassical model had the effect of portraying capitalism as a peaceful system driven by self-equilibrating competitive mechanisms – a stark contrast to the ways in which the system was depicted by Marx, as a battle between classes, full of disequilibria and far from optimal, whose resulting revolutions would have been better described by Erwin Schrödinger's concept of quantum leaps and wave mechanics.

So keen was Marshall to emphasize the equilibrating and evolutionary forces in economics, with their smooth, continuous curves that could be described by mathematical calculus, that the epigraph of his 1890 *Principles of Economics* was the Latin tag *Natura non facit saltum*, a nod to its use by Darwin in his 1859 *On the Origin of*

Species to make the point that Nature, rather than progressing in leaps and bounds, evolves in incremental steps, building on previous changes.

The equilibrium concept had a lot of appeal at the start of the twentieth century, when the rise of socialism and trade unions in Europe threatened the old, often autocratic, order and the conventional wisdom was that capitalism was largely self-regulating and government involvement was unnecessary or even dangerous.

Equilibrium was predicated on the notion of scarcity, and the effect of scarcity on diminishing returns: the more you consume, the less you enjoy each unit of consumption after a certain amount (the maximum enjoyment); and the more you produce, the less you profit from each marginal unit produced (the maximum profit). It is this concept of diminishing returns that allows economists today to draw smooth curves in diagrams, using mathematical calculus, so that maxima and minima points (e.g., the bottom of a U-shaped curve showing how costs change with increased production) provide the equilibrium targets and utility maximization.

Nineteenth-century economists liked to illustrate the importance of scarcity to value by using the water and diamond paradox. Why is water cheap, even though it is necessary for human life, and diamonds are expensive and therefore of high value, even though humans can quite easily get by without them? Marx's labour theory of value – naïvely applied – would argue that diamonds simply take a lot more time and effort to produce. But the new utility theory of value, as the marginalists defined it, explained the difference in price through the *scarcity* of diamonds. Where there is an abundance of water, it is cheap. Where there is a scarcity (as in a desert), its value can become very high. For the marginalists, this scarcity theory of value became the rationale for the price of everything, from diamonds, to water, to workers' wages.

The idea of scarcity became so important to economists that in the early 1930s it prompted one influential British economist, Lionel Robbins (1898–1984), Professor of Economics at the London School of Economics, to define the study of economics itself in terms of scarcity; his description of it as 'the study of the allocation of resources, under conditions of scarcity' is still widely used.[8] The emergence of marginalism was a pivotal moment in the history of economic thought, one that laid the foundations for today's dominant economic theory.

The Marginal Revolution

The 'marginal revolutionaries', as they have been called, used marginal utility and scarcity to determine prices and the size of the market. In their view, the supply and demand of scarce resources regulates value expressed in money. Because things exchanged in a monetary market economy have prices, price is ultimately the measure of value. This powerful new theory explained how prices were arrived at and how much of a particular thing was produced.[9] Competition ensures that the 'marginal utility' of the last item sold determines the price of that commodity. The size of the market in a particular commodity – that is, the number of items that need to be sold before marginal utility no longer covers the costs of production – is explained by the scarcity, and hence price, of the inputs into production. Price is a direct measure of value.[10] We are, then, a long way from the labour theory of value.

But what this model gains in versatility – the notion that the preferences of millions of individuals determine prices, and hence value – it loses in its ability, or, rather, lack of ability, to measure what Smith called 'the wealth of nations', the total production of an economy in terms of value. As value is now merely a relative concept – we can compare the value of two things through their prices and how the prices may change – we can no longer measure the labour that produced the goods in the economy and by this means assess how much wealth was created.

Marginal utility and scarcity need a couple of additional assumptions for price determination to work as intended. First, all humans have to be one-dimensional utility calculators who know what's best for themselves, what price to pay for what commodity and how to make an economically 'rational' choice.[11] Second, there must be no interference, for example by monopolies, in price-setting. 'Equilibrium' with 'perfect competition' – in which supply and demand are exactly balanced, an idea Jean-Baptiste Say developed back in the early nineteenth century – became a necessary and central concept in economics. These assumptions, as we will see, bear heavily on today's discussion of value creation.

The Production Boundary
Becomes Malleable

The consequences of marginal thinking for the production boundary are dramatic. As we have seen, classical thinkers differed in their definition of who was and was not productive. For Quesnay only farmers were productive; Smith put services in the 'unproductive' bracket; and even Marx defined productive workers as those who were working in capitalist production. In marginal thinking, however, such classification was swept aside. What replaced it was the notion that it is only whatever fetches a price in the market (legally) that can be termed productive activity. Moreover, productivity will fluctuate with prices, because prices determine value, not vice versa. The utility theory therefore completely changes the concept of productive and unproductive labour. In fact, the distinction effectively falls away, since every sector that produces for the market exchanges its products – which means there are now few definitively unproductive sectors. The only part of the economy which clearly lies outside the production boundary and is unproductive, as in Figure 7, consists of those who receive income simply as transfers, such as subsidies to companies or social security payments to citizens.

In Marshall's state of 'equilibrium', where prices are not distorted, everyone gets paid what they are worth – which may change if consumers alter their tastes or if technology advances. This has important consequences for how incomes are assessed and justified. What workers earn is reflected in their marginal productivity and their revealed preferences (marginal utility) for leisure versus work. There is no longer any room for the analytical distinctions that Ricardo or Marx made about a worker's contribution to production, let alone the exploitation of that worker. You are valuable because what you provide is scarce. Because we are rational utility calculators in the face of scarcity, we don't let things go to waste. Workers might choose unemployment because that gives them more marginal utility than working for that or a given wage. The corollary of this logic is that unemployment is

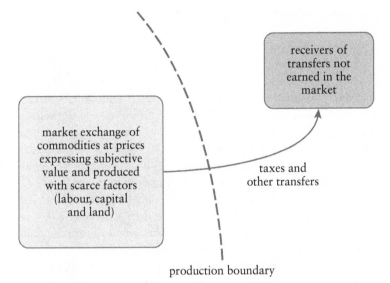

Figure 7. The marginalist revolution

voluntary. Voluntary unemployment arises from viewing economic agents as rationally choosing between work and leisure (i.e. 'inter temporal maximization' in modern theory). In other words, Marx's concept of the 'reserve army of labour' disappears into thin air.

As Lionel Robbins neatly put it,

> In the first place, isolated man wants both real income and leisure. Secondly, he has not enough of either fully to satisfy his want of each. Thirdly, he can spend his time in augmenting his real income or he can spend it in taking more leisure. Fourthly, it may be presumed that, save in most exceptional cases, his want for the different constituents of real income and leisure will be different. Therefore he has to choose. He has to economize.[12]

Inherent in equilibrium is the idea that everything is in everyone's interest. In the 1940s the Russian-born British economist Abba Lerner (1903–82) formulated what he called the 'first fundamental welfare theorem',[13] which basically states that competitive markets lead to 'optimal' outcomes for all. Once market exchange at equilibrium prices has taken place, no one can be made better off, or, in economic parlance, have their 'welfare' increased (for example, by accepting more work) without making someone else worse off.

Today, competitive markets where no one can be made better off without someone being made worse off are known as 'Pareto-optimal' – named after Walras's successor in Lausanne, Vilfredo Pareto (1848–1923), who was the first to introduce the term 'welfare maximization'. In his *Manual of Political Economy* (1906), Pareto studied economic equilibrium in terms of solutions to individual problems of 'objectives and constraints', and was the first economist to argue that utility maximization did not need to be cardinal (i.e., the exact amount that someone wanted something) just the ordinal amount (how much they wanted it more than something else – X versus Y). This made mathematical calculus even easier to use, and many welfare properties in economics today bear his name. He used his theories to argue for free trade in Italy, which did not make him popular with the Fascist government of the time, which was more protectionist.

But to get to these 'optimal' outcomes, we must ensure that equilibrium holds: all obstacles to equilibrium, such as an interfering government, monopolies, other rents arising from scarcity and so on, must be obliterated. Our problems, marginalism holds, derive solely from imperfections in, and inhibitions on, the smooth working of the capitalist machine. Rent is no longer seen as 'unearned income', as it was by the classical economists, but as an imperfection that can be competed away. Left to itself, capitalism can thus create maximal value for everyone, which is conveniently what everyone 'deserves' based on their marginal product. The contrast with the classical economists is glaring. For Marx, capitalists appropriate surplus value by paying a wage less than the value of labour. Smith and Ricardo held that value was created by effort that directly added up to the wealth of nations. But with marginal utility there are no longer classes, only individuals, and there is no objective measurement of value.

This approach has a very important consequence. It suggests that government should never intervene in the economy unless there are market failures. Market failure theory uses the first fundamental theorem (FFT) of welfare economics as its starting point. The FFT holds that markets are the most efficient allocators of resources under three specific conditions: first, that there exists a complete set of markets, so that all goods and services which are demanded and supplied are traded at publicly known prices; that all consumers and producers behave competitively; and that an equilibrium exists.

Violations of any of these three assumptions leads to the inefficient allocation of resources by markets, or what marginalists term 'market failures'. Market failures might arise when there are 'positive externalities', benefits to society such as basic science research from which it is hard for individual firms to profit; or 'negative externalities', bad things like pollution, which harm society but are not included in firms' costs. If markets are not 'Pareto-optimal', then everyone could be better off as a result of public policies that correct the market failure in question.[14] However, as we will see in Chapter 8, a body of economics referred to as Public Choice theory, advocated by Nobel Prize winner James Buchanan (1919–2013), later argued that as government failures are even worse than market failures (due to corruption and capture), so the correction of market failures by bureaucrats might make things even worse.

From the Class Struggle to Profits and Wages in 'Equilibrium'

Defining everything that commands a price as valuable led to the marginalists' conclusion that what you get is what you are worth. Profits are not determined by exploitation but by technology and the 'marginal product of capital'. Capital and labour are seen as the two main inputs into production, and so just as labour earns wages for its productive contribution (marginal product of labour), capital earns a return (marginal product of capital). John Bates Clark (1847–1938), a former critic of capitalism who converted to become one of the most ardent contributors to the marginalist revolution, argued strongly against the idea that labour was exploited. Capital could not exploit labour, he reasoned, because labour and capital were simply earning their 'just rewards' – their marginal products. In Clark's view, capital goods themselves were the rewards for capitalist self-restraint. Instead of consuming their profits, they had saved them – saving that would eventually result in higher investment in more capital goods (we will come back to this in Chapter 8).

The equilibrium view diverted attention from the tensions between capital and labour, and ultimately from alternative theories on the sources and distribution of value – which almost faded into oblivion from the late nineteenth century onwards, except in expressly Marxist circles and in the thinking of economists such as Joan Robinson (1903–1983), Professor of Economics at Cambridge, and Piero Sraffa (1898–1983), an Italian who also studied and worked in Cambridge. Both were dedicated critics of the neoclassical view of production, believing that the concept of the 'marginal' product of labour and capital was ideologically based, and was also subject to a 'fallacy of composition': the neoclassical theory of production could not apply to the entire system. They engaged actively in what was later called the Cambridge Capital Critique – a debate between the Cambridge, UK-based Robinson and Sraffa, and Solow and Samuelson, who were at MIT in Cambridge, Massachusetts.

Sraffa and Robinson argued that 'capital' is heterogeneous and so cannot be used as an aggregate concept. That is, it cannot be aggregated since it would be like adding apples to oranges. In 1952 Robinson, influenced by the writings of Sraffa, argued that the idea of profits as the value measurement of capital is a tautology: there is no way to know the value of capital without knowledge of equilibrium prices, and these require an equilibrium rate of profit that cannot be obtained unless we have estimated the value of capital. Furthermore, following the ideas of Marx, Robinson and Sraffa argued that the rate of profit was not the reward for productive contribution of 'capital'; it derived from social relations, that's to say, who owned the means of production and who was forced to work for them. The circularity of the logic of neoclassical theory was partly accepted by Samuelson in a well-known 1966 article in the prestigious *Quarterly Journal of Economics*, where he admitted the logical validity of the points being made by Robinson and Sraffa. Solow, on the other hand, claimed that neoclassical economics should not be distracted by such critiques; and indeed, the debate between the 'classicals' and the 'neoclassicals' would later disappear, so that most students of economics today don't even know it happened.

Remarkably, the neoclassical theory of value has not changed much in the last hundred years. The maximization of utility has been extended beyond the economic sphere to explain human behaviour, including crime, drug addiction and, infamously, models of divorce. This particular idea originated with Gary Becker (1930–2014), an American who was Professor of Economics and Sociology at the University of Chicago and won the Nobel Prize in Economics in 1992. In essence, Becker postulated that two individuals marry when there is a positive surplus from their union in contrast to remaining single. These gains may come from, for example, economies of scale, provision of insurance and general risk-sharing. Becker's ideas encouraged many others to pursue similar investigations.

Attempts have also been made to forge stronger links between macroeconomic patterns (the whole economy, for instance inflation, unemployment and business cycles) and microeconomic decisions made by people and firms. And, as we will see, other work has looked at the need to include non-priced goods (such as care) into GDP.

But despite the critiques, marginal utility theory prevails and is highly influential. The narrow equilibrium view that we will all benefit from perfect competition has influenced – and continues to influence – government policies and those of powerful multilateral bodies such as the International Monetary Fund and the World Bank: how, with perfect competition, individuals will supposedly maximize their preferences and companies their profits so we will all benefit. On the basis of contemporary economic assumptions, we can no longer reliably say who creates value and who extracts it and therefore how the proceeds of production – income – should reasonably be distributed. In the next chapter we will see how this subjective approach to value has also had a strong impact on the ways we *measure* national wealth and income through the concept of GDP.

THE DISAPPEARANCE OF RENT AND WHY IT MATTERS

When students learn about microeconomics in the classroom (e.g. how prices are determined, including wages), they are not told that this is only one of many different approaches to thinking about value.

It is, as far as they are concerned, the only one – and, as a result, there is no need to refer to the word 'value'. The term essentially disappears from the discourse. It is simply Microeconomics 101.

In concluding our history of economic thought, we should ask: is this only an academic exercise, or does it matter? Why it *does* matter is the subject of this book: it is crucial to our understanding of value extraction – and hence the ability to limit it.

The concept of 'rent' has changed in economic thought over the centuries, because rent is the principal means by which value is extracted. The eighteenth-century economists described rent as unearned income, which they thought of as income derived from simply moving existing resources from one hand to another. Their disapproval of unearned income partly came, as we have seen, from medieval strictures on usury – the charging of interest. But it was also practical. Adam Smith believed that a genuinely free market was a market free of rent, and so policymakers had to do their best to eliminate it. His follower David Ricardo considered landowners who collected rent without contributing to the productivity of land to be economic parasites; he denied vehemently that there was any value in the income or rent received from owning land. Rents were *unearned* income and fell squarely outside the production boundary. Both Smith and Ricardo realized that freeing the economy from rent called for strong intervention – in practice by government – to prevent value extraction. Neoclassical economists too; they see rent as an impediment to 'free competition' (free entry and exit of different types of producers and consumers). Once those impediments are removed, competition will benefit everyone.

In the subjective marginalist's approach, rent, along with wages and profits, all arise from 'maximizing': individuals maximizing utility and firms maximizing profits. Thus labour, capital and land are input factors on the same footing. The distinction between social classes, including who owns what, is obliterated, since whether one lends out capital or works for wages depends on an unexplained initial endowment of resources.[15]

Wages are determined by the worker equalizing the (diminishing) marginal utility of the money obtained from working with the 'disutility' of working, for example less leisure time. At the prevailing wage rate, the amount of time spent on work determines the income. This assumes that the amount of employment can be flexibly adjusted. If this is not the case, the marginal utility of taking a job might become less than the utility derived from an equivalent time of leisure; someone chooses not to work. As we have seen, this means that unemployment is therefore voluntary.

Profits and rent are thus determined analogously: the owners of capital (money) will lend it until the marginal utility from doing so is lower than that of consuming their capital. Landlords do the same with their land. For instance, the owner of a house might rent it out and then decide to let her daughter live there for nothing, effectively consuming capital because rent earnings are forgone. The justification for any profits is thus related to individual choices (based on psychology) and the *psychological assumption* that people derive less utility from future consumption (discounting). So the return on capital and land is seen as compensation for future marginal utility at a level which could be enjoyed today if the capital were consumed instead of lent.

In classical economics, therefore, rents are part of the 'normal' process of reproduction. In neoclassical economics, rents are an equilibrium below that which is theoretically possible – 'abnormal' profits. The main similarity is that both theories see rent as a type of monopoly income. But rent has a very different status in the two approaches. Why? Chiefly because of the divergent value theories: classical economics fairly clearly defines rent as income from non-produced scarce assets. This includes, for example, patents on new technologies which – once produced – need not be reproduced any more; the right to issue credit money, which is restricted to organizations with a banking licence; and the right to represent clients in court, which is restricted to members of a Bar association.[16] Essentially, it is a claim on what Marx called the pool of social surplus value – which is enormous compared to any individual production capitalist, circulation capitalist, landowner, patent holder and so on.

By contrast, in neoclassical economics – in general equilibrium – incomes must by definition reflect productivity. There is no space for rents, in the sense of people getting something for nothing. Tellingly, Walras wrote that the entrepreneur neither adds nor subtracts from value produced.[17] General equilibrium is static; neither rents nor innovation are allowed. A relatively recent refinement, the more flexible partial equilibrium analysis, allows us to disregard interactions with other sectors and introduce quasi-rents, and has since the 1970s led to the idea of 'rent-seeking' by creating artificial monopolies, for example tariffs on trade. The problem is that there is no hard-and-fast criterion with which to assess whether the entrepreneur creates 'good' new things or is imposing artificial barriers in order to seek rents.

The neoclassical approach to rent, which largely prevails today, lies at the heart of the rest of this book. If value derives from price, as neoclassical theory holds, income from rent must be productive. Today, the concept of *unearned income* has therefore disappeared. From being seen by Smith, Ricardo and their successors as semi-parasitic behaviour – extracting value from value-creating activity – it has in mainstream economic discourse become just a 'barrier' on the way to 'perfect competition'. Banks which are judged 'too big to fail' and therefore enjoy implicit government subsidy – a form of monopoly – contribute to GDP, as do the high earnings of their executives.

Our understanding of rent and value profoundly affects how we measure GDP, how we view finance and the 'financialization' of the economy, how we treat innovation, how we see government's role in the economy, and how we can steer the economy in a direction that is propelled by more investment and innovation, sustainable and inclusive. We begin by exploring in the next chapter what goes into – and what is omitted from – that totemic category, GDP, and the consequences of this selection for our assessment of value.

3

Measuring the Wealth of Nations

What we measure affects what we do; and if our measurements are flawed, decisions may be distorted.
Joseph Stiglitz, Amartya Sen and Jean-Paul Fitoussi,
Mismeasuring Our Lives (2010)

Scarcely a day goes by without politicians, the media or experts opining on the state of a country's GDP – the measure used to calculate the production of goods and services in an economy: the 'wealth of nations'. Success or failure – real or imagined – in managing GDP can make or break governments and careers. If GDP falls for more than two consecutive quarters, there are cries of 'recession'. If the fall is sustained over a year, it's a depression. But where does this measure come from? And how is it influenced by the way value is understood?

Marginal utility is today a major influence on the measurement of economic activity and growth. It has an effect on the rationale for the kinds of economic activities that are considered productive – which, as we saw in Chapter 2, is basically anything that fetches a (legal) price in the market. According to marginalists, because value derives from price, somebody earning a very high salary is indicative of their productivity and worth. At the same time, anybody holding down a job at all is supposed to reflect their preference for work: the utility of work against that of leisure. GDP can be measured as the total amount of products produced, the total amount demanded, or the total income earned (with adjustments reviewed below). But if income is not necessarily a sign of productivity but of something else – for example the classicals' notion of rent as 'unearned income' – what are the implications for GDP as a reliable measure of an economy's productiveness?

A rise in incomes in the financial sector, for example, would have an effect on GDP. So how sectors are valued influences our calculations of growth rates, and this may in turn influence how we decide to steer the economy. In other words, how we measure GDP is determined by how we value things, and the resulting GDP figure may determine how much of a thing we decide to produce. Performativity!

But if there are problems with the way in which we measure GDP, policymakers can receive misleading signals about what is productive and how to steer the economy. Discussion about which parts of society are productive and which non-productive has been much less explicit since the arrival of marginal utility theory. As long as products and services fetch a price on the market, they are worthy of being included in GDP; whether they contribute to value or extract it is ignored. The result is that the distinction between profits and rents is confused and value extraction (rent) can masquerade as value creation.

This chapter will look at the ways in which governments have calculated growth through national accounting methods, the relationship between these methods and value theory, and the very strange results that have ensued, including the undervaluation of certain activities (like caring for our children), and the overvaluation of others (such as polluting businesses). In Chapter 4 we will see how marginal utility theory has also failed to account for one of the key problems in modern capitalism: the extractive activities of the financial sector.

GDP: A SOCIAL CONVENTION

It is crucial to remember that all types of accounting methods are evolving social conventions, defined not by physical laws and definite 'realities' but reflecting the ideas, theories and ideologies of the age in which they are devised.[1] The way in which a spreadsheet is constructed in itself reflects values. An interesting example is the Jesuit Order. Back in the 1500s, the newly founded Order devised an innovative accounting system which blended vision with finance. In order to align finance with the values of their order, they made sure that the cash box could only be opened with two keys: one operated by the person in charge of the finances (the procurator, today's CFO) and another by the person in charge of the strategy (the rector, today's CEO).[2] As this instance shows, accounting is not neutral, nor is it set in stone; it can be moulded to fit the purpose of an organization and in so doing affect that organization's evolution.

In this same way, the modern accounting concept of GDP is affected by the underlying theory of value that is used to calculate it. GDP is based on the 'value added' of a national economy's industries. Value added is the monetary value of what those industries produce, minus the costs of material inputs or 'intermediate consumption': basically, revenue minus material input cost. Accountants call the intermediate inputs a 'balancing' item because they balance the production account: cost and value added equal the value of production. Value added, however, is a figure specifically calculated for national accounting: the residual difference (residual) between the resource side (output) and the use side (consumption).

The sum of all industry value-added residuals in the economy leads to 'gross value added', a figure equal to GDP, with some minor corrections for taxes. GDP can be calculated either through the production side, or through the income side, the latter by adding up the incomes paid in all the value-adding industries: all profits, rents, interest and royalties. As we will see below, there is a third way to calculate GDP: by adding up expenditure (demand) on final goods, whose price is equal to the sum of the value added along the entire production chain. So GDP can be looked at through production (all goods and services produced), income (all incomes generated), or demand (all goods and services consumed, including those in inventory).

So which industries add value? Following marginalist thinking, the national accounts today include in GDP all goods and services that fetch a price in the market. This is known as the 'comprehensive boundary'. As we saw in Chapter 2, according to marginalism the only economic sectors outside the production boundary are government – which depends on taxes paid by the productive sectors – and most recipients of welfare, which is financed from taxation. Adopting this principle to calculate GDP might seem logical. But in fact it throws up some real oddities which call into question the rigour of the national accounting system and the way in which value is allocated across the economy. These oddities include how government services are valued; how investments in future capacity, such as R&D, are measured; how jobs earning high incomes, as in the financial sector, are treated; and how important services with no price (such as care) or no legal price (such as the black market) are dealt with. In order to explain how these oddities have arisen, and why the system seems to be so idiosyncratic, we need briefly to look at the way in which national accounting and the idea of 'value added' has developed over the centuries.

A Brief History of National Accounts

Value theory has been at the heart of national accounting for a very long time. The most significant early initiatives took place in late-eighteenth-century France, when there were at least eight attempts by different thinkers to estimate France's national product based on Quesnay's land theory of value. Because, as we have seen, for Quesnay the production boundary encompassed only agricultural output – everyone else being classed as living off transfers from the agricultural sector – manufacturing was placed on the unproductive side of the boundary, in the process ignoring dissenting voices such as that of Say, who, taking a broadly utilitarian approach, argued that productive labour is simply labour which produces utility. If the product is something people want to buy – has utility for them – then making it is productive.

Excluding manufacturing from the national product seemed as obvious to Quesnay's followers as it is for us today to include everything that fetches a price. These early French estimators were illustrious figures. They included the writer Voltaire (1694–1778); Antoine Laurent Lavoisier (1743–94), one of the founders of modern chemistry; and his friend the mathematician Joseph Louis Lagrange (1736–1813), better known today for his work on mechanics and mathematical techniques which is still used by economists. Quesnay's ideas proved remarkably durable: as late as 1878, one French estimate of national product was based on his reasoning.[3]

Similarly influential were Adam Smith's ideas of value production. His national income estimates defined only the production or income of agricultural and industrial labour, which produced material goods – actual stuff – and excluded all services, whether government or banking ones. Smith's ideas even underpinned the first account of national product in revolutionary France when, in 1789, Napoleon commissioned Smith's disciple Charles Ganilh (1758–1836) to provide an up-to-date and accurate picture of French national income.[4]

In the late nineteenth century, marginal utility theory predominated. Although radically different from the thinking of earlier economists, it continued to underscore the importance of value theory in national accounting. Increasingly, under its influence, national accountants included everything bought with income: for them, the sum of revenue from market activity, irrespective of sector, added up to the national income. As income tax statistics became more readily available, it was easier to construct estimates based on income data and to analyse the personal distribution of income.

Alfred Marshall, the father of marginal utility theory in Britain, was the driving force behind its application to national income estimates.[5] In his highly influential *Principles of Economics* he wrote explicitly about how the national product could be estimated. An earlier book, *The Economics of Industry*, co-authored with his wife Mary Paley Marshall (1850–1944), was clear on the utility basis of national income: 'everything that is produced, in the course of a year, every service rendered, every fresh utility brought about is a part of the national income'.[6]

Meanwhile, the labour theory of value which, fully developed by Marx, rooted productivity firmly in the concept of the production of 'surplus value', was either disputed or, increasingly, ignored altogether in assessments of national income. By the early twentieth century it was associated with a revolutionary programme and therefore could not, by definition, sit easily with official statistics in the very nations of which Marxists were so critical. Things were of course different in the countries where Communists came to power: first in the Soviet Union after the 1917 Bolshevik Revolution and later in Eastern Europe after the Second World War (though in justifying their construction of a 'material product system' that valued only material goods they should technically have been invoking Smith, not Marx). With the exception of these socialist states, the idea that assessments of national income should be based on the sum total of all incomes, thus forming a 'comprehensive' production boundary, spread rapidly to many countries.[7]

In the first half of the twentieth century marginalists had become aware of their theory's limitations, and began to debate the inclusion of non-market activities in national income accounting. One of Alfred Marshall's students, the British economist Arthur Cecil Pigou (1877–1959), who succeeded him as Professor of Political Economy at Cambridge, argued that since market prices merely indicated the satisfaction (utility) gained from exchange, national income should in fact go further: it should measure welfare. Welfare, Pigou argued, is a measure of the utility that people can gain through money – in other words, the material standard of living. In his influential 1920 book *The Economics of Welfare*, Pigou further defined 'the range of our inquiry' as being 'restricted to that part of social welfare that can be brought directly or indirectly into relation with the measuring-rod of money'.[8] On the one hand, Pigou was saying that all activities which do not really improve welfare (recall the discussion of welfare principles from Pareto discussed in Chapter 2), should be excluded from national income, even if they cost money. On the other hand, he stressed, activities which do generate welfare should be included – even if they are not paid for. In these, he included free or subsidized government services.

One of Pigou's most prominent disciples was the first person to provide an estimate of the fall in national income of the United States during the Great Depression. The Belarusian-born Simon Kuznets (1901–85), a Professor of Economics at Harvard, won the Nobel Prize in Economics in 1971 for his work on national accounts. Believing that they incurred costs without adding to final economic output, Kuznets, unlike Pigou, excluded from the production boundary all government activities that did not immediately result in a flow of goods or services to households – public administration, defence, justice, international relations, provision of infrastructure and so on.[9]

Kuznets also believed that some household expenditure did not increase the material standard of living, but simply paid for the cost of modern life – in particular the 'inflated costs of urban civilization', such as having to maintain a bank account, pay trade union dues or the social obligation to be a member of a club. Kuznets estimated that between 20 and 30 per cent of consumer expenditure went on such services.[10] However, he did argue that unpaid housework should be included, because it clearly improves economic welfare. Kuznets, then, drew the production boundary according to what he believed improved the material standard of living and what did not.

Perhaps Kuznets's view would have had more traction in a peaceful world. But the exigencies of the Second World War, which forced governments to focus on the war effort, took economists down a different path: estimating output rather than concerning themselves with welfare. As a result, economists who believed that national product is the sum total of market prices prevailed.

The resulting ways in which estimates of output were used to calculate GDP appeared to follow marginal utility theory, but were in fact doubly out of sync with it. First, they ignored the idea of value as utility – the benefit it provided to the consumer – and included items that the Pigou–Kuznets welfare concept would have seen as 'necessary' for the creation of value. Rather than assess whether final consumption increased utility, they added *any* final consumption to national income. In Kuznets's own words: 'Many foods and drugs are worthless by scientific standards of nutrition and medication; many household appurtenances are irrelevant to any scientifically established needs for shelter and comfort; many service activities as well as commodities are desired for the sake of impressing foreigners or our fellow countrymen and could hardly measure up to ethical principles of behaviour in relation to the rest of mankind.'[11] From that perspective, the new national accounts overstated welfare.

Second, competition in economies is generally imperfect – a reality that has proven distinctively uncomfortable for national accountants trained in the neoclassical ideas of perfect competition and 'equilibria'. By simply adding up market prices they ignored the fact that those prices would not always produce an equilibrium and be compatible with 'perfect competition'; prices could therefore be higher or lower than if equilibrium prevailed, thereby giving a distorted impression of value creation. In short, during the war years practice became significantly detached from the prevailing theory – or, seen another way, the utility theory of value did not solve the urgent war-related problems of the time.

In many ways, the national accounts as we know them today stem from the trauma of the Great Depression of the 1930s, and the needs of the Second World War war effort. In this, as in so much else, the British economist John Maynard Keynes (1883–1946) was a pivotal figure. In his 1936 masterpiece *The General Theory of Employment, Interest and Money*, written during the Great Depression, Keynes assumed that workers would underestimate the purchasing power of their wages, and would therefore be willing to produce more than they needed to. In this way, workers' involuntary overproduction would in turn create involuntary unemployment – fewer workers being needed to do the same amount of work – and the economy could find itself in a low-output equilibrium. This is a state in which forces in the economy, such as supply and demand, are in balance and there is no incentive to change them, even though the total output of the economy is low and wages and employment are depressed. Keynes used this idea to develop a theory of the macroeconomy – the economy as a whole – in which government spending could stabilize the business cycle when business was investing too little, and even raise the economy's output.

In order to lift the economy out of the depression, governments needed information to measure how their policies were working. Up until then, they had flown mostly blind: they had no need for detailed statistics because the economy was supposed to be self-regulating. Keynes's book *How to Pay for the War*, published in 1940, introduced the idea of recording national income in a set of accounts and completely changed the way in which governments used that data.

In the late 1930s and the 1940s national accountants took up Keynes's ideas about how government could invigorate an economy, and came to view government spending as directly increasing output. For the first time in the history of modern economic thought, government spending became important – in stark contrast to Kuznets's omission of many government services from the national income. This redefinition of government as a contributor to national product was a decisive development in value theory. Keynes's ideas quickly gained acceptance and were among the main influences behind the publication of the first handbook to calculate GDP, the United Nations' System of National Accounts (SNA): a monumental work that in its fourth edition now runs to 662 pages.

THE SYSTEM OF NATIONAL ACCOUNTS COMES INTO BEING

After the Second World War, formal international rules were drawn up, standardizing national accounting for production, income and expenditure. The first version of the SNA, compiled by the United Nations, appeared in 1953.[12] The SNA describes itself as 'a statistical framework that provides a comprehensive, consistent and flexible set of macroeconomic accounts for policymaking, analysis and research purposes'.[13] It defines national accounting as measuring 'what takes place in the economy, between which agents, and for what purpose'; at its heart 'is the production of goods and services'.[14] GDP is '[i]n simple terms, the amount of value added generated by production'.[15] It is defined explicitly as a measure of value creation. It can therefore be said that the national accounts, too, have a production boundary.

The SNA's emergence in the early post-war years owed much to recent economic, political and intellectual developments. The experience of depression and war weighed heavily on policymakers' minds. Many countries saw wartime planning, which was based on unprecedented amounts of economic information, as a success. Political pressures were important too. In the US, the New Deal of the 1930s and full employment during the war led many voters to believe that government could intervene benignly and progressively in the economy. In Europe, the strength of left-wing parties after the war – exemplified by the Labour Party's 1945 election victory in the UK – also changed, and marked a change in, people's attitudes, and made fuller and more accurate national accounts essential. The crucial question was, and remains: on what theory of value were they based?

'Simple' national income estimates had to add up the price of production (minus intermediate goods) in the economy, or incomes, or the expenditure of all economic actors on final goods: *National Production = National Income = National Expenditure*. In order to carry out this estimate, we might have expected the SNA's authors to use as their methodology the prevailing economic theory of value, marginal utility. But they didn't – or, at least, not fully. In fact, the resulting model was, and is, a strange muddle in which utility is the major, but not the only, ingredient.

The SNA brings together various different ways of assessing the national income that had developed over centuries of economic thinking. Decisions about what gets included in the production boundary have been described as 'ad hoc',[16] while national accountants admit that the SNA rules on production are 'a mix of convention, judgment about data adequacy, and consensus about economic theory'.[17] These include devising solutions based on 'common sense'; making assumptions in the name of 'computational convenience' – which has important consequences for the actual numbers we come up with when assessing economic growth; and lobbying by particular economic interests.

In fairness, there have always been practical reasons for this ad hoc approach. Aspects of the economy, from R&D and housework to the environment and the black economy, proved difficult to assess using marginal utility. It was clear that a comprehensive national accounting system would have to include incomes from both market exchange *and* non-market exchange – in particular, government. With market-mediated activity lying at the heart of the marginalist concept of value, most estimators of national income wanted to adopt a broader approach.[18]

National Income Accounting Gets it All Together

National income accounting, then, incorporates many different accounting methods. The system simultaneously allows an integrated view of the different aspects of the economy – both production (output) and distribution of income – and obliges national income accountants to link each commodity produced with someone's income, thereby ensuring consistency. To maintain consistency between production, income and expenditure, the national accounts must record all value produced, income received, money paid for intermediate and finished goods and so on as transactions between actors in the economy – the government, or households or a particular sector – in which each actor has an account. This helps provide a detailed picture of the economy as a whole.

Expenditure on final goods must add up to GDP (as the price of intermediate goods goes into the price of the final goods). So it is possible to compute GDP from the expenditure side and, as we saw in Chapter 1, Petty used this method to estimate national output as early as the seventeenth century. Modern national accounts divide expenditure into the following categories:

GDP = Consumption by households (C) + Investment by companies and by residential investment in housing (I) + Government spending (G).

This can be expressed as: GDP = C + I + G.

For simplicity's sake we will ignore the contribution of net exports. Two observations are in order: first, on the expenditure side, companies only appear as investors (demanding final investment goods from other companies). The remainder of spending (aggregate demand) is split between households and the government. Government expenditure is only what it spends itself; that is, excluding the transfers it makes to households (such as pensions or unemployment benefits). It is its collective consumption expenditure on behalf of the community. By focusing on government only in terms of the spending, it is by definition assumed to be 'unproductive' – outside the production boundary.

MEASURING GOVERNMENT VALUE ADDED IN GDP

In Chapter 8 we will see that government is rarely acknowledged as a creator of value – indeed, quite the reverse. Yet national accounting conventions have in fact been quietly tracking its value-added contribution for the last half century—and it's not small! While Chapter 8 is fully dedicated to looking at the various ways in which economists, and those they advise, have considered government – as a value-creating entity or just a strain on the economy – in this chapter we focus on the relevance of this discussion to how GDP is calculated. The most striking thing to emerge from these analyses is that, contrary to the views of most economists, government certainly does add value to the economy,

Figure 8 below tracks US government value added and expenditure since 1930. During the Second World War the government bought an astonishing half of national output. In this figure we can see that government value added has hovered between 11 and 15 per cent of GDP for the post-war period. As a comparison, the finance industry adds some 4 per cent of GDP in the US and 8 per cent in the UK. But the chart reveals what looks like a strange discrepancy. It shows that government expenditure has been consistently higher than government value added, at between 20 and 25 per cent of GDP.

It is important to stress, however, that the difference between value added and final expenditure is not the government's budget deficit. Rather, the deficit is government revenue (mainly taxes) minus expenses, including transfers of funds from the government to households, such as pensions and unemployment benefit – which, since households spend the money from pensions and benefits, are defined in national

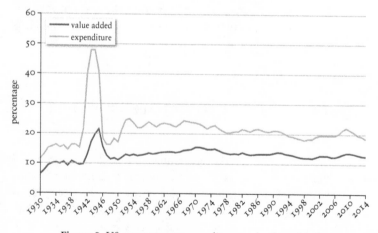

Figure 8. US government expenditure and value added
as a share of GDP, 1930–2014[19]

accounting as household, rather than government, spending (it's the final expenditure that matters, remember). It is that household spending that counts towards final demand for the whole economy. So, what is going on?

Spending and Value

Before answering this question, we have to recognize that government value added cannot be computed in the same way as that of other industries and, as a result, is a complicated issue for national statistical institutes. A lot of government activities are not sold at market prices: that is, prices that pay for all production costs (including wages, rent, interest, royalties as well as inputs into production) and yield a profit for a private-sector business. Instead, government activities are provided at lower, 'non-market' prices – or even for free. Consider schools, state-funded universities, public healthcare, public transport, parks, recreation and the arts, police and fire services, the law courts, environmental protection such as flood prevention and so on. These goods are largely financed by taxes or debt.

Given these lower prices, the usual way of calculating value added for a business doesn't work with government activities. Let's recall that value added is normally the value of output minus costs of intermediate inputs used in production. The value added by a business is basically workers' wages plus the business's operating surplus, the latter broadly similar to *gross operating profit* in business accounting terms. So adding up the non-market prices of government activities is likely to show less value added, because they are set with a different, non-commercial objective: to provide a service to the public. If the non-market prices of the output are lower than the total costs of intermediate inputs, value added would even show up as negative – indeed, government activities would 'subtract' value. However, it makes no sense to say that teachers, nurses, policewomen, firefighters and so on destroy value in the economy. Clearly, a different measurement is needed. As the British economist Charles Bean, a former Deputy Governor for Economic Policy at the Bank of England, argues in his *Independent Review of UK Economic Statistics* (2016),[20] the contribution to the economy by public-sector services has to be measured in terms of 'delivering value'.[21] But if this value is not profit, what is it?

National accountants have therefore long adopted the so-called 'inputs = outputs' approach. Once the output is defined, value added can be computed because the costs of intermediate inputs, such as the computers that employees use, are known. But since government's output is basically intermediate inputs plus labour costs, its value added is simply equal to its employees' salaries. One significant consequence of this is that the estimate of government value added – unlike that of businesses – assumes no 'profit' or operating surplus on top of wages. (In Figure 8 above, the dark-grey line shows the value added of government; it is equal – with slight adjustments – to the share of government employment income in GDP.) In a capitalist system in which earning a profit is deemed the outcome of being productive, this is important because it makes government, whose activities tend to be non-profit, seem unproductive.

But then what about the light-grey line, which represents government final consumption expenditure? We have already seen that pensions and unemployment benefits paid by government are part of household final consumption, not government spending. More broadly, it is not obvious why government should have *any* final consumption expenditure in the way that households do. After all, companies are not classed as being final consumers; their consumption is seen as intermediate, on the way to producing final goods for households. So why isn't government spending likewise classed as intermediate expenditure? After all, there are, for example, millions of school students or medical patients who are consumers of government services.

Indeed, following this logic, government is also a producer of intermediate inputs for businesses. Surely education, roads, or the police, or courts of law can be seen as necessary inputs into the production of a variety of goods? But herein lies a twist. If government spending were to increase, this would mean that government was producing more intermediate goods. Businesses would buy at least some of those goods (e.g. some public services cost money) with a fee; but because they were spending more on them (than if government was not producing anything, and therefore not buying supplies from businesses), their operating surplus and value added would inevitably fall. Government's share of GDP would rise, but the absolute size of GDP would stay the same. This does, of course, run counter to Keynesian attempts to show how increases in government demand could lift GDP.

Many economists made exactly this argument in the 1930s and 1940s – in particular Simon Kuznets, who suggested that only government non-market and free goods provided to households should be allowed to increase GDP. Nevertheless, the convention that all government spending counts as final consumption arose during the Great Depression and the Second World War, when the US needed to justify its enormous government spending (the spike in the light-grey line in Figure 8 in the early 1940s). The spending was presented as adding to GDP, and the national accounts were modified accordingly.[22]

Later in the twentieth century there were repeated attempts to clear up the confusion over whether certain kinds of government spending counted as intermediate or final consumption. This was done by identifying which government activities provided non-market and free services for households (for example, schools), as opposed to intermediate services for businesses (for example, banking regulation). The distinction is not easy to make. Governments build roads. But how much of their value accrues to families going on holiday and how much to a trucking company moving essential spare parts from factory to user? Neither family nor trucking company can build the road. But the family on holiday adds to total final demand; the trucking company is an intermediate cost for businesses.

In 1982, national accountants estimated that some 3 to 4 per cent of Swedish, German and UK GDP was government expenditure that, previously categorized as final consumption expenditure, should be reclassified as (intermediate) inputs for businesses. This had the effect of lowering government's overall value added by between 15 to 20 per cent.[23] To take an example of such reclassification, in 2017 the UK telecommunications regulator, Ofcom, compelled British Telecom (a private firm) to turn its broadband network operation Openreach into a separate company following repeated complaints from customers and other broadband providers that progress in rolling out broadband around the country had been too slow and that the service was inadequate. At least part of the cost of Ofcom could be seen as beneficial to the private telecommunications sector. Yet the convention that all government spending should count as final consumption has proved remarkably resistant to change.

Now we can see why government final consumption expenditure is bigger than its value added in Figure 8. The government's value added only includes salaries. However, the government also purchases a lot of goods and services from businesses, from coffee to cars, from pencils to plane tickets, to the office rentals for regulating bodies such as Ofcom. The producers of these goods and services, not the government, take credit for the value added. Since government is treated as a final consumer, the purchase of goods and services increases its spending. Clearly, government expenditure can be higher than what it charges (e.g. fees for services) because it raises taxes to cover the difference. But need the value of government be undermined because of the way prices are set? By not having a way to capture the production of value created by government – and by focusing more on its 'spending' role – the national accounts contribute to the myth that government is only facilitating the creation of value rather than being a lead player. As we will see in Chapter 8, this in turn affects how we view government, how it behaves and how it can get 'captured' easily by those who confidently see themselves as wealth creators.

SOMETHING ODD ABOUT THE NATIONAL ACCOUNTS: GDP FACIT SALTUS!

Apart from this curious view of government, the national accounts expose a number of other accounting oddities. GDP, for instance, does not clearly distinguish a cost from an investment in future capacity, such as R&D; services valuable to the economy such as 'care' may be exchanged without any payment, making them invisible to GDP calculators; likewise, illegal black-market activities may constitute a large part of an economy. A resource that is destroyed by pollution may not be counted as a subtraction from GDP – but when pollution is cleaned up by marketed services, GDP increases. And then there's the biggest oddity of all: the financial sector.

Does the financial sector simply facilitate the exchange of existing value, or does it create new value? As we will see in Chapters 4 and 5, this is the billion-dollar question: if it's answered wrongly, it may be that the growing size of the financial sector reflects not an increase of growth, but rent being captured by some actors in the economy. First, however, there are some other inconsistencies to be considered.

Investment in Future Capacity

First, let's look at how R&D is dealt with in the national accounts. Before 2008, the SNA considered in-house R&D to be an input into production[24] – in other words, a company's spending on R&D (research equipment, laboratories, staff and the like) was treated as a cost and subtracted from the company's final output. However, in the 2008 version of the SNA, in-house R&D was reclassified as an investment in the company's stock of knowledge, to be valued 'on the basis of the total production costs including the costs of fixed assets used in production'.[25] It became a final productive activity rather than just an intermediate cost towards that activity.

The SNA's decision to reclassify R&D was justified less by value theory than by 'common-sense' reasoning: the contribution of 'knowledge' to production seemed to be significant, and should therefore be recognized. R&D was made productive because it was considered important.

As a result, since 2008 GDP has been enlarged by the annual cost of R&D, including the depreciation of fixed assets used. When in 2013 the US implemented this change, the value from R&D added $400 billion – 2.5 per cent of US GDP – to national income overnight.[26] Of course, those sectors with the largest R&D contributions improved their share of GDP, making them look more important than others.

The Value of Housework . . . and the House

Then there's housework. Feminists in particular have long objected to the lack of recognition given to housework's contribution to the economy. The national accounts exclude all housework, and therefore a large part of women's work, from production. The architect of the first and second editions of the SNA (1953 and 1968), the Nobel Prize-winning British economist Sir Richard Stone (1913–91) – sometimes called 'the father of national income accounting' – had decided views on the matter. Writing for the UN committee that drafted the first SNA evaluation of household production, Stone commented that it 'is unnecessary to impute an income to family services or to the services of household equipment and may even prove an embarrassment to do so, since, not only are there very little data in this field, but the principles on which such imputations should be made are obscure'.[27] He simply thought it was impossible to know how to do it – and even if a solution could be devised, doing so would be socially awkward.

Now, seventy years later, since there is still no theory – beyond ignorance or shame – that explains why housewives (and house husbands) should not be included in GDP, the SNA architects have come up with a different defence. They have expressed a 'reluctance' to include such work because, although it is equivalent to work done by servants, 'By convention . . . only the wages of the domestic staff are treated as the value of output.'[28] The 'convention' here is ironically close to Marx's value theory that only someone who produces a surplus for a capitalist generates surplus value. But Marx's point was linked to his value theory and understanding of how capitalism works (or does not work), whereas in this instance the convention has been cherry-picked because it is convenient for the current system.

In explaining why housework is accounted as unproductive, national accountants are forced constantly to fall back on their 'comprehensive' production boundary, and are at pains to invoke 'common sense'. Their explanations include: 'the relative isolation and independence of these activities from markets, the extreme difficulty of making economically meaningful estimates of their values, and the adverse effects it would have on the usefulness of the accounts for policy purposes and the analysis of markets and market disequilibria'.[29]

According to this awkward logic, a nation would increase its GDP if we paid our neighbours to look after our children and do our laundry, and they paid us to do theirs.[30] Underlying this 'common-sense' approach to household work is the utility theory of value: what is valuable is what is exchanged on the market. The implicit production boundary is determined by whether money changes hands for the service. Therefore, there is 'extreme difficulty' in giving a value to work done by women (or men) who do not receive a wage in exchange for it.

By contrast, it is remarkable how national accountants go to great lengths to include inside the production boundary the house itself, the property in which the supposedly unproductive household work is done. In the national accounts, houses owned by their occupants generate services that are included in GDP. In the US, such 'work' contributes 6 per cent of GDP – that is, a cool $1 trillion – even though none of these dollars actually exist.

How do the statisticians come up with such an absurdity? They impute a rent to everyone who lives in their own home. A market rent is estimated for a property which the owner-occupier then pays herself as lessor for the services the house provides. Since the imputed rent is regarded as income, it is also recorded in the national accounts as production. Accountants justify this with the argument that 'both international and inter-temporal comparisons of the production and consumption of housing services could be distorted if no imputation were made for the value of own-account housing services'.[31]

How might this work? Let's contrast two countries. In one, there are only renters paying owners such as real-estate companies (in Switzerland in 2014 more people lived in rented homes than in owner-occupied homes). In the other, all houses are owned (in the US and UK a larger percentage of people own than rent). Since real estate adds value and income (rent) from the actual rent charged (as opposed to the 'imputed rent' calculated), the first country would have an unfairly high GDP compared to the other, at least in terms of the percentage of GDP deriving from property.

From a different perspective – one that sees no greater value in renting over owning a house, especially when there is no rent control – we could equally well ask why real-estate rents should add value in the first place. Another valid question is why a hike in rent should increase the value produced by real-estate agencies, especially if the quality of the rental service is not improving. London and New York City tenants, for example, know only too well that property management services do not improve even though rents rise – in London's case, rapidly in recent years.[32]

It's also worth noting that the national accounts treat property and real estate (both residential and commercial) as comparable to a firm. Buying a house or factory building is called an 'investment'. It is assumed that the owner goes on 'servicing' the building, investing in its upkeep or improvement, so their income is 'payment for a service' and not just rent. Capital gains on buying and selling property are treated like those that apply to a business or a financial asset – although the extent to which a building is 'productive' is debatable. Capital gains from holding property arise out of increases in land value, which itself are determined by collective investment (in roads, schools, etc.) – little to do with the effort of the property owner.

As with the absurdity of neighbours paying each other to do their housework, it is as if the statisticians are saying that a nation of owner-occupiers could artificially amplify GDP by swapping homes with their neighbours and paying rent to one another. Statisticians have fiercely defended their treatment of income from property. But when real-estate prices appreciate rapidly, as in the US and the UK before 2007 and in hot-spots such as London even after the financial crisis, there are alarming implications for measuring. Rising house prices mean rising implicit rentals, and hence rising incomes when the implicit rental is included. The paradoxical result is that a house price bubble, perhaps caused by low interest rates or relaxed lending conditions, will show up as an acceleration of GDP growth. Why? Because households' services to themselves – as their own landlords, charging themselves implicit rentals – are suddenly rising in value, and that is counted as income which adds to GDP. By the same token, if you strip out those imputed rentals, GDP can be shown to have risen more slowly in the years before the financial crash than after 2009.[33]

Prostitution, Pollution and Production

So national accountants' approach to valuation affects the production boundary, sometimes in intriguing ways. In the Netherlands, where prostitution is legal and regulated, the tax authorities have asked sex workers to declare their earnings, which count towards national income. In other countries, such as the UK, earnings from prostitution are not included in national income, except perhaps in estimates of the black economy.

Equally importantly, the boundary loops around the issue of the environment. Consider a river polluted by industrial waste. When the polluter pays to clean it up, the expenditure is treated as a cost which reduces profits and GDP. But when the government pays another company to clean up the river, the expenditure adds to GDP because paying workers adds value. If the cost of cleaning up pollution is borne by someone other than the polluter it is called an externality – the cost is 'outside' the polluter's profit-and-loss account – and increases GDP. Kuznets argued that such a calculation should be balanced by the 'disservice' that has been created by pollution, and therefore that the cost of that 'disservice' be taken out of the 'net' calculation of value added. But national accounts do not do that: instead, they state that it is not 'appropriate' or 'analytically useful' for 'economic accounts to try to correct for presumed institutional failures of this kind by attributing costs to producers that society does not choose to recognize'.[34]

National accountants present this question of whether something is 'analytically useful' or not as a vague argument, without reference to value. To be fair, they also rightly caution that it would be extremely difficult comprehensively to cost such externalities – negative or positive 'side effects' of production – which are not priced. All of which just highlights the difficulties of being consistent and drawing a clear production boundary.

So while Marshall claimed that Nature does not make jumps (recall the discussion of *natura non facit saltus* in Chapter 2), national income, it appears, can do so! If self-employment (referred to as own-account production for small farming or sex workers, for example) grows in importance, or if a way can be found to cost externalities, national income will jump when the statisticians decide to include it.

The Black Economy Gets into the SNA

Something similar happens with the black or – to use the official euphemism – 'informal' economy when countries decide that it has grown so large that they must start to include estimates of it in national accounting. Consider Italy, a 'developed' country. The Group of 7 (G7), the international club of the biggest economies, estimates that in 2015 the informal economy made up 12.6 per cent of Italy's GDP.[35] That calculation excludes illegal activities, which Italian statisticians decided to leave out of their GDP measures. Since the Great Recession which began in 2008, many more unemployed Italians have taken up informal production. The Organization for Economic Cooperation and Development (OECD), the grouping of mainly high-income countries, estimated that in 2013 Italy's black market (including illegal activities – around 1 per cent of GDP) was a massive 21 per cent of GDP.[36] The same study found that, across other European countries, informal activities comprised between 7 per cent and 28 per cent of GDP – activities which were incorporated in the national accounts upon the recommendation of the 1993 and 2008 SNA.

All this begs the question: where does one start and stop? What is, or is not, to be included in the national accounts? The very fact that these questions are so difficult to answer illustrates the idiosyncrasies and vagaries of the accounting system. And the biggest oddity of all has turned out to be the so-called 'banking problem': how to estimate the productiveness of finance.

More than any other sector, finance highlights the arbitrary way in which modern national accounting decides where to draw the production boundary. When the financial sector was small (before its boom in the 1970s), there was little difficulty in excluding it; interest was as much a question of morality (positions against usury) as of economics. But as the size of the financial sector grew it became more awkward to exclude it from national output. The tension between economists' – and indeed society's – long-held views of banks as unproductive and the steady post-war growth of the sector gave rise to what is known as the banking problem.

Until the 1970s, one of the principal sources of banks' profits – net interest payments, which are the difference between the interest that banks charge for loans they make and the interest they pay on deposits – was excluded from output in the national accounts. The only part of banks' income which was included was fees for services people actually paid for, such as the cost of opening or closing a bank account or getting mortgage advice.

Yet next came an extraordinary change. From being perceived as transferring existing value and 'rent' in the sense of 'unearned income', finance was transformed into a producer of new value. This seismic shift was justified by labelling commercial bank activities as 'financial intermediation', and investment bank activities as 'risk-taking'. It was a change that co-evolved with the deregulation of the sector, which also swelled its size even further. As this part of the story – how finance has been 'accounted' for – is too big to treat in this chapter, the next two will be devoted to it.

Profits versus Rents

As we saw in Chapter 2, the discussion about which parts of society were productive or unproductive was much more explicit before the arrival of marginal utility theory. And as we have seen in this chapter, moreover, as long as products and services fetch a price on the market, they are deemed worthy of being included in GDP; whether they contribute to value or extract it is ignored. The result is that the distinction between profits and rents is confused and value extraction (rent) can masquerade as value creation.

The complexity of assessing government value added pales in comparison with this glaring weakness in the SNA: a confusion between profits and rents. Disentangling the two is fundamental to understanding value. As we saw earlier, classical value theory held that income from activities outside the production boundary was unearned. Rent – which was regarded as unearned income – was classified as a transfer from the productive to the unproductive sector, and was therefore excluded from GDP. But if, as marginal utility holds, the 'services' of a landlord or hedge fund manager are treated as productive, they magically become part of GDP.

The SNA generally links what people earn with the industries which pay them. Steel workers are paid by steel makers, shop workers are paid by retailers, insurance workers are paid by insurance companies, and so on. But income from property, dividends and lending, for example, is different because the people receiving it are not necessarily directly linked to its source (rent, dividends, loan interest etc.). If a steel firm rents an office, the rent it pays could go to firms in other sectors, to the government or even to households. A rich investor can derive income from dividends paid by any number of productive companies. A creditor – such as a bank – can lend money to several businesses or households and receive income as interest from them. All these types of income cannot be pinned down easily in the product account.

Although the SNA 2008 tried to deal with this difficulty, it did not state that, for example, property income is a reward for production, merely that 'Property income accrues when the owners of financial assets and natural resources put them at the disposal of other institutional units.'[37]

PATCHING UP THE NATIONAL ACCOUNTS ISN'T ENOUGH

So while, in theory, balancing the national accounts between income and expenditure requires a clear sense of where the production boundary lies – where value is created – in practice the boundary is far from clear. National accounts as they stand are certainly much better than nothing and, among their merits, do permit consistent comparison between countries and over time. But despite all the effort that has gone into developing it, the SNA lacks a coherent and rigorous underlying value theory.

Government agencies such as the Bureau of Economic Analysis (BEA) in the United States and the Office of National Statistics (ONS) in the United Kingdom employ armies of people to estimate GDP, making decisions about what is producing new value that enlarges the wealth of a country. We are mesmerized into seeing this as the domain of a highly specialized profession that uses sophisticated modern statistical methods to provide precise parameters for the value that our society produces. The growth rate of our economies is forecast years in advance using complicated mathematics, with potential 'outputs' measured and GDP estimated to a tenth of a percentage every quarter.

In reality, the national accounts have been subjected to repeated attempts to patch them up and make them more relevant to changing needs and economies. Accounting for environmental damage has been mentioned. Accounting for happiness is another case. Lest the idea seems impossible, or at least nothing to do with economics, it's worth recalling something basic: there is no point to the economy unless it helps people to lead better lives – and that quite reasonably means, at least in part, happier lives. The American economist James Tobin (1918–2002), who won the Nobel Prize in Economics in 1981 and was a Professor of Economics at Yale University for many years, wrote:

> The whole purpose of the economy is the production of goods and services for consumption now or in the future. I think the burden of proof should always be on those who would produce less, rather than more, on those who would leave idle men or machines or land that could be used. It is amazing how many reasons can be found to justify such waste: fear of inflation, balance-of-payments deficits, unbalanced budgets, excessive national debt, loss of confidence in the dollar.[38]

Making decisions about which goods and services to include in GDP involves returning to the concept of the production boundary at the centre of classical economic thought – distinguishing productive from unproductive activities – and the theory of value that justifies such a distinction. Is a theory just assumed, as in the work of Petty and King? Or is it spelled out, as in Marx? And how can national accountants be persuaded that an activity that was previously seen as a transfer of existing value is actually creating new value? And above all, what do we mean by growth?

The way we define and measure growth is of course affected by our theory of value. And the resulting growth figures may guide the activities that are deemed important. And in the process possibly distort the economy.

GDP is worrying citizens and politicians everywhere: is it going up? Falling? And by how much? Understanding how GDP is constructed is thus crucial.

Unlike statisticians at the time of Smith or Marshall, modern governments have a wealth of data and a sophisticated system of national accounts that tracks the economy and the growth of each of its sectors. On the one hand, this makes it possible to see in great detail who does what in the economy – who is a 'value creator' and just how much everyone contributes to the national product. On the other hand, because of the way in which these accounts are set up, they are no more an objective metric of value than Quesnay's categorizations, or Smith's, or Marx's.

In essence, we behave as economic actors according to the vision of the world of those who devise the accounting conventions. The marginalist theory of value underlying contemporary national accounting systems leads to an indiscriminate attribution of productivity to anyone grabbing a large income, and downplays the productivity of the less fortunate. In so doing, it justifies excessive inequalities of income and wealth and turns value extraction into value creation.

Put bluntly, any activity that can be exchanged for a price counts as adding to GDP. The accountants determine what falls into this category. But what criteria do they use? The answer is a hodge-podge which combines marginal utility with statistical feasibility and some sort of common sense that invites lobbying rather than reasoning about value. It is this that determines where the production boundary is drawn in the national accounts.

The next chapter focuses on the most egregious case of boundary-hopping: that of the financial sector, formerly seen as unproductive, now a creator of value.

4

Finance: A Colossus is Born

If the UK financial system thrives in the post-Brexit world, which is the plan, it will not be ten times GDP, it will be fifteen to twenty times GDP in another quarter of a century.

Mark Carney, Governor of the Bank of
England, 3 August 2017

A large and growing financial sector has long been presented as a sign of UK and US success, credited with mobilizing capital to drive their economic development and generating exports at a time when manufacturing and farming had declined into net import. In the 1990s, comparable financial-sector expansion became an ambition for other countries seeking to follow the development path of these early industrializers, and to lessen dependence on the import of capital and services from the world's 'financial centres' located in the UK and the US. Underpinning this expansion is the belief that a country benefits from an ever-growing financial sector, in terms of its growing contribution to GDP and exports, and as total financial-sector assets (bank loans, equities, bonds and derivatives) become an ever-larger multiple of GDP.

The celebration of finance by political leaders and expert bankers is, however, not universally shared among economists. It clashes with the common experience of business investors and households, for whom financial institutions' control of the flow of money seems to guarantee the institutions' own prosperity far more readily than that of their customers. For those without large fortunes and for many with 'assets under management', the notion of finance adding value has rung increasingly hollow in the long shadow of the global financial crisis that began in 2008. This required governments around the world to rescue major banks whose 'net worth' had turned out to be fictitious; with the bailouts continuing to impose heavy social costs, ten years on, in the form of squeezed public budgets, heavy household debt and negative real returns for savers.

But for much of recent human history, in stark contrast to the current enthusiasm for financial-sector growth as a sign of (and spur to) prosperity, banks and financial markets were long regarded as a cost of doing business. Their profits reflected added value only to the extent that they improved the allocation of a country's resources, and cross-subsidized a reliable payments system. Recurrent financial crises exposed the regularity with which they threw resources in unproductive directions (basically to other parts of the financial sector itself), ultimately disrupting the flow of money and goods in the real economy. The fastest-growing financial activities in 1980–2008 were asset management (making more money by investing in liquid financial assets and property, for the segment of the population earning enough to save) and lending to households, rather than to businesses. Finance also diverted many highly trained scientists and engineers away from work in direct production, by offering them on average 70 per cent more pay than other sectors could afford. The improbable level to which financial-sector profits rose, before and after the latest crisis, reflects a deliberate decision during the twentieth century to redraw the production boundary, so that previously excluded financial institutions were now included within it – and, having redesignated finance as productive, to strip away the regulations that had previously kept its charging and risk-taking under control.

The current chapter looks at the expansion of banking, and the way in which political decisions to recognize its value in national accounts (although based on economically contentious assumptions) helped to drive a deregulation which fuelled its ultimately over-reaching growth. In the next two chapters I explore the relationship between this growth and the financialization of the rest of the economy.

BANKS AND FINANCIAL MARKETS
BECOME ALLIES

Policymakers' faith in the value of finance was undiminished by its 2008 implosion. Indeed, their reaction to the global financial crisis was to insist that more of each economy's 'capital' should be assigned to private-sector banks, and to support them with an ultra-relaxed monetary policy, in which near-zero interest rates were supplemented by central banks' buying-up of government or even corporate bonds to keep their prices high. This massively increased the 'asset' side of the world's main central banks.

Countries aspiring to achieve US levels of prosperity have long been advised, especially by their multilateral creditors, to make 'financial deepening' – the expansion and deregulation of banks and financial markets – a central part of their development strategy. At the same time, these creditors termed policies that restricted banks' growth – such as capping interest rates, or restricting cross-border lending – 'financial repression', with the implication that financial liberalization was part of wider liberation. After 2008, as after previous regional financial crises (such as those that hit much of Latin America in 1982–3 and East Asia in 1997), the economists who had urged this liberalization asked themselves whether the unleashing of financial sectors had gone too far. But they invariably concluded that the crises were mere stumbles on a road travelled faster when financial growth was unblocked. So in 2015, the IMF concluded an exhaustive study 'rethinking' financial deepening by concluding that while the positive effects of the sector's expansion might weaken at high levels of per-capita GDP, and/or if it grew too fast, 'there is very little or no conflict between promoting financial stability and financial development', and 'most emerging markets are still in the relatively safe and growth-enhancing region of financial development'.[1]

Yet the belief that economic progress requires a growing financial sector, with banks at the heart of it, is counter-intuitive on a number of counts. If financial intermediaries promote economic growth by mobilizing capital and giving it better uses, national output (GDP) could be expected to grow faster than financial-sector output, thus diminishing its share of GDP. This must indeed be the case for many of the most successful 'newly industrializing countries', if – as they claim – the US and UK financial sectors have outgrown their home economies through the export of capital and services to the rest of the world. If banks and financial markets become more efficient, firms should make increased use of their services over time, losing their early preference for internal financing of investment out of retained profit. In practice, numerous studies find that firms continue to finance most of their investment (in production and new product development) internally through retentions, because external financers know less about their activities and offset their greater risk by demanding a higher return.[2] And over time, financial markets should, by gaining efficiency, be able to expand at the expense of banks, which are usually explained as an alternative mechanism for channelling funds from savers to borrowers when equity and bond markets are insufficiently developed and information isn't flowing freely.[3] Yet even in modern capitalist economies banks have entrenched their role at the centre of the financial universe, to the extent of commanding wholesale rescue when their solvency and liquidity drained away in 2008.

THE BANKING PROBLEM

As we've seen, problems arise in national accounting with activities that appear to add value to the economy but whose output isn't priced. Many of the services provided by government and voluntary-sector organizations fall into this category, as do private-sector products that are made freely available, such as Google's search engine and Mozilla's browser. National accounts conventionally ascribe a value to these, notwithstanding the free-market critics' objection that non-marketed goods and services are cross-subsidized by (and constitute a drain on) the marketed-sector producers, thus subtracting from national productivity.[4]

But an equally serious problem arises when prices are charged for (and profits made from) a product or service that doesn't obviously confer any value. In most parts of the economy, this is classified and condemned as monopoly rent-extraction. The trader who 'corners the market' in a product and resells it at a premium by withholding supplies, or stands between buyer and seller for no other purpose than to charge a commission before the two can connect, is condemned for the same unproductive profiteering as the highwayman who relieves travellers of cash before allowing them to pass. Until the 1970s, the financial sector was perceived as a distributor, not a creator, of wealth, engaging in activities that were sterile and unproductive. At that point, through a combination of economic reappraisal of the sector and political pressure applied by it, finance was moved from outside to inside the production boundary – and in the process wreaked havoc.

Governments across nineteenth-century Europe were convinced that banks added value, and were vital for the achievement of industrial modernization and economic growth. They were especially keen to promote investment banks, which were viewed as essential both to channel funds into productive investment and to co-ordinate firms and industries to raise the efficiency and rates of return on this investment. Investment banks' importance in channelling professional investors' funds into productive industry rose up the political agenda because early savings banks, which took deposits from households, often lost them to fraudulent or excessively risky money-making schemes and so were steered by regulation into buying mainly government bonds.[5] By licensing only a few investment banks, governments granted them the monopoly power needed to co-ordinate expansion of related industries, and to achieve the profit required to absorb high risks.[6] The banks' unique role in development was recognized by some mid-twentieth-century economists, notably Joseph Schumpeter (1934) and Alexander Gerschenkron (1962).[7]

The 'banking problem' arose because, as the twentieth century progressed, banks' role in fuelling economic development steadily diminished in theory and practice – while their success in generating revenue and profit, through operations paid for by households, firms and governments, steadily increased. A fast-expanding part of the economy in the middle of the twentieth century was not being accounted for in the national accounts. The economists (like Schumpeter and Gerschenkron) who had ascribed banks a key role in development were nevertheless clear that they achieved this through exercising a degree of monopoly power, collecting rent as well as profit. Mainstream opinion, meanwhile, continued to view banks as intermediaries which, in charging to connect buyers and sellers (or borrowers and savers), made their income by capturing value from others rather than creating it themselves. Indeed today, if we use the value-added formula (wages plus profits), we find that the financial sector, far from contributing 7.2 per cent of GDP to the UK economy and 7.3 per cent to the US (as the 2016 national accounts showed), in fact makes a contribution to output that is zero, or even negative. By this yardstick it is profoundly, fundamentally unproductive to society.

The 'banking problem', therefore, presented an oddity for national accountants. Traditionally, commercial banks and most investment banks make much of their income from interest differentials: they receive higher interest on the loans they make to customers than the interest they pay on funds they borrow. The charging of interest is justified in several complementary ways. It is said, for instance, to be a 'reward for waiting', compensating lenders for not being able to enjoy their money immediately because they're allowing someone else to use it. It may also be a reward for taking risk. If money is not spent right now, it might yield less satisfaction later: if, for instance, those who use it in the meantime should lose all or part of it, or if its purchasing power is eroded by rising prices or a falling exchange rate. Unless kept in a sock, all unspent money tends to be lent to others, with no guarantee that money lent now will be repaid in full and on time. Borrowers might lose it on a failed business venture, or simply steal it and refuse to repay. Far from being 'usurious', therefore, the payment of interest can be interpreted as the lender's reward for running the risk of never seeing their money again. The greater this risk, the higher the interest they are justified in charging.

Giving interest an economic function does not in itself explain how banks create value. Economists have traditionally resolved the 'banking problem' by assuming that banks create value in other ways, and use their interest differential (the difference between borrowing and lending rates) as an indirect way to capture this value, because it comes from delivering services that cannot be directly priced. Banking, it is argued, provides three main 'services': 'maturity transformation' (the conversion of short-term deposits into mortgages and business loans); liquidity (the instant availability of cash through a short-term loan or overdraft for businesses and households that need to pay for something); and, perhaps most importantly, credit assessment (vetting loan applications to decide who is creditworthy and what the terms of the loan should be). As well as channelling funds from lenders to borrowers, banks run the various payments systems linking buyers to sellers. These activities, especially the transformation of short-term deposits into long-term loans and the guarantee of liquidity to customers with overdrafts, also mean a transfer of risk to banks from other private-sector firms. This bundle of services collectively constitutes 'financial intermediation'. It is assumed that, instead of directly charging for these services, banks impose an indirect charge by lending at higher interest rates than they borrow at.

The cost of 'financial intermediation services, indirectly measured' (FISIM) is calculated by the extent to which banks can mark up their customers' borrowing rates over the lowest available interest rate. National statisticians assume a 'reference rate' of interest that borrowers and lenders would be happy to pay and receive (the 'pure' cost of borrowing). They measure FISIM as the extent to which banks can push lenders' rates below and/or borrowers' rates above this reference rate, multiplied by the outstanding stock of loans.

The persistence of this interest differential is, according to the economists who invented FISIM, a sign that banks are doing a useful job. If the gap between their lending rates and borrowing rates goes up, they must be getting better at that job. That's especially true given that, since the late 1990s, major banks have succeeded in imposing more direct charges for their services as well as maintaining their 'indirect' charge through the interest-rate gap.[8]

According to this reasoning, banks make a positive contribution to national output, and their ability to raise the cost of borrowing above the cost of lending is a principal measure of that contribution. The addition of FISIM to the national accounts was first proposed in 1953, but until the 1990s the services it represented were assumed to be fully consumed by financial and non-financial companies, so none made it through into final output. The 1993 SNA revision, however, began the process of counting FISIM as value added, so that it contributed to GDP. This turned what had previously been viewed as a deadweight cost into a source of added value overnight. The change was formally floated at the International Association of Official Statistics conference in 2002, and incorporated into most national accounts just in time for the 2008 financial crisis.[9]

Banking services are of course necessary to keep the economy's wheels turning. But it does not follow that interest and other charges on the users of financial services are a productive 'output'. If all firms could finance their business investments through retained earnings (the profits they don't distribute to shareholders), and all households could pay for theirs through savings, the private sector would not need to borrow, no interest would be paid and bank loans would be redundant.

National accounting conventions recognize this incongruity by treating the cost of financial services (FISIM plus direct fees and charges) as a cost of production for firms or governments. This 'production' from financial institutions that funds the activities of firms and governments immediately disappears into 'intermediate consumption' by the public and non-financial private sectors. It is only the flow of goods and services from non-financial firms (and government) that counts as final production. But exceptions are made for financial services provided to a country's households and non-resident businesses; these services, as well as direct fees and charges imposed by financial institutions, are treated as a final output, counting towards GDP alongside everything else that households and non-residents consume. The steady growth in household borrowing in the UK, US and most other OECD countries since the 1990s has automatically boosted banks' measured contribution to GDP, through the rising flow of interest payments they collect from households. The increasingly hazardous nature of lending to subprime and already indebted households further boosted this measured contribution, since it resulted in a higher premium of borrowers' rates over the reference rate with inadequate adjustment for the increased risks.[10] The alleged under-reporting of key interbank lending rates, commonly used as the reference rate, may have worsened the exaggeration during the 2008 Libor scandal.

FISIM has ensured that the financial sector's contribution to GDP has kept growing since the financial turbulence of 2008–9, especially

in the US and UK. But if an intermediation service becomes more efficient, it should absorb less of its clients' output rather than more; it should make a smaller contribution to GDP the more efficient it gets. Estate agents or realtors, for example, generate income through commission on each property sale. If they become more efficient, competition will drive down commission rates and the remaining players will survive on lower commission by reducing costs – making a smaller contribution to GDP.

The rules are different for finance. National accounts now state that we are better off when more of our income flows to people who 'manage' our money, or who gamble with their own. If professional investors profit by investing in property during a boom, new ways of accounting will register the profit as a rise in their GDP contribution. Short-selling (or 'shorting'), which involves borrowing an asset and selling it in the expectation of buying it back after its price has fallen,[11] is another speculative activity whose growth contributes to GDP under the new form of measurement. If money is made by shorting property-related investments before a slump, as investors such as the hedge fund manager John Paulson famously did before the 2008 crash, the profit increases GDP. But surely if, for example, bus fares kept rising in real terms, we'd demand to know why bus companies were becoming less efficient, and take action against operators who used monopoly power to push up their prices? But when the cost of financial intermediation keeps rising in real terms, we celebrate the emergence of a vibrant and successful banking and insurance sector.

According to theories that view the financial sector as productive, ever-expanding finance does not harm the economy; indeed, it actually facilitates the circulation of goods and services. Yet all too often investment funds and banks act to increase their profits rather than channel the profits into other forms of investment, such as green technology. Macquarie, the Australian bank which used post-privatization acquisitions to become one of the world's largest infrastructure investors, quickly became known for securing additional debts against these assets so that more of their revenues were channelled into interest payments, alongside distributions to shareholders. After acquiring Thames Water in 2006, it used securitization to raise the company's debt from £3.2 billion to £7.8 billion by 2012, while avoiding major

infrastructure investment,[12] The strategy raised alarm among environmentalists when, in 2017, Macquarie acquired the Green Investment Bank, a major financer of renewable energy and conservation projects set up by the UK government five years earlier. Moreover, once financiers realize that very little value stands behind their liabilities, they try to issue even more debt to refinance themselves. When they cannot continue to do so, a debt deflation occurs, such as the one that began in the US and Europe in 2007–8 and was still depressing global growth rates ten years later. Society at large then bears the costs of the speculative mania: unemployment rises and wages are held down, especially for those left behind during the previous economic expansion. In other words, value is extracted from labour's share of earnings in order to restore corporate profits.

It is, then, difficult to think about the financial sector as anything but a *rentier*: a value extractor. This, indeed, was the economic verdict on finance before the 1970s, incorporated into national accounts, until a decision was taken to ascribe 'value added' to banks and their financial-market activities. That decision redesignated, as results of productive activity, financial profits that economists previously had little problem ascribing to banks' monopoly power, associated with economies of scale and governments' recognition that the biggest were 'too big to fail'. The redrawing of the production boundary to include finance was in part a response to banks' lobbying, which was itself a feature of their market power and influence. By showing finance as a large and growing source of national output, it overthrew the logic of previous financial regulation. Where beforehand such regulation had been seen as a safeguard against reckless and rent-seeking behaviour, it was now portrayed as a shackle suppressing a valuable trade in money and risk.

DEREGULATION AND THE SEEDS OF THE CRASH

Financial sectors were heavily regulated in the early 1970s, even in countries with large international financial centres such as the US and UK. Governments viewed regulation as essential, because a long

international history of bank crashes and failed or fraudulent investment schemes showed how, left to themselves, financial firms could
easily lose depositors' money and, in so doing, disrupt real economic
activity and even cause social unrest. When banks competed, they
tended to offer ever more improbably high returns to savers by funding ever more risky investment projects, until disaster (and bankruptcy)
struck. But while such competitive instability was averted by restricting entry, and giving banks some monopoly power, they still inflicted
damage on the rest of the economy in other ways – by artificially
inflating the price of loans, and co-ordinating their buying and selling to cause artificial boom and bust in the prices of key commodities.
Small banks were especially vulnerable because their (and clients')
activities were insufficiently spread across different industries and
geographical regions. But big banks quickly became 'too big to fail',
assured of expensive government rescue when overextended because
their collapse would do too much economic damage. Such assurances
only led them to behave even more recklessly.

Governments' appetite for financial regulation increased after the
global depression of the 1930s, heralded by the collapse of insufficiently regulated stock markets and banks, and the world war to
which this indirectly contributed. In 1933, following the Wall Street
Crash, the US had separated commercial banks (financial institutions
which took deposits) from investment banks (financial firms raising
money for companies through debt and equity issues, corporate
mergers and acquisitions, and trading in securities for their own
account) under the Glass–Steagall Act. The Act's regulations were
in some respects strengthened by the Bretton Woods Agreement of
1944. In line with the so-called 'Keynes Plan', the Bretton Woods system imposed tight curbs on international capital movements in order
to preserve a system of fixed exchange rates – thereby ruling out most
of the cross-border investments and currency trades which had previously been major sources of instability and speculative profits. The
Bretton Woods Agreement also required governments to maintain
tight restrictions on their domestic financial sectors – including high
minimum ratios of capital to assets and liquid reserves to total bank
assets, interest rate caps and, in the US, strict legal separation of
commercial and investment banking. The cornerstone of the Bretton

Woods currency system was the gold standard, under which the dollar was convertible into gold at $35 an ounce.

Such measures made it hard for financial institutions to shift their business to low-tax or low-regulation jurisdictions. The rules reflected policymakers' consensus that financial institutions acted at best like a lubricant for the 'real' motors of the economy – agriculture, manufacturing and business services – and were not significantly productive in themselves. It was feared that a deregulated financial sector could become excessively speculative, causing disruption domestically and to the external value of currencies. But in the 1960s, as the idea of 'light-touch' regulation became increasingly attractive, such measures were increasingly viewed on both sides of the Atlantic as an obstacle to circumvent.

During this time, banks never ceased to lobby against the regulations that deprived them of significant markets, and others (like the Glass–Steagall Act) which restricted their scope to combine operations in different markets. As well as pushing for an end to regulations, banks proved adept at persuading politicians that restrictive regulations were unworkable, by finding ways to work around them. Bans on speculative derivatives trading, enacted in the US in the 1930s because of its role in magnifying the 1929 Crash and Great Depression, were effectively sidestepped by the growth of unregulated over-the-counter derivatives trading, which grew explosively in the 1980s and defied subsequent efforts at re-regulation.[13] Banks' invention of 'offshore' currencies, to sidestep cross-border capital controls, was especially effective. In 1944, the Bretton Woods system had pegged the value of the dollar to gold. But when the post-war boom, based on manufacturing, tailed off around 1970, 'light-touch' financial regulation increasingly appealed to policymakers on both sides of the Atlantic. The financial sector reacted to this interest by developing a new currency, the Eurodollar.

As non-US companies, mainly in Europe, accumulated dollars from exports to the US and from oil sales, financiers realized they could borrow and lend in these dollars, which would be outside the control of European governments because they had not issued the currency. UK banks were keen as early as 1957 to mobilize their dollar-denominated deposits, as the chronic balance-of-payments deficit forced the government to impose controls on their use of sterling for foreign transactions.[14] Russian banks stepped up their use of Eurodollars in fear of financial sanctions from the US, and were joined by US banks as they correctly anticipated the suspension of convertibility by the US in response to its worsening US external deficit. London became the centre of the Eurodollar market, which grew into a global one. Rather than being reinvested in the US economy to build new factories or research laboratories, Eurodollars were siphoned off to developing countries in search of a higher yield than was available in developed economies at the time. The result was what has been called the 'dollar shortage', meaning that the currency was insufficient even for the country that issued it – the US.[15] In 1971, faced also with the cost of the Vietnam War and mounting inflation, President Richard M. Nixon stepped in to avert a vacuum in the vaults of the US Bullion Depository at Fort Knox by suspending the dollar's convertibility into gold. It was a dramatic move which signalled the end of the Bretton Woods system and the start of a search for a new way to manage international trade and payments, which was far more market-driven. There followed a period of zero growth and high inflation ('stagflation'), exacerbated by OPEC quadrupling the oil price in the 1970s. By 1980, the gold price had reached $850 an ounce.

The economic difficulties industrial economies faced were regarded by some as a crisis of capitalism. What was not anticipated at the time was that financial markets would be hailed as the way out of the crisis. Finance turned into a growth hormone that would restore and sustain economic expansion.

The deregulation and transformation of finance was both a response to, and a cause of, huge social and economic changes which began in the 1970s. Globalization increased competition, particularly in manufacturing, and in Western countries many communities built on manufacturing – from toys to steel – saw those jobs head east to Asia. The rust belts of the American Midwest, northern England and regions of Continental Europe such as Wallonia in Belgium suffered wrenching social dislocation. Energy prices soared, driving up inflation and further increasing pressure on household budgets. The resulting slower economic growth held down wage rises in richer countries, and hence also the taxes raised by governments. Inequalities of income and wealth widened as profits' share of national income relative to wages grew, in turn partly reflecting the weakening of workers' bargaining power, for example by restricting the rights of trade unions and diluting labour laws.

The competing financial centres of London and New York worked out that they could attract more business by lightening their regulatory touch, with lower costs of compliance. In the US there was perceived to be a shortage of credit for small businesses and home buyers. In fact the real issue was the price of credit, which economists tended to blame on a combination of regulation forcing costs up and banks' monopoly power pushing charges up; the response was to allow more competition between lenders. From the 1960s, Federal banking regulators, interpreting Glass–Steagall with increasing generosity, allowed financial institutions to undertake a growing range of activities. Household borrowing began to climb steeply. Under the Heath government in 1971, the UK adopted a temporary policy known as 'Competition and Credit Control', whereby quantitative ceilings on bank lending were lifted and reserve ratios for commercial banks were reduced.[16] In 1978 minimum commissions were abolished on the New York Stock Exchange, clearing the way for competition and higher trading volumes. A year later, the Thatcher government in the UK abolished exchange controls.

Then, in 1986, Big Bang financial reforms in the City of London did away with fixed commissions for buying and selling shares on the London Stock Exchange, allowed foreigners to own a majority stake in UK stockbrokers, and introduced dual capacity which allowed market makers to be brokers and vice versa. Most of London's stockbroking and market-making firms were absorbed by much bigger foreign and domestic banks. In the late 1990s, supercharged by the IT revolution, the volume of securities trading rocketed. Commercial banks could now use their huge balance sheets, based on customers' deposits, to speculate. Their investment banking arms, along with independent investment banks such as Goldman Sachs, developed financial instruments of increasingly mind-blowing complexity.

THE LORDS OF (MONEY) CREATION

Large financial firms were, however, careful to secure a lightening of regulation, rather than the complete deregulation advocated by free-marketeers such as the Nobel Prize-winning economist Friedrich Hayek. Their reasoning was as follows. To maintain their high profits, the big commercial and investment banks still needed regulators who would keep potential competitors out of the market. Existing big players are therefore helped if banking licences are restricted. Ironically, the disastrous big bank behaviour that triggered the 2008 crash forced regulators (especially in Europe) into further lengthening and complicating an already arduous process for obtaining a new licence, frustrating their plans to unleash a hungry horde of 'challenger banks'. In issuing licences sparingly, governments and central banks were quietly admitting something they were still reluctant to announce publicly: the extraordinary power of private-sector bank lending to determine the pace of money creation, and therefore economic growth.

That banks create money is still a highly contested notion. It was politically unmentionable in 1980s America and Europe, where economic policy was predicated on a 'monetarism' in which governments precisely controlled the supply of money, whose growth determined inflation. Banks traditionally presented themselves purely as financial intermediaries, usefully channelling household depositors' savings into business borrowers' investment. Mainstream economists accepted this characterization, and its implication that banks play a vital economic role in 'mobilizing' savings. Banks are not only empowered to create money as well as channel it from one part of the economy to another; they also do remarkably little to turn households' savings into business investment. In fact, in the US case, when the flow of funds is analysed in detail, households 'invest' their savings entirely in the consumption of durable goods while large businesses finance their investment through their own retained profits.[17]

They also had to overlook the fact that money appears from nowhere when firms or households invest more than their savings, and borrow the difference. When a bank makes you a loan, say for a mortgage, it does not hand over cash. It credits your account with the amount of the mortgage. Instantly, money is created. But at the same time the bank has also created a liability on itself (the new deposits in your account), and banks must ensure they have sufficient reserves or cash (both forms of central bank money) to meet requests by you for payments to other banks or cash withdrawals. They must also hold capital in reserve in case loans are not repaid, in order to prevent insolvency. Both of these create constraints on bank lending and mean that banks generally refrain from lending to people and firms that do not fulfil certain criteria such as creditworthiness or expected profitability. Money creation also occurs when you pay for dinner with a credit or debit card. As a matter of fact, only about 3 per cent of the money in the UK economy is cash (or what is sometimes called fiat money, i.e. any legal tender backed by government). Banks create all the rest. It wasn't until after the 2008 crisis that the Bank of England admitted that 'loans create deposits', and not vice versa.[18]

So licensing and regulation gave smaller banks a significant cost disadvantage compared to big ones, which can spread the bureaucratic costs (and risks) more widely and raise funds more cheaply. This made it harder for new competitors to enter the market. For existing players, there was a lot of monopoly rent to extract, and they could easily co-ordinate between them to avoid excessive competition without needing formal (illegal) cartel arrangements, while customers trusted them – rarely questioning their practices or financial health – precisely because regulators were watching over them. For example, it took an investigation by the UK's Competition Commission in 2000 to establish that the country's Big Four banks had been operating a complex monopoly on services for small businesses, using their 90 per cent market share to extract £2 billion in annual profit and push their average return on equity up to 36 per cent, by mutually agreeing not to compete.[19] If banks' gambles ever endangered their solvency, the government would have to rescue them with public money. This implicit guarantee of a public bailout lowered the biggest players' cost of raising capital, which further cemented their market power.

FINANCE AND THE
'REAL' ECONOMY

For centuries, income earned by charging interest had been viewed as a subtraction from productive enterprise rather than a symbol of it. This was both a moral and an economic judgement. As we have seen, the Roman Church banned the charging of interest for most of the Middle Ages, while Enlightenment philosophers such as John Locke, writing in 1692, saw bankers merely as middlemen, 'eating' up a share of the gains of trade rather than creating any gains themselves.[20] Even before the formal study of economics began in the late eighteenth century, many intellectuals and writers had concluded that banks did not produce value and often did not operate in the public interest at all.

For the physiocrats, finance didn't belong in the agricultural sector and was therefore seen as unproductive. Adam Smith took a similar view, though he also rarely mentioned bankers explicitly. According to Smith, bankers cannot create more than they get; for him, the idea of making money from money does not work in the aggregate – although it certainly helps the bankers fill their own pockets.

Karl Marx introduced another idea. He located the financial sector in the circulation phase of the circuit of capital, where value created in production is realized through distribution and ultimately used up in consumption. For Marx, finance is a catalyst, transforming money capital into production capital (the means of production such as factories, machinery and living labour – the labour power of workers). Hence any income is paid out of the value generated by others. Rather than adding to value, finance simply takes part of the surplus value generated through the production process – and there is no hard-and-fast rule as to how much it should take. Taking (not uncommonly) reassurance about capitalism from its arch-opponent, twentieth-century economists assumed that financial profits would always be limited by (and total less than) the sum of productive firms' profits, and might even move up and down to even out the flow of profits in the 'real' economy.

But this story came under attack after the crisis. Trade in financial instruments had vastly outgrown trade in real products and was stimulating the very price fluctuations from which profits are made – by creating opportunities to buy low and sell high. In fact, systemic fluctuations have led to a crash historically every fifteen to twenty years.[21] Crashes reveal the investment banks' 'risk-taking' service – which justified their inclusion in GDP accounting – to be a hollow boast. It is the taxpayer who is called on to take the real risk, bailing out the banks. But even the most influential critics of finance in the twentieth century – Keynes and Minsky – did not succeed in fundamentally challenging the privileged place of financial institutions in economic policy and in the national accounts. Keynes's attention was deflected (and Minsky's early warnings obscured) by the fact that financial services' share of national output was below 4 per cent and falling from 1933 to 1945, and did not move back above its 1930s level until the 1970s.

Writing in the 1930s, one of the most influential critics of finance, John Maynard Keynes, was upfront about what financial speculation entailed. In his lifetime he observed how financial markets and public attitudes to financial trading were changing, becoming ends in themselves rather than facilitators of growth in the real economy. When speculation spread from a rich leisure class to the wider population, it drove the stock market bubble that ushered in the Wall Street Crash and 1930s depression; but as public spending helped to restore people's jobs and incomes, those with money again began to gamble it on stocks and shares. Wall Street was, he said, 'regarded as an institution of which the proper social purpose is to direct new investment into the most profitable channels in terms of future yield'. By this yardstick, Keynes commented, Wall Street could not 'be claimed as one of the outstanding triumphs of *laissez-faire* capitalism – which is not surprising, if I am right in thinking that the best brains of Wall Street have been in fact directed towards a different object'.[22]

That 'different object', in Keynes's view, was not a form of production, but 'betting' – and the profits of the bookmaker were 'a mere transfer',[23] a transfer which should be limited lest individuals ruin themselves and harm others in the process. Moreover, Keynes argued, since gambling is luck, there should be no pretence that financial speculation involved skill. Any reference to skill – or productiveness on the part of speculators – was a sign that somebody was trying to trick somebody else. Keynes also thought that the proceeds from such betting and speculating should go to the state to remove the incentive – a better word might be temptation – to reap private gains from it.[24] He went on to stress the difference between this kind of speculation (value extraction) and finance for actual productive investment (value creation), which he saw as crucial for growth and which was only possible without the speculative apparatus around it. If 'the capital development of a country becomes a by-product of the activities of a casino, the job is likely to be ill-done'.[25]

Hyman Minsky, who was much influenced by Keynes, wrote extensively about the self-destabilizing dynamics of finance. In his work on financial instability[26] he nested Keynes's critique within an alternative theory of money. This theory, which began far from the mainstream but forced its way in when a bubble-bursting 'Minsky moment' broke the long boom in 2008, holds that the quantity of money in an economy is created by the interplay of economic forces rather than by an outside agency such as a central bank. Although portrayed as all-powerful (and so responsible for all financial instability) by Milton Friedman (1912–2006; Nobel Prize 1976) and the 'monetarists' propelled to prominence by 1970s stagnation, central banks such as the US Federal Reserve can only indirectly and weakly control the private-sector banks and their money creation, by setting the base interest rate. Minsky charted the way in which the banking system would eventually end up moving to 'speculative finance', pursuing returns that depended on the appreciation of asset values rather than the generation of income from productive activity.

Banks and investment funds may believe they are deriving income from new production, and their individual 'risk models' will show that they will survive most conceivable financial shocks because of the diversification of their portfolios. But their incomes are ultimately transfers from other financial firms, and can suddenly dry up when one firm's inability to meet a transfer obligation (defaulting on a loan, or withholding a dividend) forces others to do so in turn. That is what happened when Lehman Brothers, the American investment bank, collapsed in 2008, thereby precipitating the financial crisis.

As long as financial assets can be bought and sold in a reasonable amount of time without incurring losses, and debt can be rolled over to pay previous loans, markets are liquid and the economy runs smoothly. But once investors realize that borrowers are not earning enough to pay interest and principal (on which the interest is based), creditors stop financing them and try to sell their assets as soon as possible. Financial bubbles can be seen as the result of value being *extracted*; during financial crises value is actually *destroyed*. The fallout can be measured not only in output and job losses but also by the amount of money that governments had to pour into private banks because they were 'too big to fail': the quantitative easing (QE) schemes that followed the crisis might have been used to help sustain the economy, but ended up further propping up the banks. The figures involved were enormous. In the US, the Federal Reserve embarked on three different QE schemes, totalling $4.2 trillion over the period 2008–14. In the UK, the Bank of England undertook £375 billion of QE between 2009 and 2012, and in Europe, the ECB committed € 60 billion *per month* from January 2015 to March 2017.[27]

Back in the mid-1980s, to try to prevent the banking system from moving to speculative finance, Hyman Minsky formulated an economic recipe that can be summarized as 'big government, big bank'. In his vision, government creates jobs by being the 'employer of last resort' and underwrites distressed financial operators' balance sheets by being the 'lender of last resort'.[28] When the financial sector is so interconnected, it is very possible for one bank's failure to become contagious, leading to the bankruptcy of banks all over the world. In order to avoid this 'butterfly effect' (as chaos theory calls it), Minsky favoured strong regulation of financial intermediaries. In this he followed Keynes, who, as the post-war international order was being devised at Bretton Woods in 1944, advocated 'the restoration of international loans and credit for legitimate purposes', while stressing the necessity of 'controlling short-term speculative movements or flights of currency whether out of debtor countries or from one creditor country to another'.[29]

According to Keynes and Minsky, the possibility of financial crisis was always present in the way that money circulated – not as a means of exchange, but as an end in itself (an idea based predominantly on Marx's thinking). They believed that government had to intervene to avert or manage crises. Although controversial in the 1930s (due to its undertones of 'socialism' and central planning) and later (after the revival of free-market economics, including the idea of unregulated 'free' banking), the idea of intervention in markets was hardly novel or radical. Back in the eighteenth century, Adam Smith's belief that a free market was one free from rent implied government action to eliminate rent. Modern-day free marketeers, who have gagged Smith while claiming his mantle, would not agree with him.

Financial regulators have focused on introducing more competition – through the break-up of large banks and the entry of new 'challenger banks' – as an essential step towards preventing another financial crisis. But this 'quantity theory of competition' – the assumption that the problem is just size and numbers, and not fundamental behaviour – avoids the uncomfortable reality that crises develop from the uncoordinated interaction of numerous players.

There is danger in a complex system with many players. Greater stability might be achieved when a few large companies serve the real economy, subject to heavy regulation in order to make sure that they concentrate on value creation and not value extraction. By contrast, deregulation designed to reinvigorate a part of the financial sector may well promote risk-taking behaviour – the opposite of what is intended. Lord Adair Turner, who took over as Chair of the UK financial regulator (then called the Financial Services Authority) in 2008, just as the system was crashing around it, reflected when the dust settled that: 'financial services (particularly wholesale trading activities) include a large share of highly remunerated activities that are purely distributive in their indirect effects ... the ability of national income accounts to distinguish between activities that are meaningfully value-creative and activities that are essentially distributive rent extraction is far from perfect'.[30]

Neither William J. Baumol (1922–2017), whose descriptions of 'unproductive entrepreneurship' could account for much financial activity but who is now a leading contributor to mainstream portfolio and capital-market theory, nor Turner, despite his subsequent leading role in the Institute for New Economic Thinking, discuss finance much in terms of value theory. Yet their thinking implies that finance should be fundamentally reformed to create value inside the production boundary, and that those of its elements outside the boundary should be drastically reduced, eliminated or competed away. Lord Turner's more considered verdict, ten years on from the start of the crisis, was to bemoan the ever larger amount of debt needed to add an extra dollar to GDP, but then trace much of this to the bad aggregate effects of essentially good lending, which 'private lenders do not and cannot be expected to take into account'. His prescriptions, requiring more and smarter financial regulation to monitor and control the system's aggregate risks, actually imply additional and permanent effort by public authorities to make the marketplace safe for private bank (and shadow-bank) profit.

Over the past decades, Keynes's and Minsky's insights and warnings about the potentially destructive nature of an unbridled financial sector have been totally ignored. Today, the economic mainstream continues to argue that the bigger (measured by the number of actors) or 'deeper' financial markets are, the more likely they are to be efficient, revealing the 'true' price and therefore value of an asset in the sense defined by the Nobel Prize-winning US economist Eugene Fama.[31] An 'efficient' market is, in Fama's definition, one that prices every asset so that no further profit can be made by buying and reselling it. This way of thinking reconciles the case for large financial markets with the high incomes paid to employees in financial services, because incomes supposedly reflect the huge benefits of financial services to the economy.[32]

From the perspective of marginal utility, therefore, the expansion of finance is highly desirable and should increase its value added, and hence its positive contribution to GDP growth,[33] even though it was only a convenient decision to treat finance as productive in the national accounts in the first place.[34]

But it is impossible to understand the rise of finance without analysing the background dynamics which allowed it to thrive: deregulation and rising inequality.

FROM CLAIMS ON PROFIT
TO CLAIMS ON CLAIMS

Commercial banks seem literally to have been given a licence to print money, through their ability to create money in the process of lending it, and to lend it at higher interest rates than they borrow. But such lending remains a risky source of profit, if those they lend to don't pay back. And because they can only lend if a household or business wants to borrow, it's a highly cyclical source of profit, rising and falling with the scale of investment activity. So from the start, commercial bankers have sought to do more with the money they create – and the additional funds they take in from depositors – than just lend it to prospective borrowers.

They've eyed the lucrative world of financial markets – dealing in shares and bonds, on behalf of clients and on their own account – as an additional source of profit. That's why the Glass–Steagall Act and its counterparts elsewhere, forcing banks to choose between taking customer deposits or playing the markets, was so unpopular in banking circles, and why they celebrated its repeal at the turn of the twenty-first century.

The move into investment banking was made more attractive by other aspects of financial deregulation. It enabled investment banks to poach some of the commercial banks' most profitable clients: large businesses which could finance investment by issuing bonds rather than taking bank loans, and high-net-worth individuals seeking private wealth management. And it opened up a range of new financial markets for investment banks to gamble on, trading instruments which had long been known about but which past regulations had effectively banned.

Two classes of financial instrument in particular were made available to investors by deregulation from the 1970s onwards, and were central to the subsequent massive growth in financial transactions and profitability. These were *derivatives*, contracts on the future delivery of a financial instrument or commodity which allowed investors to make bets on their price movement; and *securitizations*, bundles of income-yielding instruments that turned these into tradable securities (and enabled their inclusion in derivative contracts). Commercial banks made a particular breakthrough in the early 2000s when they began to 'securitize' past lending to finance new lending. Home mortgages were the initial focus, enabling banks like the UK's Northern Rock to grow their loans at unprecedented speed, and win political praise for making these loans available to households previously dismissed as too poor to borrow. After the 2008 financial crash – triggered in part by debt securitizations rendered worthless by default on the underlying mortgages – attention turned to securitizing other forms of obligation, among them 'personal contract plans' and other car loans, student loans and residential rents.

Political leaders and financial experts praised financial markets for helping goods and services markets to work more efficiently and grease the wheels of capitalism. In his 'The Great Moderation' speech in 2004, Ben Bernanke, who later became the Chairman of the US Federal Reserve, said: 'The increased depth and sophistication of financial markets, deregulation in many industries, the shift away from manufacturing toward services, and increased openness to trade and international capital flows are other examples of structural changes that may have increased macroeconomic flexibility and stability.'[35] Spectacular growth in the volume of derivatives – which can be traded even if the underlying assets were never delivered or deliverable – was viewed as helping to reduce systemic risks and 'get prices right'. The often enormous profits were dressed up as fulfilling the worthy social objective of spreading and managing risk so that the previously unbankable and uncreditworthy could be brought in from the cold and sold products – especially homes – that the more affluent took for granted.

As we saw in Chapter 3, banks mark up borrowers' interest rates as an indication of value added (FISIM): an obvious example of fictitious financial value. But this is only the tip of the iceberg. Today, leading investment banks like Goldman Sachs and J. P. Morgan don't attribute their employees' vast salaries to success in ordinary borrowing and lending. The great bulk of these banks' profits comes from activities such as underwriting the initial public offerings (IPOs) of corporate bonds and shares, financing mergers and acquisitions, writing futures and options contracts that take over risk from non-financial businesses, and trading in these and other financial instruments for capital gain.

The subtle yet fundamental change in the way that the banking sector's productivity has been redefined over the last two decades or so has corresponded with its increasing capture of the economy's surplus. The massive and disproportionate growth of the financial sector (and with it the origins of the global financial crisis) can be traced back to the early 2000s, when banks began increasingly to lend to other financial institutions via wholesale markets, making loans not matched by deposits. In the UK the 'customer funding gap' between loans advanced and deposits from households (traditionally viewed as the most stable form of bank financing) widened from zero in 2001 to more than £900 billion ($1,300 billion) in 2008, before the crisis cut it to less than £300 billion in 2011.[36] Banks and other lenders found that wholesale funds could be raised much more cheaply than deposits from retail or business customers, especially by using their customers' existing loans, such as mortgages, as security for more borrowing. These lenders benefited from a seemingly virtuous circle in which additional lending raised financial asset prices, which strengthened their balance sheets, giving them the scope to borrow and lend more within existing minimum capital ratios, the amount of capital banks had to retain relative to their lending.

As well as lending more to one another and to retail clients, over the past three decades banks began to target their loans at riskier prospects offering higher rates of return. This is the part of the story that most people now understand, having been well covered in the media and popular culture, in books and films such as *Inside Job*, *Margin Call* and *The Big Short*. Banks felt they needed to take more risks because, with governments trying to balance budgets and reduce public borrowing requirements, the yields on low-risk assets (such as US and European government debt) had fallen very low. Banks also believed that they had become much better at handling risk: by configuring the right portfolio, insuring themselves against it (especially through credit default swaps – CDSs – that would pay out if a borrower didn't pay back), or selling it on to other investors with a greater risk appetite. Investment banks lent to hedge funds and private equity firms and developed and traded exotic instruments based on assets like subprime mortgages, because the returns were higher than lending to industry or government.

When channelling short-term deposits into long-term loans, banks traditionally took a risk – especially when the loans went to borrowers who would need a windfall gain (a business that took off, a house price that rose) to pay back their loans. Ostensibly, that risk disappeared in the 1990s and early 2000s, when securitization turned a bundle of subprime mortgages or other loans into a bond with a prime (even triple-A) credit rating in the shape of a mortgage-backed security (MBS).

Securitization can and does play a valuable role in diversifying risk and increasing liquidity in the financial system. In 2006 Alan Greenspan, then Chairman of the US Federal Reserve, and Tim Geithner, the former President of the Federal Reserve Bank of New York, claimed that derivatives were a stabilizing factor because they spread the risk among the financial institutions best equipped to deal with it.[37] Greenspan had, a decade before the crisis struck, vetoed a proposal to regulate over-the-counter (OTC) derivatives, claiming that on the contrary 'the fact that OTC markets function so effectively without the benefits of the Commodity Exchange Act [CEA] provides a strong argument for development of a less burdensome regulatory regime for financial derivatives traded on futures exchanges'. Passed in 1936, the CEA requires all futures contracts for physical commodities to be traded on an organized exchange. As was spectacularly shown in 2008, derivatives' capacity to transfer and defray risk really exists only at the individual level. At the aggregate level, the individual risk is merely transferred to other intermediaries in the form of counter-party risk. Its disappearance from the balance sheets of the original holders, and the frequent lack of clarity about who has taken it over, makes the market situation even more precarious.[38]

Securitization was also abused, sometimes in ways that bordered on fraudulence, and that abuse certainly influenced regulators in the years following the financial crisis. The transformation of relatively low-quality loans into triple-A-rated securities occurred largely because credit-rating agencies routinely gave high valuations to securitizations of low-grade debt, underestimating the likelihood of default, especially on residential mortgages. To be doubly sure that their high returns were sheltered from a comparably high risk, banks 'transferred' their risk by assigning the securitized debt to 'special purpose vehicles' (SPVs), whose liabilities did not show up on the banks' own balance sheets. When lower-income borrowers began struggling to repay their debts after 2005, the securitized bonds turned out to be much less safe than their triple-A rating suggested, and the SPVs bounced back onto the banks' balance sheets. The golden combination of high return and low risk turned out to be a statistical illusion, but one that national accounting had promoted just as enthusiastically as had banks' pre-2008 corporate accounts.

A DEBT IN THE FAMILY

Since the 1970s, the growing inequality of wealth and income has profoundly shaped the way in which finance has developed. The growth of finance has also fed the growth of inequality, not least by adding to the influence and lobbying power of financiers who tend to favour reduction of taxes and social expenditures, and promoting the financial-market volatility that boosts the fortunes of those who serially buy low and sell high.

Following deregulation, the enormous increase in finance available to households was the main reason for the rise in banks' profits. Commercial banks profited from direct loans for anything from cars to homes to holidays, and from credit cards. Investment banks made money by securitizing commercial-bank 'products' and trading the derivatives they 'manufactured'. Legislators allowed financial intermediaries to regulate themselves, or imposed only minimal regulation because their operations were too complex to be understood. Markets (following the marginalists) were considered to be 'efficient' – healthy competition would deter financial intermediaries from reckless behaviour.

As previously prudent banks bombarded customers with offers of credit – the age of tempting credit card promotions dropping almost daily through millions of letter boxes had arrived – household borrowing began to rise inexorably. Across the financial sector more broadly, the relaxation of controls on mortgage lending became another source of profit and also fuelled the increased household borrowing. Whereas in the 1970s mortgages had been rationed in the UK, by the early 2000s house buyers could borrow 100 per cent or even more of the value of a property. By 2016, total cumulative household borrowing in the UK had reached £1.5 trillion – about 83 per cent of national output, and equivalent to nearly £30,000 for each adult in the land – well above average earnings.[39]

Governments rejoiced when banks offered mortgages to low-paid, marginally employed home buyers on the assumption that their debt could be 'securitized' and quickly resold to other investors. It seemed less a reckless gamble and more a social innovation, helping to broaden property ownership and boosting the 'property-owning democracy', while increasing the flow of income to an already buoyant investor class. Greater revenue from financial-sector incomes and associated high-end purchases even pushed the US and UK government budgets into rare surpluses around the turn of the twenty-first century.[40]

Loosening the availability of credit to sustain consumption is not in itself a bad thing. But there are dangers. One is cost. It seemed to make sense to relax controls on lending when interest rates were low or falling. It makes less sense if borrowers, lulled into a sense of false security, are caught out when interest rates rise. Another fundamental danger is the tendency of the system to overexpand: for credit to become too readily available, as the Bank for International Settlements has recently recognized.[41] The system is stable when the growth in debt is matched by the growth in the value of assets whose purchase is financed by that debt. As soon as people begin to have doubts about the assets' value, however, the cracks appear. That is what happened when US property prices collapsed after the crash of 2008. Home owners may find themselves in negative equity and even have their property repossessed, although not before lenders have extracted interest. But banks can always choose to provide other services than loans. When uncertainty about the future is high, they can even decide to hoard cash rather than invest it – often a sound decision, as high interest rates are associated with a high risk of not obtaining enough for the investment.

The rise in private debt in the US and UK has resulted in household savings falling as a percentage of disposable income – income minus taxes – especially in periods of sustained economic growth (during the 1980s, the late 1990s and the beginning of the 2000s). Simultaneously, household consumption expenditure has been buoyant. It has outpaced any rise in disposable income, and its contribution to GDP has grown.[42]

Income inequality has been on the rise in most advanced

economies, especially in the US and in the UK, over the past four decades. Increasing inequality in the US has taken three complementary forms.[43] First, real wages have fallen or stagnated for many low- and middle-income households. For instance, OECD data on the US economy indicate that the annual real minimum wage (in 2015 US dollars) fell from $19,237 in 1975 to $13,000 in 2005 (in 2016 it was $14,892). Second, in almost every OECD country wage shares have declined by several percentage points in favour of rising profit shares, even when real employee compensation has gone up.[44] As Figure 9 below shows, this was the result of average productivity growth rising faster than average or median real-wage growth in many countries, especially in the US.

Third, personal distribution of income and wealth has become more and more unequal. In both the US and the UK, and in many other OECD countries, those with the highest incomes have enjoyed an increasing share of total national income ever since the 1970s, as can been seen in Figure 10. Furthermore, income distribution is extremely skewed towards very high incomes, not just the top 10 per cent and 1 per cent, but especially the top 0.1 per cent.[45] Wealth distribution reveals a similar pattern. A 2017 Oxfam report, *An Economy for the 99%*, found that in 2016 eight men own the same

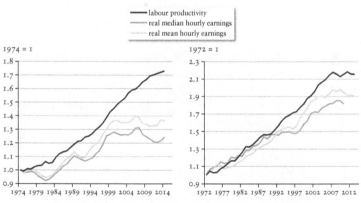

Figure 9. Labour productivity and wages in the US since 1974 *(left)* and the UK since 1972 *(right)*[46]

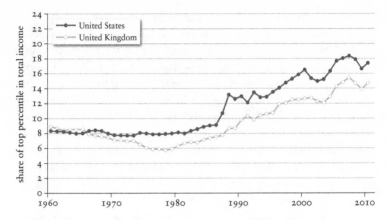

Figure 10. Income inequality in the US and the UK, 1960–2010[47]

wealth as the poorest half of the world's population. In a report published a year earlier, *An Economy for the 1%*, Oxfam calculated that
the club of the wealthiest 1 per cent of individuals globally shrank
from 388 members in 2010 to just sixty-two in 2015; in other words,
the very richest were getting even richer relative to others who were
also by any sensible standard very rich. The wealth of the sixty-two
very richest individuals increased by 45 per cent in the five years to
2015, a jump of more than half a trillion dollars in total. Over the
same period, the wealth of the bottom half fell by just over a trillion
dollars – a drop of 38 per cent.[48]

The upshot of growing inequality of income and wealth was that,
to maintain the living standards they had enjoyed from the Second
World War to the 1980s, workers had to shoulder an increasing debt
burden from the 1980s onwards. Looking at the broader economic
picture, without growing household debt, demand might have been
weaker and sales by businesses lower. Finance bridged the gap, in the
form of new forms of credit whose resultant interest flows and charges
underpinned the sector's expansion.

As a result, private debt, and particularly household debt, increased
substantially as a percentage of disposable income. Figure 11 below
shows that total household debt as a percentage of net disposable

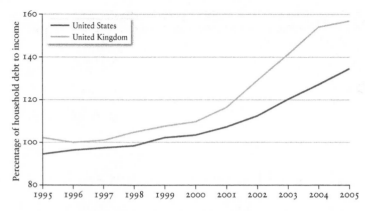

Figure 11. Household debt and income in the US and the UK, 1995–2005[49]

income grew by 42 per cent in the US and by 53 per cent in the UK from 1995 to 2005.

In the US, mortgage loans were a principal cause of rising household indebtedness (Figure 12), partially a reflection of households' propensity to extract equity from the rising value of their houses.[50]

In 2007, the US Congressional Budget Office lent weight to the argument that the increased value of real estate represented a typical 'wealth effect': the assumption that as people's assets such as their houses go up in value, they are psychologically more disposed to spend. The rise in US real-estate prices translated into higher rates of mortgage-equity withdrawal and ultimately boosted consumer spending.[51]

The *Survey of Consumer Finances* produced by the US Federal

	Consumer credit	Home mortgages	Other	Total debt
1980	17.8	46.2	8.1	72.1
1990	19.2	58.3	9.1	86.7
2000	24.2	66.7	11.7	102.8
2010	24.5	97.5	11.1	134.1

Figure 12. Household debt as a percentage of disposable personal income[52]

Percentile of income	Percentage with debt ratio >40%
less than 20	27.0
20–39.99	18.6
40–59.99	13.7
60–79.99	7.1
80–89.99	2.4
90–100	1.8

Figure 13. Indebtedness and family income (2004)[53]

Reserve shows that the poorer a family is, the more heavily indebted it is likely to be. Using data for the 2004 (pre-crisis) period, Figure 13 is based on all families whose ratio of debt payments relative to their disposable income is greater than 40 per cent. The families are broken down into groups according to their income bands (measured as percentiles) and levels of indebtedness. In the group with the lowest income, the poorest 20 per cent of the income distribution, 27 per cent of families were 'heavily indebted'. Among the richest 10 per cent, it was only 1.8 per cent. This means that poorer families were much more indebted than richer ones in relative terms. The stagnation or outright decline in real incomes of the poorest group forced them to borrow to finance current consumption.

Sustaining economic growth through household borrowing has been aptly defined as 'privatized Keynesianism',[54] because 'instead of governments taking on debt to stimulate the economy, individuals did so'.[55] But it was an unsustainable solution to the lack of wage-led demand growth. Aided and abetted by government policy, central banks, instead of being the lenders of last resort, became the lenders of *first* resort to the financial sector, cutting interest rates to avert financial crises. But this policy drove up the price of assets such as shares and houses and further encouraged households to borrow. The result was that households were enrolled in an indirect – if not in fact 'private' – management of effective demand, through highly financialized consumption that left many ever more impoverished and indebted.

CONCLUSION

By the late twentieth century, finance was perceived as being much more productive than before. Finance, too, became increasingly valuable to policymakers, in order to maintain economic growth and manage inequality of wealth and income. The cost was mounting household debt and increasing government dependence on tax revenues from the financial sector.

To ignore the question of value in relation to finance is, then, highly irresponsible. But in the end, the real challenge is not to label finance as value-creating or value-extracting, but to fundamentally transform it so that it *is* genuinely value-creating. This requires paying attention to characteristics such as timeframe. Impatient finance – the quest for short-term returns – can hurt the productive capacity of the economy and its potential for innovation.

Indeed, the crash of 2008 vindicated the warnings of Keynes, Minsky and others about the dangers of excessive financialization. Yet while the crash and the ensuing crisis weakened banks, it still left them in a dominant position in the economy, sparing the embarrassment of those who had extolled the value of financial services in the years before they imploded into bankruptcy and fraud.

In the intervening years, there has, unsurprisingly, been a regulatory reversal – or at least a partial one. Under political pressure, and recognizing that they may have gone too far in allowing commercial and investment banks to share the same roof, regulators in the US and Europe have since 2008 sought to distance one from the other. Reforms such as the US Dodd–Frank Act of 2010 attempt to prevent investment banks from using the deposits of their commercial-bank parents (which are ultimately backed by government under deposit insurance schemes) to finance their riskier income-generating activities. New rules have tried, at least partly, to steer investment banks back to their original function of using borrowed money raised in wholesale markets to finance risky transactions – which even mainstream economists sometimes liken to a casino.

Yet today financialization appears to be thriving again despite its questionable productivity. Financialization remains a powerful force and its capacity for value extraction is scarcely diminished. Attempts to end excessively dangerous and socially useless financial processes, or at least shine a light on them, have merely displaced them into darker corners. Tighter regulation of the activities that caused the last crash has encouraged banks to seek ways around the new curbs, while still lobbying to relax them (except where they conveniently keep out new competitors). It has led less regulated 'non-bank financial institutions' or 'shadow banks' to expand where banks were forced to contract. What we must now look at is the wider web of different financial intermediaries that have cropped up, with their desire to make a quick, high return and their effect on company organization and the evolution of industry.

5

The Rise of Casino Capitalism

Rather than the financial conservatism that pension funds,
mutual funds and insurance companies were supposed to
bring, money manager capitalism has ushered in a new era of
pervasive casino capitalism.

Hyman Minsky, 1992[1]

When we talk about finance, we should bear in mind its many different forms. While traditional activities like bank lending remain important, they have been eclipsed by others. One is 'shadow banking', a term coined in 2007 to describe diverse financial intermediaries that carry out bank-like activities but are not regulated as banks.[2] These include pawnbrokers, payday lenders, peer-to-peer lenders, mortgage lenders, mobile payment systems and bond-trading platforms established by tech firms and money market funds. Between 2004 and 2014, the value of assets serviced by the 'informal lending sector' globally rose from $26 trillion to $80 trillion and may account for as much as a quarter of the global financial system. Shadow-banking activities – borrowing, lending and asset-trading by firms that are not banks and escape their more onerous regulation – all have one thing in common: they funnel finance to finance, making money from moving existing money around. Another significant boost to finance has been the rise of the asset management industry and its different components, from widely marketed retail investment funds to hedge funds and private equity. While average incomes have grown, enabling a build-up of savings especially by the better-off, rising longevity and governments' reduced appetite for social insurance and pension provision have put pressure on households around the world to make their savings work harder. Those who 'manage' investments on their behalf can often claim a fee – often a percentage of the funds under management – whether or not their stock-picks and strategies have demonstrably added value. Taken together with traditional banking, and released from the regulations that previously kept financial firms' size and risk appetite in check, these forces caused the sector to grow disproportionately large.

There are two key aspects to the long-term growth of the financial sector and its effect on the real economy. These two aspects of financialization are covered in this and the next chapter. I will focus on the UK and the US, where both forms of financialization have been developing most. The first, covered in this chapter, is its expansion in absolute terms and as a share of total economic activity. Today, the sector has sprawled way beyond the limits of traditional finance, mainly banking, to cover an immense array of financial instruments and has created a new force in modern capitalism: asset management. The financial sector now accounts for a significant and growing share of the economy's value added and profits. But only 15 per cent of the funds generated go to businesses in non-financial industries.[3] The rest is traded between financial institutions, making money simply from money changing hands, a phenomenon that has developed hugely, giving rise to what Hyman Minsky called 'money manager capitalism'.[4] Or, put another way: when finance makes money by serving not the 'real' economy, but itself.

The second aspect, covered in the next chapter, is the effect of financial motives on non-financial sectors, e.g. industries such as energy, pharmaceuticals and IT. Such financialization can include the provision of financial instruments for customers – for example, car manufacturers offering finance to their customers – and, more importantly, the use of profits to boost share prices rather than reinvest in actual production.

Both these aspects of financialization show how, in the growth of the financial sector, value creation has been confused with value extraction, with serious economic and social consequences. Finance has both benefited from and partly caused widening inequality of income and wealth, initially in the main 'Anglo-Saxon' countries, but spreading since the 1990s to previously less financialized European and Asian economies. Rising inequality might be 'justified' by economic gains if it promotes faster growth that raises basic or average incomes, for example by giving richer entrepreneurs the means and incentive to invest more. But recent increases in inequality have been associated with slower growth,[5] linked to its social impact as well as the deflationary effect of reducing already-low incomes. The key issue is: what role does finance, in all its complexity, play in the economy? Does it justify its size and pervasiveness? Are the sometimes huge rewards that can be earned from financial activities such as hedge funds (an investment fund that speculates using borrowed capital or credit) or private equity proportional to the actual risks taken?

PROMETHEUS (WITH A PILOT'S LICENCE) UNBOUND

Such questions are not new. Back in 1925, Winston Churchill, then Chancellor of the Exchequer, had begun to get itchy about the way in which finance was changing. He famously claimed that he would 'rather see finance less proud and industry more content'.[6] The suspicion troubling policymakers (and their newly emerging economic advisers) was that financiers were positioned in relation to industrial producers in the same way as pre-industrial landowners related to agricultural producers – extracting a significant share of the revenue, without playing any active part in the process of production. Investors who passively collected interest on loans and dividends from shares were 'rentiers' in the classic sense, exploiting their (often inherited) control over large sums of money to generate unearned income, which – if not used for conspicuous consumption – added to their wealth, especially in an age of low taxation.

The profits extracted by lenders and stock market investors could not be used for investment in industrial expansion and modernization. This was a growing concern, especially in the UK, whose inexorable fall behind the industrial power of Germany and America (especially in industries that could convert to military use) had been the subject of increasingly anxious parliamentary enquiries since the late nineteenth century. The inclination of British-based banking families and trusts to channel funds abroad in search of higher returns, while foreign-based investors brought British assets through its stock market, amplified these concerns as more of the country's colonies began to agitate for independence, and the storm clouds that had heralded the First World War began to gather again. Churchill's Chancellorship had also alerted him to rent-seeking behaviour – lobbying government for rules and entry barriers that would enhance financial profit, and making loans to investors who expected to repay out of share price gains – which was soon to rebound internationally in the Wall Street Crash of 1929.

Yet at the time he wrote, the financial sector in the UK was only 6.4 per cent of the entire economy.[7] Finance trundled along at the same pace in the first thirty years after the Second World War. Then, after a process of deregulation begun during the 1970s, and the shifts in the production boundary reviewed in the previous chapter, it powered ahead of the real economy – manufacturing and the non-financial services provided by private-sector companies, voluntary organizations and the state. By reclassifying them from collectors of rent to creators of financial 'value added', the newly ignited bundle of finance, insurance and real estate (FIRE) was transformed into a productive sector at which economists of the eighteenth, nineteenth and even the first half of the twentieth century would have marvelled.

In the US, from 1960 to 2014, finance's share of gross value added more than doubled, from 3.7 to 8.4 per cent; over the same period, manufacturing's share of output fell by more than half, from 25 per cent to 12 per cent. The same happened in the UK: manufacturing's share fell from over 30 per cent of total value added in 1970 to 10 per cent in 2014, while that of finance and insurance rose from less than 5 per cent to a peak of over 9 per cent in 2009, dropping slightly to 8 per cent in 2014.[8] So in the three decades following deregulation, the financial sector comprehensively outpaced the 'real' economy. This can be seen clearly for the UK in Figure 14.

As regulations started to be lifted in the early 1980s, US private-sector financial corporations' profits as a share of total corporate

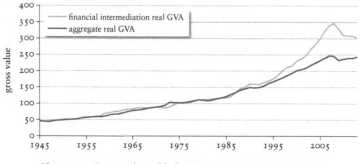

Figure 14. Gross value added, UK 1945–2013 (1975 = 100)[9]

Figure 15. US financial corporate profits as share of domestic total profits[10]

profits – stable at around 10–15 per cent in the first forty years after the Second World War – rose to over 20 per cent, peaking at 40 per cent at the beginning of the twenty-first century (Figure 15).

The proportion of wages that goes to financial-sector workers also illustrates the sector's growth. Until 1980, finance's share of employment and income was almost identical (the ratio is 1). After that, the ratio spiked: by 2009 it had almost doubled to 1.7 (Figure 16).[11]

The financial sector's profits were fabulous, especially in the UK and US with their global financial hubs in London and New York City, and were contributing an increasing share of GDP. It was hardly surprising that the public went along with 'financial innovation'.

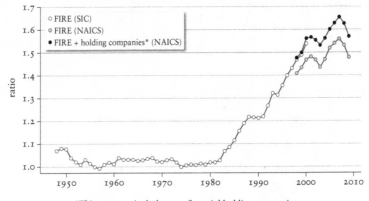

*This category includes non-financial holding companies.

Figure 16. Ratio of finance employee compensation share
to national employment share[12]

People spent. From London to Hong Kong the retail and leisure sectors of the world's financial centres were doing a roaring trade.

From the 1980s onwards the financial sector was on a mission to convince governments that it was productive. In the minds of policymakers, finance had become an increasingly productive industry, an idea they were keen to convey to the public.

Strange as it might seem now, policymakers largely ignored the danger of financial turmoil. Only a few years after his 2004 Mansion House speech, in which he paid fulsome tribute to the productivity of the City of London's financial and business elite, then Labour Chancellor of the Exchequer Gordon Brown voiced the hubris which financiers, regulators, politicians and many economists shared when the economy was still apparently robust. In his 2007 Budget Statement, months before the first signs of the coming crash appeared on the horizon, Brown solemnly declared (not for the first time): 'We will not return to the old boom and bust.'

How could Brown – and so many others – have got it so horribly wrong? The key to this catastrophic misjudgement lies in their losing sight of one crucial factor: the distinction between 'price' and 'value', which over the previous decades had been lost from sight. The marginalist revolution that had changed the centuries-old theory of value to one of price had exposed marginalism's ultimate tautology: finance is valuable because it is valued, and its extraordinary profits are proof of that value.

So when the global financial crisis arrived in 2007 it blew apart the ideology that had promoted financialization above all else. Yet the crisis did not fundamentally change how the sector is valued: two years later the head of Goldman Sachs could still keep a straight face when arguing that his bankers were the most productive in the world. And the fact that ex-Goldman Sachs employees were abundant in both the Obama and Trump administrations shows the power of the 'story' of the value created by Goldman Sachs across political parties.

In modern capitalism, the financial sector has greatly diversified as well as grown in overall size. Asset management in particular is a sector which has risen rapidly and secured influence and prominence; it comprises the banks which have traditionally been at the centre of the value debate but also, now, a broad range of actors. Hyman Minsky argued it was reshaping the economy into what he called 'money manager capitalism'. But how much value does it actually create?

During the three decades after the Second World War, Western economies grew robustly, in the process accumulating massive savings. These 'thirty golden years', better known by their French name of the *trente glorieuses*, also saw a huge rise in pension commitments as people lived longer and were able to save more. The wealth built up in savings and pensions had to be managed. Investment management developed to meet the demand and gave an enormous fillip to the size and profits of the financial sector as a whole. Individual investors, who had made up a significant part of stock market activity, gave way to massive institutions run by professional fund managers, many of whom shared the attitudes and remuneration of the executives running the companies in which the fund managers invested their clients' money.

The financial system evolved to meet savers' needs in an uncertain future several decades away. Investment had to be long-term, reasonably liquid and yield an attractive return, particularly to counter inflation's inevitable corrosion of savings. Pensions are central to such investments, especially in the Anglo-Saxon countries, where they make up about half of wage earners' retirement funds. Today, it is hard to overstate the importance of pensions for individual beneficiaries and the economy: pensions sustain aggregate demand by enabling the elderly to consume after they retire. But they are also crucial for the whole financial system, partly by virtue of size – the volume of assets held in pension funds – and, even more significantly, because the private pensions industry is driven by profit and returns to shareholders. The number of mutual pension providers – companies owned by their members – has steadily declined as they convert to shareholder-owned companies or consolidate in order to compete with them.

Although the pensions industry existed in the early twentieth century, it came of age in the post-war years with the rise of the welfare state. In an era of full employment, often in large enterprises, compulsory pension schemes to which employers and employees contributed piled up enormous assets. Voluntary pension savings were common too. Life insurance has also been an important savings vehicle, but payments into life insurance policies have not generally been compulsory. In the UK and the US, governments have long given pension savings significant tax advantages, partly to encourage private savings and reduce the burden on state pension provision.

Here, I look at how the investment industry and investment banks, despite seeming to be highly competitive, often behave more like monopolies protected from competition. They extract rent for the benefit of managers and shareholders while the ultimate clients – ordinary customers and investors in shares, pensions and insurance policies – frequently pay fees for mediocre returns that do not pass on the benefits of fund management's expansion and profitability.

NEW ACTORS IN THE ECONOMY

The post-war accumulation of savings placed asset managers centre-stage. They were not completely new on the scene. Mutual funds, called unit trusts in the UK, had existed before the war, and in the UK investment trusts were a popular form of middle-class saving.

But the sheer scale of the investment required – and the social responsibilities that went with it – turned asset managers into a new set of actors in the economy. Their job was not to invest in productive assets like entrepreneurs, but to be the temporary stewards of savings which they invested in liquid and, generally, financial assets (as opposed to, say, property). In the US, assets under management (AUM) grew dramatically from $3.1 billion in 1951 to some $17 trillion in 2015.[13] In the UK, the asset management industry accounted for £5.7 trillion by the end of 2015, more than three times the size of GDP in the same year.[14]

Changes in regulation played an important role in the expansion of asset management. In the US, pension funds had been obliged to avoid speculative and risky investment, precisely as a prudent man would have done. But in the 1970s, the relaxation of the 'prudent man' investment rule allowed pension funds to invest in less conventional ways, such as private equity (PE) and venture capital (VC), while the Employee Retirement Security Act of 1974 permitted pension funds and insurance companies to invest in a greater variety of funds, such as equities, high-yield debt, PE and VC. Fund managers pushed for this relaxation as a way to make higher-returning investments, but governments were keen to allow it because faster-growing private-sector funds would lessen demand for state-provided pensions. During this time, the rise in the number of very wealthy people – dubbed high-net-worth individuals (HNWIs) – also increased demand for professional asset management. An HNWI is now generally defined as someone with net financial assets (excluding property) of more than $1 million. Originally a rich-country phenomenon, it is now global as the ranks of millionaires and billionaires swell in emerging countries, notably in Asia and Latin America. According to the consultancy Capgemini, the number of HNWIs rose from 4.5 million in 1997 to 14.5 million in 2014. China now has more billionaires than the US.[15] In 2015 the city with the most HNWIs was London (370,000), followed by New York (320,000).[16]

As fund management expanded, so the proportion of private investors shrank. Individual ownership of stocks fell in the US from 92 per cent of the total in 1950 to about 30 per cent today.[17] The percentage held by private investors is even lower elsewhere – 18 per cent in

Japan and just 11 per cent in the UK.[18] In 1963, UK individual investors owned more than 50 per cent of the stock market; insurance groups, pension groups, unit trusts and overseas investors together accounted for about 10 per cent. Since then the trend has reversed: pension funds and, particularly, overseas investors have rapidly acquired a larger stake in the UK stock market, with the latter owning more than 50 per cent of quoted UK companies' shares in 2014.[19] In the US, some 60 per cent of publicly issued shares (equities) are held in mutual funds. Moreover, the fund management industry is now quite concentrated, especially in the US, where about twenty-five fund managers control 60 per cent of all the equities in the hands of investment institutions.[20]

In the last two decades the types of fund management have diversified, most noticeably into hedge funds, private equity and venture capital. The US has about 5,000 hedge funds, managing total assets of $2 trillion. Hedge funds have a glamorous image – in London many are clustered in the exclusive enclave of Mayfair – and some hedge fund managers have made a great deal of money: in 2016, forty-two were listed among the world's billionaires.[21] Some are even household names. George Soros shot into the headlines when on 16 September 1992 he reputedly 'broke the Bank of England', making $1 billion betting against British membership of the European Exchange Rate Mechanism (ERM), forcing the UK out of the ERM; the day became known as 'Black Wednesday'.

Hedge funds, though, are a little tricky to define. One of their chief characteristics is shorting (betting on the price of investments falling) as well as going long (betting on the price of investments rising). Ironically, this was originally intended to take the risk out of their speculative investments, by enabling them to 'hedge' upwards against downward price movements. In practice, it lets them chase superior returns by placing expensive one-way bets, often using high borrowing ('leverage') to multiply their gains from tiny differences in price. Compared to other managed funds, hedge funds also have a high portfolio turnover and invest in a wide range of assets, from property to commodities. Many conventional investment funds are much more restricted in how and where they invest.

Private equity (PE) firms invest in companies, usually to take ownership and manage them, later – typically after three to seven years – selling them at a profit. They make their profit, if successful, from the increase in the equity value of the company after the debt has been paid off. They then realize the equity value by selling the company (sometimes to another PE firm) or through an IPO (initial public offering – in other words, a stock market launch).

These firms are called private equity because the companies they acquire are not quoted on the stock exchange, and because they themselves are also privately owned rather than through shares issued in the (public) stock market. In the US, PE firms control about $3.9 trillion of assets, 5 per cent of the asset management market,[22] and own some well-known and large companies. For example, in the UK the American PE firm Kohlberg Kravis Roberts (KKR) paid almost $25 billion to acquire a stake in Alliance Boots, the UK high-street chemist chain. After KKR sold the final part of its stake in Alliance Boots in 2015 it was reported to have quadrupled its money.[23] Other prominent PE firms include Bain Capital, BC Partners, Blackstone Capital and Carlyle Group.

Private equity firms claim to make companies more efficient and profitable, in part because they are the direct owners of these companies. In theory, separating owners (shareholders) and managers should resolve the vested interests that the latter have in increasing their own financial compensation rather than the price of the companies' stocks. (This is the main reason why the overriding objective for the contemporary asset manager is to maximize shareholder value, as measured by the shares' price.) Critics, however, say that private equity firms have a deleterious impact on companies: their aim is to cut costs in the short term, for example by firing workers and reducing investment, in order to make a quick profit selling the business, at the expense of long-term corporate health.

The owners of private equity firms are called general partners (GPs). The funds they use to buy companies come from investors such as pension funds, foundations, insurance companies and wealthy individuals. Public and private pension funds contribute about a third of the value of the total funds PE firms invest. All these types of investors are called limited partners (LPs). They commit their money for a fixed time, say ten years, during which time they usually cannot withdraw funds. However, a good deal of PE firms' investment funds can be classified as debt, used to buy the equity stakes in the anticipation of repaying it with gains in equity value. PE firms are often criticized for placing that debt on the balance sheets of the companies they buy, while continuing to extract dividends from the companies rather than service the debt. KKR's first high-profile acquisition, the leveraged buyout of cereal and tobacco group RJR Nabisco in 1988, captured in the book and film *Barbarians at the Gate*,[24] loaded the Shredded Wheat manufacturer with debt from which it never fully recovered, but launched the PE firm on its continuing global expansion. PE firms have become particularly adept at borrowing to acquire a firm and then arranging a 'special dividend', often for a similar sum, which ensures a rapid profit from the deal even if the borrowings, transferred to the acquired firm, depress its resale price or even doom its existence. The PE firm TA Associates demonstrated how far this technique could be stretched when in 2014 it secured a $1.77 billion 'syndication loan' (a type made possible by banks immediately securitizing and reselling them) against drug-testing firm Millennium Laboratories – and immediately arranged a $1.29 billion special dividend. The transaction conformed to all rules imposed after 2008 to prevent 'asset-stripping' by private acquirers. When Millennium declared bankruptcy the following year, a court indemnified TA and other shareholders (the firm's former managers) against any effort by creditors to claw back the dividend, even after it was revealed that the owners and their loan arrangers had not informed them that its biggest client, the US government, had successfully sued it for $256 million over fraudulent tests.[25]

HOW FINANCE EXTRACTS VALUE

How does finance extract value? There are broadly three related answers: by inserting a wedge, in the form of transaction costs, between providers and receivers of finance; through monopoly power, especially in the case of banks; and with high charges relative to risks run, notably in fund management.

In certain areas of the economy, such transaction costs are regarded as reducing efficiency and destroying value, not creating it. Governments are accused of inefficiency whenever they impose an income tax – which puts a wedge between what people receive for work and the value they place on leisure – or when they try to finance social security through a payroll tax, which disconnects wage costs from total labour costs. When they secure a pay rise for their members, trade unions are accused of increasing workers' pay while their contribution to production remains the same.

As far as banks are concerned, their efficiency as useful intermediaries between borrowers and lenders might reasonably be judged by their ability to narrow the 'wedge', or cost gap, between the two. Maximum efficiency, friction-free capitalism, would in theory be reached when the interest differential disappears. Yet the 'indirect' measure of financial intermediation services adopted by national accounts (FISIM, explained in Chapter 4) assumes that a rise in added value will be reflected in a wider wedge (or, if the wedge narrows, by increased fees and charges through which intermediaries can obtain payment directly). The point, of course, is not to eliminate interest but – if interest is the price of financial intermediation – to make sure that it reflects increased efficiencies in the system, driven by appropriate investments in technological change, as some fintech (financial technology) developments have done.

Banks stand in sharp contrast to supermarkets. As we have seen, the cost of financial services probably *rose* in the twentieth century, despite the dramatic growth of the financial industry, suggesting that financial consumers did not benefit from economies of scale in the same way as they did with supermarkets, epitomized by Walmart in the US and Tesco in the UK. A large part of the explanation for the difference is the monopolistic – or more strictly, oligopolistic – nature of banking.

In 2010, five big US banks controlled over 96 per cent of the derivative contracts in place.[26] In the UK, ten financial institutions accounted for 85 per cent of over-the-counter derivatives turnover in 2016, and 77 per cent of foreign exchange turnover.[27] Only the biggest banks can take the risk of large-scale writing and trading in derivatives, since they need a comfortable cushion of equity between the value of their assets and liabilities to stay solvent if asset prices fall. Only a few banks worldwide have grown big enough to sustain the high risks of proprietary trading – trading on their own account rather than for a client – and to be worthy of state-supported rescue if the risks prove too great.

As a result, there are few banks with whom governments and large corporations can place new bond or share issues and expect subsequent market-making in those securities. The paucity of players, even in large financial centres such as London and New York, inevitably gives each bank considerable price-setting power, irrespective of whether or not they collude among themselves to do so. In retail markets, minimum core capital requirements for banks (raised after 2008, to 4.5 per cent of risk-weighted assets in 2013, 5.5 per cent in 2015 and 6 per cent from 2016)[28] and the need for prudential regulation limits the number of banking licences that governments and central banks can issue, and confers significant market power on the few banks who hold such licences. This power enabled banks to secure 40 per cent of total US corporate profits in 2002 (up from 13 per cent in 1985). They still enjoyed 23 per cent in 2010 and almost 30 per cent in 2012 – just two years after rebounding after a brief plunge to 10 per cent in 2008, in a period when corporate profits were growing much faster than labour income or GDP.[29]

The high degree of monopoly in wholesale and retail banking is closely linked to its continuing ability to extract rents from the private and public sectors, even when these were shrinking in the aftermath of the 2008 crash. In the UK, since the financial crisis regulators have aimed to promote new banks and alternative forms of financial intermediation, such as peer-to-peer lending, in order to spur competition. The handful of new banks started in the UK since the crisis are somewhat optimistically called 'challenger banks' – a challenge that so far has not put much of a dent in the oligopoly of UK 'high street' banks. Nor are alternative forms of financial intermediation effective substitutes for the dominant banks. Only licensed banks can create money through loans,[30] as distinct from merely shifting money between savers and borrowers. Once banks' profitability has been swelled by the market power that allows them to extract rents from other sectors, their top employees can in turn exert internal labour-market power to channel a share of those rents to themselves, helping to give the financial sector its unique and entrenched bonus culture.

On top of monopoly rent, financial markets give investment banks and other professional 'players' another significant route to high financial returns, divorced from the high risk that is traditionally understood to justify those returns. Financial markets instantly adjust the price of company shares and bonds to the future profits those companies are expected to make. They can therefore instantly capture (and 'capitalize') the jump in expected future profit when, for example, a new drug wins approval for hospital use, a social media platform finds a way to monetize its millions of users, or a mining company learns that its once-exotic metal is to be used in the next generation of mobile phones. Owning an asset that suddenly jumps in value has always been a faster way to get rich than patiently saving and investing out of income;[31] and the speed differential of asset 'revaluation' over asset accumulation has been amplified in the present era of historically low interest rates.

Revaluation gains in the 'real' economy are widely hailed as economically efficient and socially progressive. Entrepreneurs who cash in on a genuinely useful invention can claim to have reaped just rewards from genuinely productive risk-taking, especially when they are shown to have displaced hereditary landowners in the charts of ultra-high net worth. But when – as is usually the case by the time the revaluation occurs – shares have passed beyond the original inventors and become owned by private equity or quoted on financial markets, it is passive rather than active investors who capture most of the revaluation gains. Financialization enables investment bankers and fund managers who picked the right stock – often by chance – to make profits that would previously have gone to those who built the right product, by painstaking design. And, having captured this value, they invariably race to extract it – channelling the gain into real estate or other financial investments designed to hold their 'value' – rather than reinvesting it in more innovative production, which rarely yields a comparable crock of gold a second time.

The relationship between finance's share of employment and its share of income gives an idea of what has happened. Until 1980, finance's share of employment and income in the US were almost

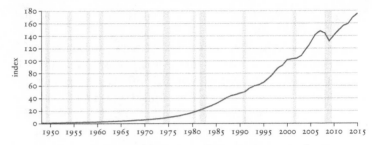

Figure 17. Ratio of finance employee compensation share
to national employment share[32]

identical (the ratio is 1). But, as Figure 17 reveals, by 2015 it had almost doubled to 1.8. This steep rise in average income per employee – scarcely interrupted by the crash of 2008 – was, according to its supporters, a sign of the financial sector's rising productivity and a justification for channelling more resources into finance. But the productivity gain was, as seen in Chapter 4, highly dependent on a redefinition that boosts banks' and other lenders' 'value added'. An alternative explanation for the rising income-to-employment ratio is that finance was reinforcing its power to extract value, and gain monopoly rents from other private-sector activities.

The concentration of banking and financial-market trading among a few large players, which is at its most extreme in the derivatives markets (Figure 18) underlines the extent to which financial 'value added' may be traceable to monopoly and oligopoly rents.[33] It is in financial regulators' interest to keep the number of players small, despite the risk of collusive behaviour: they want to maintain an overview of all market players' exposure so as to guard against systemic risk, and the decision (after the 2008 crisis) to bring over-the-counter derivatives trades (derivatives that are not listed on a stock exchange and are often bespoke deals between professional investors such as banks) onto a more viewable transparent central platform works in their favour. Indeed, the rigging of a key interest rate (the London interbank offered rate, Libor, used to set many private-sector borrowing rates globally) in the aftermath of the crisis may have occurred with the connivance of some regulators, at least according to traders

	Top five banks	% of total derivatives	Other banks	% of total derivatives	All banks	% of total derivatives
Futures and forwards	32,934	14.2	2,775	1.2	35,709	15.4
Swaps	145,440	62.9	3,807	1.6	149,247	64.6
Options	31,136	13.5	939	0.4	32,075	13.9
Credit derivatives	13,407	5.8	743	0.3	14,150	6.1
Total	222,917	96.4	8,264	3.6	231,181	100.0

Figure 18. Concentration of US derivatives contracts
($ billions; fourth quarter, 2010)[34]

who successfully defended themselves against fraud charges.[35] The rigging, and subsequent arguments over who gained and lost from it, highlight the extent to which banks and other financial market players today battle over, and perhaps collude in, the distribution of a surplus created by mainly non-financial businesses.

Banks are without doubt instrumental in moving funds from less to more productive parts of the economy. Instruments such as derivatives, futures and options can genuinely help to hedge against risks, particularly for the economy's producers who are confronting uncertainty over future prices and exchange rates. Yet it must be said that some bank activities are clearly not productive, especially when they become too complex or too large relative to the real economy's needs. Take the mortgage-backed security (MBS) market mentioned earlier. In 2009, mortgage-related debt in the US totalled around $9 trillion, having grown an astonishing 400 per cent in fifteen years to stand at more than a quarter of all outstanding US bond market debt. The revenue generated through interest payments on this debt has been estimated at $20 billion a year between 2001 and 2007.[36] After the 2008 financial crisis, this line of business dried up completely. Around the world, holders of these US MBSs took huge losses, leading to a cascade of financial crises in other countries as borrowers who held them as collateral proved unable to repay their debt. Banks had extracted revenue for 'managing' and 'laying off' risk – but their own activities had actually increased risk in the process.

Credit default swaps (CDSs) are another example. Originally an insurance against a borrower defaulting on their loan, CDSs have largely become a way to bet on someone else being unable to repay their debts. CDSs may have their uses for people whose own solvency might depend on the debtor's ability to repay. But their speculative use was literally stripped bare in the case of 'naked' CDSs, which played a major role in promoting sovereign and corporate debt defaults on both sides of the Atlantic. Naked CDSs are so called when the buyer of a swap has no vested interest in the credit-taking party being able to repay; in fact, the buyer, in order to collect his or her winnings, actively wants the debtor to default. It's like taking out fire insurance on a neighbour's house and hoping it will burn down. Far from seeking to keep the borrower's (and the whole system's) risks down, the swap buyer has every incentive to help the fire break out.

But even if creditors only ever bought CDSs as an insurance policy, they are still inherently dangerous because of systemic risk – where default risk is no longer confined to a few borrowers and spreads to all. At times of crisis, defaults become highly correlated. One failure to repay triggers others. Banks or insurers who write CDSs end up underwriting this systemic risk, as they found to their own – and countless others' – enormous cost in 2007–8. By 2010, due to the cost of bailing out banks and the economic recessions that followed their cessation of business lending, a number of European countries were experiencing sovereign debt crises. They were struggling to service their public debts, and in order to do so severely cut provision of public goods and services. The same banks that had benefited from the bailout now profited from governments' plight, earning some 20 per cent of their entire derivative revenues from such naked CDSs.

Financial intermediation – the cost of financial services – is a form of value extraction, the scale of which lies in the relationship between what finance charges and what risks it actually runs. Charges are called the cost of financial intermediation. But as we have seen, while finance has grown and risks have not appreciably changed, the cost of financial intermediation has barely fallen, apart from some web-based services that remain peripheral to global financial flows. In other words, the financial sector has not become more productive. Another way to grasp this simple fact is to measure the amount of fees charged by institutional investors and compare them with the performance of the funds they manage. The ratio between the two can be interpreted as a sort of degree of value extraction: the higher the fee, the lower is the gain for the investor and the greater the profit for the manager. So the ways in which manufacturers and non-financial service firms have used their size to hold down costs and prices do not seem to apply to finance. An excellent study on this topic concludes: 'The finance industry of 1900 was just as able as the finance industry of 2000 to produce bonds and stocks, and it was certainly doing it more cheaply.'[37]

Let's now take some of the main parts of the fund management business, a huge financial intermediation machine, and look in more detail at fees and risks.

Millions of savers invest in funds – usually mutual funds or unit trusts – either directly themselves or more often indirectly, for example through pensions. The objective of any fund manager is to produce a rate of return for the funds he or she oversees. The benchmark for that return will be the relevant markets in which that fund manager is investing, be it the US stock market, the European bond market, Australian mining companies and so on. Managing your fund to outperform the average market return (or the benchmark) is called 'active management', or, more pointedly, 'picking winners'. Succeeding in doing better than the benchmark is said to be achieving 'alpha' (alpha of 1 per cent means that the return on the investment over a selected period is 1 per cent better than the market during that same period). The alternative basic investment management strategy is called 'passive'. A passive fund is usually an 'index' or 'tracker' fund, where the manager simply buys shares in proportion to a stock market index and tracks that benchmark.

But performance must be balanced with fees. Consider investing long-term, say over the forty-year working life of a given employee. One of the leading figures in the US fund management industry is John Bogle. He founded Vanguard, a very large index investment group (not an active investor) which charges low fees. Bogle has estimated an all-in cost for actively managed funds of 2.27 per cent of the funds' value. The amounts may not seem excessive. But Bogle never tires of saying to fund investors: 'Do not allow the tyranny of compounding costs to overwhelm the magic of compounding returns.'[38] In fact, if you assume Bogle's estimate of fund management costs and also assume an annual return of 7 per cent, the total return to a saver over forty years will be 65 per cent higher without the charges. In hard cash, the difference could mean retiring with $100,000 or $165,000.[39] It's a good deal for the fund manager; rather less so for the investor.

Let's concede for a moment that there is a role for active management and the associated fees. Let's also allow for the increase in the volume of assets under management and the application of IT to assess investments, manage them and communicate with clients, which ought to give fund management benefits of scale and efficiency. What size should we expect those fees to be? In a presentation to the Asset Management Unit of the Securities and Exchange Commission, the US regulator, Bogle presented the following statistics (Figure 19):

	1951 assets ($ millions)	1951 expense ratio	2015 assets ($ billions)	2015 expense ratio
MIT	472	0.42%	180	1.29%
Fidelity	64	0.63%	1.615	1.06%
Putnam	52	0.66%	81	1.31%
American	27	0.84%	1.216	0.99%
T Rowe Price	1	0.50%	493	0.84%
Total average top 9	$1.474	0.62%	$7.195	1.13%

Figure 19. US mutual fund assets and charges 1951 and 2015

The striking and perhaps surprising conclusion is that over more than sixty years, expense ratios, even among the same firms, have not gone down but have gone *up* – and significantly. Why has this happened?

Fund managers deserve much of the blame. First, fund management's strategy of divide and conquer is part of the explanation. In the interest of diversification and providing investors with plenty of choice in investment strategies, fund managers have multiplied the number of funds they manage. They have also handed control of funds to individual portfolio managers who take a more short-term view of returns than investment committees of, say, a whole fund management group, which on the whole takes a broader view. The result has been much more aggressive investing and a significant increase in asset turnover as managers buy and sell stocks to try to boost returns. According to Bogle, portfolio turnover rose from 30 per cent in the 1950s and 1960s to 140 per cent in the last decades.[40] Another measure of asset management quality is volatility: the degree of uncertainty or risk about the size of fluctuations in a share's value. Just as turnover has risen, so the volatility of funds has increased significantly from 0.84 to 1.11 over the same period.

Second, there are transaction costs. Greater turnover – buying and selling more shares – keeps fees higher than they might have been, adding to transaction costs without adding to investors' capital gains given the zero-sum nature of the market. Crucially for the investor, additional fees reduce returns by increasing the cost of managing money. While transaction costs for each trade have fallen over the last thirty years, the frequency of trading has increased exponentially in recent years. Thus, the total amount of fees has risen as well. As Bogle notes:

> When I entered this business in 1951, right out of college, annual turnover of U.S. stocks was about 15 per cent. Over the next 15 years, turnover averaged about 35 per cent. By the late 1990s, it had gradually increased to the 100 per cent range, and hit 150 per cent in 2005. In 2008, stock turnover soared to the remarkable level of 280 per cent, declining modestly to 250 per cent in 2011. Think for a moment about the numbers that create these rates. When I came into this field 60 years ago, stock-trading volumes averaged about 2 million shares per day. In recent years, we have traded about 8.5 billion shares of stock daily – 4,250 times as many. Annualized, the total comes to more than 2 trillion shares – in dollar terms, I estimate the trading to be worth some $33 trillion. That figure, in turn, is 220 per cent of the $15 trillion market capitalisation of U.S. stocks.[41]

Moreover, this massive trading is often between fund managers, which makes it truly a zero-sum game within the industry. The idea of a financial transaction tax (related to the Tobin Tax, named after the Nobel Prize-winning economist James Tobin, an early advocate) is to reduce this 'churn' and make investors hold their stocks for longer, by raising the cost of each sale. It satisfies the conditions for an efficient tax in deterring a practice which imposes deadweight costs – the main obstacle to its introduction being that all large exchanges would have to impose it, to stop trade migrating to those that choose not to.

Hedge funds are in many ways a response to demands from the increasing number of HNWIs for superior returns on their portfolios. As more active share traders, hedge fund managers tend to pride themselves on their ability to pick stocks on the basis of proprietary information. This information may be obtained legally, for example by detailed research by an in-house team, although it might also be obtained in some unlawful way. Superior information should lead to superior returns, but it is also costly. To the extent that superior returns are obtained, the cost may be justified. But we should remember that in the end it is a game that balances winners and losers and has little social value: the gains or above-average returns that some investors enjoy will be offset by losses or below-average returns others suffer.

While some hedge funds have certainly been very successful, moreover, average returns have been less impressive. About 20 per cent of hedge funds fail each year. Even when returns have been high they often owe as much to idiosyncratic gambles as to investment genius. A spectacular example is the American John Paulson, who made $2 billion from betting in the run-up to the financial crisis that US house prices would crash. Since then, however, his firm Paulson and Co. has done less well and some investors have withdrawn their funds.

The middling investment performance of hedge funds stands in sharp contrast to their glamorous image and – more importantly for investors – their high fees. For many years typical hedge fund fees have been called '2 and 20' – a 2 per cent fee on the volume of assets managed and a hefty 20 per cent of realized and unrealized profits. Some hedge funds specialize in high-frequency trading – buying and selling assets very fast and in large volume, sometimes within fractions of a second, by the use of special computers – which raises costs for investors. All this adds up to a total yearly cost of 3 per cent.[42]

This same '2 and 20' model is also used in venture capital. Like hedge funds, VC claims special skill in picking profitable opportunities in young businesses and technologies. In practice, VC usually enters the fray after others, notably taxpayer-funded basic research, have taken the biggest risks and the technology is already proven.

Private equity firms provide a case study of how fund managers increase their likelihood of making a profit. PE firms also charge annual management fees of the order of 2 per cent. Over the, say, ten-year lifetime of a fund, this fee represents a commitment of 20 per cent, leaving only 80 per cent which is actually free to earn a return. So limited partners, rather like investors in mutual funds or hedge funds, start out with an embedded cost to catch up on – which is hard to do. What's more, as the *New York Times* revealed in 2015, some companies in which PE firms invest end up paying fees to the PE firms for years after they have been taken public again.[43]

In addition to the management fees, PE funds have found many other ways to get paid in order to avoid relying on their portfolios' actual performance. These include paying themselves fees (on top of fees paid to consultants, investment bankers, lawyers, accountants and the like) for any transactions undertaken (the acquisition itself, acquisitions of other companies, the sale of divisions and so on), paying themselves monitoring fees as part of their role on the boards of these companies, and other service fees. All in all, this results in a fixed component for them of about two-thirds of the general partners' compensation.[44]

The final element of the PE firm's compensation is carried interest – the investment manager's share of the profits of an investment above the amount the manager committed to the partnership. For many years now, market practice has been that carried interest is 20 per cent of the profits generated over and above an agreed hurdle rate – i.e. a return on an investment below which a company will not pursue an investment opportunity or project. This element of the compensation is specifically meant to motivate general partners to perform, and PE capital gains are taxed at a favourable rate. But in practice, fees are so high that carried interest amounts to only about a third of general partners' compensation.

PE firms also protect themselves by loading down the companies they acquire with debt, typically 60–80 per cent of the cost of an acquisition. Consider this: if an asset worth 100 is bought with 30 put in as equity by the investment manager and 70 from debt, the investment manager can make a 100 per cent return if the debt is paid off and the equity value goes up to 60. And yet PE firms hold on average only 2 per cent of the value of the funds they manage.

What do PE investors get for their money? When PE firms present their results to investors, they usually highlight their internal rates of return – the rate of return on capital invested (technically, the discount rate which makes the net present value of all cash flows [positive and negative] from an investment equal to zero). One may well argue that all the charges and compensation could be justified if they resulted in outsized returns. And in fact, there are many studies that claim superior returns for PE firms compared to other investment vehicles. Figure 20, from one highly cited work, appears to show that in recent years PE has outperformed by 27 per cent (average and median for the 2000s). But that performance should be viewed over the ten-year lifetime of a fund, so it actually represents an outperformance of just 2.4 per cent per year.

To be fair, this is still outperformance in absolute terms. But several factors effectively negate it. The performance has been achieved through highly indebted investments that are relatively illiquid (hard to sell). In fact, limited partners often require extra outperformance to take account of this additional risk – a premium of the order of 3 per cent – in recognition that PE's superior performance is otherwise offset by its increased risk-taking. Furthermore, the basis for comparison in the table below, the Standard & Poor's (S&P) 500 index, is less relevant than an index of small- and medium-sized companies in the US such as the Russell 2000 or 3000. Relative to these indices, the outperformance is significantly lower, about 1–1.5 per cent.

Funds	Buyout funds PMEs			
	funds	average	median	weighted average
Average 2000s	411	1.27	1.27	1.29
Average 1990s	157	1.27	1.17	1.34
Average 1980s	30	1.04	1.03	1.11

Figure 20. Buyout funds performance vs S&P 500[45]

In short, once the returns reported by private equity are adjusted for risk and compared to appropriate benchmarks, it becomes much harder to justify their high charges.

The fund management industry naturally argues that the returns it can make – seeking 'alpha' – for clients justify the fees it charges. In an influential article,[46] Joanne Hill, a Goldman Sachs partner, identifies conditions in which trying to achieve alpha need not be a zero-sum game – conveniently showing that investment banks' proprietary trading might have some social and economic value. But these conditions include an assumption that the market is divided into traders with short- or long-term horizons, who are pursuing alpha over different time periods and measuring it against different benchmarks. Without this artificial separation, alpha is indeed zero-sum – and turns into a negative-sum game once active managers deduct the extra fees they must charge for selecting stocks rather than just buying them in proportion to the relevant index.

CONCLUSION

Asset management has grown into one of modern capitalism's defining characteristics. If nothing else, its sheer scale and central importance to the financial security of many millions of men and women have given financial management its influence. But at least as significant is that many of its activities extract value rather than create it. Financial markets merely distribute income generated by activity elsewhere and do not add to that income. Chasing alpha – selecting and over- or under-weighting stocks so as to outperform an index – is essentially a game that will produce as many losers as winners. This is why actively managed funds frequently fail to beat the performance of passive funds. Much of fund management is a massive exercise in rent-seeking of a sort that would have caused raised eyebrows among the classical economists.

Reform is not impossible. Financial regulation can be used to reward long-termism and also help to direct finance towards the real economy, as opposed to feeding on itself. Indeed, the point of the financial transaction tax – which has yet to be implemented – is precisely to reward long-term investments over quick millisecond trades.

Furthermore, the fees being earned by asset managers should reflect real value creation, not the 'buy, strip and flip' strategy common in PE, or the '2 and 20' fee model common to PE, VC and hedge funds. Were the fees more accurately to reflect risks run (or not run – such as the large taxpayer-funded investments that often precede the entrance of VCs), the percentage of realized and unrealized profits retained would be lower than the customary 20 per cent. It is not that financial actors should not make money, or that they do not create value; but that the collective effort involved in the value-creation mechanism should be reflected in a more equitable share of the rewards. This is tied to Keynes's notion of 'socialization of investment'. He argued that the economy could grow and be better stabilized, and hence guarantee full employment, if the quantity and quality of public investment was increased. By this he meant that funding investment in infrastructure and innovation (capital development) ought to be done by public utilities, public banks or co-operatives which direct public funds towards medium- and long-term growth rather than short-term returns.

But rent-seeking is not limited to the financial sector. It has pervaded non-financial industries as well – through the pressures that financial-sector profitability, exaggerated by monopoly power and implicit public guarantees, place on the corporate governance of non-financial firms. If investors can expect a certain return by putting their money into a fund, spreading the risks across a wide range of money-making instruments, they will only sink the same funds into one industrial project if it offers a much higher return. The return on financial-sector investment sets a minimum for the return on 'real' fixed investment, a floor which rises as financial operations become more profitable. Non-financial companies that cannot beat the financial investors' return are forced to join them, by 'financializing' their production and distribution activities.

6

Financialization of the Real Economy

On the face of it, shareholder value is the dumbest idea in the world.

Jack Welch, former General Electric CEO, 2009[1]

Finance's extraordinary growth into an economic colossus over the past thirty years has not been confined to the financial sector; it has also permeated companies in the broader economy, such as manufacturing and non-financial services. The financialization of the real economy is in some respects a more extraordinary phenomenon than the expansion of the financial sector itself and is a central social, political and economic development of modern times.

In exploring this phenomenon, I will look chiefly at the US and the UK, where financialization tends to be most advanced. As we have seen, businesses such as manufacturing and non-financial services have often been classed as the 'productive sector', unambiguously creating value, whereas finance is often a cost of doing business, and only contributes to value creation rather than creating value by itself. More loosely, the productive sector is often called 'the real economy'.

It's a truism to say that the modern corporation is among the most important forces in the economy. In 2015, the 500 largest public US companies (those listed on a stock exchange) employed almost 25 million people worldwide and generated revenues of over $9 trillion. In the same year, the 500 largest UK companies on the stock market had more than 8 million employees and their total annual turnover was well over £1.5 trillion.[2] What's more, many of the largest companies at the forefront of innovation in the economy are publicly listed;

to these we must add the many companies that are privately owned but controlled by financially minded owners such as private equity (PE) or venture capital (VC). The decisions these corporations take, particularly capital allocation, are critical to value creation.

This is why it is so important to understand the huge extent of the financialization of the productive sector. In the 2000s, for example, the US arm of Ford made more money by selling loans for cars than by selling the cars themselves. Ford sped up the car's transition from physical product to financial commodity by pioneering the Personal Contract Plan (PCP), which allowed a 'buyer' to pay monthly instalments that only covered the predicted depreciation, and trade up to a new model after two or three years rather than pay off the balance (thus resulting in a higher loan amount than the new car's price). Adopted by most other auto-makers, and with the additional merit of being bundled into securitizations and resold on financial markets, PCPs drove sales to record levels, alarming only the regulators, who wondered what would happen if (as with houses in 2008) cash-strapped contractees walked away from their vehicles and handed back the keys. Over the same period GE Capital, the finance arm of the enormous General Electric (GE) group, made around half of the whole group's earnings.[3] Companies such as Ford and GE contributed heavily to the sharp rise in the value of financial assets relative to US GDP in the quarter-century after 1980.

Lending money to customers to buy your cars does not necessarily mean that you are extracting value to the extent discussed in the previous chapter. But, as we shall see, financialization more generally can profoundly affect how companies behave. The strongest evidence of how financial value can damage real economic value can be found in the widespread practice of share buy-backs by public companies listed in the US and UK.

THE BUY-BACK BLOWBACK

Share buy-backs are a way of transferring money from a corporation to its shareholders. The company buys some of its own shares from existing shareholders. As a pure matter of finance and economics, these transactions are just like money paid out as dividends: shareholders receive, and the company pays out, the same amount. The only difference is that dividends are paid out evenly to all shareholders, while buy-backs give cash only to those who want to sell; and, what's more, buy-backs avoid any penalty taxes imposed on dividends by governments that want more profit reinvested.

A switch from dividends to buy-backs can, however, make a big difference to executive pay, because (unlike dividends) they reduce the number of shares. This automatically boosts earnings per share (EPS), which is one of the key measures of corporate success. Buy-backs typically increase the pace of EPS growth – a measure which is often used to determine just how exorbitant the rewards of senior executives will be. So bosses prefer buy-backs to dividends. Two basically equivalent measures have been made to diverge, unless accountants adjust the share count to ensure that identical transactions have the same effect on the reported results. But bosses are hardly likely to prod them to standardize their measures of corporate payouts.[4]

Shareholders also seem impressed by rising EPS, preferring not to notice that buy-backs remove just as much cash as dividends from the funds available for investment. They also seem to ignore the fact that companies are more likely to buy back shares when the price is high than when the price is low,[5] despite the inefficiency of this market timing.

In any case, the numbers are striking. In 2014 the American economist William Lazonick chronicled the scale of share buy-backs in the top US companies in recent years.[6] Between 2003 and 2012, 449 companies listed in the S&P 500 index deployed $2.4 trillion in buying back their own shares, mostly through open-market purchases. That sum constituted 54 per cent of their collective earnings. Add in dividends, which took out a further 37 per cent, and only 9 per cent of profits were available for capital investment. Over the same period, the ten biggest re-purchasers in the US shelled out a staggering $859 billion on share buy-backs, equivalent to 68 per cent of their combined net income. As illustrated in Figure 21 below, seven of those companies committed more than *100 per cent* of their net income to buy-backs and dividends.

Until recently, few investors seemed to grasp the scale of these disbursements. While regular dividends are often used by shareholders as a source of income – which is why shareholders get so upset when they're cut – buy-backs, on the other hand, are often considered special payments. This ignores their status as an active choice *not* to invest to create long-term value.

Some investors are finally waking up. In March 2014, Larry Fink, the CEO of Blackrock, one of the largest institutional investors in the world, wrote to the CEOs of the S&P 500 companies about excessive profit distributions. Observing that too many companies 'have cut capital expenditure and even increased debt to boost dividends and increase share buy-backs', Fink stated that while 'returning cash to shareholders should be part of a balanced capital strategy', such a practice could, 'when done for the wrong reasons and at the expense of capital investment . . . jeopardize a company's ability to generate sustainable long-term returns'.[7]

However, Fink's message has not been widely echoed by investors. The ratio of buy-backs and dividends to reported earnings has hardly

Company	Net income	Repurchases plus dividends (of which repurchases)	Repurchases plus dividends over net income
Exxon Mobil	$347 bn	$287 bn ($207 bn)	83%
Microsoft	$148 bn	$185 bn ($114 bn)	125%
IBM	$117 bn	$130 bn ($107 bn)	111%
Cisco Systems	$64 bn	$77 bn ($75 bn)	121%
Procter & Gamble	$93 bn	$108 bn ($66 bn)	116%
Hewlett-Packard	$41 bn	$73 bn ($64 bn)	177%
Walmart	$134 bn	$97 bn ($62 bn)	73%
Intel	$79 bn	$87 bn ($60 bn)	109%
Pfizer	$84 bn	$122 bn ($59 bn)	146%
General Electric	$165 bn	$132 bn ($45 bn)	81%

Figure 21. Top ten stock repurchasers in the US (2004–2012),
ranked by the absolute amount of share buy-backs[8]

declined. Having set a required return on reinvested funds that few managements feel able to meet, shareholders have grown accustomed to having a steady stream of funds paid out instead.

MAXIMIZING SHAREHOLDER VALUE

Share buy-backs boost executive pay. To defend the idea that incentive pay realigns executive and shareholder interests, it is often claimed that share buy-backs maximize shareholder value (MSV) and thus improve the efficiency of companies.[9] Financial techniques, it is argued, are a legitimate way for managers to improve productivity and therefore benefit workers and customers as well as shareholders. If a company can earn a higher return at any given time from putting capital to work financially rather than directly selling cars or software, it is behaving rationally and in the best interests of the business. Having a choice between a financial or a productive use for capital helps to keep the (supposedly) core business of cars or software on its toes because it has to produce returns which compete with financial alternatives. By extension, it is argued that making it easier for customers to obtain credit, especially to buy your own products, is a service to ordinary people. There is something to this – but not much. Where did these ideas come from? And do they have validity?

Back in the 1970s, as the economic crisis and stagnation of the decade impaired the performance and profitability of the corporate sector, shareholder dissatisfaction made shareholder returns the principal aim of the corporation. In 1970, Milton Friedman published in the *New York Times Magazine* an article which became the founding text of the shareholder value movement and, in many ways, of corporate management in general. Titled 'The Social Responsibility of Business Is to Increase its Profits', Friedman's article advanced the idea that America's economic performance was declining because a cardinal principle of mainstream economics – that firms maximize profits – was being violated. There was no longer any punishment for managers who failed to profit-maximize. Shareholders could not inflict such punishment because they were too dispersed and un-co-ordinated; and markets could not do so, because listed companies had monopoly power and would not be assailed by new competitors if their costs and prices drifted upwards. Some 1960s economists had viewed 'managerialism' as potentially good for society, if bosses allowed profit to be eroded by paying better wages to employees, meeting higher environmental or health and safety standards and investing more in new products. Friedman reset the debate by suggesting that bosses were more likely to be sacrificing profit to their own expense accounts and luxury lifestyles; and that even letting costs rise through 'corporate social responsibility' was fundamentally wrong. The piece spawned an academic literature that would become known as 'agency theory'.

Friedman's idea was developed further by the University of Chicago-trained Michael Jensen, who was steeped in its 'free market' ideas. In 1976 Jensen, now a professor at the University of Rochester, wrote a paper with the Dean of Rochester's business school, William Meckling (who, like Jensen, was a student of Friedman at Chicago), on how to implement Friedman's idea. It was called 'Theory of the firm: Managerial behavior, agency costs, and ownership structure'. The key argument was that managers (the agents) were not being disciplined by competitive financial markets or product markets, since they could misallocate resources or run up unnecessary expenses without incurring losses or endangering their jobs, and so it was hard for investors (the principals) to keep them accountable. The only way to do so was through strengthening the 'market', which was neutral and objective enough to make sure the company thrived. The result was a body of theory that argued that the only way for companies to be well run was if they maximized their 'shareholder value'. In this way, investors would indirectly keep company managers accountable.

In the decades that followed, an entire intellectual apparatus was created around 'maximizing shareholder value', with new developments in law, economics and business studies. It became the dominant perspective of leading business schools and economic departments. The overriding goal of the corporation became that of maximizing shareholder value, as captured in the corporation's share price.

However, far from being a lodestar for corporate management, maximizing shareholder value turned into a catalyst for a set of mutually reinforcing trends, which played up short-termism while downplaying the long-term view and a broader interpretation of whom the corporation should benefit. In the name of MSV, managers sought profits anywhere they could, directly fuelling globalization and outsourcing production to locations from China to Mexico. Jobs were lost and communities wrecked. Meanwhile, the added external pressures on corporate management did little to enhance its quality. Rather than become properly trained managers with sectoral expertise, who could make decisions on what to produce and how to produce it, top graduates in business schools preferred to go to Wall Street. While in 1965 only 11 per cent of Harvard Business School MBAs went into the financial sector, by 1985 the figure had reached 41 per cent and has risen since then.

Figure 22 shows how the influence of PE, one of the most aggressive manifestations of MSV, grew in the US in the first decade and a half of the twenty-first century. The arguments of Friedman, Jensen and Meckling suggested that shareholder value was going to waste. So a new type of investor that could capture this leaking value would be instantly rewarded, through bigger dividends or share price gains. PE funds and acquisition vehicles led the pack of new, value-hungry investors that now assailed the world's stock markets.

PE is MSV turbo-charged. Many of the companies in which PE

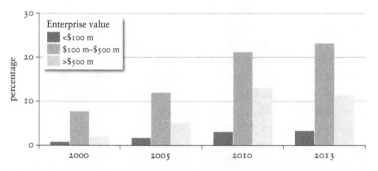

Notes: All values are estimated; calculations are based on data only for companies with more than $10 million in revenues.

Figure 22. PE-backed companies as a percentage of all US companies (by enterprise size)[10]

firms invest are not financial ones; often, indeed, they can be found on the productive side of the production boundary. But whereas traditional institutional investors were often satisfied to 'buy and hold', and to await share price gains via profit being reinvested rather than paid out, PE seeks to buy and resell at a higher price within a few years. What this means is that many firms owned by PE funds are pushed into taking a significantly shorter-term view than they might have done otherwise – the exact reverse of 'patient capital' and raising productivity to benefit society in the long run. If the influence of PE on the productive economy seems exaggerated, consider this: Blackstone, one of the largest PE companies, has a portfolio of over seventy-seven companies, which together generate over $64 billion in combined annual revenues and employ more than 514,000 people globally.[11]

The recent history of the care home and water industries in the UK shows how PE can change a business – and not necessarily for the better. Until the mid-1990s the country's care homes were owned either by small family firms or by local authorities.[12] Today, for a combination of political and financial reasons, many local authority homes have closed. A new breed of financial operator has moved into the market, largely following a PE model, often 'selling' many of its places to local authorities but also generating private profit. In 2015, the five biggest care home chains controlled about a fifth of the total number of care home beds in the UK. These operators were attracted by stable cash flows, part of which came from local authorities, and opportunities for financial engineering: cheap debt; property which could be sold and leased back; tax breaks on debt interest payments and carried interest; and – ultimately – frail and vulnerable residents whom the state would have to look after if the business failed. The corporate structures of some care home owners became exceedingly complex and often hidden in tax havens, while corporation tax payments were low or nil. Given that local authorities still funded many care home placements and that the nurses employed in the homes had been state-trained, opaque corporate structures and minimal tax payments are hardly the way to provide an essential public service.

Four Seasons Health Care displays many of these characteristics. The company owns the biggest chain of care homes in the UK, with 23,000 beds in 2015. But it was only a small Scottish chain until its acquisition by Alchemy Partners, a PE firm, in 1999. Having enlarged the company, Alchemy sold it in 2004 to Allianz Capital Partners, another private firm, which two years later sold it to Three Delta, yet another PE firm. By 2008, during this game of pass the parcel, the company's external debt had ballooned to £1.5 billion, carrying an annual interest charge of over £100 million – or an unsustainable £100 per bed per *week*. In 2012 the company was bought by Terra Firma – you've guessed it, a PE firm – controlled by Guy Hands, a well-known British financier who had cut his teeth at Goldman Sachs. Despite a financial restructuring involving losses for equity holders, bondholders and banks before Terra Firma acquired the business, by 2014 Four Seasons was losing money, and a pre-tax loss of £70.1 million in 2015 deepened to £264 million.[13] The cost of debt-servicing was at least partly to blame. The company blamed local authorities for freezing the amount they would pay for residents, although the authorities themselves were suffering severe budget cuts under the Conservative-led government's austerity programme. The Care Quality Commission, the government body which monitors standards in care homes, was sufficiently concerned about the business health of Four Seasons that at one point it embargoed twenty-eight of Four Seasons' homes, meaning that they could not take in new residents.

Similar patterns can be seen in England and Wales's water industry, which was privatized in 1989.[14] The ten water and sewerage companies (WSCs) were listed on the London Stock Exchange as part of the then government's policy of creating a 'shareholder democracy'. Today, only two remain listed. Asian infrastructure conglomerates own three of the companies; another is a mutual company (Welsh Water, or Dŵr Cymru); and PE firms own four – Anglian Water, Thames Water (the biggest water company), Southern Water and Yorkshire Water.

As with care homes, the ratio of debt to equity in the water companies has increased sharply: a typical feature of companies owned by PE firms, as we saw in the previous chapter. Between 2003 and 2013 average net debt rose by 74 per cent while equity fell by 37 per cent in nine of the companies: Anglian, Thames, Northumbrian, Severn Trent, Southern, South West, United Utilities, Wessex and Yorkshire. The companies with the highest net debt – about 80 per cent of capital or more – were all PE-owned. Net interest payments by the nine English WSCs went up from £288 million in 1993 to an eye-watering £2 billion in 2012. Interestingly, the company with the lowest gearing (ratio of debt to equity) and the highest credit rating was Welsh Water, which is mutually owned. The four companies with the highest gearing and the lowest credit ratings were all PE-owned.

Just like some of the care home groups, WSC ownership structures are often opaque. The combination of shadowy corporate structures and complex financial engineering may well explain high payouts to water company owners. Between 2009 and 2013 Anglian, Thames, United Utilities, Wessex and Yorkshire paid out more in dividends than they made in after-tax profits. Directors saw their share of the companies' income rise from 13.18 per cent in 1993 to 20.52 per cent in 2013. Over the same period the share of the water companies' income going to salaries and wages fell from 15.37 per cent to 10.22 per cent: in other words, the workers' loss seemed to be diametrically opposed to the owners' gain. It is true that the water companies have invested more than £100 billion in the country's water and sewerage infrastructure since privatization. But the financialization of the industry was not anticipated in 1989, and neither price controls nor limits to returns on capital imposed on the companies by the Water Services Regulation Authority (Ofwat), the industry's economic regulator, appear to have prevented what looks like value extraction.

The cases of care homes and water in Britain are not a blanket argument against PE or financialization. But they do illustrate how financial engineering of socially essential services can change the nature of an industry. It is at the very least debatable whether the opaque ownership and excessive financialization which characterize these PE-owned businesses serve their customers more than their owners.

THE RETREAT OF 'PATIENT' CAPITAL

Agency theory and MSV, then, are essentially straightforward concepts. The purpose of the firm is to return as much value to its shareholders – the equity owners of the company – as possible. In public companies especially, the shareholder is detached from the running of the business even though he or she is legally an owner; professional managers run it. Here is the crux of agency theory: the agents (the managers) are in law answerable to the principals (the shareholders). But, in relation to managers, shareholders are disadvantaged: they have less information about the business; they are numerous where the managers are few; and they are last in the queue for rewards – after the managers, the workers, the suppliers, the debt holders and the landlords. They only see a return for their investment after the other recipients have been paid. The shareholders are the 'residual' claimants, as they are assumed to be the only actors who do not have a guaranteed return from their contribution to the business. They are justified in claiming the return the company generates in excess of the costs associated with other stakeholders in the company.[15]

For a public company, maximizing shareholder value is effectively the same as maximizing the value of the equity shareholders' investment, as captured in the share price. The same is true, for practical purposes, of private companies: the owners – whether a family, PE or venture capital – will value a company by what they can expect to get for selling it or listing it on a stock exchange. That value will be substantially determined by that of similar public companies, as revealed by their share price.

MSV's origins are often traced to the development of the 'portfolio theory of the firm', a popular explanation for the development of the large industrial conglomerates of the 1950s and 1960s. The portfolio theory of the firm held that companies – like other investors – could spread their risks by owning assets in diverse industries. It assumed that corporations were only a collection of asset-generating cash flows and that professional managers, who were emerging as the heroes of modern capitalism, were capable of running any type of industry equally well. Business schools aimed to train managers with exactly this purpose in mind. Perhaps the epitome of the conglomerate of the time was the Transamerica Corporation, which at one stage counted among its sprawling interests the Bank of America, the United Artists film studio, Transamerica Airlines, Budget Rent a Car and various insurance operations.

Advocates of MSV argued that conglomerates were 'destroying' value, because managers (however competent and well trained) could not possibly be experts in getting the best out of such diverse operations. Diversification was more appropriately left to the shareholders, with the bosses of each company 'sticking to the knitting' and not venturing beyond their narrow zone of expertise. Conglomerates' inefficiency could be practically demonstrated if their constituent parts, broken up and floated separately, could command a higher total share price than the coagulated whole. Whether right or wrong, the assumption about managers' professionalism did not address the problem that they might not always act in the best interests of shareholders. When the US and other Western economies slowed down in the 1970s, Friedman and other agency theorists argued that because principals and agents are motivated by self-interest, the inevitable conflicts could best be resolved by giving the ultimate owner, the shareholder, the overriding interest. Conventional wisdom was turned on its head and conglomerates were broken up, a step also justified by seeing corporations as nothing more than a collection of cash flows. The interests of managers and shareholders should, the agency theorists reasoned, be 'aligned': if managers were also paid in the company's shares or options on those shares, the argument went, they would be motivated to maximize the interests of all shareholders.

Another constituency shared the managers' interest in rent-seeking: the asset managers, a driving force behind the fashion for breaking up conglomerates to extract greater shareholder value. Economically and socially, asset managers were closer to corporate managers than they were to their real customers, the remote and probably poorly informed members of pension funds or holders of life insurance policies. MSV offered asset managers the chance to get rich alongside the managers of the companies in which they invested their clients' money. Asset managers became the major holders of public equities, the 'residual' shareholder acting at least nominally on behalf of others. Their demands on the public corporation and later – through PE – the private corporation would profoundly affect the behaviour of the productive economy.

As we saw in the previous chapter, fund managers have played a central role in the development of contemporary capitalism. In theory, equity shareholders – largely institutional shareholders – monitor corporate performance. They act as gatekeepers, resolving the agent–principal problem generally and in particular monitoring how corporations use and allocate their capital. Their role should lead to better distribution of productive resources and make better use of resources already employed: for example, drawing on agency theory, a positive link has been made between institutional ownership and innovation.[16] But these assessments often seem to neglect the broader picture. It is no coincidence that the case for shareholder activism and supervision often accompanies palpable breakdown of corporate governance: witness the string of corporate scandals such as Enron and WorldCom in the US, Sports Direct in the UK and Volkswagen cheating on diesel engine emissions.

Shareholders are not the only gatekeepers. Others include auditors, rating agencies, government regulators, the media and equity analysts – specialists who assess companies for investors. The cause of many of the corporate scandals of recent years, the standard argument goes, is the failure of these gatekeepers to do their job. Rather than being critical observers of companies, equity analysts have become their cheerleaders, and largely failed to see that banks were heading for the rocks. Independent auditors and rating agencies became business partners of the companies they oversaw instead of guarding the interests of investors and the wider community. Governments moved to 'light-touch' regulation of finance, often under pressure from the industry lobby. The media were slow to spot the scandals and uncover them. Corporate directors – who, let's not forget, in the UK have a legal responsibility to act in the best interests of shareholders – were only a limited counterweight to managerial overreach.[17] There is no doubt that the incentive to generate fees – from advising, analysing and auditing companies, for example – resulted in collusion and conflicts of interest between the gatekeepers and the public corporations that led to failures of governance.

But the failure of the gatekeepers to fulfil their responsibility also owed much to the MSV mindset with which they perceived the fundamental role of the public corporation. And the key actors in the economy whose interests were most closely aligned with MSV's objective were the institutional investors. Principal and agent were meant to eye each other warily, but instead an unholy alliance developed between them to extract value from the company. Their relationship worked against other stakeholders, not least workers, whose pay lagged further and further behind that of CEOs and senior managers.

SHORT-TERMISM AND UNPRODUCTIVE INVESTMENT

In the Great Depression of the 1930s, long before financialization entered the modern lexicon, Keynes observed that:

> [most] expert professionals, possessing judgment and knowledge beyond that of the average private investor . . . are, in fact, largely concerned, not with making superior long-term forecasts of the probable yield of an investment over its whole life, but with foreseeing changes in the conventional valuation a short time ahead of the general public.[18]

A successful speculator himself, Keynes knew what he was talking about. He warned that the stock market would become 'a battle of wits to anticipate the basis of conventional valuation a few months hence, rather than the prospective yield of an investment over a long term of years'.[19] He would be proved right. The time within which shareholders seek to make profit, through a flow of dividends or a share price movement, is determined by the time for which they hold a particular share. And the average holding time for equity invest-ment, whether by individuals or institutions, has relentlessly fallen: from four years in 1945 to eight months in 2000, two months in 2008 and (with the rise of high-frequency trading) twenty-two seconds by

2011 in the US.[20] Average PE holding times jumped to almost six years when stock markets froze in the wake of the 2008 global financial crash, but were on a firm downward course again by 2015.[21]

The 'short-termism' which Keynes anticipated is encapsulated in index fund pioneer John Bogle's concept that institutional investors rent the shares of the companies they invest in rather than take ownership for the long term. Consider the increased turnover of domestic shares: according to the World Federation of Exchanges, which represents the world's publicly regulated stock exchanges, in the US turnover of domestic shares was around 20 per cent a year in the 1970s, rising steeply to consistently over 100 per cent a year in the 2000s. Turnover measures how often a share changes hands and is calculated by dividing the number of shares traded in a given period by the number of shares outstanding in the same period. Increasing turnover is a sign that institutional investors' sights were trained on the short-term movement of stock prices rather the intrinsic, long-term value of the corporation. High turnover can be more profitable for institutional investors than passive, long-term holding of shares. It should also be said that the short-termist behaviour of institutional investors reflects mounting pressure over the last four decades from clients who, expecting quick results and with a dislike of surprises, quickly withdraw their funds when disappointed. The result has been a corporate fixation on quarterly performance, which encourages consistent earnings growth to generate acceptable share price performance.

In 2013 the management consultants McKinsey and Company and the Canadian Pension Plan Investment Board surveyed 1,000 board members and senior company executives around the world to assess how they ran their businesses.[22] The majority of respondents said that the pressure to generate strong short-term results had increased during the past five years to a point where managers felt obliged to demonstrate strong financial performance. But while roughly half of the respondents claimed to be using a time horizon of less than three years in setting strategy, almost all of them said that taking a longer-term view would improve corporate performance, strengthen financial returns and increase innovation.[23]

Another important trend that further demonstrates the scale of

MSV's impact on corporate behaviour is that of rising hurdle rates. A hurdle rate, as we saw in the previous chapter, is a return on investment below which a company will not pursue an investment opportunity or project. It could be that, over time, there are fewer suitable opportunities available because the most profitable projects have already been taken up. Excess capacity in car-manufacturing, for instance, would naturally suggest that building a new plant would not be logical (though investing in other technologies very well might be). Fundamental economic forces may also be at work. Yet what has been happening to the hurdle rate seems to suggest that something else is also going on.

Hurdle rates are critical to the way in which companies allocate capital, but they are deeply affected by expectations – or what Keynes called 'animal spirits'.[24] The hurdle rate of a project is usually determined relative to the cost of capital – basically, interest rates on borrowing and dividends to shareholders. The project should generate returns, calculated as an Internal Rate of Return (IRR) or Return on Invested Capital (ROIC),[25] higher than the firm's cost of capital. But an odd discrepancy has appeared. On the one hand, the cost of debt-financing has been at record lows and could reasonably have been expected to encourage finance for new investment projects. On the other hand, according to J. P. Morgan,[26] the weighted average cost of capital remains quite low at 8.5 per cent but the median hurdle rate (minimum return on investment needed to justify a new project) reported by S&P 500 companies is 18 per cent. This suggests that companies are not pursuing investment opportunities unless the differential between their expected returns and their cost of capital is around 10 percentage points. Why would they leave such opportunities on the table? One explanation, given the exigencies of MSV, is that they have easier alternatives – such as share repurchases.

MSV, then, sets off a vicious circle. Short-term decisions such as share buy-backs reduce long-term investment in real capital goods and innovation such as R&D. In the long run, this will hold back productivity. With lower productivity, the scope for higher wages will be limited, thus lowering domestic demand and the propensity to invest in the economy as a whole. The spread of financialization deep into corporate decision-making therefore goes well beyond the immediate benefits it brings to shareholders and managers. As Hyman

Minsky observed, there appears to be an inevitable dynamic of the capitalist system: unless properly regulated or with the right buffers, it will expand too fast. Steady growth caused by increased borrowing – which speeds up value extraction – is matched by the rising value of assets. Everything seems to be fine – until people start to query the value of assets. Then trouble brews.

FINANCIALIZATION AND INEQUALITY

One of the key precepts of MSV, as we've seen, is that the incentives of management and shareholders need to be aligned, and that the best way to do this is to compensate management by awarding them shares. Senior managers soon embraced MSV when they realized how it could help them to increase their pay (Figure 23). The original spirit of MSV has been perverted: the massive share options which have been a major part of many CEOs' pay packages do not really align with managers' and shareholders' interests. Managers – depending on the terms on which they are granted options – enjoy an almost free upside, with no downside. They are partly insulated against the ups and downs of share prices that are the lot of long-term investors via

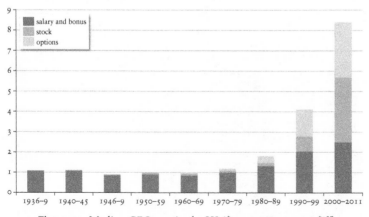

Figure 23. Median CEO pay in the US ($m, constant 2011 $)[27]

anti-takeover devices such as the 'golden parachute', a cash reward if they lose their job, or 'poison pills', which trigger an event such as the sale of a valuable corporate division to reduce the company's value when faced with an unwelcome takeover attempt.

Shareholders were not the only stakeholders whose interests were imperfectly aligned with those of managers. Despite a period of down-sizing (corporate speak for firings), which – especially after the late-1980s conquest of conglomerates – was meant to strip away surplus manage-ment and raise the productivity of employees who survived the cull, the ratio of CEO pay to workers' pay also soared (Figure 24).

The emphasis on short-term results has also led to another self-fulfilling outcome: the reduced tenure of management. As seen in Figure 25, the average tenure of CEOs has over the past few decades dropped from ten years to six. When one considers that CEO pay is heavily weighted towards share price performance, the need for com-panies to perform in the short term can be viewed not as pressure from an external gatekeeper gone rogue but as a mutually advanta-geous set-up that has served the interests of an elite few at the expense of the many.

The importance of EPS (earnings per share) growth as a measure of corporate success has become as much a proxy for MSV as the

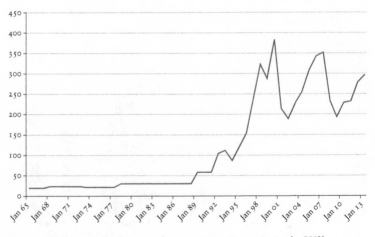

Figure 24. CEO-to-worker compensation ratio in the US[28]

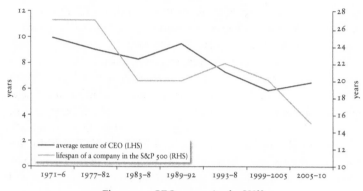

Figure 25. CEO tenure in the US[29]

share price. But EPS has not always enjoyed this totemic status. While Samuel Palmisano (IBM President from 2000 to 2011, and CEO from 2002 to 2011) argued that IBM's main aim was to double earnings per share over the next five years, half a century earlier in 1968 Tom Watson Jr (IBM President from 1952 to 1971) argued that IBM's three core priorities were (1) respect for individual employees, (2) a commitment to customer service and (3) achieving excellence. Although they are anecdotal, the two pronouncements by two different CEOs of IBM at two different times illustrate how priorities have evolved.

Palmisano's statement reflects what most corporate CEOs would parrot to their investors these days. This measure of a company's performance comes down to its two major components: earnings and the number of shares. The first, earnings, is an output from the profit and loss account of a company. It is notoriously vulnerable to manipulation. Earnings are usually calculated according to the Generally Agreed Accounting Principles (GAAP), the widely accepted framework of standards, rules and conventions accountants follow in drawing up financial statements. But within GAAP there is scope to adjust earnings to allow for exceptional items (which must be reported but can recur for several years), such as company restructuring charges, and extraordinary items (isolated events which do not need to be reported), such as hurricane damage. Managers therefore have some leeway to massage earnings. More than that, earnings are fundamentally determined by the company's operating profits, which in turn are the product of sales growth and earnings margins.

The number of shares outstanding is less vulnerable to accounting manipulation, but corporate actions can definitely influence it: for example by granting shares and share options for CEO and management compensation, and via share buy-backs. A delicate balance must be struck. Awarding shares to managers as part of their pay reduces EPS growth. Buying back shares can raise EPS, provided that the cost does not offset the gains from lowering the number of shares in issue.

Sales growth and improved profit margins, the two components of earnings growth, are positively influenced by investment, whether in plant and equipment (capital expenditure) or R&D. Investment is the story corporate managers like to tell. But there is another, quicker and more predictable way to improve margins, about which managers are less forthcoming: cutting costs. It's a process that companies have embraced – to the detriment of investment.

Figure 26 shows how business investment in the US is now around its lowest level for more than sixty years, an amazing and disturbing phenomenon.

At the same time, as discussed in the previous chapter, the decoupling of average productivity and earnings means that the share of total value added going to wage earners has also steadily declined.

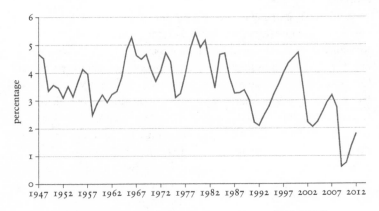

Figure 26. Business investment as percentage of US GDP[30]

William Lazonick, the chronicler of share buy-backs, has character-ized these two trends, when taken together, as a shift from a model of 'Retain and Invest' to 'Downsize and Distribute'. The first strategy – 'Retain and Invest' – uses finance only to set up a company and start production. Once profits are being made loans are likely to be at least partly repaid because retained earnings are a cheap way of financing the next production cycle and investments to expand market share. The second strategy – 'Downsize and Distribute' – is entirely different. It views companies merely as 'cash cows' whose least productive branches have to be sold. The resulting surplus is then distributed to managers and owners, rather than to others such as the workers who have also contributed to the business. The result may hamper the growth of the company and even cut the work-force – 'Downsize'. If the shareholders are happy, however, the strategy is justified.

One way of testing whether 'Downsize and Distribute' is a neces-sary corporate strategy is to compare public and private companies. Figure 27 shows that on several basic criteria such as size, sales, growth and return on assets (ROA), private companies seem to invest more than public ones.

It could be said that public companies are less profitable and

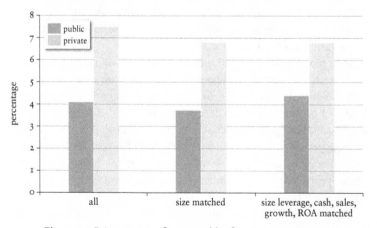

Figure 27. Private-sector firm vs public firm investment rates
(percentage of total assets)[31]

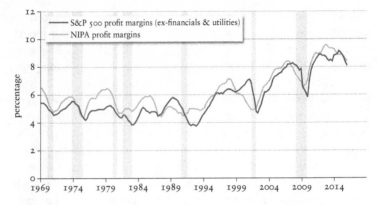

Figure 28. Non-financial sector public company profitability (GMR)[32]

therefore have less money to invest. But that doesn't seem to be true. Figure 28 illustrates that there is little difference between the profit margins of major US public companies (the S&P's 500) and those of all US firms derived from the National Income and Product Account (NIPA) compiled by the Bureau of Economic Analysis, which is part of the US Department of Commerce. The graph clearly shows a steady rise in profitability over forty-five years, culminating in record highs in recent years: truly 'profits without prosperity'. In other words, the agent–principal problem does not have to result in declining investment and short-termism.

So, if margins are high but investment is low, what have companies done with their profits? Following the money leads us directly to shareholders. As we can see from Figure 29, corporations have largely returned profits to shareholders in the form of dividends and share buy-backs. Having averaged 10–20 per cent in the 1970s, the percentage of cash flow returned to shareholders has remained above 30, and sometimes substantially more than that for most of the past thirty years, although it dipped during the tech boom in the early 1990s when companies were investing.

What emerges from the evidence presented so far is that, just like finance, the financialization of the productive sector extracts value – objectively, rent. But not only in the productive sector. In recent years

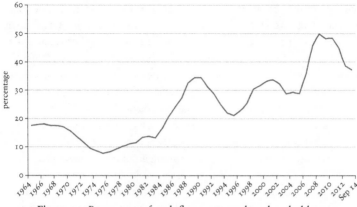

Figure 29. Percentage of cash flows returned to shareholders
(US non-financials five-year moving average)[33]

a wide range of businesses in the UK, from social providers like care homes to utilities such as water, both of which had previously been regarded as steady and unexciting investments, have been subject to financial engineering by new owners, often PE firms. The result is a transformation of public goods into private goods.

Financialization has a long arm. It reaches into society as well as the economy, and despite claims that its encroachment into the productive economy is a solution to issues such as average earnings, skills and inequality, the evidence is not encouraging. As John Bogle has noted: 'The highest-earning 0.01 per cent of U.S. families (150,000 in number), for example, now receives 10 per cent of all of the income earned by the remaining 150 million families, three times the 3 to 4 per cent share that prevailed from 1945 to 1980. It is no secret that about 35,000 of those families have made their fortunes on Wall Street.'[34]

FROM MAXIMIZING SHAREHOLDER VALUE TO STAKEHOLDER VALUE

Shareholder-value ideology is based on shareholders being the 'residual claimants'. They are the lead risk takers, with no guaranteed rate of return. Friedman summarized the classic view of entrepreneurial firms as eternally struggling to stay afloat in a turbulent market (while hinting at the temptation to escape by subverting that market) by defining the purpose of a business as being to 'use its resources and engage in activities designed to increase profits so long as it stays within the rules of the game, which is to say, engages in open and free competition, without deception or fraud'.[35]

A truth more complex than the primacy of the shareholders, however, is that wealth creation is a collective process. After all, important as shareholders are, it is hard to imagine a company being successful without the involvement of many groups, including employees, suppliers, distributors, the broader community in which the company's plants and headquarters are located, and even local and central government. Moreover, it is wrong to assume that these groups have a guaranteed return while shareholders are stuck at the back of queue. Indeed, as we shall see in the next chapter, governments which make risky investments in new technologies and basic research – both of which are later adopted by companies reluctant to assume this high level of early risk – have no guaranteed return at all.

Recognizing the collective nature of value creation takes us from a shareholder to a stakeholder view. Whereas MSV boils valuation down to a single measure – the share price – an opposing argument is that corporations should focus on maximizing stakeholder *value*: creating as much value as possible for all stakeholders and seeing any decision as a balance of interests and trade-offs to achieve that goal – hardly an easy task, given the complexity of many business decisions. The charge which proponents of stakeholder value level against MSV is that the 'pursuit of gains for shareholders at the expense of other stakeholders [is] a pursuit which ultimately destroys both shareholder and stakeholder value'.[36] Even Jack Welch, whose twenty years as General Electric CEO were often hailed as a triumph for the MSV approach, begged to differ when in 2009 he cited customers, employees and products as the key to that success, denouncing shareholder value as 'the dumbest idea in the world'.

The stakeholder theory of business is more than a theory of how to run a company better; it also has far-reaching social and economic implications. It answers the question, 'What makes a business successful?' very differently to the proponents of MSV. In sharp contrast to Friedman and Michael Jensen, who advocated strongly that a company succeeds simply through profit maximization, a stakeholder view emphasizes the social relationships between management and employees, between the company and the community, the quality of the products produced, and so on. These relationships give the company social goals as well as financial ones. Together they can create more sustainable 'competitive advantage'. And because value is created collectively, through investments of resources by a multitude of actors, it should also be distributed more collectively – not just to the shareholders.

In contrast to MSV and its goal of short-term profit maximization and its marginalization of human capital and R&D, stakeholder value sees people not just as inputs but as essential contributors who need to be nurtured. Trust – critical for any enterprise – is then built between workers and managers, in a process that acknowledges the vital role of workers in value creation. Investing in people is an admission that workers add value.

We have seen how short-termism distorts finance, making it more speculative. A stakeholder understanding of value denotes a very different type of finance: one that is more 'patient' and supports necessary long-term investments. In some countries this is achieved through public banks, such as the Kreditanstalt für Wiederaufbau (KfW) in Germany. KfW was intimately involved in Germany's postwar recovery and economic growth, lending more than €1 trillion since its founding in 1948.[37] Most of the countries that have public banks tend to follow a stakeholder model of corporate governance, for example by having workers on company boards.

Of course, no form of corporate governance is perfect – as the recent Volkswagen (VW) 'dieselgate' scandal proves. The car maker boasted several attributes which agency theorists consider helpful for far-sighted investment and honest practice, widening the shareholder base and extending its interests beyond short-term profit. German workers, who would have little to gain from tricking US consumers, had a powerful say in the company's affairs. A family holding company, a German state and a Middle Eastern sovereign fund control 90 per cent of the shareholder votes. All are very long-term investors.

The company had a reputation among customers and industry specialists for engineering excellence. It did not seem like the sort of company that would get into serious trouble.

But it did. VW wilfully designed a system to reduce emissions during testing but not during driving, and has paid fines of $20 billion and lost roughly $100 billion of stock market capitalization as a result. Half a century earlier, Ford incurred similar financial and reputational damage when top managers very deliberately calculated that the cost of fixing a fatal flaw in its Pinto model exceeded the cost of paying compensation for the customers it killed.[38] At VW, a hidden design flaw (potentially just as injurious to life and health) arose less through cynical calculation at the top than through pressures placed on subordinates to promote financial performance. The problem seems to have been a culture of competitiveness and fear which drove some engineers to take desperate measures to drive sales and many others to remain quiet about what they knew was a deception. There was long-term thinking at the top – but only about increasing market share, not about reputation. The unspoken but clear message to the employees who could have refused to comply was that failure to pass emissions tests was unacceptable, so it was preferable to cheat than admit defeat. In short, the VW scandal tells us that corporate governance structures and rules are unlikely to work unless corporate values are aligned with public values (a concept we will visit in Chapter 8).

CONCLUSION

Sky-rocketing rewards for the lucky few have widened social divisions and increased inequality in much of the Western world, notably in the US, the home of financialization.

This state of affairs can be – and is – attacked on moral grounds. Inequality reveals what we think of millions of our fellow humans. The economic issue with value extraction is not normative, however. As we have seen, in a capitalist economy some rent is necessary: there is an unavoidable price tag to maintaining the circulation of capital in the economic system. But the scale of the financial sector and of financialization generally has increased value extraction to the point where two critical questions must be answered: where is value created, extracted and even destroyed? And how can we steer the economy away from excessive financialization towards true value creation? Proposals such as taxing away very high incomes and accumulations of wealth may treat some of the symptoms of excessive finance. They do not, however, treat the causes, which lie deep in a system of value extraction which has grown up over the last forty years or so.

If the objective is long-term growth, the private sector must be rewarded for making decisions that target the long-term over the short-term. While some companies might be focusing on boosting their stock prices through share buy-backs, aimed at increasing stock prices and hence stock options (through which executives are paid), others may be taking on the difficult investments to increase the training needed for workers, introduce risky new technology, and investment in R&D, eventually leading, with luck, to new technology and more likely leading to nowhere. Companies could be rewarded for doing more of the latter and less of the former.

Executive pay should be kept in check through an understanding that there are many other stakeholders who are critical to value creation, from workers and the state to civil society movements. Reinvestment of profits back into the real economy – rather than hoarding or engaging in share buy-backs – should be a condition attached to any type of government support, whether through subsidies or government grants and loans.

The British-Venezuelan scholar Carlota Perez has argued that the decoupling of finance from the real economy is not 'natural' but an artefact of deregulation and excess belief in the power of free markets. Her groundbreaking work has identified a pattern of intense financialization followed by its reversal in each technological revolution.[39] She shows that the early decades of each of the five revolutions to date (from the steam engine to the IT revolution) have been times of financial mania and increasing inequality. But after the financial bubbles collapse, and amid the ensuing recession and social turmoil, governments have tended to rein in finance and promote a period that favours the expansion of production, benefiting society more broadly and making finance serve its real purpose. But if and when government does not step in and play its part, financialization can have no end.[40]

The next chapter turns to the world of innovation, a glamorous arena of inspired inventors and fearless entrepreneurs where 'wealth creation' is not all it is claimed to be.

7

Extracting Value through the Innovation Economy

*First, only invest in companies that have the potential to
return the value of the entire fund.*

Peter Thiel, *Zero to One:
Notes on Startups, or How to Build the Future* (2014)[1]

STORIES ABOUT VALUE CREATION

The epicentre of a still-unfolding technological revolution, Silicon
Valley is the most dynamic industrial district in the world for high-
tech start-ups. Since the 1980s it has made millionaires of many
thousands of founders, early-stage employees, executives and venture
capitalists – and billionaires of a significant number too. The ingenuity of these people has undoubtedly been instrumental in changing
how we communicate, transact business and live our lives. Their
products and services epitomize our contemporary idea of progress.

Silicon Valley's entrepreneurs are often viewed as heroic do-
gooders. Indeed, Google's stated mission is *Do No Evil*. In April
2016 a front cover of the *Economist* showed the Facebook founder
Mark Zuckerberg dressed like a Roman emperor under the headline
'Imperial Ambition'. Meanwhile, innovation is seen as the new force
in modern capitalism, not just in Silicon Valley but globally. Phrases
like the 'new economy', 'the innovation economy', 'the information
society' or 'smart growth' encapsulate the idea that it is entrepreneurs, garage tinkerers and their patents that unleash the 'creative

destruction' from which the jobs of the future come. We are told to welcome the likes of Uber and Airbnb because they are the forces of renewal that sweep away the old incumbents, whether black cabs in London or 'dinosaur' hotel chains like Hilton.

The success of some of the companies has been extraordinary. Google's share of the global desktop search engine market is more than 80 per cent,[2] while just five US companies (Google, Microsoft, Amazon, Facebook and IBM) own most of the world's data, with China's Baidu being the only foreign company coming close. This market share also results in immense wealth: Apple's cash pile was over $250 billion in 2017.

These companies' huge profits, and their domination of their respective markets, are claimed to be justified in terms of the value they create: such profits and such domination are simply a reflection of their enormous wealth-creating power. Similarly, big pharmaceutical companies have justified the enormous increase in drug prices – where cures for diseases like hepatitis C can cost up to a million dollars – through stories about their extraordinary innovation capability and associated costs, or – when those costs are revealed to be much lower and/or actually picked up by the taxpayer – through the notion of 'value'-based pricing.

This chapter takes a critical look at the innovation economy and the stories around it. It explores how the dominant narratives about innovators and the reasons for their success fundamentally ignore the deeply collective and cumulative process behind innovation. This failure to recognize these processes has in turn led to a problematic distribution of the rewards for innovation, and to policies which, in the name of innovation, have enabled a few companies to extract value from the economy.

Value extraction in the innovation economy occurs in various ways. First, in the way that the financial sector – in particular venture capital and the stock market – has interacted with the process of technology creation. Second, in the way that the system of intellectual property rights (IPR) has evolved: a system that now allows not just the products of research but also the tools for research to be patented and their use ring-fenced, thereby creating what the economist

William J. Baumol termed 'unproductive entrepreneurship'. Third, in the way that prices of innovative products do not reflect the collective contribution to the products concerned, in fields as diverse as health, energy or broadband. And fourth, through the network dynamics characteristic of modern technologies, where first-mover advantages in a network allow large companies to reap monopolistic advantages through economies of scale and the fact that customers using the network get locked in (finding it too cumbersome or disadvantageous to switch service). The chapter will argue that the most modern form of rent-seeking in the twenty-first-century knowledge economy is through the way in which risks in the innovation economy are socialized, while the rewards are privatized.

WHERE DOES INNOVATION COME FROM?

Before looking at these four areas of value extraction, I want to consider three key characteristics of innovation processes. Innovation rarely occurs in isolation. Rather it is by nature deeply cumulative: innovation today is often the result of pre-existing investment. Innovation is, moreover, collective, with long lead-times: what might appear as a radical discovery today is actually the fruit of decades of hard work by different researchers. It is also profoundly uncertain, in that most attempts at innovation fail and many results are unexpected. (Viagra, for instance, was initially developed for heart problems.)

(i) Cumulative Innovation

If there is one thing that economists agree on (and there are not many), it is that technological and organizational changes are the principal source of long-term economic growth and wealth creation. Investments in science, technology, skills and new organizational forms of production (such as Adam Smith's emphasis on the division of labour) drive productivity and long-term increases in GDP.

Building on the work of Marx, who highlighted the role of techno-logical change in capitalism, Joseph Schumpeter (1883–1950) is probably the economist who has most emphasized the importance of innovation in capitalism. He coined the term 'creative destruction' to describe the way that product innovations (new products replacing old) and process innovations (new ways to organize production and distribution of goods and services) caused a dynamic process of renewal but also a process of destruction, with old ways falling aside and in the process causing many companies to go bankrupt. Schum-peter was particularly fascinated by 'waves' of innovations, which he believed occurred every thirty or so years. While Marx's interest in technological change led him to look at the crises that capitalism would experience due to the effect of innovation on capital's ability to create surplus value (or, to put it another way, if machines replace labour, how will the exploitation of labour – the source of profits – occur?), later economists focused mainly on the positive side of innovation that Schumpeter had underscored: its role in increasing the productive capacity of national economies.

In 1987 Robert Solow, a professor at the Massachusetts Institute of Technology, won the Nobel Prize in Economics for showing that improvements in the use of technology explained over 80 per cent of economic growth. Following many before him who were readers of Schumpeter, Solow argued that economic theory had to better under-stand how to describe technological change.[3] Practising what they preached, they explored what forces drive technological change. But where does innovation come from? Is it lone entrepreneurs working in their garages, genius scientists having a eureka moment in the laboratory, heroic small businesses and venture capitalists struggling against the commercial odds? No, they concluded that inventions are overwhelmingly the fruits of long-term investments that build on each other over years.

To take one obvious example: innovation in personal computers, which replaced clunky mainframes, came after decades of innov-ation in semiconductors, in memory capacity and in the box itself (reducing the size of mainframes to much smaller units). Individual companies such as IBM were key to the introduction of personal computers in the late 1970s and 1980s. But there would have been little innovation without the contribution to that lengthy process of other actors, such as the US government's investment in semiconductor research and its procurement power in the 1950s and 1960s. Or, later, the investments made by the US government in the Internet, or that made by companies like Xerox Parc – itself a beneficiary of large amounts of public co-funding – in the development of the graphical user interface, which Steve Jobs later made use of in Apple's first Macintosh, Lisa.

(ii) Uncertain Innovation

Innovation is uncertain, in the sense that most attempts to innovate fail. It also can take a very long time: decades can pass from the conception of an idea to its realization and commercialization. The types, sources and magnitude of risks vary across technologies, sectors and innovations. Technological risks, for instance, can increase with the complexity of the target (e.g. going to the moon, solving climate change) or the paucity of knowledge within the organizations involved.[4] The longer the time required to devise certain solutions, the greater the chance of a competitor reaching the market first, establishing what are known as first-mover advantages. Additional risks that militate against recouping the initial investment or the viability of the business include spillover effects (an event brought on by an apparently unrelated event elsewhere); the lack of demand for goods even if they make it to the market; investors' exposure to labour or tax problems; and changing economic conditions. These are all reasons why an appetite for risk – in both the public and private sectors involved in innovation – is essential.

Yet contrary to the prevailing image of fearless, risk-taking entrepreneurs, business often does not want to take on such risk. This is especially the case in areas where a lot of capital is needed and the technological and market risks are high – pharmaceuticals, for instance, and the very early stages of sectors, from the Internet to biotech and nanotech. At this point the public sector can, and does, step in where private finance fears to tread, to provide vital long-term finance.

(iii) Collective Innovation

Understanding both the role of the public sector in providing strategic finance, and the contribution of employees inside companies, means understanding that innovation is collective: the interactions between different people in different roles and sectors (private, public, third sectors) are a critical part of the process. Those who might otherwise be seen as lone entrepreneurs in fact benefit from such collectivity; moreover, they stand on the shoulders of both previous entrepreneurs and taxpayers who, as we will see, often contribute to the underlying infrastructure and technologies on which innovation builds.

Such processes are evident in the technologies underpinning some of today's most ubiquitous products: the iPhone, for instance, depends on publicly funded smartphone technology, while both the Internet and SIRI were funded by the Defense Advanced Research Projects Agency (DARPA) in the US Department of Defense; GPS by the US Navy; and touchscreen display by the CIA. In the pharmaceutical sector, research has shown that two-thirds of the most innovative drugs (new molecular entities with priority rating) trace their research back to funding by the US National Institutes of Health. Meanwhile, some of the greatest advances in energy – from nuclear to solar to fracking – have been funded by the US Department of Energy, including recent battery storage innovations by ARPA-E, DARPA's sister organization. Both Bill Gates, CEO of Microsoft,[5] and Eric Schmidt, Executive Chairman of Alphabet (the parent company of Google),[6] have recently written about the immense benefits their companies gained from public investments: as well as the Internet and the html code behind the worldwide web written in CERN, a public lab in Europe, Google's very algorithm was funded by a National Science Foundation grant.

The collective role of innovation can be seen not only in the co-operation between public and private but also in the role that workers play. Countries that have a more 'stakeholder' approach to corporate governance, many of which are to be found in Northern Europe, tend to involve workers more directly in the innovation process and to train them through well-developed vocational programmes: worker skills are most heavily invested in; they contribute more, and thereby are more able to share in the rewards that their work generates. When trade union representatives sit on the boards of companies, they are more likely to demand that any sacrifices in wages are compensated by higher investments in areas that eventually create more and better jobs. And countries with a more stakeholder-driven economy are more likely to embrace the kinds of public and private collaborations that are required for value creation: the strength of German manufacturing, for instance, is closely related to the strong links between science and industry fostered by public-private organizations like the German Fraunhofer Institutes.[7]

An understanding of the uncertain, collective and cumulative characteristics of innovation is helpful to understand both value creation, as indicated above, but also value extraction. There are four key ways in which value extraction occurs in the innovation economy. The first is to be found in the economy's interaction with the financial markets.

FINANCING INNOVATION

Given the lengthy and cumulative process of innovation, understanding which actors enter the innovation process, how they do it and at what point is key. In Figure 30 we can see how financial returns to innovation evolve through the innovation process. In the early days returns are low due to the very high risks; then, if the innovation proves successful, returns increase, often exponentially, before flattening out. This cumulative process is shown through a cumulative distribution (Figure 30). But it's also true that who is doing what changes over that time period. In the very early days it is often public R&D agencies or universities that fund the science base, and only when innovation is close to having a commercial application do private actors enter. Public R&D agencies include organizations like DARPA and ARPA-E and even public sources of early seed money for innovative firms often tend to precede private venture capital. These include public venture capital funds (like Yozma in the Israeli government); the funding of small enterprises linked to

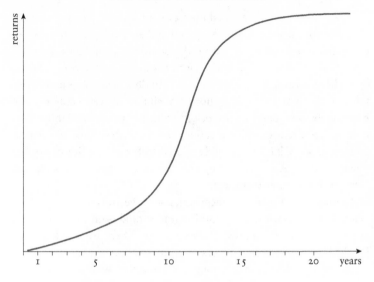

Figure 30. Cumulative returns for innovation

public procurement programmes (such as the Small Business Innovation Research Programme in the USA); or through innovation
funds inside public banks like the European Investment Bank, the
KfW in Germany or the Chinese Development Bank. Evidence shows
that it is only after these high-risk patient funds have been invested
that the more risk-averse private financial funds enter, for example
private VC.[8]

In the case of venture capitalists, their real genius appears to lie in
their timing: their ability to enter a sector late, after the highest development risks had already been taken, but at an optimum moment
to make a killing. While many such investments fail, the few that
succeed can make the investment fund in question a fortune, as
exemplified by the success of the VC company Kleiner Perkins. In
1976, Kleiner Perkins invested $100,000 in the biotechnology com-
pany Genentech, which four years later, during its initial public
offering on the stock market, was valued at $300 million. In 2009,
Genentech was acquired by a Swiss-based healthcare company, Roche,
for $47 billion, making a fortune for the investors. Similarly, Peter

Theil's $500,000 investment in Facebook back in 2004, which bought him a 10.2 per cent stake in the company, made him £1 billion when he sold the majority of his shares in 2012. These early investors are doubtless crucial to the innovation process. The critical question here is: are their rewards proportionate to the risks they take?

You might imagine, in the instances where public funds have made the initial risky investments – the private VC only entering at the point where investment looks more of a sure bet – that these funds would receive appropriate remuneration for their boldness. But in fact, the opposite is true. In these cases, the private VC industry's share of the rewards tends to be about 20 per cent, excluding other fees and charges; by contrast, the public sector's direct share is close to nil. The public sector is generally deemed to reap its rewards in other, more indirect ways: through taxation or from the benefits of products with high quality and low cost. Not only is this a way of thinking that all but ignores the crucial and risky early investments made by public funds in innovation; it disproportionally privileges the later, private investors in terms of rewards.

Let's look at this a bit more closely.

VC – *Timing is All*

The VC industry began in the USA in 1946 when the American Research and Development Corporation (ARD) was set up to raise funds from wealthy people and college endowments to invest in entrepreneurial start-ups in technology-based manufacturing. It was soon making eye-catching investments. In 1957, ARD invested a total of $70,000 in DEC, a computer company; nine years later, this same investment was already valued at $37 million. Nevertheless, the VC industry's growth was sedate until the 1980s, when it boomed, the role of pension funds upboosting its capital.

From the start of the VC industry, entrepreneurs and venture capitalists had often surfed on a wave created by decades of government investment. Starting after the Second World War, government investment in high-tech ventures grew significantly in the 1950s as part of the military-industrial complex, largely due to the Cold War.[9] Before becoming famous around the world as 'Silicon Valley', a name coined in 1971, the San Francisco Bay area was producing technology for military use or, from the 1960s, spin-offs of military technology for commercial purposes.[10] The first formal VC firm in Silicon Valley – Draper, Gaither and Anderson – was headed by two former US Army generals and the author of a secret report to President Eisenhower on how the US should respond to the USSR's launching of Sputnik.[11]

Much of the work to commercialize military technology was done in the research labs of established ICT companies like General Electric, Texas Instruments, AT&T, Xerox and IBM. Employees of these companies left to found their own start-ups. The Small Business Investment Company, set up in 1958 by the government's Small Business Administration, itself founded in 1953, helped many of the start-ups to raise capital.

The establishment in 1971 of NASDAQ – a new stock market that did not have the stringent listing requirements of the New York Stock Exchange – complemented the government's programmes. The creation of a highly liquid national market for more speculative corporate securities was important for attracting venture capitalists to invest in the IT industry, secure in the knowledge that there was now a feasible exit route from their investments.[12] Venture capitalists typically look to exit from investments within three to five years, impatient to make a buck in one enterprise and start again elsewhere.

In 1972, the Silicon Valley VC industry began to coalesce at 3000 Sand Hill Road in Palo Alto; a year later the National Venture Capital Association (NVCA) was formed. The NVCA quickly became an influential lobby. By the early 1980s it persuaded Congress to halve capital gains tax rates, arguing that it would be an incentive to greater VC investment. Warren Buffett became a lead critic of this policy, admitting that he and most investors don't look at tax, they look at opportunities.[13] Indeed, the VC industry, from when it began, followed the opportunities created by direct 'mission-oriented' government investments in areas like the Internet, biotech, nanotech and cleantech.

As we saw in Chapter 5, another crucial success for the NVCA came when it persuaded the US government to relax the interpretation of the 'prudent man' investment rule (keeping pensions funds out of high-risk investments) to allow pension fund managers to invest up to 5 per cent of pension funds in riskier investments like VC ones. It meant that, from 1979 onwards, large sums of workers' pensions savings flowed into VC funds – funds on which venture capitalists typically received a management fee of 2 per cent of total volume, as well as 20 per cent 'carried interest' of profits (i.e. the share of the profits that go to those managing the funds), like private equity.[14]

In 1984, during a tour of Silicon Valley by the then French President, François Mitterrand, the discrepancy between the venture capitalists' newfound bullishness and their actual achievements was picked up in an exchange between Paul Berg, one of the winners of the Nobel Prize in Chemistry that year, and Tom Perkins (the co-founder of Kleiner-Perkins) boasting about his sector's role in biotech. Berg said: 'Where were you guys in the '50s and '60s when all the funding had to be done in the basic science? Most of the discoveries that have fuelled [the industry] were created back then.'[15] For the venture capitalists, however, the prospect of astonishing profits now lay before them. Nothing summed up this new spirit of enterprise better than the upstart company that went public the same year: Apple.[16]

Heads I Win, Tails You Lose

Apple Computer Company had been founded in a Californian garage in 1976. When it went public in 1980 it was the largest IPO (initial public offering) since the venerable fifty-three-year-old Ford Motor Company's back in 1956.[17] Apple turned into a legend overnight. It also blazed a trail: the IPO has since become the rite of passage for hundreds of hopeful high-tech start-ups, synonymous in the public mind with the success of Silicon Valley – and for very good reasons.

An IPO is the point at which expectation and potential come face to face with the realities of the marketplace. IPOs capture in one moment value generated over a long period, capitalizing the future profit potential of a business into a market price. For VC, in other words, timing is all.

By orchestrating this moment of alchemy – when the long and winding, always uncertain, usually collaborative, journey of innovation is crystallized into hard cash – venture capitalists, other investors, founders and early-stage employees have been able to reap extraordinary rewards. In that one moment, the 'trapped equity' – the sum of all the ingenuity, effort, risk-taking, collaboration and persistence that went into developing the new idea – is released and paid out to the flotation's controllers, who may not have been the original innovators or risk takers.

IPOs are, first, a way for early investors to get their money out. The very possibility of an IPO encourages investment – although it has to be said that investors with one eye on the exit door and the other on the clock might not be ideal for nurturing a company to its potential. Second, IPOs can raise new capital for business expansion, which can be valuable in some sectors but less significant in others (like software), where the most important capital is human. Third, founders can realize the value of their ingenuity and sweat equity that has remained latent in the company. Fourth, employees, who may have been induced to leave secure jobs by the promise of equity in a risky venture, can realize the value of that equity – or at least see the possibility of doing so now that there is some liquidity in the company's stock. This, indeed, was the primary motivation for Microsoft's IPO in 1986, having awarded stock options to its employees since 1982.[18]

To restate: investments in early-stage businesses are risky and most will fail. The volatility of returns to VC across the business cycle reveals the perils.[19] Nonetheless, many venture capitalists have found themselves among the super-rich as a result of the success of high-tech firms in Silicon Valley. How has this happened? They have taken risks, of course – although mostly with other people's money – which deserve to be rewarded. Yet the returns have come from investing in companies whose value was often created by decades of prior government investment. When the investment bets have paid off in a successful IPO or sale, the venture capitalists have benefited disproportionately from their favourable position as insiders. Then they have gained again from the increasingly favourable tax treatment of their capital gains within a tax system their industry has worked hard to shape.

The allocation of shares during an IPO favours insiders, including investment banks that underwrite the deal. The insiders have incentives to encourage hype about the IPO, setting the price low and limiting the stock's availability to encourage the price to spike. As outsiders clamour to get their hands on the latest hot tech stock, insiders can sell at a large profit.[20] It is as close to a 'heads I win, tails you lose' bet as it is possible to make.

All of which was writ large in the developing microelectronics industry of the 1980s, a fertile test bed for the evolution of the American VC industry. Previous post-war decades of US government investment meant that new companies in the sector could produce marketable products within the time horizons that VC investors demanded. Gradually the VC model migrated to other emerging sectors. The biopharmaceuticals industry, again, was built on massive US government investment, this time through the life sciences knowledge base, the National Institutes of Health (NIH), since 1938. Between 2009 and 2016, the NIH have been spending an average of $31.5 billion a year (in constant 2009 dollars), twice the level of the 1990s, and three times the level of the 1980s. In 2016 the amount totalled $32.3 billion. But in the biopharmaceutical sector the product cycles are much longer and more speculative than in microelectronics: less obviously a good fit with the VC financing model of exiting within five years.[21] Along with firms like Amgen, Genzyme and Biogen, Genentech (now part of Roche) is one of only a small number of biopharmaceutical companies to keep their promise of producing a blockbuster drug (sales over $1 billion), of which the sector has generated only thirty in total.[22]

Despite this patchy record, hundreds of biopharmaceutical start-ups have been able to raise finance through IPOs and continue in business for many years, often without the encumbrance of an actual product. These product-less IPOs (or PLIPOs) survive through R&D contracts with big pharmaceutical companies and through the speculative trading of their shares on NASDAQ, fermented by news about the success or failure of the latest clinical trial. Yet, if it has proved hard to make reliable money from the development of actual new blockbuster drugs, it seems that there have been plenty of ways to derive income by speculating about the possibilities of doing so. Nor has this unremarkable history of turning taxpayer-funded investments in life sciences into successful products prevented top executives in those companies being well rewarded in salaries and stock.

The classical economists would have had little time for the way in which the VC industry has extracted value by shifting money around rather than creating value: for them the point was to nurture the production of value rather than its simple circulation.

Yet the examples of the fortunes made in the 1990s and early 2000s by founders, venture capitalists, early-stage employees and senior executives from the Silicon Valley tech boom rippled out, resetting the norms and expectations for what leaders in more established sectors ought to be paid. Similarly, inflated expectations have also been built into the patent system, and more pervasively in innovative industries like ICT, biotech and pharmaceuticals. Patents, indeed, have become synonymous with value extraction.

PATENTED VALUE EXTRACTION

The second key way in which value has been extracted from the innovation economy is by the appropriation of returns through the patent system (IPR). In the last century patents, and associated tools like copyrights and trademarks, have gone from being devices to stimulate innovation to means of blocking it.

Patents are protections granted to inventions that are novel, inventive (non-obvious) and suitable for industrial application. In theory they protect the innovator from having his or her idea copied. In practice, however, most innovations are not patented, which in itself shows that patents are not really necessary, as there are other ways to protect innovations, including lead-times and trade secrecy. One study found that between 1977 and 2004, only 10 per cent of 'important' innovations were patented.[23] Patents tend to be granted for two reasons, which must be held in constant tension for the system to function effectively. The first is to reward and incentivize inventors for developing new ideas by granting them a time-limited monopoly entitlement over their inventions,[24] or what is known as the *appropriability function* of patents. In exchange for this monopoly entitlement, the inventor must reveal detailed information about his or her invention. Which brings us to the second reason: once the patent has expired, the invention can diffuse rapidly through the economy in a process known as the *disclosure function* of patents. If the system works well, the appropriability function is properly balanced against the disclosure function and the public gains from the rapid diffusion of this new knowledge through the economy.[25]

Looked at in this light, patents are best understood not as intellectual property 'rights' in the sense of something that is universal or immutable, but as a contract or deal based on a set of policy choices. Something is given up (information about the invention) in exchange for something gained (the ability to exploit the invention exclusively for a limited period). In balancing the private benefits with the broader public good, policymakers must make trade-offs. Granting patents can help increase the incentives for inventors, which in the long run can result in higher rates of technical progress. But such grants also increase the market power of patent holders, resulting in less 'economic efficiency' during the time patents are enforceable, and slower knowledge diffusion.

The original purpose of patents is value creation. Patenting your brilliantly cheap and effective innovation is meant to ensure that the hard work you put into the invention is protected for a period during which it earns profits until others are allowed to copy it. That period is currently twenty years. Not all industries make equal use of patents; they tend to be less important for areas like software[26] and more so for science-based industries like pharmaceuticals. Indeed, there are also other ways to maintain market dominance, for example through first-mover advantages and secrecy.

To understand how patents relate to the dynamics of value extraction, we must look both at what exactly is being patented and at the structure of the patents themselves. The current dominance of the narrative of entrepreneurs as wealth creators has, I would contend, shifted the balance of the patent system away from an emphasis on the diffusion of knowledge towards private reward.[27]

Patents Can Inhibit Innovation

Today, the patent 'deal' has become unbalanced, to the extent that the patent system no longer aids the innovation economy but inhibits it. Changes in four major areas are responsible for this unbalancing: what is being patented; the length of patent protection; the ease with which patents can be obtained; and the reasons for seeking patent protection.

First, since the 1980s the patentability domain has been expanding in the US. The domain has moved 'upstream': that is, patents are no longer restricted to actual 'inventions' (products), but now include 'discoveries' (the knowledge behind products). This means that patents are no longer confined to inventions with 'practical or commercial utility'. Now, they may also apply to discoveries that help in the exploration of future innovative possibilities, such as diagnostic procedures, databases, analytic methods, or scientific principles with some potential practical application. Patents, in other words, are now gatekeepers to the knowledge base.

Instrumental in this shift was the US Bayh–Dole Act of 1980, which made it possible for universities and government research laboratories to hold patents on the results of publicly funded research.

The aim of the Bayh–Dole Act was to strengthen university–industry interactions and incentivize commercialization. Yet granting an exclusive licence on a university-owned patent deters follow-on innovations. Firms must now negotiate – and pay for – a licence before entering a market to access proprietary information that would previously have been available in publications.[28] Instead of encouraging better technology transfer – for example, of human stem cell patents held by the University of Wisconsin – the system has delayed technology diffusion.[29]

Where the US led, the rest of the world has followed. Such university licensing challenges the traditional 'open science model', where basic research outcomes were – as they should be – freely and equally available to everyone. Today, a more proprietary and exclusionary model has taken over, as the university-licensed patents on online search engines such as Google and Netscape illustrate.

Second, legal changes have extended the protection patents offer:

now, patents can be renewed. These changes came on the back of persistent lobbying, for instance by pharmaceutical companies, whose pressure resulted in the US Hatch–Waxman Act of 1984, which besides getting the generics industry off the ground (by being able to circumvent some FDA regulations), also resulted in the extension of the patent life for brand-name drugs. And since then the Act has been manipulated by industry lawyers to get patents extended even more.[30] There is a parallel here with copyright laws: over the last century the entertainment industry has increased copyright protection from fourteen years to ninety-five.[31]

Third, patents are now much easier to obtain. The squeeze on budgets for courts and the FDA, which licenses medical drugs, has cut the number of staff checking patents, leaving them often more likely to grant a patent than not.

And fourth, large companies have increasingly used 'strategic' patenting to patent around areas with a view to blocking competitors. This goes against the second role of patents, which is to allow the diffusion of resources. Such strategic patenting can be especially effective when a patent is obtained at an early stage of the development of a technology, before the technical standard is properly determined, or in fast-paced and patent-intensive fields such as ICT or biotech, where innovations are highly interdependent or complementary.[32] An early patent gives its owner the chance of setting the dominant standard and blocking improvements others might make. The risk of infringing the patent can also prevent other firms from marketing their products or services.

Another related and growing practice is 'patent-trolling': the strategic holding of patents, not to develop or commercialize the underlying idea but deliberately to collect royalties through patent enforcement. A market for patents has emerged in which the value of the patent is divorced – or effectively monetized – from the value of the production of goods or services the patent makes possible. It has been argued that strategic patenting can aid innovation by providing small firms with liquidity as they seek to bear the costs of development and commercialization[33] – but the evidence suggests that this practice is also causing harm. James Bessen and Michael J. Meurer, authors of *The Patent Litigation Explosion*, estimate that 'patent trolls cost defendant firms $29 billion per year in direct out-of-pocket costs'.[34] Another study finds that in aggregate, 'patent litigation destroys over $60 billion in firm wealth each year',[35] with the costs falling more heavily on smaller firms.[36]

UNPRODUCTIVE ENTREPRENEURSHIP

It might be said that these changes have, collectively, caused patents to result not in productive but in *unproductive* entrepreneurship. We cannot assume that entrepreneurship will always be 'productive', in the sense of leading to the discovery of new products, services or processes that increase society's wealth. In many circumstances, entrepreneurship can be unproductive: where it involves innovations in rent-seeking, for instance, or discovering unused but effective legal gambits to deploy against competitors. Today, the patent system offers many opportunities for these kinds of 'unproductive entrepreneurship'; patents can reinforce monopolies and intensify abuse of market power, block the diffusion of knowledge and follow-on innovations, and make it easier to privatize research that is publicly funded and collectively created. Indeed, in the words of economist William J. Baumol, 'at times the entrepreneur may even lead a parasitical existence that is actually damaging to the economy'.[37]

A common assumption is that rents are simply the result of imperfections in the competitive process that otherwise would lead to beneficial results for all. An alternative view, following Marx, is that rents (including those generated from patents) arise from value creation itself – i.e. not from cheating or breaking the rules of the system, but from the rules of the system itself. The way the modern-day patenting system is structured (e.g. allowing upstream patenting, and strategic patenting), I would contend, is analogous to what Marx called 'unproductive labour', because it extracts rather than creates value. The patent holder derives rents from enforceable property rights over productive resources simply by excluding others from access to those resources. Holders of patents can appropriate surplus value generated by labour and not paid out in wages. In the modern economy there are few limits to the accumulation of such IPR, and therefore few constraints on the scale of value appropriation. Duncan Foley, a heterodox economist in New York studying the relationship between modern value extraction practices and the classical approach to rent, claims: 'Any individual creator [of strategically located intellectual property] can expand her or his income effectively without limit, but this does nothing to expand social value production.'[38]

Today's narrative, which plays up the role of the private sector in innovation and plays down that of the state, has created space for broader and stronger patents to proliferate. Such patents are justified as rewarding the efforts of entrepreneurs, who can then continue to shoulder the risks of innovation. But neither the risks of innovation nor support for future innovation – both undeniably important – are enough to justify tipping the balance so far in the direction of this prevailing story. Instead of the creation of value, the expansion of patents has fuelled rent-seeking, value extraction, value destruction, strategic gaming and the privatizing of the results of publicly funded scientific research. As *The Economist* has observed: 'Patents are supposed to spread knowledge, by obliging holders to lay out their innovation for all to see . . . Instead, the system has created a parasitic ecology of trolls and defensive patent-holders, who aim to block innovation, or at least to stand in its way unless they can grab a share of the spoils.'[39]

All of which has major implications for global development. Industrialization in today's advanced economies like the US, Britain and Germany actually took place under much narrower and more flexible IPR rules than those we have today. And while later industrializing countries such as Japan and South Korea benefited from a 'friendly' or 'loose' international IPR environment, developing economies now encounter a more closed and privatized knowledge creation system, supported by international trade agreements.[40]

PRICING PHARMACEUTICALS

Perhaps nowhere is the modern patent system more pernicious than in pharmaceutical pricing. It is a vivid lesson in how the concept of value is abused. In patent-intensive sectors like pharmaceuticals, greater patent protection has not led to increases in innovation. In fact, the opposite has happened. We have more drugs with little or no therapeutic value.[41] At the same time, there have been numerous lawsuits attempting to extend patent validity on existing drugs by reshuffling old combinations of compounds. These suits lend weight to the claim that the patent legal system has become the main source of value extraction, rather than providing incentives for value creation through pharmaceutical innovations. Worse, because public institutions funded most of the key scientific discoveries behind health innovations,[42] taxpayers are now paying twice: first for the research and second for the premium that pharmaceutical companies charge for their drugs. Furthermore, increasing returns from patents reinforce the position of incumbents and lock out competitors.

A recent case illustrates how patents lead to monopoly pricing. In early 2014, the pharmaceutical giant Gilead brought a new treatment for the hepatitis C virus to the market. The drug is called Sovaldi. It is a remarkable advance over existing therapies against this life-threatening disease, which affects around 3 million people in the US and 15 million in Europe.[43] Later that year, Gilead released an improved version of Sovaldi called Harvoni. The launch of these two new drugs had wide media coverage. The reason, however, was not their therapeutic power. It was their price. A three-month treatment costs $84,000 (exactly $1,000 a pill) for Sovaldi and $94,500 for Harvoni.[44]

Sovaldi and Harvoni are not isolated cases. The price of 'specialty' drugs – which treat complex chronic conditions such as cancer, HIV or inflammatory disease – has skyrocketed in recent years, fuelling a heated debate about why prices are so high and whether they are justified. Anti-cancer drugs that only add a few months to patients' life expectancy cost hundreds of dollars a day. The case of Sovaldi drew the attention of the US Congress: two members of the Senate Finance Committee, including the then Chairman Ron Wyden, sent a letter to Gilead expressing concern and demanding a detailed account of how the price of Sovaldi had been determined.[45] It was a good question to ask. Prices of specialty drugs are completely unrelated to manufacturing costs. For example, researchers have put the manufacturing

cost of a twelve-week course of Sovaldi at between $68 and $136.[46]
So how does the pharmaceutical industry justify charging prices that
are hundreds of times higher than production costs?

Patient Health and Impatient Profits

The standard defence by pharmaceutical companies used to be that
these high prices are necessary to cover the R&D costs of developing
new drugs and of compensating for the risks associated with both
the research and the clinical trials. But public opinion is increasingly
sceptical about this argument, and for good reason: research has dis-
proved it.[47]

First, basic research expenditure by pharmaceutical companies is
very small compared to the profits they make.[48] It is also much less
than what they spend on marketing,[49] and often less than what they
spend on share buy-backs aimed at boosting short-term stock prices,
stock options and executive pay.[50]

Second, the research leading to real pharmaceutical innovation,[51]
broadly defined as new molecular entities, has come mostly from
publicly funded laboratories.[52] The pharmaceutical industry has
increasingly concentrated its R&D spending on the much less risky
development phase and on 'me too drugs' – slight variations on existing products.

For example, NIH and the US Veterans Administration funded
the research leading to the main compound in both Sovaldi and
Harvoni – from early-stage science even into later-stage clinical
trials. Private investors spent no more (and perhaps much less) than
$300 million in R&D outlays for Sovaldi and Harvoni over the course
of a decade.[53] If we consider that in the first six months of 2015 the
two drugs combined produced around $9.4 billion in sales (and $45
billion in the first three years since launch from 2014 to 2016) it is
clear that their price bears no relation to R&D costs.[54]

So, unsurprisingly, pharmaceutical companies are turning to a different line of defence. They argue that these prices are proportionate
to the intrinsic 'value' of the drugs. 'Price is the wrong discussion,'
declared Gilead's Executive Vice-President Gregg Alton, responding
to criticism over the price of Sovaldi: 'value should be the subject.'[55]

John LaMattina, former Vice-President of Pfizer and a leading figure in the pharmaceutical industry, was even more explicit. In a 2014 piece published in *Forbes* under the title 'Politicians shouldn't question drug costs but rather their value', he argued that:

> in the mind of patients, physicians, and payers, the pricing of drugs should have little to do with the expense of biomedical R&D, nor should it be associated with recouping R&D investment. Pricing should be based on only one thing – the value that the drug brings to healthcare in terms of:
>
> 1) saving lives;
> 2) mitigating pain/suffering and improving the quality of life of patients;
> 3) reducing overall healthcare costs.

Interestingly, LaMattina was also explicit that value-based pricing is meant to justify charging prices that are completely out of line with production costs and R&D expenses. Commenting on the world's most expensive drug, Alexion's Soliris, which is used to treat a rare form of anemia and also a rare kidney disorder, Mattina noted that the price (Alexion charges $440,000/year per patient) 'is really not related to the R&D costs needed to bring this drug to the market'. Yet, he continued:

> private insurers and national health agencies in Europe willingly pay for this drug. Why? Because the costs of caring for patients with these conditions can run into millions each year. Soliris, even at this high price, actually saves the healthcare system money because using it results in dramatic decreases in other healthcare system expenses generated by these patients.[56]

The high price of specialty drugs – the argument goes – is justified by how beneficial they are for patients and for society in general. In practice, this means relating the price of a drug to the costs that the disease would cause to society if not treated, or if treated with the second-best therapy. So we read, in a 'fact sheet' prepared by the US industry trade body PhRMA to justify high prices, that 'every additional dollar spent on medicines for adherent patients with congestive heart failure, high blood pressure, diabetes and high cholesterol generated $3 to $10 in savings on emergency room visits and in patient hospitalizations', that 'a 10 per cent decrease in the cancer death rate is worth roughly $4.4 trillion in economic value to current and future generations' and that 'research and medicines from the biopharmaceutical sector are the only chance for survival for patients and their families'.[57] While these claims may be true, it is striking that they are used as an explanation (or justification) for high drug prices.

Critics have replied that there is in fact no discernible link between specialty drug prices and the medical benefits they provide. They have some evidence on their side. Case studies have shown no correlation between the price of cancer drugs and their benefits.[58] One 2015 study, based on a sample of fifty-eight anti-cancer drugs approved in the US between 1995 and 2013, illustrates that their survival benefits for patients do not explain their mounting cost. Dr Peter Bach, a renowned oncologist, put online an interactive calculator with which you can establish the 'correct' price of a cancer drug on the basis of its valuable characteristics – increase in life expectancy, side effects and so on. The calculator shows that the value-based price of most drugs is lower than their market price.[59]

Unfortunately, however, most of the pharmaceutical industry's critics fight its arguments on the field big pharma has chosen. In other words, they implicitly accept the idea that prices should be linked to some intrinsic value of a drug, measured by the monetary value of the benefits – or avoided costs – to patients and society. This is not as odd as it might sound.

The idea of value-based pricing was initially developed by scholars and policymakers to *counteract* rising drug prices and to allocate public healthcare budgets more rationally. In the UK, for example, the National Institute for Health and Care Excellence (NICE) calculates the value of drugs in terms of the number of quality-adjusted life years (QALY) that each class of patients receives. One QALY is a year of perfect health; if health is less than perfect, QALYs accrue at less than one a year. Cost-effectiveness is assessed by calculating how much per QALY a drug or treatment costs. Generally, NICE considers a pharmaceutical product cost-effective if it costs less than £20,000–£30,000 per QALY provided. A price-based assessment of this sort is powerful: NICE advises the UK National Health Service (NHS) on its choice of drugs.

A cost-effectiveness analysis like the one NICE conducts makes sense for allocating a national healthcare system's finite budget. In the US, where there is no cost-effectiveness analysis and the national insurance system is forbidden by law from bargaining with drug companies, drug prices are much higher than in the UK and are increasing more rapidly. The outcome is that, measured by a yardstick such as QALY, specialty drug prices in the US are not related to the medical benefits they provide.

Basic mainstream analysis of elasticity of demand (that is, how sensitive consumers are to changes in prices, depending on the characteristics of goods) is sufficient to explain the very high prices of specialty drugs, which makes pharma's vague and rhetorical arguments about value all the more unconvincing. Specialty drugs like Sovaldi and Harvoni are covered by patents, so their producers are monopolists and competition does not constrain the prices they set. Normally, however, you would expect the elasticity of demand to be a constraint: the higher the price, the lower the demand for the monopolist's product. But the elasticity of demand for specialty drugs is of course very low: peoples' lives are at stake. They need these drugs to have some chance of surviving, and medical insurers, whether public or private, are under an obligation to pay for them.

The logical outcome of a combination of monopoly and rigid demand is sky-high prices, and this is precisely what is happening with specialty drugs. It explains why pharmaceutical companies enjoy absurdly high profit margins: in addition to the normal profit rate, they earn huge monopoly rents.[60] A value-based assessment of the kind NICE carries out can be helpful because it reduces demand for the monopolists' drugs and prevents them from charging whatever price they choose. The downside, however, is that increased elasticity of demand for drugs comes at the cost of leaving some patients without the medicines they need, because pharmaceutical companies may not cut their prices enough to treat everyone who needs the drug if doing so would reduce profit margins by more than the companies want. This is already happening in the UK, where

NICE has rejected some cancer drugs for use in the NHS because of their price. It is also happening in the US, where some private and public insurers refused to provide Harvoni to insured patients until they reached a very advanced stage of the disease.

What is not being pointed out, however, is that the principle that a specialty drug's price should equal the costs it saves society is fundamentally flawed. If we took such a principle seriously, basic therapies or vaccines should cost a fortune. For that matter, how high should the price of water be, given its indispensable value to society?

The con around drug pricing has created a constant battle between government-funded healthcare systems (where they exist), private and public insurance programmes, and the big pharmaceutical firms. Only by debunking the ideas about value underpinning these drugs can a long-lasting solution be found which results in access to genuinely affordable drugs.

NETWORK EFFECTS AND FIRST-MOVER ADVANTAGES

I have looked at how innovation, something inherently uncertain and cumulative, is financed, and at the dynamics of that finance. We have also explored how the risks and rewards of innovation have been shared problematically, with medical drugs being the most severe case in point. Now, I want to look at another aspect of innovation: the effect of modern digital networks on the ability of a few firms to achieve monopolies in their markets.

In just a few years, firms such as Google, Facebook, Twitter, Amazon and eBay have come from nowhere to being almost indispensable in the lives of billions of people around the world. These companies increasingly dominate how we find information, connect and communicate, maintain our friendships, document our lives, shop and share our thoughts with anyone who cares to listen. The new technologies behind these companies have revealed – or created – in us new wants and needs. Any number of firms, each with broadly similar technologies, might have met these needs. Many have tried. But what is interesting is how quickly and how comprehensively such a small number of firms have come to dominate. And with this dominance comes the ability to extract value on a massive scale.

How has this happened? The answer lies in the characteristics of innovation, where small differences of timing, foresight or chance can have consequences out of all proportion to the initial disparity. Anyone who gains an initial advantage – in setting a standard or capturing part of a 'sticky' market – can be very hard to displace. And as their dominance becomes entrenched, they are able to capture a disproportionate share of the value in the market.

The history of many innovations demonstrates these dynamics very well. The internal combustion engine has retained its dominance for over a hundred years, not because it is the best possible engine, but because through historical accident it gained an initial advantage. Subsequent innovations did not seek to supplant it, but clustered around improvements to it, so that it *became* post factum the best engine.[61] The same goes for the QWERTY keyboard layout, named for the first six letters on the top from left to right. In the days of mechanical typewriters, the very inefficiency of this keyboard layout gave it an advantage over alternatives such as the faster DVORAK layout because the mechanical keys would jam less frequently. The mechanical necessity for the QWERTY layout has long passed in these days of electronic keyboards, but its advantage has remained. Once people learned how to type using the QWERTY layout they resisted change. This social inertia meant its arbitrary initial advantage got locked in.

Such examples show the potential for dynamic increasing returns to scale (the more subscribers the better), from innovation due to path dependency (continuing to use a practice or product because of past preference for it) or social inertia, even when the initial advantage may be slight or arbitrary. Another example of the phenomenon are so-called 'network externalities'. Just as the value of a telephone increases as the number of people its owner can connect to rises, so a social network becomes more valuable to its owner if more people join. Facebook or Twitter do all they can to increase the number of subscribers: the bigger the network, the stronger the company's position.

Networking Profits

All this sounds fine until you ask yourself what it might mean for the size of companies. A strong source of increasing returns to scale necessarily expands companies. Google's size is a direct result of the network effects typical of Internet-based services. Google is not just a search engine. It is also an email address (Gmail), a conference call maker (Google Hangout), a document creator and editor – all designed to maximize the advantages of sticking to Google: you cannot use Google Hangout without a Gmail address.

What's the problem? Giant online firms like Facebook, Amazon and Google are often portrayed by their managers and by their apologists as 'forces for good' and for the progress of society rather than as profit-oriented businesses.[62] Excited advocates have talked of a rising and revolutionary 'sharing economy', or even of 'digital socialism',[63] advancing a rosy view according to which digital platforms 'empower' people, giving us free access to a wide range of services, from social networking to GPS positioning and health-monitoring. Silicon Valley is starkly and favourably contrasted with Wall Street. The Valley bridges the consumption gap by providing services that everyone can access, almost independently of their income; the Street intensifies the concentration of power and wealth in the hands of the 1 per cent.[64]

Of course the Internet giants are valuable to their users, sometimes greatly so. They can add to people's well-being and in some cases increase their productivity, for instance by making it easier and faster to find some web content, route, person or book. But the view that these services are offered to everyone for free out of Silicon Valley's goodwill, with the aim of 'empowering' people and creating a more open world, is exceedingly naïve. A more realistic analysis should start from a grasp of how these firms work and where their profits come from, with an eye to assessing their overall social impact in terms of value creation and value extraction.

Firms like Google, Facebook and Amazon – and new 'sharing-economy' firms like Airbnb and Uber – like to define themselves as 'platforms'. They don't face a traditional market, in which the firm produces a good or service and sells it to a population of potential consumers. They operate, instead, in what economists call two-sided markets, developing the supply and demand sides of the market as the lynchpin, connector or gatekeeper between them. On the one side, there is a service offering to users. On the other side, there is a market offering to other firms – from sales to advertising space to information on users' behaviour. Firms have long operated in more than one market. The peculiarity of two-sided markets, however, lies in how the two sides are connected. As the number of users on one side of the market (using a search engine or joining a social network) rises, clicks on ads and information on consumers' behaviour also increases, boosting profitability in the other side of the market. It suits Google and Facebook to charge their users nothing: they need as many people as possible to join to make the product they sell to firms on the other side of the market more attractive. 'Socialism', digital or otherwise, doesn't come into it.

We should not see Google, for example, as providing services for free to its users. Rather, it is users who provide Google with necessary inputs for its production process: their looks on ads and, most importantly, their personal data. In return, they obtain online searches and other services. The bulk of Google's profits come from selling advertising space and users' data to firms. If something is free online, you are not the customer, you are the product.[65] Facebook's and Google's business models are built on the commodification of personal data, transforming through the alchemy of a two-sided market our friendships, interests, beliefs and preferences into sellable propositions. The so-called 'sharing economy' is based on the same idea. For all the hype about 'sharing', it is less about altruism and more about allowing market exchange to reach into areas of our lives – our homes, our vehicles, even our private relationships – that were previously beyond its scope and to commodify them.[66] As Evgeny Morozov has warned, it risks turning us all into 'perpetual hustlers',[67] with all of our lives up for sale, while at the same time undermining the basis for stable employment and a good standard of living.

Standing on Platform Capitalism

'Platform capitalism' is often referred to as the new way in which goods and services are produced, shared and delivered – more horizontally, with consumers interacting with each other, and less intermediation by old institutions (e.g. travel agents). The so-called sharing economy, based on this framework, works by reducing the frictions between the two sides of the market: connecting buyers to sellers, potential customers to advertisers, in more efficient ways. It is presented as a radical transformation in the way that goods and services are produced, shared and delivered. It adds value by taking what was previously peripheral to the service – in Uber's case, ordering, selecting, tracking and paying for a cab – into its core. But when disabled users have complained to Uber about their drivers refusing to put wheelchairs in the boot of the car, Uber has sought to evade responsibility on the basis that it is not a taxi company, merely a platform.[68] Likewise, there is increasing evidence that Airbnb is similarly reluctant to take responsibility for such matters as the safety of premises offered on its site or racial discrimination against renters by property owners.

Furthermore, Uber's pursuit of economies of scale (based on the size of the network) and economies of scope (based on the breadth of different services, including UberEats) has led to higher profits on the backs of the key contributors to value creation for the company: the drivers. Indeed, while costs have been falling for the consumer, they have been rising for the drivers: in 2012 Uber Black (one of the company's car services) cost riders in San Francisco $4.90 per mile or $1.25 per minute. When, in 2016, charges fell to $3.75 per mile or $0.65 per minute, consumers gained. But the result of this sharing economy is that Uber Black drivers are paid less, 'standards' rise (with pressure for drivers to offer 'pool' services to customers) and competition from Uber's other services intensifies.[69] While drivers are increasingly complaining, Uber's market reach is higher than ever and growing every day: as of October 2016 it had 40 million monthly riders worldwide.[70] In 2016 it had 160,000 drivers in the US, with millions more spread across 500 cities globally – all working as 'independent contractors', so that Uber does not have to provide them with the kind of healthcare and other benefits which they would receive as full-time employees.

Uber, like Google, Facebook and Amazon, seems to have no limit to its size. The network effects that pervade online markets add an

THE VALUE OF EVERYTHING

important peculiarity: once a firm establishes leadership in a market its dominance increases and becomes self-perpetuating almost automatically. If everyone is on Facebook, no one wants to join a different social network. As most people search on Google, the gap between Google and its competitors grows wider because it can elaborate on more data. And as its market share rises, so does its capacity to attract users, which in turn increases its market dominance.[71]

Contrary to the pious pronouncements of Internet pioneers, network effects are increasingly centralizing the Internet, thereby placing an enormous concentration of market power in the hands of a few firms. Google alone accounts for 70 per cent of online searches in the US, and 90 per cent in Europe. Facebook has more than 1.5 billion users, a quarter of the planet's population and streets ahead of its competitors. Amazon now accounts for around half of the US books market, not to mention e-books. Six firms (Facebook, Google, Yahoo, AOL, Twitter and Amazon) account for around 53 per cent of the digital advertising market (with just Google and Facebook making up 39 per cent).[72] Such dominance implies that online giants can impose their conditions on users and customer firms. Many book publishers, for example, are unhappy with the conditions Amazon insists upon and are asking for better ones. But they have no leverage at all, because – as Evgeny Morozov puts it – 'there is no second Amazon they can turn to'.[73] The powerful network effects in the two-sided market have entrenched these companies' position. Companies like Google are de facto monopolies.[74] But they are not recognized as such and have not attracted the kind of anti-trust legislation that large companies in more traditional industries – tobacco, autos, food – have done.

The dominant position of a platform provider in core markets can then be used to favour their products and services in satellite markets, further extending the company's reach. The European Commission is investigating Google precisely because it is alleged systematically to tilt its search results in favour of its own products. By the same token, many users are not happy about Facebook appropriating, storing, analysing and selling to third parties so much of their personal data. But as long as all their friends are on Facebook, there is no equivalent competitor they can turn to. The standard defence of companies such as Facebook that 'competition is just one click away' is simply false in markets where network effects are so important.

A recent study by researchers at the University of Pennsylvania surveyed 1,500 American Internet users to understand why they agree to give up some privacy in return for access to Internet services and applications. The standard explanation is that consumers compare the cost of losing some privacy with the benefit of accessing these services for free, and accept the deal when benefits exceed costs. A competing explanation is that many users are simply unaware of the extent to which online companies invade their privacy. But, interestingly, the results of the Pennsylvania survey are inconsistent with both explanations. Instead, they suggest that consumers accept being tracked and surrendering their personal data, even if ideally they would prefer not to, not because they have happily embraced this quid pro quo, but out of resignation and frustration.

It is understandable that people feel they have no choice. In today's society, it is hard to live and work without using a well-functioning search engine, a crowded social network and a well-supplied online shopping platform. But the price of accessing these services is to accept the conditions the dominant provider imposes on a 'take it or leave it' basis, given that there are no comparable alternatives.

CREATING AND EXTRACTING DIGITAL VALUE

The digital giants' enormous market power raises critical issues about privacy protection, social control and political power. But what concerns us here is the impact of this market power on the relationship between value creation and value extraction.

The particular dynamics of innovation – the power of early adoption of standards and associated network effects tending towards market dominance – have profound consequences for how the value created is shared and measured.

The first major consequence is monopoly. Historically, industries naturally prone to being monopolies, for example railways and water, have been either taken into public ownership (e.g. in Europe) or heavily regulated (e.g. in the US) to protect the public against abuses of corporate power. But monopolistic online platforms remain privately owned and largely unregulated despite all the issues they raise: privacy, control of information and their sheer commercial power in the market, to name a few. In the absence of strong, transnational, countervailing regulatory forces, firms that first establish market control can reap extraordinary rewards. The low rates of tax that technology companies are typically paying on these rewards are also paradoxical, given that their success was built on technologies funded and developed by high-risk public investments.[75] If anything, companies owing their fortunes to taxpayer investment should be repaying the taxpayer, not seeking tax breaks. Moreover, the rise of the 'sharing economy' is likely to extend market exchange into new areas, where the dynamics of market dominance look set to repeat themselves.

The second major consequence of the dynamics of innovation is about how value is created, how this is measured, and how and by whom this value is extracted. If we go by national accounts, the contribution of Internet platforms to national income (as measured for example by GDP) is represented by the advertisement-related services they sell to firms. It is not very clear why advertisements should contribute to the real national product, let alone social well-being, which should be the aim of economic activity. But national accounts, in this respect, are consistent with standard neoclassical economics, which tends to interpret any voluntary market-based transaction as signalling the production of some kind of output – whether financial services or advertising, as long as a price is received, it must be valuable.[76] That is misleading: if online giants contribute to social well-being, they do it through the services they provide to users, not through the accompanying advertisements.

The classical economists' approach appears much more fruitful for analysing these new digital markets. As discussed in Chapter 1, they distinguished between 'productive' labour, which contributes to an increase in the value of what is produced, and 'unproductive' labour, which does not. The activities which make profits for online platforms – advertising and analyses of users' private information and behaviour – do not increase the value of what is produced, which is services to users such as posting a message on Facebook or making a search on Google. Rather, these activities help firms competing against one another to appropriate, individually, a larger share of the value produced.[77] The confused and misleading approach to the concept of value that is currently dominating economics is generating a truly paradoxical result: unproductive advertising activities are counted as a net contribution of online giants to national income, while the more valuable services that they provide to users are not.

The rise of big data is often talked about as a win-win opportunity for both producers and consumers. But this depends on who owns the data and how it is 'governed'. The fact that IPR has become wider and stronger, and more upstream, is due to the way it is governed – or not. Markets of any type must be actively shaped in order for knowledge to be governed in ways that produce the market outcomes that we as a society want. Indeed, regulation is not about interference, as is commonly perceived, but about managing a process that produces the results that are best for society as a whole. In the case of big data, the 'big five' – Facebook, Google, Amazon, IBM and Microsoft – virtually monopolize it. But the problem is not just a question of competition – the size and number of firms in the sector. It could be argued that a few large companies can achieve the economies of scale required to drive down costs and make data cheaper – not a bad thing given falling real incomes.

The key issue is the relationship between the Internet monopolies and these falling incomes. The privatization of data to serve corporate profits rather than the common good produces a new form of inequality – the skewed access to the profits generated from big data. Merely lowering the price monopolists charge for access to data is not the solution. The infrastructure that companies like Amazon rely on is not only publicly financed (as discussed, the Internet was paid for by tax dollars), but it feeds off network effects which are collectively produced. While it is of course OK for companies to create services around new forms of data, the critical issue is how to ensure that the ownership and management of the data remains as collective as its source: the public. As Morozov argues, 'Instead of us paying Amazon a fee to use its AI capabilities – built with our data – Amazon should be required to pay that fee to us.'[78]

SHARING RISKS AND REWARDS

Acknowledging the collective nature of innovation should result in more sharing of the rewards that accrue from the process of innovation. And yet ignoring the collective story, and only giving credit to a narrow group of individuals, has affected thinking about who should own IPR, how high a medicine's price can acceptably be, who should or should not retain equity in a new firm or a new technological advance, and the fair share of tax contributions. It is this gap between the collective distribution of risk-taking in innovation and the more individualized, privatized way in which the returns are distributed that is the most modern form of rent.

Current stories about value, wealth creation and risk-taking that privilege the contribution of individual inventors and capitalists lead to ways of thinking whereby it is acceptable to divide up the fruits of innovation between them – the concept of 'just deserts'. The term comes from the English philosopher John Locke (1632–1704). His concept of individual entitlement – 'just deserts' – to the product of work was based on a production system where individual labour was more important, and was easier to identify, than it is today when collective contributions have been central to technology-driven growth. This point was made by Herbert Simon (1916–2001), who made his name in the study of organizational decision-making, and who won the Nobel Prize in Economics in 1978. 'If we are generous with ourselves,' Simon considered, 'I suppose that we might claim that we "earned" as much as one-fifth of our income. The rest of the patrimony [is] associated with being a member of an enormously productive social system, which has accumulated a vast store of physical capital, and an even larger store of intellectual capital – including knowledge, skills, and organizational know-how held by all of us.'[79] Ignoring this collectively produced social system, certain individuals feel justified in earning a much higher proportion of a nation's income than their own contribution warrants. But, more specifically, it has affected policies on taxes, patents and prices, thus fuelling the dynamics of inequality.

The question is: what can we do about it?

Policymaking should start from understanding that innovation is a collective process. Given the immense risks the taxpayer takes when the government invests in visionary new areas like the Internet, couldn't we construct ways for rewards from innovation to be just as social as the risks taken? These ways might include: capping prices of publicly developed medicines; attaching conditions to public support, such as the requirement that profits be reinvested back into production rather than spent on speculative share buy-backs; allowing public agencies to retain equity or royalties in technologies for which they provided downstream funding; or by making income-contingent loans to businesses as we do for students.

As is the nature of early-stage investment in technologies with uncertain prospects, some investments are winners, but many are losers. For every Internet (a success story of US government financing), there are many Concordes (a white elephant funded by the British and French governments). Consider the twin tales of Solyndra and Tesla Motors. In 2009, Solyndra, a solar-power-panel start-up, received a $535 million guaranteed loan from the US Department of Energy; that same year, Tesla, the electric-car manufacturer, got approval for a similar loan, of $465 million. In the years afterwards, Tesla was wildly successful, and the firm repaid its loan in 2013. Solyndra, by contrast, filed for bankruptcy in 2011, and among fiscal conservatives became a byword for the government's sorry track record when it comes to picking winners. Of course, if the government is to act like a venture capitalist, it will necessarily encounter many failures. The problem, however, is that governments, unlike venture capital firms, are often saddled with the costs of the failures while earning next to nothing from the successes. Taxpayers footed the bill for Solyndra's losses – yet got hardly any of Tesla's profits. Strangely, the US government had put in a claim for 3 million shares into Tesla only if it did not pay back the loan – almost as if the US government has an interest in owning a part of failed companies! Tesla did pay back the loan in 2013, and so had the US government taken a stake in Tesla as a success rather than as a failure, it would have been able to more than cover its losses from Solyndra. The year Tesla received its government loan, the company went public at an opening price of $17 a share; that figure had risen to $93 by the time the loan was repaid, and doubled soon after.

In the case of prices of drugs, instead of focusing on the debatable and arbitrary quantification of 'what it would cost society not to treat', we should try to understand the production side of the pharmaceutical industry and its interdependencies with related industries such as the biochemical industry and the medical devices industry. We could engineer prices to ensure continuous production of drugs that are actually needed (reducing the amount of 'me too' drugs which have little extra benefit); supply the drugs to whomever needs them; and maintain a steady and well-targeted flow of R&D to develop new drugs. A system of this kind does not necessarily need drug prices to be above manufacturing costs. We could, for example, abolish patents on pharmaceutical products and at the same time establish a competitive prize system to reward and incentivize public and private entities to come up with well-targeted pharmaceutical innovation. If we make more use of generic drugs – drugs which are the same medically as branded ones – we can make then widely available and push pharmaceutical companies to concentrate on breakthrough innovations rather than on producing 'me too' drugs or running share repurchasing programmes to boost their stock prices.

Policymakers should have a clear understanding of who the different actors in the process are in order to prevent free-riding on publicly funded innovation and a 'winner-takes-all' outcome. Rather than creating myths about actors in the innovation economy such as venture capitalists, it is important to recognize the stages at which each of these actors is important. Tax policy could be changed to encourage truly dynamic links between the different participants in innovation, for example by bringing the rewards and tax breaks that venture capitalists enjoy more into line with the risks they actually take compared with other stakeholders. Understanding that the state's role is to do what the business sector is not willing to do – engage in high-risk early-stage development and fundamental research – also means that particular policies such as R&D tax credits must be devised so that the subsidy encourages investment in needed innovations over and above random potentially profitable ones.

Treatment of employees is also very important here. When, typically in the name of maximizing shareholder value, a successful company fires experienced employees, it is quite probable that the unlucky victims committed their time to the enterprise in the expectation of sharing in the returns if and when it succeeded. They are now cut off from the rewards that they deserve, while others such as venture capitalists who came in at a later stage receive a disproportionately large share of the rewards. Employees' contribution to the enterprise deserves to be better protected.

Deals are being developed in European capitals, such as Berlin and Paris, to place limits or conditions on the operations of companies like Airbnb, Uber and Netflix.[80] Patent pools can be set up that guarantee the use of patents for common goals. Government can earn equity stakes or royalties when investing in high-risk areas, whether in products or technologies. Prices of products that have received public support can be negotiated to reflect the public contribution. Big data can be governed so that it reflects the public data and publicly funded infrastructure upon which it rests. This means that we must not hype up technological advances, but recognize the collective contribution that created them, and govern them so that they produce a public good.

CONCLUSION

Economic growth without innovation is hard to imagine. But innovation must be properly governed to make sure that what is produced and how it is produced leads to value creation and not gimmicks for value appropriation. This means paying attention both to the rate and direction of innovation (what is produced), and to the deals that are struck between the different creators of that new value.

First, it is crucial to understand that innovation is not a neutral concept. It can be used for different purposes – in the same way a hammer can be used to build a house or as a weapon. The big data revolution itself can go either way. It can become a way for public data (on health, on energy use, on shopping preferences) to serve private profits, or it can be used to improve the services that consumers and citizens receive. Citizenship should in the process not be confused with being a client. As citizens, we have rights to enjoy the opportunities that innovation presents us with, to make use of public space, to be able to contest authority, and to share experiences and tastes without our stories and preferences ending up on a website or a database. In this sense movements for 'inclusive' innovation are important in how they focus on who is involved in envisioning change and benefiting from it.

Second, innovation has both a rate and a direction. A democratic debate about the direction is just as important as those that occur about the rate of growth – and key to understanding the multiple pathways that innovation may take, and how policy affects this. The assumption is that policy should be about 'levelling the playing field'. But achieving innovation-led growth and innovation of a particular type (e.g. green innovation) will require not levelling but tilting the playing field. And furthermore, this requires not only a different policy mindset but also a different organizational structure: the ability to explore, experiment and strategically deliberate inside the public sector. It was this capacity that was central to the organizations that fostered some of the most radical innovations of our age, from the Internet to GPS to fracking. More discussion is needed on how to use mission-oriented innovation to battle societal and technological grand challenges – like climate change or social care.[81] Just as the IT revolution was chosen and directed, we can choose and direct green and care as the new paths for innovation. This does not mean top-down dictation of what should be produced, and which actors are 'productive' and how each must behave. Rather, it requires new types of contracts between public and private actors (as well as the third sector and civil society) in order to foster symbiotic relationships, sharing the kinds of investments that will be needed to redirect economies away from high material content and energy based on fossil fuels. There are lessons from 'mission-oriented' investments such as going to the moon. Making sure our earth remains habitable demands the same ambition, organization, planning, bottom-up experimentation, public-private risk-sharing and sense of purpose and urgency as the Apollo project.[82] But it is also true that because these investments are transformational, more debate should also be had on why it is that some technologies are pursued, and what is done with them. It is curious, for example, that there was so little debate about fracking – which was government-financed – until after its arrival.

Third, as argued in the previous section, innovation is produced collectively, and hence the benefits should be shared collectively. The deeply flawed reasoning behind pharma prices, patents and the dynamics of big data is a good example of how a confused and misleading approach to the concept of value can be costly, allowing large monopolies to get away with huge rents at the expense of society. But it need not be this way if we think radically.

Patents themselves should not be seen as 'rights' (IPR), but rather as a tool with which to incentivize innovation in the sectors where they are relevant – but in such a way that the public sector also gets its return; drug prices could become 'fairer', reflecting the collective contribution of different actors and making a healthcare system sustainable. The sharing economy would not be based on the ability of a few companies to use public infrastructure for free and the dynamics of network economies to monopolize a market. A true sharing economy must by definition respect the hard-won gains of all workers, irrespective of race, gender or ability. The eight-hour day, the weekend and holiday and sick pay fought for by workers' movements and trade unions were no less important economic innovations than antibiotics, the microchip and the Internet.

In an era in which profits are being hoarded at record levels, it's important to understand what led to the agreements whereby business reinvested profits instead of hoarding them. And the answer is confident and capable government, which has built up its own capacity to invest in technological opportunities and, just as important, to negotiate the landscape that they create. Monopolies like patents are contracts which must be negotiated. One party (business) receives protection of its profits, the other party (government) receives benefits for the public, whether through lower costs and prices (by economies of scale), diffusion of innovation (by the way patents disclose information), or through reinvestment of the profits in specific areas considered beneficial for growth – in this case, innovation.

Developing countries are used to such deals over foreign investment: you come and make use of our resources as long as you reinvest profits locally to benefit us. But negotiation of this sort is largely absent from modern Western capitalism. Just as governments have allowed companies to use patents for unproductive rather than productive entrepreneurship, they have also allowed companies to stop reinvesting profits. That would be fine (perhaps) if those profits were generated from their own activity, independent of public funds. But, as I have argued throughout this chapter, the technology and the underlying networks have been produced collectively. They should therefore be negotiated collectively.

A key issue behind all these considerations is government's contribution to economic growth – public value. Why, historically, have no economists referred to it? And, more importantly, why have governments now lost their confidence in fighting for public value, while previously they limited the scope of patents or put pressure on monopolies to reinvest profits? We will turn to these matters in the next chapter.

8

Undervaluing the Public Sector

> *The important thing for Government is not to do things which individuals are doing already, and to do them a little better or a little worse; but to do those things which at present are not done at all.*
>
> John M. Keynes, *The End of Laissez-Faire* (1926)[1]

The January 2010 edition of *The Economist* was devoted to the dangers of big government. A large picture of a monster adorned the magazine's cover. The editorial opined: 'The rich world has a clear choice: learn from the mistakes of the past, or else watch Leviathan grow into a true monster.' In a more recent issue, dedicated to future technological revolutions, the magazine was explicit that government should stick to setting the rules of the game: invest in basic goods like education and infrastructure, but then get out of the way so that revolutionary businesses can do their thing.[2]

This, of course, is hardly a novel view. Throughout the history of economic thought, government has long been seen as necessary but unproductive, a spender and regulator, rather than a value creator.

Previous chapters revealed how actors in both the financial sector and Silicon Valley have been particularly vociferous in their self-aggrandized claims about wealth creation, using these claims to lobby for favourable treatment that has in turn enabled them to reap rewards disproportionate to the value they actually created. By the same token, others have widely but mistakenly been regarded as 'unproductive'.

As we have seen, finance has, ultimately, been less productive than

it claims to be. In this chapter I want to look at government, an actor that has done more than it has been given credit for, and whose ability to produce value has been seriously underestimated – and this has in effect enabled others to have a stronger claim on their wealth creation role. But it is hard to make the pitch for government when the term 'public value' doesn't even currently exist in economics. It is assumed that value is created in the private sector; at best, the public sector 'enables' value.

The concept of 'public value' has existed for millennia, debated in philosophy and society at least from the time of Aristotle's *Nicomachean Ethics*. It is, however, a Cinderella subject as far as the study of economics is concerned. There is of course the important concept of 'public goods' in economics – goods whose production benefits everyone, and which hence require public provision since they are under-produced by the private sector – but, as we shall see, the concept has also been used to hinder government activity (restricting specific areas in which it is OK for the public sector to tread) rather than help government think creatively about how it produces value in the economy.

The narrative that government is inefficient and its optimum role should be 'limited' to avoid disrupting the market is extremely powerful. At best, the story goes, government should simply focus on creating the conditions that allow businesses to invest and on maintaining the fundamentals for a prosperous economy: the protection of private property, investment in infrastructure, the rule of law, an efficient patenting system. After that, it must get out of the way. Know its place. Not interfere too much. Not regulate too much. Importantly, we are told, government does not 'create value'; it simply 'facilitates' its creation and – if allowed – redistributes value through taxation. Such ideas are carefully crafted, eloquently expressed and persuasive. They have resulted in the view that pervades society today: government is a drain on the energy of the market, an ever-present threat to the dynamism of the private sector.

But there is one area of mainstream economic theory which recognizes – indeed, emphasizes – where governments can play a positive role: fixing 'market failures'. As discussed, market failures arise when the private sector does not invest enough in an area considered good for the public benefit (e.g. basic research, as it's so hard to make profits from this output) or invests too much in areas considered bad for public benefit (e.g. polluting industries, creating a negative externality not embodied in company costs). A government subsidy may be placed on the good and a tax on the bad. But the current message to government is: intervene only if there is a problem, otherwise sit back, focus on getting the 'conditions' right for business and let the business sector do its thing, which is to create value.

But while this is the accepted view of government's role, a brief glance at the history of capitalism reveals some other powerful, if less simplistic, stories about government's place in the economy. In the middle of the Second World War Karl Polanyi, a radical Austro-Hungarian thinker who combined the reasoning of political economy with a deep understanding of anthropology, history and philosophy, wrote a very important book: *The Great Transformation*. In it, he argued that markets were far from 'natural' or inevitable – rather, they resulted from purposeful policymaking: 'The road to the free market was opened and kept open by an enormous increase in continuous, centrally organized and controlled interventionism . . .

Administrators had to be constantly on the watch to ensure the free working of the system.'[3]

Polanyi traced the long history of local and international markets. In the process, he showed that the national capitalist market – the one studied in economics classes with supply and demand curves – was actually forced into existence by the state. Government, Polanyi asserted, does not 'distort' the market. Rather, it creates the market. Put bluntly: no state, no market. This is not a normative point – the government can of course invest in areas that are considered problematic, from wartime technologies to fracking technology, which some have argued strongly against. And it is precisely this potentially powerful role that should alert us all to better understand what taxpayers' money (or printed money) is being invested in.

As discussed in the previous chapter, government policy has been crucial to envisioning and funding key technologies such as the Internet, critical to Silicon Valley's success. In the process, government has given life to new markets that have sprung from these technologies (the dot.com economy).

This historical and institutional view of markets' relationship with government contrasts sharply with the current prevailing orthodoxy and is not to be found in mainstream economics. Here – to get technical for a moment – you only find government as a player in the macroeconomic models that look at the effect of regulation or the effect of a stimulus programme on GDP (through the multiplier which we discuss later in the chapter). But government is totally missing from what in microeconomics is known as the 'production function': the relationship between the quantity of outputs of a good and the quantity of inputs needed to make it, or, to put it simply, the analysis of how firms behave. And thus it is assumed that it is only in firms that value is created. Government is left outside the production boundary.

Some theories go further. Government, they argue, is innately corrupt and liable to 'capture' by vested interests. Because government is inherently unproductive, if we can restrict what it does we can reduce unproductive activities, thereby improving conditions for productive ones, steering economies towards growth. The logical conclusion is that government should be curbed, stripped back: perhaps by budget cuts, privatization of public assets, or outsourcing. In contemporary parlance, 'austerity'.

This chapter will argue that the prevailing view of government is wrong, that it is more the product of ideological bias than anything else. The stories told about government have undermined its confidence, limited the part it can play in shaping the economy, undervalued its contribution to national output, wrongly led to excessive privatization and outsourcing, ignored the case for the taxpayer sharing in the rewards of a collective – public – process of value creation, and enabled more value extraction. Yet these stories have become accepted as 'common sense' – always a term to be treated circumspectly. We have become accustomed to much talk about the pros and cons of austerity. The debate about government, though, should not be about its size or its budget. The real question is what value government creates – because to ask about the role of government in the economy is inevitably to question its intrinsic value. Is it productive or unproductive? How do we measure the value of government activities?

THE MYTHS OF AUSTERITY

After the 2008 financial crash – a crisis chiefly brought about by private, not public, debt – governments saved the capitalist system from breakdown. Not only did they pump money into the financial system: they took over private assets. A few months after Lehman Brothers collapsed, the US government was in charge of General Motors and Chrysler, the British government was running high street banks and, across the OECD, governments had committed the equivalent of 2.5 per cent of GDP to rescuing the system.

And yet, even though the crisis was caused by a combination of high private debt and reckless financial-sector behaviour, the extraordinary policy conclusion was that governments were to blame – despite the fact that, through bailouts and counter-cyclical stimulus, they had saved the financial system from crumbling. Instead of being seen as the heroes that stepped in to fix the mess created by private finance, they became the villains. Of course there had been failings on all sides – abnormal interest rates had contributed to the rise in debt – but the narrative became twisted out of all recognition. This distortion was enabled by a view held since the 1970s that somehow the public sector is less able to engineer growth than the private sector. What followed was a drive towards austerity across Europe. And tragically, instead of being allowed to invest their way back to pre-recessionary levels of output and employment, weaker European countries were repeatedly told by the 'troika' (the IMF, European Central Bank and European Commission) to cut public spending to the bone. Any country whose budget deficits rose beyond the level stipulated in the Maastricht Treaty were penalized severely, with conditions placed on bailouts that even the pro-austerity IMF later admitted were self-defeating.

In a nutshell, austerity assumes that public debt is bad for growth, and that the only way to reduce it is to cut government spending and debt by running a budget surplus, irrespective of the possible social cost. With debt down to an unspecified level and government finances 'sound', the private sector will be freed to reignite prosperity.

The politics of 'austerity' has framed the policies of successive UK Chancellors of the Exchequer and European finance ministers for almost a decade. In the US, from Newt Gingrich in the 1990s to the legally mandated spending cuts – sequestration – after the last financial crisis, Congress has threatened periodically to shut down the Federal government unless lower budget targets are met.

But this fixation on austerity to reduce debt misses a basic point: what matters is long-run growth, its source (what is being invested in), and its distribution (who reaps the rewards). If, through austerity, cuts are made to essential areas that create the capacity for future growth (education, infrastructure, care for a healthy population), then GDP (however ill defined) will not grow. Moreover, the irony is that just cutting the deficit may have little effect on the debt/GDP if the denominator of the ratio is being badly affected. And if the cuts cause more inequality – as the Institute for Fiscal Studies has shown was the case with the UK austerity measures of the last years – consumption can only grow through debt (e.g. credit cards), which maintains purchasing power. Instead, if public investment is made in areas like infrastructure, innovation, education and health, giving rise to healthy societies and creating opportunities for all, tax revenues will most likely rise and debt fall relative to GDP.

It is crucial to understand that economic policy is not scientifically ordained. You can impose austerity and hope the economy grows, even though such a policy deprives it of demand; or you can focus on investing in areas like health, training, education, research and infrastructure with the belief that these areas are critical for long-run growth in GDP. In the end, the choice of policy depends heavily on one's perspective on the role of government in the economy – is it key to creating value, or at best a cheerleader on the sidelines?

Magic Numbers

The current debate about austerity has avoided any mention of public value. Neither budget doves nor budget hawks have seriously questioned the theory of value that underpins much 'common-sense' understanding of market processes. A major reason for this lack of curiosity is that both camps seem to have been in thrall to the so-called 'magic' numbers which have framed the debate.

When, in 1992, European integration came into being through the Maastricht Treaty, there were various obligations that the signatory countries signed up to, one of which was to keep spending in check. Total public debt was to be limited to 60 per cent of GDP, with annual deficits (debt is the accumulation of deficits) not larger than 3 per cent of GDP. These numbers purport to set objective limits to government indebtedness. But where do they come from? You might imagine they are arrived at through some kind of scientific process – but if so, you'd be wrong. These numbers are taken out of thin air, supported by neither theory nor practice.

Let's start with debt. In 2010 the *American Economic Review* published an article by two top economists, professors at Harvard University: Carmen Reinhart, ranked the following year by the *Bloomberg Markets* magazine among the 'Most Influential 50 in Finance'; and Kenneth Rogoff, a former chief economist of the IMF.[4] In this piece the pair claimed that when the size of government debt (as a proportion of GDP) is over 90 per cent (much higher than the 60 per cent of the Maastricht Treaty, but still lower than that of many countries), economic growth falls. The results showed that rich countries whose public debt exceeded that percentage experienced a sharp drop in growth rate for the period 1946–2009. This was a very important finding, as so many countries' public debt levels are close to or exceed this percentage. According to IMF data the US debt/ GDP ratio stood at 64 per cent in 2007, and 105 per cent in 2014. For the UK the equivalent numbers were 44 per cent and 81 per cent; for the European Union 58 per cent and 88 per cent, and for the Eurozone 65 per cent and 94 per cent.

Aware that the argument clearly gave ammunition to advocates of the smaller state, the authors hastened to reassure their readers that they had no skin in the game: that their argument had no ideological foundation, but was based purely on empirical data. They even went so far as to stress that their research had no underlying theory of government: 'our approach here', they emphasized, 'is decidedly empirical'.[5]

Predictably enough, politicians and technocrats eager to 'balance' public spending seized on Reinhart and Rogoff's research, which proved highly influential in the post-2008 crisis debate about austerity measures. In his Federal Budget Plan for 2013, passed by the US House of Representatives, the Republican Congressman Paul Ryan cited the study as evidence for the negative impact of high government debt on economic growth. It also informed austerity policies proposed by then UK Chancellor George Osborne and the EU Economy Commissioner, Olli Rehn.

Also in 2013, as part of his PhD studies, Thomas Herndon, a twenty-eight-year-old student at the University of Massachusetts Amherst, tested Reinhart and Rogoff's data.[6] He couldn't replicate their results: his calculations showed no steep drop in growth rates when debt was high. Examining the professors' data sheet, Herndon found a simple spreadsheet error. He also discovered inconsistencies in the countries and data cited.[7] In two articles in the *New York Times*,[8] the professors defended their general results, but accepted the spreadsheet error. Magic numbers were not so magic after all.

Now on to the other magic number held so dear by EU economists: the number 3. The 'periphery' countries of the Eurozone have been urged to restore their competitiveness by downsizing the state. In line with the Maastricht criteria, bailouts for countries like Cyprus, Greece, Ireland and Portugal have been conditional on their cutting spending. If that spending goes above 3 per cent of GDP then bailouts are jeopardized. Between 2010 and 2017, Greece received €260 billion in bailout aid, in exchange for cutting state expenditure. However, since its problems were too structural to be solved by a simple 'austerity' measure, the cuts pitched it into a deep recession, turning into full-blown depression. And, rather than decreasing Greece's debt, the lack of growth has caused the debt/GDP ratio to rise to 179 per cent. The cure is killing the patient.

This obsessive focus on countries' deficits ignores a stark reality. Some of the weakest Eurozone countries have had lower deficits than the stronger countries – Germany, for instance. What matters is not the deficit but what government is doing with its funds. As long as these funds are invested productively in sectors like healthcare, education, research and others that increase productivity, then the debt/GDP denominator will rise, keeping the ratio in check.

Italy is another glaring example of how magic numbers don't work. For the last two decades Italy's budget deficit has been lower than Germany's, rarely exceeding the 3 per cent limit specified for euro membership. Indeed, Italy has been running a primary budget surplus since 1991, the only exception being 2009. And yet Italy has a high and rising debt/GDP ratio: 133 per cent in 2015,[9] way above the 60 per cent ceiling. The ratio is less affected by the numerator (the budget deficit) than by the lack of public and private investment determining the denominator (growth of GDP). After three successive years of austerity, GDP grew by just 1 per cent in 2015 (0.1 per cent in 2014, 0.9 per cent in 2016). (In fact, the austerity years were responsible for an outstanding fall in real GDP: −2.8 per cent in 2012, −1.7 per cent in 2013.) So why has the economy stagnated? The answer is complicated, but in part it is the result of inadequate investment in areas that raise GDP, such as vocational training, new technology and R&D. To make matters worse, a prolonged squeeze on government spending has weakened demand in the Italian economy and lowered the incentive to invest.

Yet Eurozone policy blindly persists in the conventional view that austerity is the solution, and that inadequate growth indicates insufficient austerity. Back in 2014, in a stinging attack on Eurozone political economy,[10] Joseph Stiglitz wrote: 'Austerity has failed. But its defenders are willing to claim victory on the basis of the weakest possible evidence: the economy is no longer collapsing, so austerity must be working! But if that is the benchmark, we could say that jumping off a cliff is the best way to get down from a mountain; after all, the descent has been stopped.' The austerity policy of cutting taxes and government spending does not revive investment and economic growth, when the real problem is weak demand. And in countries like Greece and Spain, where 50 per cent of young people cannot find work, pursuing policies that don't actually affect investment – and hence jobs – means that an entire generation can lose its right to a prosperous future.

Questions of government debt and budget deficits are often also confused with ones about the size of government, usually measured as the ratio of government spending to the size of the economy. And yet there are no magic numbers for what is too big or too small. France, frequently touted as an example of 'big government', has a government expenditure/GDP ratio of 58 per cent. The UK government's spending is also often regarded as quite big, but at about 40 per cent its ratio is not much different to that of the US at 36 per cent – although the US is often cited as an example of 'small government'. Surprisingly, China, often perceived as a state-run economy, has a ratio of only 30 per cent.

However, recent research into the impact of government size on economic growth has found almost unanimously that small government is 'bad' if, for example, it cannot even maintain basic infrastructure, rule of law (e.g. funding of police) and the educational needs of the population. Conversely, the same research concludes that bigger government might be 'bad' if it is a result of activity that 'crowds out' (reduces) the private sector[11] or unduly restricts private-sector activity and interferes too much in people's lives.[12] But within these rather obvious limits, the ideal size of government is hard to quantify – not least because it depends heavily on what you want government to do and how you value government activity. And here we have a problem: there has been a dearth of thinking by economists – both historically and in recent decades – about the value created by government.

GOVERNMENT VALUE IN THE HISTORY OF ECONOMIC THOUGHT

Economics emerged as a discipline in large part to assert the productive primacy of the private sector.

Starting with the French physiocrats, economists found that government was required for the orderly functioning of society and thus for setting conditions for the production of value. But in itself, government was not inherently productive; rather, it was a stabilizing background force. The physiocrats pleaded with King Louis XV to *laissez-faire* – not to micro-manage the economy by siphoning off as much gold as possible, and thereby upset the intricate mechanism by which value was really created[13] – through productivity of the land, not by accumulating precious metal. We saw in Chapter 1 how, according to Quesnay's *Tableau Économique*, value produced in agriculture flowed through the economy. But government was absent, 'unproductive'. As part of the ruling class, members of the government got a share of the value apportioned simply because they were in power.[14]

Nevertheless, Quesnay knew, the *Tableau* did not work by itself. There was something to be 'governed'. Quesnay argued that the wealth of the nation could only be upheld through 'proper management by the general administration' – what we would call government regulation.[15] He thought that free competition would best benefit the economy – but to achieve this, far from excluding government, he favoured an activist state that would break monopolies and establish the institutional conditions necessary for competition and free trade to flourish and value creation to thrive.[16]

Adam Smith, meanwhile, devoted the fifth book of his *The Wealth of Nations* to the role of government in the economy. His aim was not only to explain the prosperity of the nation, but also 'to supply the state or commonwealth with a revenue sufficient for the public services'.[17] Like Quesnay, Smith believed the state was necessary. Indeed, he was convinced that national wealth could only be increased through division of labour in 'a well-governed society',[18] in which he singled out three crucial functions of government: the military, the judiciary and other public services such as provision of infrastructure.[19] These are public goods – producers cannot exclude anyone from consuming them. For Smith, such public goods had to be paid for by the state;[20] some sort of taxation was therefore necessary.

David Ricardo was perhaps the most anti-government of the classical economists. Although the title of his *The Principles of Political Economy and Taxation* contains a key activity of government (taxation), he never considered how taxation could allow government spending to encourage production and hence value creation. For Ricardo, taxes are the 'portion of the produce of land and labour, placed at the disposal of government' to spend on areas such as education.[21] If these expenditures are too high, he writes, the capital of the country is diminished, and 'distress and ruin will follow'.[22] Ricardo never asks, as Smith did, whether some taxes are necessary to help capitalists carry out production. He assumes infrastructure – the judiciary and so on – as a given. In effect, Ricardo narrows the production of economic value strictly to the private sphere. Admiring Ricardo's rigorous analytical arguments, in comparison with Smith's more fluid and interdisciplinary philosophical and political approach, economists followed him and excluded government from the productive sector.

Marx's view of government, meanwhile, derived from his materialist view of history, whereby the organization of society (including government structures) reflects the economic system (which he called the mode of production) and the underlying social relations: the interaction between classes. So, in his view, under the capitalist 'mode of production' – based on surplus value generated from exploitation of labour – government and law reflected the needs of capitalists. Marx ridiculed some followers of Smith and Ricardo for haranguing state officials as 'parasites on the actual producers', then realizing that they were after all necessary to support the capitalist system. Nevertheless Marx, like Smith before him, while stressing the necessity of some functions of the state, placed state officials in the category of unproductive labourers outside the production boundary. The capitalist class had an interest in maintaining the state in a position strong enough to guarantee the rule of law and advance their class interests – but nothing more than that: 'The executive of the modern state is nothing but a committee for managing the common affairs of the whole bourgeoisie.'[23] The question concerning Marx was what constituted the 'right' size of government to provide the necessary services without taking away any additional profits.

While the neoclassical economists broke with the labour theory of value, they did not depart from their predecessors' view that government was necessary but unproductive. Marginal utility, as we have seen, locates value in the price of any transaction that takes place freely in the market. According to this perspective, government produces nothing: it cannot create value. And government's main source of income is taxes, which are a transfer of existing value created in the private sector.

The immensely influential Alfred Marshall was quite nuanced in his discussion of economic life in his *Principles*, but still recommended that economics should avoid 'as far as possible' the discussion of matters associated with government.[24] He believed that government interference in, or regulation of, the market would often happen in response to attempts by vested interests to rig the market in their favour (i.e. government would be 'captured' by such interests) – thus only hurting a particular competitor rather than benefiting society as a whole.[25]

KEYNES AND COUNTER-CYCLICAL GOVERNMENT

To the humble citizen, however, it might not be so obvious that government does not create value. We have already seen three ways in which it does so: bailing out the banks; investing in infrastructure, education and basic science; and funding radical, innovative technologies which are transforming our lives.

The crucial point is that many of these activities involve taking *risks* and *investing* – exactly what austerity doesn't do – and in so doing they create value. But that value is not easily visible, for the simple reason that much of it goes into the pockets of the private sector. One man at least partly understood this problem: John Maynard Keynes.

When in 1929 the global economic crisis struck, recovery seemed elusive. The Great Depression shattered the idea of unbounded economic progress because, contrary to the prevailing theoretical consensus, the economy did not recover by itself. Keynes's explanation for this was a radical departure from the conventional wisdom of the time.[26] Markets, he claimed, are inherently unstable and, in a recession, may remain 'in a chronic condition of sub-normal activity for a considerable period without any marked tendency, either towards recovery or towards complete collapse'.[27] In these circumstances, he stressed, the role of government is crucial: it is the 'spender of last resort'.

Let's remind ourselves that Keynes was concerned in his *General Theory* to explain how an economy might find itself in a state of 'involuntary unemployment' due to insufficient demand – that is, workers who wanted work would not be able to find it. This, he argued, would produce a low level of GDP, compared to a situation in which the economy would be running at full capacity (and full employment). Neoclassical economic theory is ill suited to explain this situation because it assumes that people choose what they prefer, including how much labour they 'supply' to the market at a given price (the wage), and that the market makes sure to sort things out so that everyone gets the maximum utility out of it. In such a view, unemployment becomes voluntary.

Keynes disposed of the assumption that supply creates its own demand. He argued instead that producers' expectations of demand and consumption determine their investment, and consequently the employment and production that follow from it;[28] therefore, low expectations could lead to underemployment. This he called the 'principle of effective demand': investment can fall as a result of expectations or bets on the future – and we know, not least from the 2008 financial crisis, that such bets can go horribly wrong.

On the back of this theory, Keynes proposed a new role for government. When the private sector cuts production in times of downbeat expectations about demand, he argued, government could intervene positively, increasing demand through additional spending, which in turn would lead to more positive expectations of future consumption and induce the private sector to invest, with higher GDP as a result.

In Keynes's macroeconomics, therefore, government creates value in that it allows the economy to produce more goods and services than it would without government involvement. This was a pivotal shift in the way we regard government's role in the economy. For Keynes, government was in fact essential because it could create value by reviving demand – precisely when demand might be low, as in recessions, or when business confidence is low.

Of course, government would have to borrow to finance this spending, which means bigger government debt in a recessionary economy. But higher debt is a result of a crisis, not its cause. Keynes argued that this increased debt should not overly worry the government. Once the recovery was under way, the need for big deficits would pass and the debt could be paid off.

Keynes's concept of a deficit-led recovery quickly won over governments. It was applied most intensively at the end of the 1930s to stimulate post-depression growth, and at the beginning of the 1940s as wartime spending. Spreading rapidly after the Second World War, Keynes's ideas were widely credited with generating the unprecedented prosperity of the three post-war decades – the *trente glorieuses*. Towards the end of the twentieth century, Keynes's ideas earned him a place in *Time* magazine's list of the 100 most important people of the century: 'His radical idea that governments should spend money they don't have may have saved capitalism.'[29] As it turned out, these words were prophetic. Some eighty years after the publication of the *General Theory*, in the wake of the financial crisis governments around the world introduced stimulus packages: a move that owed much to Keynes.

In the end, however, Keynes only went part of the way. He changed our thinking about how government can create value in the bad times, through counter-cyclical policies; but he, and his followers, had much less to say about how it can do so in good times as well. Even as Keynesianism and the post-war boom were at their height, dissenting voices could be heard. With great ingenuity, the American Paul Samuelson (1915–2009) – one of the most influential economists of the second half of the twentieth century, a professor at the Massachusetts Institute of Technology and the first American to win the Nobel Prize in Economics – attempted to prove that neoclassical theory could explain how the economy behaved in normal times, except when recessionary periods made monetary policy have little effect: i.e. when increasing the money supply does not lower interest rates and only adds to idle balances rather than spurring growth (what is known as the 'liquidity trap'). In essence, Samuelson argued that in normal economic times there was little need for governments to try to manage the economy along Keynesian lines and that government intervention (e.g. aimed at increasing employment) in these cases would only lead to higher inflation.

In the 1970s, inflation began to increase, opening the way for the monetarists, led by Milton Friedman. A libertarian, Friedman rejected the idea that government spending is beneficial, arguing that it most likely leads to inflation, ignoring that this assumes that the economy is already operating at full capacity so that any extra demand (stimulated by government) would result in higher prices. But Keynes's whole point was that the economy would often be working at under-utilized capacity. For Friedman, what mattered was controlling the quantity of money in the economy. The new classicals also challenged Keynes by arguing that government spending was useless and only crowded out private investment. According to them, an increase in the public deficit raises the rate of interest (due to the effect of issuing bonds on interest rates) which, in turn, decreases the amount of private investment. For these reasons, government's role should be restricted to incentivizing individual producers and workers to supply more output and labour – for example by cutting taxes.

The new classicals, however, misunderstood how interest rates affect investment. First, interest rates are not a market phenomenon determined by supply and demand. Rather, they are set and controlled by the central bank through monetary policy,[30] and an increase in government expenditure financed by the deficit does not raise the interest rate. Second, lower interest rates do not necessarily lead to more investment, since firms tend to be less sensitive to interest rates and more sensitive to expectations of where future growth opportunities lie. And it is precisely these opportunities that are shaped by active government investment, as we saw in Chapter 7.

GOVERNMENT IN THE
NATIONAL ACCOUNTS

As we saw in Chapter 3, national accounts were highly influenced by Keynes's thinking. GDP can be calculated in three ways: production, income and expenditure. Despite its size and importance in the economy, however, the word 'government' rarely appears in discussions of production and income. Instead, it is usually examined simply in terms of expenditure – how the value produced and earned is spent.

For Keynes, additional public spending was needed to make sure economies were not constantly prone to recessions and depressions; by purchasing goods, government added to GDP on the expenditure side to make up for what was often too low business investment. The accounting method adopted was simply to add up the costs of government production, subtract intermediate material inputs and equate the difference – basically, government employees' salaries – with the output of government. Although government played an active part in national accounting, its image was still as a big spender rather than a producer.

This is all extremely important. The accounts seem to say that government is just spending what it taxes away from value-adding companies. But can that be true?

The national accounts fail to capture the full amount of this government value added and have several major flawed assumptions. First of all, national accounts regard most of government value added only as costs, mainly pay to government employees; government activity lacks an operating surplus, which would increase its value added. Let's compare it with the private sector. The share of pay in private-sector value added is rarely above 70 per cent. On that basis, you could say that government value added is on average only 70 per cent of what it should be.

Second, the return on investment by government is assumed to be zero; by this logic it does not earn a surplus. If it were more than zero it would show up as operating surplus. The US did not officially separate public current expenditures (e.g. costs to run the everyday business of government, such as civil servants' salaries) and capital expenditure (e.g. to fund new infrastructure) until the 1990s, which strengthened accountants' impression that the government only *spent* money. But of course vital government investments abound: obvious examples include infrastructure projects like the Federal interstate highway system in the US or motorways in the UK. It makes no sense simply to assume that the return on enormous government investments is zero, when similar investments by the private sector do produce a return. Moreover, it is perfectly possible to estimate a return. One way of doing this is to assume a market rate of return such as the yield on municipal bonds – the overall return on bonds issued by cities.[31] The crucial point here is that zero government return on investment is a political choice, not a scientific inevitability.

Third, to assume that the value of government output equals the value of input means that government activities cannot increase the economy's productivity in any meaningful way: an increase in productivity, after all, is obtained by growth of output outpacing the growth of inputs. But if the output of government is defined simply as what it costs to do something, then an increase in output will always require the same increase in inputs. In 1998, the UK's Office for National Statistics began to measure public-sector output by deploying different physical indicators, for example the number of people benefiting from public services (in areas such as health, education and social security) for every pound spent. In 2005 the British economist Sir Anthony Atkinson (1944–2017) improved on this by introducing important changes to the quantity measures of each public service, along with elaborating some quality measures for health and education.[32] Intriguingly, when these changes were applied, it was found that productivity fell on average by 0.3 per cent per year between 1998 and 2008.[33] Productivity increased significantly only after the financial crisis. But the increase was the result of fewer inputs, not improved outputs. Austerity aimed to cut back the inputs (government spending) while producing the 'same' outputs.[34] It is hardly surprising that this kind of productivity 'improvement' does not result in better services – we only have to look at the long NHS waiting times to see this.

Fourth, governments often own productive businesses such as railways, postal services or energy providers. But, by accounting convention, state-owned enterprises that sell products at market prices are counted as private enterprises in the value added of the relevant sector: public railways are part of the transport sector, not the government sector. Even though state-owned corporations earn profits (and in the stats, higher profits means higher value added), their profits are accounted for in the industrial sector they work for, not the 'government' sector. So if the state-owned railway makes huge sales and profits (high value added), it boosts the transport sector value added, even if that sector is perhaps only successful because of state ownership. Only government-owned entities that don't sell at market prices are by definition included in the government sector. In short, from the perspective of national accounting, you don't count as government if you are doing market production. So, in the case of free public education, while increasing the number of teachers might add to GDP (because they are paid), the value they actually produce does not increase GDP. All of which means that government can only increase its value added with non-market production, thereby obscuring the true importance of government in the economy: value that government businesses *do* add is not shown in official statistics, nor is the value that education or health generate.

These rules have been made in order to find a straightforward way to account for economic activity. Yet, when you consider the combined weaknesses of accounting conventions – government is lumped with households as a 'final' consumer; government cannot make a surplus, earn returns, increase its productivity or raise value added through market production – you can't help but notice that, while every effort has been made to depict finance as productive, the opposite seems to be true for government. Simply because of the way that productivity is defined, the fact that government expenditure is higher than value added reinforces the widely held idea that 'unproductive' government has to take before it can spend. This thinking by definition restricts how much government can influence the course of the economy. It underpins the theory of austerity. And it is a consequence of fables about government told over several centuries.

Multiplying Value

National accounts do not consider the interaction between public expenditure and other components of output, consumption, investment and net exports.

In order to understand this interconnection, economists estimate the value of what is called the 'multiplier'. The multiplier was an important reason for Keynes's positive view of government. Developed by Keynes's Cambridge student and colleague Richard Kahn (1905–1989) and used by Keynes himself, it formalized the idea that government spending would stimulate the economy. Quite literally: every pound that the government spent would be multiplied, because the demand it created would lead to several rounds of additional spending. Importantly, the Keynesian approach also quantified the size of the multiplier, so policymakers – who quickly took up the idea – could support their arguments for stimulus spending with hard numbers.[35]

More precisely, the multiplier refers to the effect that an increase in expenditure (demand) has on total production. Its significance lies in the fact that, in the view of Keynes and Kahn, government spending benefits the economy way beyond the amount of demand that spending generates. The company from whom the government purchases its additional goods – let's say concrete for motorways – pays incomes to its workers, who go out and spend those extra incomes on new goods – let's say wide-screen TVs – which another company produces, and that company's employees have more to spend – let's say on holidays in Cornwall – and so it goes on multiplying through the economy. Additional government demand creates several subsequent rounds of spending, multiplying the original amount spent. Government spending in recession was seen as especially powerful in getting the economy back on track, since its effect on overall output was much greater than the actual amount invested.

This powerful and important idea has inevitably attracted controversy, particularly over the size of the multiplier – that is, how much £1 of government spending generates in the economy. The sizeable literature on the subject can be divided into two schools of thought: the 'new classical' and the Keynesian.

According to the 'new classicals', the proponents of fiscal austerity measures, the multiplier's value is less than one, or even negative.[36] On this basis they can argue that public expenditure has a non-Keynesian effect on output. In other words, an increase of £1 of public expenditure is supposed to generate less than £1 or even have a negative effect on total GDP because it crowds out private investment. In the case of a negative multiplier they assume that public expenditure *destroys* value, since the increase of £1 in public expenditure is more than offset by a decrease in the other components of GDP: consumption, investment and net exports.

However, the Keynesian view has been revived recently, since it has been shown that austerity measures implemented in, for example, southern European countries have led to a fall in total output and consequently a rise in unemployment, rather than GDP growth and increased employment. The poor economic performance of these countries calls into question the austerity prescription of the 'new classical' authors. Recent IMF studies have also suggested that government spending has a positive effect on output[37] and that the value of the multiplier is greater than one – to be precise, 1.5.[38] An increase of £1 of public expenditure leads to an increase in total output of £1.50. In short, more credence is being given to the view that government expenditure does not destroy private value but can create value added by stimulating private investment and consumption.

PUBLIC CHOICE THEORY: RATIONALIZING PRIVATIZATION AND OUTSOURCING

The 1980s backlash against government was in part driven by the notion that economies should worry more about 'government failure' than 'market failure'. Government failure emerged as a concept from Public Choice theory, a set of ideas closely associated with economists like the American James Buchanan and the University of Chicago, where Buchanan studied. In 1986 he was awarded the Nobel Prize in Economics.

Public Choice theory argues that government failure is caused by private interests 'capturing' policymakers through nepotism, cronyism, corruption or rent-seeking,[39] misallocation of resources such as investing public money in unsuccessful new technologies (picking losers),[40] or undue competition with private initiatives ('crowding out' what might otherwise be successful private investment).[41]

Public Choice theory stresses that policy must be vigilant to make sure that the gains from government intervention in the economy outweigh the costs of government failures.[42] The idea is that there is a trade-off between two inefficient outcomes: one generated by free markets (market failure) and the other by governmental intervention (government failure). The solution advocated by a group of economists called the neo-Keynesians (people who built on Keynes's ideas) is to focus on correcting only some failures, such as those that arise from positive or negative externalities. The former might include 'public goods' like basic research, which the government needs to fund when the private sector doesn't (because it's hard to make profits), while the latter could involve the costs of pollution which companies do not include in their regular cost-accounting, so government might have to add that cost through a carbon tax.[43] So while Public Choice theorists worry more about government failures and neo-Keynesians more about market failures, in the end their debates about policy intervention have not seriously challenged the primacy of marginal utility theory.

Taken to its extreme, Public Choice theory, which derives from marginalism, calls for government to intervene as little as possible in the economy in order to minimize the risk of government failure. The public sector should be insulated from the private sector, for example to avoid agency capture – when a regulatory body grows too close to the industry it is meant to regulate.

Fear of government failure has convinced many governments that they should emulate the private sector as far as they can. The premise here is that government is inevitably prone to corruption and laziness because agent and principal are too close to each other. It is essential, therefore, to make public services more 'efficient'. From the 1980s onwards, private-sector measurements of efficiency were applied to the public sector and in the process 'marketized' government. Even the very language changed: hospital patients, social-service beneficiaries and even students all became 'clients' or 'customers'.

The logic of Public Choice theory resulted inexorably in government shedding responsibilities, reducing its investment in its own capacity-building, and eventually to privatization. Privatization can occur through the actual sale of a unit, as has happened with public banks. Or it may be indirect privatization through 'outsourcing', whereby a private contractor is paid by government to provide a service – such as publicly funded education, housing, health, transport and even prisons, road traffic management and benefits assessment.

The 1980s, when Public Choice began heavily to influence public policy, saw a wave of privatizations and outsourcing, first in the UK and the US, and then slowly spreading across much of Europe. It was also the decade when, as we have seen, financialization started to take hold. The idea (or ideology) that government control of productive enterprises was inefficient and wasteful became accepted wisdom. In the UK it chimed with the Thatcherite ideological purpose of creating a nation of asset owners, whether of shares or privatized council houses. These were the years of 'If you see Sid, tell him', the famous advertising campaign to persuade British citizens to buy shares in British Gas, which was privatized in 1986, and the privatizations of British Telecom and British Airways, the electricity and water industries and a host of smaller government-owned enterprises. The following decade saw the privatization of the railways.

Many other countries did not always embrace privatization with the same enthusiasm as the UK – the French electricity industry, for example, remains basically state-controlled – but it quickly became a worldwide trend. The IMF and World Bank often deployed their considerable weight to persuade developing countries to sell state-owned enterprises. Even in countries where the privatization wave has weakened – if only because most suitable assets have been sold – the idea that the state should not own but only fund (if that) is firmly lodged in the public mind. Today, few governments or politicians argue for wholesale nationalization and government ownership.

But Public Choice theory always ran the risk of throwing out the baby with the bath water. By insisting that government could not create value – indeed, was likely to destroy value – it shouted down the subtler but no less substantive debate about what value government did produce. There may be a strong case for retaining a significant public share in industries that have a natural tendency towards monopoly – essential utilities such as water, gas and electricity – in order to benefit from economies of scale in provision, and also to avoid speculative rent-seeking on basic goods needed. In more consumer-oriented industries, especially ones in which technology is transforming the market (mobile phones, for example), the case for a strong public presence may be less strong – though history shows that often a hybrid public-private form might prove the most interesting, as with French Telecom (which later became Orange).

The solution to the problem of natural monopolies was regulation. In the UK a series of regulatory agencies sprang up, each intended to stand between the public and industry. Regulatory capitalism replaced state capitalism. It was not what pure Public Choice theorists intended; indeed, regulatory capitalism resulted in exactly the kind of government cronyism and corruption that they had warned about.

Another consequence of Public Choice theory has been the rise of intermediary mechanisms to fund public activity. This has mainly taken two forms. One is private finance initiatives (PFIs), for example to build hospitals. The other, mentioned earlier, is outsourcing to private providers to run a wide range of services. In both cases, public activity is financed privately. Turning to PFIs in this way has been called 'pseudo-privatization', because the private firms receive their income not from clients in the 'market' but from government through a guaranteed profit margin. An outsourcing contract is in effect a type of monopoly which locks the government in as the sole customer. In the UK, moreover, the degree of competition between providers of outsourcing services is questionable: only a handful, dominated by Capita, G4S and Serco, account for most the contracts.[44]

The aim of PFI financing is to share costs and remove from the government's balance sheet the debt associated with large projects such as hospitals; however, it can be costly for the public sector because projects are financed with private debt and equity, which is significantly more expensive than public borrowing. Governments also pay private contractors an annual charge, running for decades and usually indexed

to inflation, to cover the capital repayment plus interest and maintenance costs. So exclusive PFI contracts in effect create monopoly
licences. The end result can be one where the costs to government are
often more than if it had provided the service/s itself. We look at two
examples below, healthcare and infrastructure.

Privatizing and Outsourcing Healthcare

In 1948, when the UK was still undergoing a long and difficult post-
war reconstruction (public debt was well above 200 per cent over
GDP in that year), British citizens received a leaflet on which was
stated: 'Your new National Health Service begins on 5th July. What
is it? How do you get it? It will provide you with all medical, dental,
and nursing care. Everyone – rich or poor, man, woman or child –
can use it or any part of it.' The National Health Service (NHS) was
created that year, following the initiative of the Minister of Health,
Aneurin Bevan. The following three core principles were behind its
establishment:[45]

- that it meets the needs of everyone
- that it be free at the point of delivery
- that it be based on clinical need, not ability to pay

Over its almost seventy years of existence, the NHS has become one
of the most efficient and equitable healthcare systems in the world,
as recognized by the World Health Organization[46] and also more
recently by the Commonwealth Foundation.[47] In the UK it is considered a national treasure, sharing its place in the pantheon with the
Queen and the BBC. The NHS is also among the cheapest healthcare
systems in advanced economies: according to OECD figures from
2015,[48] health expenditure relative to GDP in the UK was only 9.9
per cent, much less than what the US has spent (16.9 per cent) on its
far less efficient semi-private system.

The NHS owes much of its past successes to its public mission and
to its universality principle, translated into an efficient central provision of healthcare services aimed at reducing transaction costs. UK
citizens have repeatedly recognized the importance of its public
nature: currently, 84 per cent of them think that it should be run

in the public sector.[49] Even Prime Minister Thatcher stated: 'The National Health Service is safe with us' during the 1982 Conservative Party conferences, temporarily discarding plans for outright privatization set out by the Central Policy Review Staff within the Cabinet Office.

Nevertheless, such positive rhetoric on the merits of the NHS soon became the cover for a long series of reforms that have progressively introduced elements of private provision in the British healthcare system. With the National Health Service and Community Care Act of 1990, management and patient care were forced to behave as part of an 'internal market', with health authorities and general practitioners becoming autonomous purchasers of services under a limited budget. Hospitals were transformed into self-governing NHS trusts and their resources became dependent on contracts stipulated with purchasers. Contracting out to the lowest bidder was also introduced as a first element of outsourcing, with the NHS progressively moving away from its role of provider towards becoming a mere customer. Since 1992, the outsourcing process created by the Private Financing Initiative (PFI) has involved also the building of NHS hospitals. Through PFI, private companies were allowed to build hospitals which were then rented back to the NHS for a substantially high price. PFI was widely used throughout the 'New Labour' governments to save on infrastructure investment, with the renting price of hospitals subsequently burdening the NHS budget. Finally, the 2012 Health and Social Care Act de facto abolished the second principle of the original NHS, by introducing user charges and an insurance-based system that resembles the US healthcare model, passing costs and risks to patients, now customers in a market for healthcare provision. This final reform has also further increased the scope for outsourcing in many different areas, such as cleaning, facilities management, GP 'out of hours' services, clinical services, IT and so on.[50]

Those reforms were aimed at producing a more efficient and cost-effective NHS, through the introduction of market elements in the provision of healthcare. In reality the efficiency has hardly improved, while ever-scarcer resources are largely misallocated. This is what Colin Crouch has called 'the paradox of public service outsourcing'.[51] Market-oriented reforms of healthcare fail to appreciate the evidence that there is no such thing as a competitive market for those services: contracts run for several years and they are granted to a small number of firms which come to dominate the outsourcing market. Those firms become effectively specialized in winning contracts from the public sector across different fields in which they do not have a corresponding expertise. As a result, the market is highly concentrated and the diversity of tasks makes it difficult to obtain a quality-efficient outcome in all the services provided.

A study by Graham Kirkwood and Allyson Pollock shows that increased private-sector provision is associated with a significant decrease in direct NHS provision, a reduction in quality, and costs being propped up by the public sector.[52] There are many examples of inefficient outcomes created by the outsourcing process, for example Coperform with the NHS's South East Coast ambulance service and Serco with out-of-hours GPs contracts in Cornwall;[53] in some cases the public had to cover losses when private contractors withdrew from their obligations. Moreover, the whole system of contracting out has a distortive effect on the activities of NHS personnel. As noted by Pollock, 'clinicians, nurses, managers and armies of consultants and lawyers spend their days preparing multiple bids, tenders and awarding contracts, instead of providing patient care'.[54]

Finally, outsourcing appears to be immensely cost-inefficient. Contracting activities create a 'new market bureaucracy' that has to deal with the cumbersome process. These administrative burdens are effectively transaction costs that in the US represent around 30 per cent of total healthcare expenditure, while in the UK the actual figure is not known, although it was in the order of 6 per cent in the pre-marketization NHS.[55] Yet, perhaps the elephant in the room will be the huge burden for the public that the PFIs will have created by the time their contracts expire. Especially in the case of NHS hospitals, that cost is estimated to be several times higher than the actual worth of the underlying assets.[56]

Although reaching a more efficient provision of healthcare services for a lower cost has always been the stated purpose of outsourcing in the NHS, recent evidence seems to suggest that this might just be the second phase of what Noam Chomsky has called the 'standard technique of privatization: 'defund, make sure things don't work, people get angry, you hand it over to private capital'.[57]

Outsourcing Scotland's Infrastructure

Use of PFI financing was particularly prevalent in Scotland between 1993 and 2006. Data published by the Scottish government show that the eighty projects completed in Scotland during this period will cost the public sector £30.2 billion over the coming decades – more than five times the £5.7 billion initial estimate. As well as poor value for money, there is a real concern that PFI projects may be low-quality and even dangerous: in April 2016, seventeen PFI schools in Edinburgh were closed because of safety concerns about construction defects.

In response to growing concerns about PFI, the Scottish government developed after 2010 the Non-Profit Distribution (NPD) model to fund a range of projects in three main sectors – education, health and transport. In this new model, there is no dividend-bearing equity and private-sector returns are capped; however, financing is still by private loan with the expectation of a market rate of return. Projects funded under the NPD model are therefore still significantly more expensive than they would be if they were paid for by direct public borrowing.[58] A recent study by the New Economics Foundation found, for example, that between 1998 and 2015 the Scottish government would have saved a total of £26 billion if the projects financed through the Private Finance Initiative (PFI) and Non-Profit Distribution (NPD) schemes had instead been funded directly through a Scottish public investment bank.[59]

As we have seen, outsourcing often increases costs and is a form of monopoly. Social Enterprise UK, which promotes organizations such as the *Big Issue*, Cafédirect and the Eden Project, has referred to the oligopoly of outsourcing providers as the 'Shadow State'. Capita, G4S and Serco continue to win contracts in both the UK and US, even though they have all been fined for improper management.[60] In 2016, for example, an investigative article revealed that G4S has been fined for at least 100 breaches of prison contracts between 2010 and 2016, including 'failure to achieve search targets, smuggling of contraband items, failure of security procedures, serious cases of "concerted indiscipline", hostage taking, and roof climbing. Other cases include failure to lock doors, poor hygiene and a reduction in staffing levels.'[61]

The fines, however, are minuscule in proportion to the profits made by both Serco and G4S – and such companies, rather than being penalized for carelessness and reckless cost-cutting, are being rewarded with more contracts. The applications procedures for Obamacare were outsourced in 2013 to Serco in a $1.2 billion contract.[62]

Indeed, US Federal government outsourcing contracts to such companies are rapidly rising. A recent GAO report shows that in 2000 contract spending was $200 billion, while in 2015 it was $438 billion.[63] This amount represented almost 40 per cent of government's discretionary spending. The GAO report also distinguished spending on contracts for goods from contracts for services. Among civilian agencies, 80 per cent of contractor expenditures were for services, of which 'professional support services' was the largest category. The GAO report notes that 'contractors performing these types of services are at a heightened risk of performing inherently governmental work'. Indeed, one of the most worrying aspects is probably not the *amount* of money spent on contractors, but that such a *big proportion* of it is for 'professional support services'. This often means that inherently governmental work has been contracted out.

The cost to the taxpayer of all the contract workers is double that of civil servants, not because contract workers are paid better – they often have to put up with low wages and poor conditions – but because the contractors' fees, overheads and profit margins, and the ratio of the number of contract workers to the number of civil servants is sometimes as high as four, revealing how bloated and inefficient the outsourcing process can become.[64] A recent study shows that the 'federal government approves service contract billing rates – deemed fair and reasonable – that pay contractors 1.83 times more than the government pays federal employees in total compensation, and more than 2 times the total compensation paid in the private sector for comparable services'.[65] Again, it is not the contracted workers who get the higher amounts, but the firms that win the public contracts.

The mantra of higher efficiency through privatization, therefore, is unsupported by the facts – if you can get hold of them, that is. Such facts can be hard to ferret out, despite claims of greater transparency in the private sector. Rather than increase competition through more consumer choice, privatization has often resulted in less choice and less democracy – as is clearly evidenced by the above description of the outsourcing of many NHS services and the high cost of PFI contracts to build and maintain hospitals.[66] What the public gets is frequently less transparency, lower quality, higher costs and monopoly – exactly the opposite of what in theory privatization (poorly justified as it was in the first place) is supposed to achieve.

Good Private, Bad Public

What is also striking is the commonplace assumption that when the public does own something, it will privatize that asset by retaining in the public hands the 'bad' company and selling off the 'good' company. The narrative of good private versus bad public could not be more clear! A salient example is the privatization of Royal Mail, which delivers post, and runs a chain of some 11,000 post offices across the UK. But, as is well known over the last two decades, email and the Internet have caused a dramatic fall in the level of postal traffic. In 2008 an independent review commissioned by the government, led by Richard Hooper CBE (the former Deputy Chairman of the government's competition authority, Ofcom), concluded that the Royal Mail and the post offices be split into two separate private companies. Five years later, the Conservative-led government privatized Royal Mail by floating it on the London Stock Exchange, while retaining a 30 per cent stake. The now separate Post Office Ltd remains wholly in public ownership. But the government was strongly criticized for selling Royal Mail at too low a price: on the day of flotation the share price rocketed from the official price of 330p a share to 455p within hours. According to some critics, the flotation valuation of £3.3 billion should have been more like £5.5 billion. Moreover, fees to banks, lawyers, accountants and other advisers came to £12.7 million. The sweetener that greatly added to the attraction of the privatization for investors was that the Treasury took responsibility for the Royal Mail Pension Plan, the biggest in the country, which covers workers in both Royal Mail and the post offices. This was to all intents and purposes the 'bad company' dumped on the taxpayer.

Similar situations have occurred with banks which are affected by bad loans, such as RBS in the UK. Such banks end up with balance sheets full of worthless loans that then prevent the banks in question from making any further loans. The default answer in such cases has often been to take out all the toxic assets from the 'good' part of the bank, and to put them in a government-run 'bad bank'. The idea is that doing so will allow the private bank to get back on its feet, with the taxpayer taking on the responsibility of managing or selling off the bad assets. But this has resulted in the socialization of risks and privatization of rewards that we examined in Chapter 7: in the same way that the US government picked up the bill for the failed Solyndra, and let the profits from the similar investment made in Tesla go private, the taxpayer picks up the bill for those parts of public assets that are less efficient, and sells off the better bits to the private sector – and often at a garage sale discount. Similar examples have occurred in other companies: in 2014 Italy's national airline Alitalia was split into a good company, sold privately, and a bad company which remained in government hands.

The use of the words good versus bad in the above examples could not be more stark: private is good, public is bad. If you are constantly told that you are an impediment to dynamism and competition, you might begin to believe it.

REGAINING CONFIDENCE AND SETTING MISSIONS

Public Choice theory's interpretation of government failures as worse than market failures, and the drive towards making government 'efficient', has had the effect of eroding the ethos and purpose of public services. It has also reduced government capacity and confidence (gaslighting), and eroded civil servants' ability to 'think big'.

The epigraph opening this chapter, in which Keynes argues the need for governments to think big – to do what is not being done – shows that he believed that government needs to be bold, with a sense of mission, not merely to replicate the private sector but to achieve something fundamentally different from it. It is wrong to interpret him as believing that what is needed from policy is to simply *fix* what the private sector does not do, or does badly, or at best invest 'counter-cyclically' (i.e. increase investments during the downside of the business cycle). After the Great Depression, he claimed that even paying men simply to dig ditches and fill them up again could revive the economy – but his work inspired Roosevelt to be more ambitious than just advocating what today would be called 'shovel-ready projects' (easy infrastructure). The New Deal included creative activities under the Works Progress Administration, the Civilian Conservation Corps and the National Youth Administration. Equally, it is not enough to create money in the economy through quantitative easing; what is needed is the creation of new opportunities for investment and growth – infrastructure and finance must be embedded within the greater systemic plans for change.

President John F. Kennedy, who hoped to send the first US astronaut to the moon, used bold language when talking about the need for government to be mission-oriented. In a 1962 speech to Rice University he said:

> We choose to go to the moon in this decade and do the other things, not because they are easy, but because they are hard, because that goal will serve to organize and measure the best of our energies and skills, because that challenge is one that we are willing to accept, one we are unwilling to postpone, and one which we intend to win, and the others, too.[67]

In other words, it is a government's duty to think big and confront difficulties – exactly the opposite of the facilitating role predicated by Public Choice theory, the inevitable result of which is timid and lacklustre public agencies which will be easier to privatize later.

Replacing these bold ambitions with financial cost-benefit analysis has dismissed the public value that governments can create. Civil servants are told to step back, minimize costs, think like the private sector and be fearful of making mistakes. Government departments are ordered to cut costs, inevitably also diminishing the skills and capacity of the public structures in questions (departments, agencies, etc.). When government stops investing in its own capacity, it becomes more unsure of itself, less able, and the probability of failure increases. It becomes harder to justify the existence of a particular government function, leading to further cuts or eventually to privatization. This lack of belief in government thereby becomes a self-fulfilling prophecy: when we don't believe in government's ability to create value, it eventually cannot do so. And, when it does create value, such value is treated as a private-sector success or goes unnoticed.

In Chapter 7 we saw the importance of government in developing the key infrastructure and technology upon which twentieth-century capitalism was built, even though it has received inadequate recognition for doing so. Of course, the story is not always positive. The Concorde aircraft did not result in a commercialized plane. Most R&D in new drugs leads to nothing. And guaranteed loans are made to companies which fail, a recent example, as we have seen, being the $528 million provided by the US Department of Energy to the company Solyndra in 2005 for the production of solar cells. When the price of silicon chips fell dramatically soon after, Solyndra went bankrupt, leaving the taxpayer to pick up the bill.[68]

Yet any venture capitalist will say that innovation involves exploring new and difficult paths, and that occasional failure is part of that journey. The guaranteed loan ($465 million) provided to Tesla for the development of the Model S electric car was, as we saw in Chapter 7, a success. This trial-and-error process is accepted in the private sector – but when governments experience failure they are regarded as incompetent and are accused of being unable to 'pick winners'. As a result, public organizations are frequently told to stick to the straight and narrow, to promote competition without 'distorting' the market by choosing specific technologies, sectors or companies in which to invest.[69]

To limit government in this way is to completely ignore its track record, from the development of touchscreen technology to innovation in the renewables sector. Government has often been at its best when mission-oriented – precisely because, as President Kennedy said, it is hard.

Doing 'hard' things means being willing to explore, experiment, make mistakes and to learn from those mistakes. But this is almost impossible in a context in which government 'failure' is deemed the worst of all sins, and in which the guns are loaded, waiting for government to make the slightest mistake.

This does not of course mean that mistakes should be welcome under any conditions. Mistakes that arise from rent-seeking behaviour can lead to vested interests influencing government. As we know, rent occurs when value is extracted through special privileges, for example a subsidy or tax break, and when a company or individual grabs a large share of wealth without having created it. Profit-maximizing firms can try to increase their profits by soliciting special policy-related favours, and are often successful because politicians and policymakers are open to influence and even corruption. The possibility of this sort of capture (of government by vested interests) is a problem, but it becomes even more acute when there is no clear appreciation of government value. If the state is seen as irrelevant, it will over time also become less confident and more easily corrupted by the so-called 'wealth creators' – who can then convince policymakers to hand out favours which increase their wealth and power.

Lazy assumptions about the role of public investment are misleading. Business investment is mainly driven by perceptions of future opportunities, whether these be in a new sector (the emergence of nanotechnology), or in a region that is perceived as an exciting place for new ideas. As we have seen, such opportunities have historically been funded directly by governments, whether by DARPA-type investments in what later became the Internet, or the Danish government's investment in renewable energy. All of which means that policies constructed on the assumption that business always wants to invest, and simply needs a tax incentive to do so, are simplistic, not to say naïve. The incentives (indirect spending through a tax cut), unless complemented by strategic direct investment by government, will rarely make things happen that *would not have happened anyway* (in economics speak, there is no 'additionality'). As a result, a company or individual will often experience an increase in profits (through a tax cut) without increasing investment and without generating any new value. And the primary objective of the policymaker should be to increase business investment, not profits. Indeed, as seen earlier the relationship between profits and wages is at record levels. There is no profits problem, but an investment problem.[70]

PUBLIC AND PRIVATE JUST DESERTS

Once we recognize that the state is not just a spender but an investor and risk taker, it becomes only sensible to ensure that policy leads to the socialization not only of risks but also of rewards. A better realignment between risks and rewards, across public and private actors, can turn smart, innovation-led growth into inclusive growth.

As we have seen, neoclassical value theory for the most part disregards the value created by government, such as an educated workforce, human capital and the technology which ends up in our smart products. Government is ignored in microeconomics – the study of production – except in regulating the prices of inputs and outputs. It plays a bigger part in macroeconomics, which deals with the economy as a whole, but at best as a redistributor of the wealth created by companies and an investor in the 'enabling' conditions companies need – infrastructure, education, skills and so on.

The marginal theory has fostered the idea that collectively produced value derives from individual contributions. Yet, as the American economist George Akerlof, who shared the Nobel Prize in Economics in 2001, said: 'Our marginal products are not ours alone'[71] – they are the fruits of a cumulative process of learning and investment. Collective value creation entails a risk-taking public sector – and yet the usual relationship between risks and rewards, as taught in economics classes, does not seem to apply. So the crucial question is not just about accounting for government value but also *rewarding* it: how should rewards from investment be divided between the public and private sectors?

As Robert Solow showed, most of the gains in productivity of the first half of the twentieth century can be attributed not to labour and capital but to technical change. And this is due not only to improved education and infrastructure, but also, as discussed in the previous chapter, to the collective efforts behind some of the most radical technical changes where the public sector has historically taken a lead role – 'the entrepreneurial state'.[72] But the socialization of risks has not been accompanied by socialization of rewards.

The issue, then, is how the state can reap some return from its successful investments (the 'upside') to cover the inevitable losses (the 'downside') – not least, to finance the next round of investments. This can be done in various ways, as discussed in Chapter 7, whether through equity-holding, conditions on reinvestment, caps on prices, or the need to keep patents as narrow as possible.

FROM PUBLIC GOODS TO PUBLIC VALUE

In this chapter we have considered the biased way in which government activity in the economy is viewed. The role of government is often limited to 'fixing problems'; it must not over-reach itself, government failures being regarded as worse than market failures. It should have a light touch on the economic tiller and fix the basics by investing in areas like skills, education and research, but not go as far as to produce anything. And should government be productive, as state-owned enterprises are, our way of accounting for GDP does not recognize it as public production.

Indeed, almost nothing that government does is considered to fall within the production boundary. Government spending is seen purely as expenditure and not as productive investment. While that spending might be regarded by some as socially necessary and by others as unnecessary and better done by the private sector, neither side has made a robust case for government activity as productive and essential to creating a dynamic capitalist economy. Too often ideology has won over experience.

Keynes was critical in showing the dynamic role of public expenditure in creating a multiplier effect that can lead to higher growth. Yet there is still debate as to whether the multiplier exists at all, and advocates of government economic stimulus are often on the defensive. Part of the problem is that the argument for fiscal spending continues to be tied mainly to taming the business cycle (through counter-cyclical measures), with too little creative thinking about how to direct the economy in the longer term.

It is especially important to rethink the terminology with which we describe government. Portraying government as a more active value creator – investing, not just spending, and entitled to earn a rate of return – can eventually modify how it is regarded and how it behaves. All too often governments see themselves only as 'facilitators' of a market system, as opposed to co-creators of wealth and markets. And, ironically, this produces exactly the type of government that the critics like to bash: weak and apparently 'business-friendly', but open to capture and corruption, privatizing parts of the economy that should be creating public and collective goods.

A new discourse on value, then, should not simply reverse the preference for the private sector over the public. What is required is a new and deeper understanding of public value, an expression found in philosophy but almost lost in today's economics. This value is not created exclusively inside or outside a private-sector market, but rather by a whole society; it is also a goal which can be used to shape markets. Once the notion of public value is understood and accepted, reappraisals are urgently required – of the idea of public and private and of the nature of value itself. 'Public values are those providing normative consensus about (1) the rights, benefits, and prerogatives to which citizens should (and should not) be entitled; (2) the obligations of citizens to society, the state, and one another; (3) and the principles on which governments and policies should be based.'[73]

The idea of public value is broader than the currently more popular term 'public good'. The latter phrase tends to be used in a negative way, to limit the conception of what governments are allowed to do, rather than to stimulate the imagination to find the best ways to confront the challenges of the future. So the state-owned BBC is thought to serve the public good when it makes documentaries about giraffes in Africa, but is questioned if it makes soap operas or talk shows. State agencies can often fund basic science due to the 'positive externalities', but not downstream applications. Public banks can provide counter-cyclical lending, but they cannot direct their lending to socially valuable areas like the green economy. These arbitrary distinctions reflect a narrow view of the economy which often results in a public actor being accused of 'crowding out' a private one – or, worse still, delving into the dangerous waters of 'picking winners': the state is only supposed to do what the private sector does not want to do, rather than have its own vision of a desirable and achievable future.

Public institutions can reclaim their rightful role as servants of the common good. They must think big and play a full part in the great transformations to come, squaring up to the issues of climate change, ageing populations and the need for twenty-first-century infrastructure and innovation. They must get over the self-fulfilling fear of failure, and realize that experimentation and trial and error (and error and error) are part of the learning process. With confidence and responsibility, they can expect success, and in so doing will recruit and retain top-quality employees. They can change the discourse. Instead of de-risking projects, there will be risk-sharing – and reward-sharing.

It might also make sense for private enterprises – which benefit from different types of public investments and subsidies – in return to engage in a fair share of activities which are not immediately profitable. There is much to be learned from the history of Bell Labs, which was born out of the US government's demand that the monopolist AT&T invest its profits rather than hoard cash, as is so common today. Bell Labs invested in areas that its managers and its government contractors thought could create the greatest possible public value. Its remit went well beyond any narrow definition of telecommunications. The partnership of purely government-funded research and work co-financed by Bell Labs and agencies like DARPA led to phenomenal tangible results – many found in our handbags and pockets today.[74]

A bold view of the role of public policy also requires a change in the metrics used for evaluation of those policies. Today's typical static cost-benefit analysis is inadequate for decisions which will inevitably have many indirect consequences. A much more dynamic analysis, one which can capture more of the market-shaping process, is urgently required. For example, any measure of the success of a government project to organize a charging infrastructure for electric cars must try to take into account the opportunities offered for further technical development, the reduction of pollution and the political and ecological gains of lessening reliance on non-renewable oil from countries with objectionable governments.

It is crucial to find metrics which favour long-run investments and innovation. In the 1980s, it was not cost-benefit analysis that encouraged the BBC to establish a dynamic 'learning programme' to get kids to code. The activity led to the development of the BBC Microcomputer, which found its way into all British classrooms. While the Micro did not itself become a commercial success, procurement for its parts supported Acorn Computers and eventually led to the creation of ARM Holdings, one of the most successful UK technology companies of recent decades. However, to recognize that the public sector creates value we must find ways to assess that value, including the spillovers from this sort of ambitious public funding. The BBC initiative helped kids learn to code and increased their interest in socially and economically beneficial new technologies. It also had direct and indirect effects in different sectors, helping new companies to scale up and bringing new investors into the UK tech landscape. Similarly, there would almost certainly be more European high-tech successes if there existed greater interaction between innovation systems and public procurement policies. However, to recognize that the public sector creates value we must first find ways to assess that value, including the spill-overs from this sort of ambitions public funding.

Governing Public Value

The work of Elinor Ostrom (1933–2012), an economist from Indiana University who received the Nobel Prize in 2009, helps clarify the richness of the way in which new metrics can affect behaviour and vice versa, in defusing the conflict between government and market. Ostrom shows how the crude state–private divide that dominates current thinking fails to encapsulate the complexity of institutional structures and relationships – from non-partisan government regulators to state-funded universities and state-run research projects – that span this divide. Rather, she emphasizes common pooled resources, and the shaping of systems that take into account collective behaviour.

Ostrom's work supports Polanyi's historical conclusion in *The Great Transformation*: governments, along with the many institutions and traditions of a society, are the womb in which markets are nourished, and later the parent which helps them serve the common good. One vital government responsibility in the modern economy – which Ostrom also finds in successful pre-industrial economies – is to limit the amount of rent that emerges from any non-collective approach to wealth creation. This brings us back to Adam Smith's definition of the 'free market' as being free from rent.

Today, these ways of thinking could significantly benefit many crucial institutions which are neither fully private nor fully public. Universities could proudly promote the pursuit of knowledge, without having to worry about generating immediately profitable patents and spin-off companies. Medical research institutes could expect strong funding, with much less pressure to fight for attention. Think tanks could shake off the taint of lobbying, once they present their work as being supportive of common values. And co-operative, mutual and other not-for-profit enterprises could flourish without having to decide which side of the great private–public divide they are really on.

In the new discourse, there would certainly be no more talk of the public sector interfering with or rescuing the private sector. Instead, it would be widely accepted that the two sectors, and all the institutions in between, nourish and reinforce each other in pursuit of the common goal of economic value creation. The sectors' interactions would be less marked by hostility, and more infused with mutual respect.

Once the story telling about value creation is corrected, changes can embolden private institutions as well as their public partners. The private sector can be transformed by the simple but profound expedient of replacing shareholder value with stakeholder value. This idea has been around for decades, most countries continue to have companies run by shareholder value focused on maximizing quarterly returns. Stakeholder value recognizes that corporations are not really the exclusive private property of one group of providers of profit-sharing financial capital. As social entities, companies must take into account the good of employees, customers and suppliers.

They benefit from the shared intellectual and cultural heritage of the societies in which they are embedded and from their governments' provision of the rule of law, not to mention the state-funded training of educated workers and valuable research; they should in return deliver benefit to all these constituencies. Of course, there is no easy way to agree on the right balance, but a lively discussion is far preferable to the current practice of maximizing profits for shareholders. Indeed, the presence of co-operatives run on a stakeholder understanding of value creation, such as John Lewis in the UK or Mondragon in Spain, should serve as evidence that there is more than one way to govern a business. And governments that want to achieve innovation-led growth should ask themselves whether employees are more likely to share great ideas in businesses in which they are valued, or in ones where they are simply appendages to a profit-making machine that is then siphoned off to a few shareholders.

This is no easy task, but one that will not even begin without a new positioning of all actors as being central to the collective value creation process.

In sum, it is only by thinking big and differently that government can create value – and hope.

9

The Economics of Hope

The global financial crisis, which began in 2008 and whose repercussions will continue to echo round the world for years to come, has triggered myriad criticisms of the modern capitalist system: it is too 'speculative'; it rewards 'rent-seekers' over true 'wealth creators'; and it has permitted the rampant growth of finance, allowing speculative exchanges of financial assets to be compensated more than investments that lead to new physical assets and job creation. Debates about unsustainable growth have become louder, with concerns not only about the *rate* of growth but also its *direction*.

Recipes for serious reforms of this 'dysfunctional' system include making the financial sector more focused on long-run investments; changing the governance structures of corporations so they are less focussed on their share prices and quarterly returns; taxing quick speculative trades more heavily; and legally curbing the excesses of executive pay.

In this book, I have argued that such critiques are important but will remain powerless – in their ability to bring about real reform of the economic system – until they become firmly grounded in a discussion about the processes by which economic value is created. It is not enough to argue for less value extraction and more value creation. First, 'value', a term that once lay at the heart of economic thinking, must be revived and better understood.

Value has gone from being a category at the core of economic theory, tied to the dynamics of production (the division of labour, changing costs of production), to a subjective category tied to the 'preferences' of economic agents. Many ills, such as stagnant real wages, are interpreted in terms of the 'choices' that particular agents in the system make, for example unemployment is seen as related to the choice that workers make between working and leisure. And entrepreneurship – the praised motor of capitalism – is seen as a result of such individualized choices rather than of the productive system surrounding entrepreneurs – or, to put it another way, the fruit of a collective effort. At the same time, price has become the indicator of value: as long as a good is bought and sold in the market, it must have value. So rather than a theory of value determining price, it is the theory of price that determines value.

Along with this fundamental shift in the idea of value, a different narrative has taken hold. Focused on wealth creators, risk taking and entrepreneurship, this narrative has seeped into political and public discourse. It is now so rampant that even 'progressives' critiquing the system sometimes unintentionally espouse it. When the UK Labour Party lost the 2015 election, leaders of the party claimed they had lost because they had not embraced the 'wealth creators'.[1] And who did they think the wealth creators were? Businesses and the entrepreneurs leading them. Feeding the idea that value is created in the private sector and redistributed by the public sector. But how can a party that has the word 'labour' in its title not see workers and the state as equally vital parts of the wealth *creation* process?

Such assumptions about the generation of wealth have become entrenched, and have gone unchallenged. As a result, those who claim to be wealth creators have monopolised the attention of governments with the now well-worn mantra of: give us less tax, less regulation, less state and more market.

By losing our ability to recognize the difference between value creation and value extraction, we have made it easier for some to call themselves value creators and in the process extract value. Understanding how the stories about value creation are around us everywhere – even though the category itself is not – is a key concern of the book, and essential for the future viability of capitalism.

To offer real change we must go beyond fixing isolated problems, and develop a framework that allows us to shape a new type of economy: one that will work for the common good. The change has to be profound. It is not enough to redefine GDP to encompass quality-of-life indicators, including measures of happiness,[2] the imputed value of unpaid 'caring' labour and free information, education and communication via the Internet.[3] It is also not enough to tax wealth. While such measures are important in themselves, they do not address the greatest challenge: defining and measuring the collective contribution to wealth creation, so that value extraction is less able to pass for value creation. As we have seen, the idea that price determines value and that markets are best at determining prices has all sorts of nefarious consequences. To sum up, four stand out.

First, this narrative emboldens value extractors in finance and other sectors of the economy. Here, the crucial questions – which kinds of activities add value to the economy and which simply extract value for the sellers – are never asked. In the current way of thinking, financial trading, rapacious lending, funding property price bubbles are all value-added by definition, because price determines value: if there is a deal to be done, then there is value. By the same token, if a pharma company can sell a drug at a hundred or a thousand times more than it costs to produce, there is no problem: the market has determined the value. The same goes for chief executives who earn 340 times more than the average worker (the actual ratio in 2015 for companies in the S&P 500).[4] The market has decided the value of their services – there is nothing more to be said. Economists are aware that some markets are not fair, for example when Google has something close to a monopoly on search advertising; but they are too often enthralled by the narrative of market efficiency to worry whether the gains are actually justly earned profits, or merely rents. Indeed, the distinction between profits and rents is not made.

Price-equals-value thinking encourages companies to put financial markets and shareholders first, and to offer as little as possible to other stakeholders. This ignores the reality of value creation – as a collective process. In truth, everything concerning a company's business – especially the underlying innovation and technological development – is intimately interwoven with decisions made by elected governments, investments made by schools, universities, public agencies and even movements by not-for-profit institutions. Corporate leaders are not telling the whole truth when they say that shareholders are the only real risk takers and hence deserve the lion's share of the gains from doing business.

Second, the conventional discourse devalues and frightens actual and would-be value creators outside the private business sector. It's not easy to feel good about yourself when you are constantly being told you're rubbish and/or part of the problem. That's often the situation for people working in the public sector, whether these be nurses, civil servants or teachers. The static metrics used to measure the contribution of the public sector, and the influence of Public Choice theory on making governments more 'efficient', has convinced many civil-sector workers they are second-best. It's enough to depress any bureaucrat and induce him or her to get up, leave and join the private sector, where there is often more money to be made.

So public actors are forced to emulate private ones, with their almost exclusive interest in projects with fast paybacks. After all, price determines value. You, the civil servant, won't dare to propose that your agency could take charge, bring a helpful long-term perspective to a problem, consider all sides of an issue (not just profitability), spend the necessary funds (borrow if required) and – whisper it softly – add *public value*. You leave the big ideas to the private sector which you are told to simply 'facilitate' and enable. And when Apple or whichever private company makes billions of dollars for shareholders and many millions for top executives, you probably won't think that these gains actually come largely from leveraging the work done by others – whether these be government agencies, not-for-profit institutions, or achievements fought for by civil society organizations including trade unions that have been critical for fighting for workers' training programmes.

Third, this market story confuses policymakers. By and large, policymakers of all stripes want to help their communities and their country, and they think the way to do so is to put more trust in market mechanisms, with policy just a matter of tinkering at the edges. The crucial thing is to be seen as progressive while also 'business-friendly'. But with a very limited understanding of where value comes from, politicians and all too many government employees are like putty in the hands of those who claim to be value creators. Regulators end up being lobbied by businesses and induced to endorse policies which make incumbents even richer – increasing profits but with little effect on investment. Examples include ways in which governments across much of the Western world have been persuaded to reduce capital gains tax, even though there is no reason to do so if the aim is to promote long-term investments rather than short-term ones. And lobbyists with their innovation stories have pushed through the Patent Box policy, which reduces tax on the profits generated from 20-year patent-based monopolies – even though the policy's main impact has been merely to reduce government revenue, rather than increasing the types of investments that led to the patents in the first place.[5] All of which serves only to subtract value from the economy and make for a less attractive future for almost everyone. Not having a clear view of the collective value creation process, the public sector is thus 'captured' – entranced by stories about wealth creation which have led to regressive tax policies that increase inequality.

Fourth, and last, the confusion between profits and rents appears in the ways we measure growth itself: GDP. Indeed, it is here that the production boundary comes back to haunt us: if anything that fetches a price is value, then the way national accounting is done wont be able to distinguish value creation from value extraction and thus policies aimed at the former might simply lead to the latter. This is not only true for the environment where picking up the mess of pollution will definitely increase GDP (due to the cleaning services paid for) while a cleaner environment won't necessarily (indeed if it leads to less 'things' produced it could decrease GDP), but also as we saw to the world of finance where the distinction between financial services that feed industry's need for long-term credit versus those financial services that simply feed other parts of the financial sector are not distinguished.

Only with a clear debate about value can rent-extracting activities in every sector, including the public one, be better identified and deprived of political and ideological strength.

MARKETS AS OUTCOMES

Redefining value must start with a deeper interrogation of the concepts on which much of today's policy is based. First and most fundamental, what are markets? They are not things-in-themselves. They are shaped by society, and are outcomes of multi-agent processes in a specific context. If we regard markets this way, our view of government policy changes too. Rather than a series of intrusive 'interventions' in an otherwise free-standing market economy, government policy can be seen for what it is: part of the social process which co-shapes and co-creates competitive markets. Second, what are private–public partnerships? Or, more precisely, what kinds of private–public partnerships will provide society with its desired outcomes? To answer that question economists should abandon their desire to think like physicists and turn instead to biology, and consider how functional partnerships are those that emulate a mutualistic eco-system rather than a parasitic or predator–prey one.

As Karl Polanyi wrote, markets are deeply embedded in social and political institutions.[6] They are outcomes of complex processes, of interactions between different actors in the economy, including government. This is not a normative point but a structural one: how new socio-economic arrangements come about. The very fact that the market is co-shaped by different actors – including, crucially, policymakers – offers hope that a better future *can* be constructed. We can fashion markets in ways that produce desirable outcomes such as 'green growth' or a more 'caring' society with care influencing the type of social and physical infrastructure that is built. By the same token, we can allow speculative short-term finance to triumph over long-term investment. As we have already seen, even Adam Smith was of the opinion that markets needed to be shaped. Contrary to the modern interpretation of his work as 'laissez-faire' (leave the market alone), he believed that the right kind of freedom is not the absence of government policy, but freedom from rent extraction. Smith would have been baffled by the current understanding of economic freedom as a minimum of non-private activity. His *Wealth of Nations* is a huge book, largely because even in that simpler economic world there were so many varieties of rent-seeking to discuss. He devoted many pages to productive and unproductive activities, often simplistically putting some inside the production boundary and some outside. Karl Marx was subtler: it was not the sector itself that mattered, but how exactly it interacted with the creation of value and the important concept in his analysis of *surplus value*.

Polanyi helps us to go beyond both Smith and Marx. Rather than focusing on which activities are inside or outside the production boundary, today we can work to ensure that all activities – in both the real economy and in the financial sector – promote the outcomes that we want: if the quality and characteristics of an activity in question help deliver true value, then it should be rewarded for being inside the boundary. Policymakers must be emboldened to broker 'deals' that generate symbiotic public–private partnerships. In the case of finance, it would mean favouring long-term investment over short-term (through measures like a financial transaction tax), but, even more, founding new financial institutions (like mission-oriented state investment banks) that can provide the strategic, long-term finance crucial to the high risk investments required for exploration and research underlying value creation.

Beyond the financial sector, patent law and regulation should encourage big pharma to foster research into needed essential drugs rather than, as is currently so often the case, block competition and innovation through the use of strong and wide patents. One possibility is to grant fewer patents upstream, leaving the tools for research open-access. And the prices of the drugs should reflect the overall 'deal' between public and private actors, not force the taxpayer to pay twice. Furthermore, the high level of share buybacks in the sector should be questioned before government handouts are provided. In general, government support should be made conditional on an increase in committed investment by business – reducing the trends of hoarding and financialization.

In the ICT and digital sectors, more thinking is required about the appropriate tax system for companies like Uber and Airbnb, which would never have existed without publicly funded technology such as GPS and the Internet and which exploited network effects to create their potentially highly profitable first-mover advantages. It should be clear that many people – not just company employees – have contributed to their competitive advantage. How we govern technology affects who shares in the benefits. The digital revolution requires participatory democracy, keeping the citizen, not big business or big government, at the centre of technological change. Take smart meters, for example; Morozov argues that if they are closed boxes transferring information, 'what we are doing is essentially introducing more and more closed systems which simply seek to capture rent from infrastructure that has been funded by us, without letting us the citizens take advantage of the same infrastructure for our own purposes and our own monitoring of the government, whether it is the city, or the national government'.[7]

With this in mind, we can move beyond the idea of public goods as 'corrections', that is being limited to areas that need fixing (due to positive externalities that they generate), to being 'objectives'. This requires a new understanding of policy as actively 'shaping' and 'creating' markets that achieve public value, benefitting society more widely.

Making public value better justified, appreciated and evaluated would potentially open up a new vocabulary for policy makers. Rather than being mere 'regulators' of health care or the digital agenda, as co-creators of that care and digital transformation policymakers would have a more justifiable right to make sure that the benefits are accessible to all. A different vocabulary, and a new policymaking framework, would also reduce the timidity which has kept politicians from funding much-needed infrastructure investments for decades, and which led to a bare-minimum fiscal and legislative response to the 2008 financial crisis and subsequent recession. Once the potential of the executive and legislative branches to promote the good of society is fully recognized, then elected officials can start to live up to higher, but still realistic, expectations. Young, ambitious people might start choose electoral politics, or careers in the civil service, over jobs in the City or business – but only if they see that such choices are valuable and valued.

TAKING THE ECONOMY ON A MISSION

The question remains: what direction should the economy take if it is to benefit the greatest number of people? Maximum GDP growth, one standard answer these days, is far too crude to be helpful: it sweeps away all the serious questions about value. Another common answer is fiscal probity, governments running balanced budgets or even, as in Germany, a surplus. This, however, is not only crude but wrong-headed. The drive to reduce government deficits after the 2009 recession continues to impede a proper European economic recovery. A low fiscal deficit is a misplaced target. The real question is how government spending and investment can create long-term growth. And while such investments might require short-term deficits to increase, in the long term by raising GDP, the debt–GDP ratio will be kept in check by the effects of such value-creating investments. This is indeed why so many countries that continue to have modest deficits might also have a high debt–GDP ratio.

The question of growth must thus focus less on the rate of growth and more on its direction. A more open discussion of economic value could, I believe, also help shape discussions about directionality. Progressive arguments against fiscal austerity too often default to a cry for investing in infrastructure (or 'shovel ready' projects) as though that were a panacea. That is a very modest demand. The discussion of the kind of infrastructure, and its relationship to greater social goals, has been puerile. Just roads and bridges? Public investment that is driven by ambition and a vision cannot be limited to a laundry list of traditional physical infrastructure projects. The first step should be to think seriously about the problem in question. A green transformation requires not only green infrastructure but a clear vision of what living a green life means. It means transforming all sectors, including traditional ones like steel to lower its material content.

Indeed, a key way to tackle some of society's most pressing problems today is to learn lessons from historical periods in which bold ambitions were set to tackle difficult technological problems. Consider two lessons from the man on moon mission. First, the agencies involved, from NASA to DARPA, built up their own capacity and competences. They did not outsource their tasks, or the resulting knowledge, to the private sector. This practice should be borne in mind when considering the currently fashionable public–private partnership arrangements. They will only succeed as dynamic knowledge-intensive collaborations, with both sides equally committed to investing in in-house competencies and capabilities.

Second, the Apollo mission required different types of actors and sectors to collaborate, from aerospace to innovations in textiles. The focus was not on subsidising a sector (aeronautics) but on solving problems together, which required many sectors and different types of public and private actors to collaborate – even those in low-tech sectors like textiles. Similarly, today's challenge to reverse human damage to the environment is not something that can be solved solely by increased investment in renewable energy – although that is already a daunting technological challenge – but requires a societal commitment to new, less physically materialist approaches to the way we live. Concrete missions that involve different types of collaboration are required to drive the fight against climate change or the fight to eradicate cancer – with clear targets, a multitude of sectors and actors, co-investing and exploring new landscapes, but also patience in achieving long-term goals. Past periods of technological upheaval have been associated with changes in lifestyle, such as the connection between mass-production and suburbanization.[8] A green revolution will require deliberate and conscious changes in social values: a redirection of the entire economy, transforming production, distribution and consumption in all sectors.

A BETTER FUTURE FOR ALL

The concept of value must once again find its rightful place at the centre of economic thinking. More fulfilling jobs, less pollution, better care, more equal pay – what sort of economy do we want? When that question is answered, we can decide how to shape our economic activities, thereby moving activities that fulfill these goals inside the production boundary so they are rewarded for steering growth in the ways we deem desirable. And in the meantime we can also make a much better job of reducing activities that are purely about rent-seeking and calibrating rewards more closely with truly productive activity.

I began the book stating that the goal was not to argue that one value theory is better than another. My aim is for the book to stir a new debate, putting value back at the centre of economic reasoning. This is not about drawing firm and static fences around the production boundary, arguing that some actors are parasitic or takers, while others are glorious producers and makers. Rather we should have a more dynamic understanding of what making and taking are in the context of the societal objectives we have. Both objective and subjective factors will no doubt come into play, but the subjective ones should not reduce everything to an individual choice, stripped from the social, political and economic context in which decisions are made. It is those very contexts that are affected by the (objective) dynamics of technological change and corporate governance structures. The latter will affect the way that income distribution is determined, as will the strength of workers to bargain their share. These structural forces are results of decision-making inside organizations. There is nothing inevitable or deterministic about it.

I have tried to open the new dialogue by showing that the creation of value is collective, that policy can be more active around co-shaping and co-creating markets, and that real progress requires a dynamic division of labour focused on the problems that twenty-first-century societies are facing. If I have been critical, it's because such criticism is badly needed; it is, moreover, a necessary preliminary to the creation of a new economics: an economics of hope. After all, if we cannot dream of a better future and try to make it happen, there is no real reason why we should care about value. And this perhaps is the greatest lesson of all.

Bibliography

Aghion, P., Van Reenen, J. and Zingales, L., 'Innovation and institutional ownership', *American Economic Review*, 103(1) (2013), pp. 277–304.

Alperovitz, G. and Daly, L., 'Who is really "deserving"? Inequality and the ethics of social inheritance', *Dissent*, Fall 2009, p. 90.

Arrow, K., *Social Choice and Individual Values* (New Haven: Cowles Foundation, 1951).

Atkinson, T., *Atkinson Review: Final Report. Measurement of Government Output and Productivity for the National Accounts* (Basingstoke and New York: Palgrave Macmillan, 2005).

Barba, A. and Pivetti, M., 'Rising household debt: Its causes and macroeconomic implications – A long-period analysis', *Cambridge Journal of Economics*, 33(1) (2009), pp. 113–37.

Barba, A. and de Vivo, G., 'An "unproductive labour" view of finance', *Cambridge Journal of Economics*, 36(6) (2012): http://doi.org/10.1093/cje/ber022

Barrett, P. and Langreth, R., 'Pharma execs don't know why anyone is upset by a $94,500 miracle cure', *Bloomberg Businessweek*, 3 June 2015: https://www.bloomberg.com/news/articles/2015-06-03/specialty-drug-costs-gilead-s-hepatitis-c-cures-spur-backlash

Barro, R. J. and Redlick, C. J., 'Macroeconomic effects from government purchases and taxes', *Quarterly Journal of Economics*, 126(1) (2011), pp. 51–102: https://doi/org:10.1093/qje/qjq002

Barton, D. and Wiseman, M., 'Focusing capital on the long term', *Harvard Business Review*, January–February 2014.

Baumol, W. J., 'Contestable markets: An uprising in the theory of industry structure', *American Economic Review*, 72(1) (1982).

Baumol, W. J., 'Entrepreneurship: Productive, unproductive, and destructive', *Journal of Political Economy*, 98(5) (1990), pp. 893–921.

Baumol, W. J., *Entrepreneurship, Management and the Nature of Payoffs* (Cambridge, MA: MIT Press, 1993).

Bayliss, K., *Case Study: The Financialisation of Water in England and Wales*, FESSUD (Financialisation, Economy, Society and Sustainable Development) Working Paper series no. 52 (2014).

BEA, *Measuring the Economy: A Primer on GDP and the National Income and Product Accounts* (Washington, DC: Bureau of Economic Analysis, US Department of Commerce, 2014): http://www.bea.gov/national/pdf/nipa_primer.pdf

Beesley, A. and Barker, A., 'Apple tax deal: How it worked and what the EU ruling means', *Financial Times*, 30 August 2016: https://www.ft.com/content/cc58c190-6ec3-11e6-a0c9-1365ce54b926

Bentham, J., *A Fragment on Government* (London: 1776).

Bergh, A. and Henrekson, M., 'Government size and growth: A survey and interpretation of the evidence', *Journal of Economic Surveys*, 25(5) (2011), pp. 872–97: http://doi.org/10.1111/j.1467-6419.2011.00697.x

Bernanke, B. S., 'The Great Moderation', remarks at the meetings of the Eastern Economic Association, Washington, DC, 20 February 2004.

Bessen, J. and Meurer, M. J., *The Patent Litigation Explosion*, 45 Loy. U. Chi. L. J. 401 (2013): http://lawcommons.luc.edu/luclj/vol45/iss2/5

Bessen, J. and Meurer, M. J., 'The direct costs from NPE disputes', *Cornell Law Review*, 99(2) (2015).

Bogle, J. C., *The Clash of the Cultures: Investment vs. Speculation* (Hoboken, NJ: John Wiley and Sons, 2012).

Bogle, J. C., 'The arithmetic of "all-in" investment expenses', *Financial Analysts Journal*, 70(1) (2014).

Borio, C., Drehmann, M. and Tsatsaronis, K., 'Anchoring countercyclical capital buffers: The role of credit aggregates', BIS Working Paper no. 355 (November 2011).

Boss, H. H., *Theories of Surplus and Transfer: Parasites and Producers in Economic Thought* (Boston, MA: Unwin Hyman, 1990).

The Boston Consulting Group, *Doubling Down on Data*, Global Asset Management (2016): http://www.agefi.fr/sites/agefi.fr/files/fichiers/2016/07/bcg-doubling-down-on-data-july-2016_tcm80-2113701.pdf

Bozeman, B., *Public Values and Public Interest: Counterbalancing Economic Individualism* (Washington, DC: Georgetown University Press, 2007).

Brown, G., '2007 Financial Statement at the House of Commons': http://www.publications.parliament.uk/pa/cm200607/cmhansrd/cm070321/debtext/70321-0004.htm

Buchanan, J. M., 'Public Choice: The origins and development of a research program', *Champions of Freedom*, 31 (2003), pp. 13–32.

Buffett, W. E., 'Stop coddling the super-rich', *New York Times*, 14 August 2011: http://www.nytimes.com/2011/08/15/opinion/stop-coddling-the-super-rich.html?_r=2&hp

Buiter, W., 'Housing wealth isn't wealth', National Bureau of Economic Research Working Paper no. 14204, July 2008.

Burns, D., Cowie, L., Earles, J., Folkman, P., Froud, J., Hyde, P., Johal, S., Rees Jones, I., Killett, A. and Williams, K., *Where Does the Money Go? Financialised Chains and the Crisis in Residential Care*, CRESC Public Interest Report, March 2015.

Business Week, 'Blue-ribbon venture capital', 29 October 1960.

Butler, S., 'How Philip Green's family made millions as value of BHS plummeted', the *Guardian*, 25 April 2016: https://www.theguardian.com/business/2016/apr/25/bhs-philip-green-family-millions-administration-arcadia

Chien, C. V., 'Startups and patent trolls', *Stanford Technology Law Review*, 17 (2014), pp. 461–506.

Christophers, B., 'Making finance productive', *Economy and Society*, 40(1) (2011), pp. 112–40.

Christophers, B., *Banking Across Boundaries* (Chichester: Wiley-Blackwell, 2013).

Churchill, W., 'WSC to Sir Otto Niemeyer, 22 February 1925', Churchill College, Cambridge, CHAR 18/12A-B.

Clark, J. B., *The Distribution of Wealth: A Theory of Wages, Interest and Profits* (New York: Macmillan, 1899).

Cohen, L., Coval, J. and Malloy, C., 'Do powerful politicians cause corporate downsizing?', *Journal of Political Economy*, 119(6) (2011), pp. 1015–60: https://doi.org/10.1086/664820

Cohen, W. M., Goto, A., Nagata, A., Nelson, R. R. and Walsh, J. P., 'R&D spillovers, patents and the incentives to innovate in Japan and the United States', *Research Policy*, 31(8–9) (2002), pp. 1349–67: http://doi.org/10.1016/S0048-7333(02)00068-9

Cournède, B. and Denk, O., 'Finance and economic growth in OECD and G20 countries', OECD Economics Department Working Paper no. 1223 (2015).

Coyle, D., *GDP: A Brief but Affectionate History* (Princeton, NJ: University Press, 2014).

Crane, E., *Ownership of UK Quoted Shares: 2014* (London: Office for National Statistics, 2015): https://www.ons.gov.uk/economy/investmentspensionsand trusts/bulletins/ownershipofukquotedshares/2015-09-02

Crouch, C., 'Privatised Keynesianism: An unacknowledged policy regime', *British Journal of Politics and International Relations*, 11(3) (2009), pp. 382–99.

Crouch, C., *The Knowledge Corrupters: Hidden Consequences of the Financial Takeover of Public Life* (Cambridge: Polity Press, 2016).

Dahl, R., *Charlie and the Chocolate Factory* (New York: Knopf, 1964).

David, P., 'Clio and the economics of QWERTY', *American Economic Review*, 75(2), *Papers and Proceedings of the Ninety-Seventh Annual Meeting of the American Economic Association* (May 1985), pp. 332–7.

Davidoff, S., 'Why I.P.O.s get underpriced', Dealbook, *New York Times*, 27 May 2011.

Davies, R., 'Uber suffers legal setbacks in France and Germany', the *Guardian*, 9 June 2016: https://www.theguardian.com/technology/2016/jun/09/uber-suffers-legal-setbacks-in-france-and-germany

Dezember, R., 'KKR to earn big payout from Walgreen–Alliance Boots deal', *Wall Street Journal*, 1 January 2015.

Dosi, G., 'Sources, procedures, and microeconomic effects of innovation', *Journal of Economic Literature*, 26 (1988), pp. 1120–71.

Dilulio, J., *Bring Back the Bureaucrats: Why More Federal Workers Will Lead to Better (and Smaller!) Government* (West Conshohocken, PA: Templeton Press, 2014).

The *Economist*, 'The third industrial revolution', 21 April 2012: http://www.economist.com/node/21553017

The *Economist*, 'Time to fix the patents', 8 August 2015: http://www.economist.com/news/leaders/21660522-ideas-fuel-economy-todays-patent-systems-are-rotten-way-rewarding-them-time-fix

Eichengreen, B., *The European Economy since 1945: Coordinated Capitalism and Beyond* (Princeton, NJ: University Press, 2008).

Ellis, K., Michaely, R. and O'Hara, M., 'When the underwriter is the market maker: An examination of trading in the IPO aftermarket', *Journal of Finance*, 55(3) (1999), pp. 1039–74.

Elson, D., *Macroeconomics and Macroeconomic Policy from a Gender Perspective*, Public Hearing of Study Commission on Globalization of the World Economy – Challenges and Responses, Deutscher Bundestag, Berlin, 18 February 2002.

Epstein, G. A., *Financialization and the World Economy* (Cheltenham and Northampton, MA: Edward Elgar Publishing, 2005).

Evans, P., *Embedded Autonomy: States and Industrial Transformation* (Princeton, NJ: University Press, 1995).

Falck, O., Gollier, C. and Woessmann, L., 'Arguments for and against policies to promote national champions', in Falck, O., Gollier, C. and Woessmann, L. (eds), *Industrial Policy for National Champions* (Cambridge, MA: MIT Press, 2011), pp. 3–9.

Fama, E., 'Efficient capital markets: A review of theory and empirical work', *Journal of Finance*, 25(2) (1970).

Farrell, G., 'Blankfein defends pay levels for "more productive" Goldman staff', *Financial Times*, 11 November 2009: http://www.ft.com/intl/cms/s/0/c99bf08e-ce62-11de-a1ea-00144feabdc0.html

Farrell, M., 'The Internet of things – Who wins, who loses?', the *Guardian*, 14 August 2015.

Fioramonti, L., *Gross Domestic Problem* (London: Zed Books, 2013).

Foley, D. K., *Adam's Fallacy: A Guide to Economic Theology* (Cambridge, MA: Belknap Press, 2006).

Foley, D. K., 'Rethinking financial capitalism and the "information" economy', *Review of Radical Political Economics*, 45(3) (2013), pp. 257–68: http://doi.org/10.1177/0486613413487154

Forero-Pineda, C., 'The Impact of stronger intellectual property rights on science and technology in developing countries', *Research Policy*, 36(6) (2006), pp. 808–24.

Foroohar, R., *Makers and Takers* (New York: Crown, 2016).

Fortado, L., 'Hedge funds fees take a trim', *Financial Times*, 22 December 2016: https://www.ft.com/content/ab1ce98e-c5da-11e6-9043-7e34c07b46ef

Freeman, R. E., Harrison, J. S., Wicks, A. C., Parmar, B. L. and de Colle, S., *Stakeholder Theory: The State of the Art* (Cambridge: University Press, 2010).

Friedman, B. M., 'Crowding out or crowding in? Economic consequences of financing government deficits', *Brookings Papers on Economic Activity*, 3 (1979), pp. 593–654.

Friedman, M., *Capitalism and Freedom* (Chicago, Ill.: University Press, 1962).

Furceri, D. and Mourougane, A., 'Financial crises: Past lessons and policy implications', *OECD Economics Department Working Papers* no. 668 (2009): http://www.oecd.org/officialdocuments/publicdisplaydocumentpdf/?doclanguage=en&cote=eco/wkp(2009)9

Gaus, G. F., *Value and Justification: The Foundations of Liberal Theory* (New York: Cambridge University Press, 1990).

Gertner, J., *The Idea Factory: Bell Labs and the Great Age of American Innovation* (London and New York: Penguin, 2013).

Gimein, M., Dash, E., Munoz, L. and Sung, J., 'You bought. They SOLD', *Fortune*, 146(4) (2002), pp. 64–8, 72, 74.

Glyn, A., *Capitalism Unleashed: Finance, Globalization and Welfare* (Oxford: University Press, 2006).

Gompers, P. A. and Lerner, J., *The Venture Capital Cycle* (Cambridge, MA: MIT Press, 2002).

Goodhart, C. A. E., 'Competition and credit control', Financial Markets Group, London School of Economics, Special Paper no. 229 (2014).

Greenspan, A. and Kennedy, J., *Estimates of Home Mortgage Originations, Repayments, and Debt on One-to-Four-Family Residences*, Finance and Economic Discussion Series 2005-41 (Washington, DC: Board of Governors of the Federal Reserve System, 2005).

Haber, S. and Werfel, S. H., 'Patent trolls as financial intermediaries? Experimental evidence', *Economics Letters*, 149 (2016), pp. 64–6: http://dx.doi.org/10.2139/ssrn.2552734

Hadas, E., 'Seeing straight: Why buybacks should be banned', *Breakingviews*, 14 December 2014: https://www.breakingviews.com/features/why-buy backs-should-be-banned/

Haywood, W. D., *Bill Haywood's Book: The Autobiography of Big Bill Haywood* (New York: International Publishers, 1929).

Henderson, N. and Schrage, M., 'The roots of biotechnology: Government R&D spawns a new industry', *Washington Post*, 16 December 1984: https://www.washingtonpost.com/archive/politics/1984/12/16/government-r38/cb 580e3d-4ce2-4950-bf12-a717b4d3ca36/?utm_term=.27fd51946872

Herndon, T., Ash, M. and Pollin, R., 'Does high public debt consistently stifle economic growth? A critique of Reinhart and Rogoff', *Cambridge Journal of Economics*, 38(2) (2014), pp. 257–79: http://doi.org/10.1093/cje/beto75

Hill, A., Khoo, S., Fortunak J., Simmons, B. and Ford, N., 'Minimum costs for producing Hepatitis C direct-acting antivirals for use in large-scale treatment access programs in developing countries', *Clinical Infectious Diseases*, 58(7) (2014), pp. 928–36: https://doi.org/10.1093/cid/ciuo12

Hill, C., *The Century of Revolution 1603–1714* (London: Nelson, 1980).

Hill, J. M., 'Alpha as a net zero-sum game: How serious a constraint?', *Journal of Portfolio Management*, 32(4) (2006), pp. 24–32: https://doi.org/10.3905/jpm.2006.644189

Hill, P., 'The services of financial intermediaries, or FISIM revisited', paper presented to the Joint UNECE/Eurostat/ OECD Meeting on National Accounts, Geneva, 30 April–3 May 1996: http://www.oecd.org/dataoecd /13/62/2790061.pdf.

Hilner, B. E. and Smith, T. J., 'Efficacy does not necessarily translate to cost effectiveness: A case study in the challenges associated with 21st-century cancer drug prices', *Journal of Clinical Oncology*, 27(13) (2009).

Hooper, R., 'Saving the Royal Mail's universal postal service in the digital age: An update of the 2008 *Independent Review of the UK Postal Services Sector*, September 2010: https://www.gov.uk/government/uploads/

system/uploads/attachment_data/file/31808/10-1143-saving-royal-mail-univ
ersal-postal-service.pdf

Houlder, V., Beesley, A. and Barker, A., 'Apple's EU tax dispute explained', *Financial Times*, 30 August 2016: https://www.ft.com/content/3e0172a0-6e1b-11e6-9ac1-1055824ca907

Hutton, D., Smith, I. R. and Hooper, R., *Modernise or Decline: Policies to Maintain the Universal Postal Service in the United Kingdom, Independent Review of the UK Postal Services Sector*: https://www.gov.uk/government/uploads/system/uploads/attachment_data/file/228786/7529.pdf

'Fiscal policy as a countercyclical tool', *World Economic Outlook*, ch. 5 (Washington, DC: International Monetary Fund, October 2008).

Jacobs, M. and Mazzucato, M. (eds), *Rethinking Capitalism: Economics and Policy for Sustainable and Inclusive Growth* (Chichester: Wiley-Blackwell, 2016).

Jensen, M. J. and Meckling, W. H., 'Theory of the firm: Managerial behavior, agency costs and ownership structure', *Journal of Financial Economics*, 3(4) (1976), pp. 305–60.

Jevons, W. S., *The Theory of Political Economy*, 2nd edn, ed. Collison Black, R. D. (Harmondsworth: Penguin, 1970).

Jorgenson, D. W., 'A new architecture for the U.S. national accounts', *Review of Income and Wealth*, 55(1) (2009), pp. 1–42.

J. P. Morgan, 'Bridging the gap between interest rates and investments', JPM Corporate Finance Advisory, September 2014.

Kantarjian, H. and Rajkumar, S. V., 'Why are cancer drugs so expensive in the United States, and what are the solutions?', *Mayo Clinic Proceedings*, April 2015.

Kasperkevic, J., 'America's top CEOs pocket 340 times more than average workers', the *Guardian*, 17 May 2016: https://www.theguardian.com/us-news/2016/may/17/ceo-pay-ratio-average-worker-afl-cio

Keller, M. R. and Block, F., 'Explaining the transformation in the US innovation system: The impact of a small government program', *Socio-Economic Review*, 11(4) (2013), pp. 629–56: https://doi.org/10.1093/ser/mws021

Kelly, K., 'The new socialism: Global collectivist society is coming online', *Wired* magazine, 17 June 2009.

Kendrick, J., 'The historical development of national-income accounts', *History of Political Economy*, 2(2) (1970), pp. 284–315.

Kennedy, J. F., 'Moon speech', Rice Stadium, 12 September 1962: https://er.jsc.nasa.gov/seh/ricetalk.htm

Kennedy, J. F., 'Address before the Irish Parliament in Dublin', 28 June 1963: https://www.jfklibrary.org/Asset-Viewer/lPAi7jx2soi7kePPdJnUXA.aspx

Kenney, M. and Patton, D., 'Reconsidering the Bayh-Dole Act and the current university invention ownership model', *Research Policy*, 38(9) (2009), pp. 1407–22.

Keynes, J. M., *The End of Laissez Faire* (London: Hogarth Press, 1926).

Keynes, J. M., *The General Theory of Employment, Interest and Money* (London: Macmillan, 1936).

Keynes, J. M., *How to Pay for the War* (New York: Harcourt, 1940).

Keynes, J. M., 'Proposals for an International Clearing Union', in *The Collected Writings of John Maynard Keynes*, ed. Moggridge, D., vol. 25: *Activities 1940–1944. Shaping the Post-War World. The Clearing Union* (Cambridge: University Press, 1943).

Kirkwood, G. and Pollock, A. M., 'Patient choice and private provision decreased public provision and increased inequalities in Scotland: A case study of elective hip arthroplasty', *Journal of Public Health*, 39(3) (2017), pp. 593–60.

Kliff, S., 'Meet Serco, the private firm getting $1.2 billion to process your Obamacare application', *Washington Post*, 16 July 2013: https://www.washingtonpost.com/news/wonk/wp/2013/07/16/meet-serco-the-private-firm-getting-1-2-billion-to-process-your-obamacare-application/?utm_term=.33eeeadf4a01

Kokalitcheva, K., 'Uber now has 40 million monthly riders worldwide', *Fortune*, 20 October 2016: http://fortune.com/2016/10/20/uber-app-riders/

Krueger, A. O., 'The political economy of the rent-seeking society', *American Economic Review*, 64(3) (1974), pp. 291–303.

Kuznets, S., *National Income: A Summary of Findings* (New York: National Bureau of Economic Research, 1946).

LaMattina, J., 'Politicians shouldn't question drug costs but rather their value. Lessons from Soliris and Sovaldi', *Forbes*, 4 August 2014: https://www.forbes.com/sites/johnlamattina/2014/08/04/politicians-shouldnt-question-drug-costs-but-rather-their-value-lessons-from-soliris-and-sovaldi/#5d9664502675

La Roche, J. and Crowe, P., 'The richest hedge fund managers in the world', *Business Insider*, 2 March 2016.

Lavoie, M., *Introduction to Post-Keynesian Economics* (Basingstoke: Palgrave Macmillan, 2009).

Lazonick, W., *Sustainable Prosperity in the New Economy? Business Organization and High-Tech Employment in the United States* (Kalamazoo, MI: W. E. Upjohn Institute for Employment Research, 2009): https://doi.org/10.17848/9781441639851

Lazonick, W., 'Profits without prosperity', *Harvard Business Review*, September 2014.

Lazonick, W., 'Innovative enterprise or sweatshop economics? In search of foundations of economic analysis', ISIGrowth Working Paper no. 17 (2016).

Lazonick, W. and Tulum, Ö., 'US biopharmaceutical finance and the sustainability of the biotech business model', *Research Policy*, 40(9) (2011), pp. 1170–87.

Lazonick, W. and Mazzucato, M., 'The risk–reward nexus in the innovation–inequality relationship: Who takes the risks? Who gets the rewards?', *Industrial and Corporate Change*, 22(4) (2013), pp. 1093–128: https://doi.org/10.1093/icc/dtt019

Lazonick, W., Mazzucato, M. and Tulum, Ö., 'Apple's changing business model: What should the world's richest company do with its profits?', *Accounting Forum*, 37 (2013), pp. 249–67.

Leigh, D. and Blanchard, O. J., 'Growth forecast errors and fiscal multipliers', Working Paper no. 13/1 (Washington, DC: International Monetary Fund, 2013).

Leigh, D., Devries, P., Freedman, C., Guajardo, J., Laxton, D. and Pescatori, A., 'Will it hurt? Macroeconomic effects of fiscal consolidation', IMF *World Economic Outlook* (2010), pp. 93–124.

Lemley, M. A., 'Software patents and the return of functional claiming', *Wisconsin Law Review*, 2013(4), pp. 905–64.

Lemley, M. A. and Shapiro, C., 'Probabilistic patents', *Journal of Economic Perspectives*, 19(2) (2005), pp. 75–98: DOI: 10.1257/0895330054048650.

Lequiller, F. and Blades, D., 'The general government account', in *Understanding National Accounts*, 2nd edn (Paris?: OECD Publishing, 2014): http://doi.org/10.1787/9789264214637-en

Leslie, S. W., *The Cold War and American Science: The Military-Industrial-Academic Complex at MIT and Stanford* (New York: Columbia University Press, 1993).

Levina, I., 'A puzzling rise in financial profits and the role of capital gain-like revenues', Political Economy Research Institute Working Paper no. 347 (April 2014).

Light, D. W. and Lexchin, J. R., 'Pharmaceutical research and development: What do we get for all that money?', *BMJ*, 2012;345:e4348: http://dx.doi.org/10.1136/bmj.e4348

MacFarlane, L., *Blueprint for a Scottish National Investment Bank* (London: New Economics Foundation, 2016).

Malthus, T. R., *An Essay on the Principle of Population*, critical edn ed. James, P. (1798; Cambridge: University Press, 1989).

Marshall, A., *Elements of Economics of Industry* (London: Macmillan, 1892).

Marshall, A., *Principles of Economics* (1890; London: Macmillan, 1920).

Marx, K., *Theories of Surplus Value* (vol. 4 of *Capital*), Part I (Moscow: Progress Publishers, 1863).

Marx, K., *Capital*, vol. 1 (London: Penguin Classics, 2004).

Marx, K., *Capital*, vol. 3 (London: Penguin Classics, 1992).

Marx, K. and Engels, F., *The Communist Manifesto* (1848; London: Penguin Classics, 2010).

Mason, R., 'G4S fined 100 times since 2010 for breaching prison contracts', the *Guardian*, 15 April 2016: https://www.theguardian.com/society/2016/apr/15/g4s-fined-100-times-since-2010-prison-contracts

Mazzoleni, R. and Nelson, R., 'The benefit and costs of strong patent protection: A contribution to the current debate', *Research Policy*, 27 (1998), pp. 273–84.

Mazzucato, M., *The Entrepreneurial State: Debunking Public vs. Private Sector Myths* (London: Anthem Press, 2013).

Mazzucato, M., 'From market-fixing to market-creating: A new framework for innovation policy', special issue of *Industry and Innovation*: 'Innovation policy – Can it make a difference?', 23(2) (2016).

Mazzucato, M. and Penna, C., 'Beyond market failures: The market creating and shaping roles of state investment banks', *Journal of Economic Policy Reform*, 19(4) (2016), pp. 305–26.

Mazzucato, M. and Shipman, A., 'Accounting for productive investment and value creation', *Industrial and Corporate Change*, 23(4) (2014), pp. 1059–85: http://doi.org/10.1093/icc/dtt037

Mazzucato, M. and Wray, L. R., 'Financing the capital development of the economy: A Keynes-Schumpeter-Minsky Synthesis', Levy Economics Institute Working Paper no. 837 (2015).

McLeay, M., Radia, A. and Thomas, L. R., 'Money creation in the modern economy', *Bank of England Quarterly Bulletin*, 54(1) (2014), pp. 1–14.

Meek, R. L., *The Economics of Physiocracy: Essays and Translations* (London: George Allen & Unwin, 1962).

Merler, S. and Hüttl, P., 'Welcome to the dark side: GDP revision and the non-observed economy', Bruegel, 2 March 2015: http://bruegel.org/2015/03/welcome-to-the-dark-side-gdp-revision-and-the-non-observed-economy/

Metrick, A. and Yasuda, A., 'The economics of private equity', *Review of Financial Studies*, 23(6) (2011), pp. 2303–41: https://doi.org/10.1093/rfs/hhq020

Minsky, H. P., 'The financial instability hypothesis: An interpretation of Keynes and an alternative to "standard" theory', *Challenge*, 20(1) (1977), pp. 20–27.

Minsky, H. P., *Stabilizing an Unstable Economy* (New Haven and London: Yale University Press, 1986).

Minsky, H. P., 'Reconstituting the United States' financial structure', Levy Economics Institute Working Paper no. 69 (1992).

Minsky, H. P., 'The capital development of the economy and the structure of financial institutions', Hyman P. Minsky Archive, Paper no. 179 (1992).

Minsky, H. P., 'Finance and stability: The limits of capitalism', Levy Economics Institute Working Paper no. 93 (1993).

Mirowski, P., *More Heat than Light: Economics as Social Physics, Physics as Nature's Economics* (Cambridge: University Press, 1989).

Mirowski, P., 'Learning the meaning of a dollar: Conservation principles and the social theory of value in economic theory', *Social Research* 57(3) (1990), pp. 689–718.

Mishan, E. J., *The Costs of Economic Growth* (New York: Praeger, 1967).

Morozov, E., 'Don't believe the hype, the "sharing economy" masks a failing economy', the *Guardian*, 28 September 2014: http://www.theguardian. com/commentisfree/2014/sep/28/sharing-economy-internet-hype-benefits-overstated-evgeny-morozov

Morozov, E., 'Silicon Valley likes to promise "digital socialism" – but it is selling a fairy tale', the *Guardian*, 28 February 2015.

Morozov, E., 'Where Uber and Amazon rule: Welcome to the world of the platform', the *Guardian*, 6 June 2015.

Morozov, E., 'Cheap cab ride? You must have missed Uber's true cost', the *Guardian*, 31 January 2016: http://www.theguardian.com/commentisfree/ 2016/jan/31/cheap-cab-ride-uber-true-cost-google-wealth-taxation

Morozov, E., 'Data populists must seize our information – for the benefit of us all', the *Guardian*, 4 December 2016: https://www.theguardian.com/ commentisfree/2016/dec/04/data-populists-must-seize-information-for-benefit-of-all-evgeny-morozov

Moulton, B. R., *The System of National Accounts for the New Economy: What Should Change?* (Washington, DC: Bureau of Economic Analysis, US Department of Commerce, 2003): http://www.bea.gov/about/pdf/ sna_neweconomy_1003.pdf

Moulton, B. R., 'SNA 2008 in the US national income and product accounts' (Eurostat Conference: 'The Accounts of Society', Luxembourg, 12–13 June 2014).

Mukunda, G., 'The price of Wall Street's power', *Harvard Business Review*, June 2014.

Mun, T., *England's Treasure by Forraign Trade* (1664; London: Macmillan, 1865).

Newcomer, E., 'In video, Uber CEO argues with driver over falling fares', *Bloomberg*, 28 February 2017: https://www.bloomberg.com/news/articles/ 2017-02-28/in-video-uber-ceo-argues-with-driver-over-falling-fares

Oltermann, P., 'Berlin ban on Airbnb short-term rentals upheld by city court', the *Guardian*, 8 June 2016: https://www.theguardian.com/technology/2016/jun/08/berlin-ban-airbnb-short-term-rentals-upheld-city-court

ONS (Office for National Statistics), *Public Service Productivity Estimates: Total Public Services, 2012* (2015): http://www.ons.gov.uk/ons/dcp171766_394117.pdf

Osborne, G., Mansion House speech by the Chancellor of the Exchequer, 10 June 2015: https://www.gov.uk/government/speeches/mansion-house-2015-speech-by-the-chancellor-of-the-exchequer

Ostrom, E., *Governing the Commons: The Evolution of Institutions for Collective Action* (Cambridge: University Press, 1990).

Ostrom, E., *Understanding Institutional Diversity* (Princeton, NJ: University Press 2005).

Owen, G., *Industrial Policy in Europe Since the Second World War: What Has Been Learnt?* ECIPE Occasional Paper no. 1, 2012 (Brussels: The European Centre for International Political Economy): http://eprints.lse.ac.uk/41902/

Oxfam, *An Economy for the 1%*, Oxfam Briefing Paper, January 2016: https://www.oxfam.org/sites/www.oxfam.org/files/file_attachments/bp210-economy-one-percent-tax-havens-180116-en_0.pdf

Oxfam, *An Economy for the 99%*, Oxfam Briefing Paper, January 2017: https://www.oxfam.org/sites/www.oxfam.org/files/file_attachments/bp-economy-for-99-percent-160117-en.pdf

Palin, A., 'Chart that tells a story – UK share ownership', *Financial Times*, 4 September 2015: https://www.ft.com/content/14cda94c-5163-11e5-b029-b9d50a74fd14

Perez, C., 'Capitalism, technology and a green global golden age: The role of history in helping to shape the future', in Jacobs, M. and Mazzucato, M. (eds), *Rethinking Capitalism: Economics and Policy for Sustainable and Inclusive Growth* (Chichester: Wiley-Blackwell, 2016).

Pessoa, J. P. and Van Reenen, J., 'The UK productivity and jobs puzzle: Does the answer lie in labour market flexibility?', Centre for Economic Performance, Special Paper no. 31 (2013).

Petty, W., *A Treatise of Taxes and Contributions* (London: 1662), in Charles Henry Hull (ed.), *The Economic Writings of Sir William Petty*, 2 vols (Cambridge: University Press, 1899).

Petty, W., *Several Essays in Political Arithmetick* (London: 1699), in Charles Henry Hull (ed.), *The Economic Writings of Sir William Petty*, 2 vols (Cambridge: University Press, 1899).

Phelps, M. G., Kamarudeen, S., Mills, K. and Wild, R., 'Total public service output, inputs and productivity', *Economic and Labour Market Review*, 4(10) (2010), pp. 89–112: http://doi.org/10.1057/elmr.2010.145

Philippon, T., 'Finance vs Wal-Mart: Why are financial services so expensive?', in Blinder, A., Lo, A. and Solow, R. (eds), *Rethinking the Financial Crisis* (New York: Russell Sage Foundation, 2012): http://www.russellsage.org/sites/all/files/Rethinking-Finance/Philippon_v3.pdf

Pigou, A. C., *The Economics of Welfare* (London: Macmillan, 1926).

Piketty, T., *Capital in the Twenty-First Century* (Cambridge, MA: Harvard University Press, 2014).

Pisano, G., *Science Business: The Promise, the Reality, and the Future of Biotech* (Boston, MA: Harvard Business School Press, 2006).

Polanyi, K., *The Great Transformation: The Political and Economic Origins of Our Time* (1944; Boston, MA: Beacon Press, 2001).

Pollitt, C. and Bouckaert, G., *Public Management Reform: A Comparative Analysis* (Oxford: University Press, 2004).

Porter, M. E., *Competitive Advantage* (New York: Free Press, 1985).

Porter, M. E. and Kramer, M. R., 'Creating shared value', *Harvard Business Review*, 89 (2011), pp. 62–77.

Poterba, J. M., 'Venture capital and capital gains taxation', in L. H. Summers (ed.), *Tax Policy and the Economy*, Vol. 3 (Cambridge, MA: MIT Press, 1989), pp. 47–68.

Protess, B. and Corkery, M., 'Just how much do the top private equity earners make?', Dealbook, *New York Times*, 10 December 2016.

Reich, R. B., *The Work of Nations: Preparing Ourselves for the 21st Century Capitalism* (New York: Knopf, 1991).

Reich, R. B., 'Economist John Maynard Keynes', *TIME* magazine, 29 March 1999.

Reich, U. P. and Horz, K., 'Dividing government product between intermediate and final uses', *Review of Income and Wealth*, 28(3) (1982), pp. 325–44.

Reinert, E. S., *How Rich Countries Got Rich and Why Poor Countries Stay Poor* (London: Constable, 2008).

Reinhart, C. M. and Rogoff, K. S., 'Growth in a time of debt', *American Economic Review*, 100(2) (2010), pp. 573–8.

Reinhart, C. M. and Rogoff, K. S., 'Debt, growth and the austerity debate', *New York Times*, 25 April 2013: http://www.nytimes.com/2013/04/26/opinion/debt-growth-and-the-austerity-debate.html?_r=0

Reinhart, C. M. and Rogoff, K. S., 'Reinhart and Rogoff: Responding to our critics', *New York Times*, 25 April 2013: http://www.nytimes.com/2013/04/26/opinion/reinhart-and-rogoff-responding-to-our-critics.html

Ricardo, D., *The Works and Correspondence of David Ricardo*, ed. Sraffa, P. with the collaboration of Dobb, M. H., vol. 1: *On the Principles of Political Economy and Taxation* (Cambridge: University Press, 1951).

Ritter, J., IPO data website, 2012: http://bear.warrington.ufl.edu/ritter/ipodata.htm.

Ro, S., 'Chart of the day: Here's who owns the stock market', *Business Insider*, 13 March 2013: http://www.businessinsider.com/chart-stock-market-ownership-2013-3?IR=T

Robbins, L., *An Essay on the Nature and Significance of Economic Science* (London: Macmillan, 1932).

Rogers, C., *Money, Interest and Capital: A Study in the Foundations of Monetary Theory* (Cambridge: University Press, 1989).

Roncaglia, A., *The Wealth of Ideas: A History of Economic Thought* (Cambridge: University Press, 2005).

Roose, K., 'Silicon Valley's secessionist movement is growing', *New York* magazine, 21 October 2013: http://nymag.com/daily/intelligencer/2013/10/silicon-valleys-secessionists.html

Rubin, I. I., *Essays on Marx's Theory of Value* (1928; Detroit, Ill: Black and Red Press, 1972).

Rubin, I. I., *A History of Economic Thought* (1929; London: Pluto Press, 1989).

Saez, E., 'Striking it richer: The evolution of top incomes in the United States' (University of California, Berkeley, Department of Economics, 2015).

Samuelson, P., *Economics*, 3rd edn (New York: McGraw-Hill, 1955).

Sandel, M. J., *What Money Can't Buy: The Moral Limits of Markets* (London and New York: Allen Lane and Farrar, Straus and Giroux, 2013).

Say, J.-B., *Traité d'économie politique* (Paris: 1803).

Schumpeter, J. A., *History of Economic Analysis* (New York: Oxford University Press, 1954).

Sekera, J. A., *The Public Economy in Crisis: A Call for a New Public Economics* (Switzerland: Springer International Publishing, 2016).

Simon, H. A., 'Public administration in today's world of organizations and markets', *PS: Political Science and Politics*, December 2000.

Smith, A., ed. Skinner, A., *The Wealth of Nations* (1776; London: Penguin, 1999)

SNA 1968: *A System of National Accounts* (New York: United Nations, 1968).

SNA 2008: *System of National Accounts 2008* (New York: United Nations, 2009).

Snowdon, B. and Vane, H., *A Macroeconomics Reader* (London: Routledge, 1997).

Steiner, P., 'Wealth and power: Quesnay's political economy of the "agricultural kingdom"', *Journal of the History of Economic Thought*, 24(1) (2002), pp. 91–110.

Stiglitz, J. E., *The Price of Inequality: How Today's Divided Society Endangers our Future* (London: Allen Lane, 2012)

Stiglitz, J. E., 'Austerity has been an utter disaster for the Eurozone', the *Guardian*, 1 October 2014: https://www.theguardian.com/business/2014/oct/01/austerity-eurozone-disaster-joseph-stiglitz

Stiglitz, J. E., Sen, A. and Fitoussi, J.P., *Mismeasuring Our Lives: Why GDP Doesn't Add Up* (New York: The New Press, 2010)

Stiglitz, J. E., Sen, A. and Fitoussi, J.P., *Report by the Commission on the Measurement of Economic Performance and Social Progress* (Paris: Commission on the Measurement of Economic Performance and Social Progress, 2010).

Stiglitz, J. E. and Weiss, A., 'Credit rationing in markets with imperfect information', *American Economic Review*, 3(71) (1981), pp. 393–410.

Stone, R., 'Definition of the national income and related totals', in Subcommittee on National Income Statistics, *Measurement of National Income and the Construction of Social Accounts* (Geneva: United Nations, 1947).

Studenski, P., *Income of Nations* (New York: University Press, 1958).

Stuvel, G., *National Accounts Analysis* (Basingstoke: Macmillan, 1986).

Sunga, P. S., 'An Alternative to the current treatment of interest as transfer in the United Nations and Canadian systems of national accounts', *Review of Income and Wealth*, 30(4) (1984), pp. 385–402: http://doi.org/10.1111/j.1475-4991.1984.tb00487.x

Swanson, A., 'Big pharmaceutical companies are spending far more on marketing than research', *Washington Post*, 11 February 2015: http://www.washingtonpost.com/news/wonkblog/wp/2015/02/11/big-pharmaceutical-companies-are-spending-far-more-on-marketing-than-research/

Sweney, M., 'Netflix and Amazon must guarantee 20% of content is European', the *Guardian*, 25 May 2016: https://www.theguardian.com/media/2016/may/25/netflix-and-amazon-must-guarantee-20-of-content-is-european

't Hoen, E. F. M., *The Global Politics of Pharmaceutical Monopoly Power* (Diemen: AMB Publishers, 2009): https://www.msfaccess.org/sites/default/files/MSF_assets/Access/Docs/ACCESS_book_GlobalPolitics_tHoen_ENG_2009.pdf

Tassey, G., 'Underinvestment in public good technologies', *Journal of Technology Transfer*, 30(2) (2005), pp. 89–113.

Teece, D. J., 'Profiting from technological innovation', *Research Policy*, 15(6) (1986), pp. 285–305.

Thiel, P. and Masters, B., *Zero to One: Notes on Startups, or How to Build the Future* (New York: Crown, 2014).

Tomaskovic-Devey, D. and Lin, K. H., 'Income dynamics, economic rents, and the financialization of the U.S. Economy', *American Sociological Review*, 76(4) (2011), pp. 538–559: http://doi.org/10.1177/0003122411414827

Tullock, G., Seldon, A. and Brady, G. L., *Government Failure: A Primer in Public Choice* (Washington, DC: Cato Institute, 2002).

Turner, A., *Economics After the Crisis: Objectives and Means* (Cambridge, MA: MIT Press, 2012).

Tversky, A. and Kahneman, D., 'Advances in prospect theory: Cumulative representation of uncertainty', *Journal of Risk and Uncertainty*, 5(4) (1992), pp. 297–323: doi:10.1007/BF00122574. ISSN 0895-5646.

Vanoli, A., *A History of National Accounting* (Washington, DC: IOS Press, 2005).

Veblen, T., 'The limitations of marginal utility', *Journal of Political Economy*, 17(9) (1909), pp. 620–36.

Verkuil, P. R., *Outsourcing Sovereignty: Why Privatization of Government Functions Threatens Democracy and What We Can Do about It* (Cambridge: University Press, 2007).

Walker, D. A. and van Daal, J. (eds and trans.), *Léon Walras, Elements of Theoretical Economics: Or the Theory of Social Wealth* (Cambridge: University Press, 2014).

Walras, L., *Elements of Theoretical Economics*, trans. and ed. by Donald A. Walker and Jan van Daal (1883; Cambridge: University Press, 2014).

Wolff, E. N., *Growth, Accumulation, and Unproductive Activity: An Analysis of the Postwar U.S. Economy* (Cambridge: University Press, 1987).

Wood, R., 'Fallen Solyndra won bankruptcy battle but faces tax war', *Forbes*, 11 June 2012.

Wray, L. R., *Modern Money Theory* (Basingstoke: Palgrave Macmillan, 2012).

Zirkelbach, R., 'The Five essential truths about prescription drug spending', March 2015, available on PhRMA website at http://catalyst.phrma.org/the-five-essential-truths-about-prescription-drug-spending

Notes

PREFACE

1. http://www.multpl.com/us-gdp-inflation-adjusted/table.
2. http://www.epi.org/publication/stagnant-wages-in-2014/
3. 'I often hear references to higher compensation at Goldman,' said Mr Blankfein. 'What people fail to mention is that net income generated per head is a multiple of our peer average. The people of Goldman Sachs are among the most productive in the world.' http://www.businessinsider.com/henry-blodget-blankfeins-new-defense-of-goldman-bonuses-goldman-employees-are-better-than-you-2009-11?IR=T
4. Goldman Sachs Annual Report, 2010.
5. http://www.forbes.com/sites/mikecollins/2015/07/14/the-big-bank-bail out/#66d600ee3723
6. Goldman Sachs Annual Report, 2016.
7. Goldman Sachs Annual Report, 2010.
8. GDP (Gross domestic product) superseded GNP as the standard measure of output in the 1980s. The difference is not relevant to value creation.
9. See for example B. E. Hilner and T. J. Smith, 'Efficacy Does not Necessarily Translate to Cost Effectiveness: A Case Study in the Challenges Associated with 21st-Century Cancer Drug Prices', *Journal of Clinical Oncology*, 27(13) (2009).
10. Peter Bach's interactive calculator can be accessed at www.drugabacus.org
11. http://nymag.com/daily/intelligencer/2013/10/silicon-valleys-secession-ists.html
12. Plato, *The Republic*, translated and with an Introduction by H. D. P. Lee (London: Penguin Books, 1955), p. 115.

INTRODUCTION: THE MAKERS VERSUS THE TAKERS

1. Bill Haywood, *Bill Haywood's Book: The Autobiography of Big Bill Haywood* (New York: International Publishers,1929).
2. https://www.theguardian.com/business/2016/apr/25/bhs-philip-green-family-millions-administration-arcadia
3. https://www.ft.com/content/cc58c190-6ec3-11e6-a0c9-1365ce54b926
4. https://www.ft.com/content/3e0172a0-6e1b-11e6-9ac1-1055824ca907
5. http://databank.worldbank.org/data/download/GDP.pdf
6. M. Mazzucato, *The Entrepreneurial State: Debunking Public vs. Private Sector Myths* (London: Anthem Press, 2013).
7. W. Lazonick, M. Mazzucato and Ö. Tulum, 'Apple's changing business model: What should the world's richest company do with its profits?', *Accounting Forum* 37 (2103), pp. 249–67.
8. Oxfam, *An Economy for the 99%*, Oxfam Briefing Paper, January 2017: https://www.oxfam.org/sites/www.oxfam.org/files/file_attachments/bp-economy-for-99-percent-160117-en.pdf
9. And even conservative forces have liked to play with the takers versus makers analogy, with Mitt Romney calling his private equity firm the locus of 'wealth creation', while also making many remarks about those parasitic elements of society that extract wealth through the welfare state. G. Monbiot, 'Mitt Romney and the myth of self-created millionaires', the *Guardian*, 24 September 2012: https://www.theguardian.com/commentisfree/2012/sep/24/mitt-romney-self-creation-myth
10. J. Stiglitz, *The Price of Inequality: How Today's Divided Society Endangers our Future* (London: Allen Lane, 2012).
11. A recent excellent book by the journalist Rana Foroohar, called *Makers and Takers*, looks at the way in which productive industry has been undermined by the growth of a financial sector that serves itself and managers in industry that serve the objectives of finance rather than long-term growth. R. Foroohar, *Makers and Takers: The Rise of Finance and the Fall of American Business* (New York: Crown Business, 2016).
12. While I was writing this book, Michael Hudson wrote a stinging critique of modern finance, also building on this concept of unearned income: M. Hudson, *Killing the Host: How Financial Parasites and Debt Bondage Destroy the Global Economy* (Dresden: ISLET Verlag, 2015).
13. M. C. Jensen and W. H. Meckling, 'Theory of the firm: Managerial behavior, agency costs and ownership structure', *Journal of Financial Economics* 3(4) (1976), p. 308.
14. M. E. Porter and M. R. Kramer, 'Creating shared value', *Harvard Business Review*, 89 (2011), pp. 62–77.

15. M. E. Porter, *Competitive Advantage* (New York: Free Press, 1985).
16. SNA 2008 (New York: United Nations, 2009), p. 6. Also discussion of production boundary in D. Coyle, *GDP: A Brief but Affectionate History* (Princeton: University Press, 2014), pp. 37–9. And a discussion of the production boundary in H. H. Boss, *Theories of Surplus and Transfer: Parasites and Producers in Economic Thought* (Boston: Unwin Hyman, 1990).
17. It is fundamental not to interpret this statement as meaning that other forms of discussion of value in economics are not crucial. (See B. Bozeman, *Public Values and Public Interest: Counterbalancing Economic Individualism* (Washington DC: Georgetown University Press, 2007) for an excellent discussion about 'public value' in economics; J. E. Stiglitz, A. Sen and J-P. Fitoussi, *Mismeasuring Our Lives: Why GDP Doesn't Add Up* (New York: The New Press, 2010) for implications on GDP; and G. F. Gaus, *Value and Justification: The Foundations of Liberal Theory* (New York: Cambridge University Press, 1990) for issues of morality and ethics in liberal thought. But the thesis of this present book is specific to the way that economic measurements of value in production have fundamentally changed the ability to differentiate value creators from value extractors, and consequently the distinction between rents and profits which, as we will see in Chapter 2, affects GDP in a different way from the problems identified in Stiglitz.
18. https://www.usatoday.com/story/news/2017/08/22/breakthrough-cancer-drug-astronomical-price/589442001/
19. European Commission Horizon 2020 agenda; OECD, UN.
20. W. J. Baumol, 'Entrepreneurship: Productive, unproductive, and destructive', *Journal of Political Economy* 98(5) (1990), pp. 893–921.

1. A BRIEF HISTORY OF VALUE

1. *De Republica* and *Nicomachean Ethics*.
2. Matthew 19:24.
3. E. S. Reinert, *How Rich Countries Got Rich and Why Poor Countries Stay Poor* (London: Constable, 2008).
4. T. Mun, *England's Treasure by Forraign Trade* (1664; London: Macmillan, 1865), p. 7.
5. P. Studenski, *Income of Nations* (New York: University Press, 1958), p. 27.
6. Ibid.
7. W. Petty, *A Treatise of Taxes and Contributions*, in C. H. Hull (ed.), *The Economic Writings of Sir William Petty* (Cambridge: University

Press, 1899), vol. 1, p. 306: 'Where a People thrive, there the income is greater than the expence, and consequently the tenth part of the expence is not a tenth part of the income.'

8. Petty, *Verbum Sapienti*, ibid., p. 105.

9. Petty, *Several Essays in Political Arithmetick*, ibid., p. 177.

10. Ibid., p. 267.

11. Ibid., p. 256.

12. Boss, *Theories of Surplus and Transfer*, p. 21.

13. A. Smith, *The Wealth of Nations*, Books I–III, ed. A. Skinner (London: Penguin Classics, 1999), Book I, p. 180: 'In 1688, Mr Gregory King, whose skill in political arithmetic is much extolled by Doctor Davenant, computed the ordinary income of labourers and out-servants to be fifteen pounds a year to a family, which he supposed to consist, one with another, of three and a half persons.'

14. King's table redrawn in Boss, *Theories of Surplus and Transfer*, p. 20.

15. Ibid., p. 32.

16. In Quesnay's own words: 'Productive expenditure [which] is employed in agriculture, grasslands, pastures, forests, mines, fishing etc., in order to perpetuate wealth in the form of grain, beverages, wood, live-stock raw materials for manufactured goods, etc.' Quesnay in R. L. Meek, *The Economics of Physiocracy: Essays and Translations* (London: George Allen & Unwin, 1962), p. 128. The sterile class is outside the production boundary; that is, the value production boundary. They work but they do not increase the wealth. 'Sterile expenditure [which] is on manufactured commodities, house-room, clothing, interest on money, servants, commercial costs, foreign produce, etc.' Ibid., p. 128.

17. Notice also that the money for circulation is 2 billion and suffices to exchange products worth 5 billion. The 'velocity of money' is 2.5; money changes hands two and a half times per production period.

18. I. I. Rubin, *A History of Economic Thought* (1929; London: Pluto Press, 1989), p. 135 and Meek, *The Economics of Physiocracy*, p. 158.

19. Turgot also distinguished between 'necessary' reproduction and luxury production, a theme prominent in Ricardo and later the Italian-born economist Piero Sraffa (1898–1983).

20. Smith, *The Wealth of Nations*, Book I, p. 110.

21. Ibid., p. 119.

22. A. Smith, *The Wealth of Nations*, Books IV–V, ed. A. Skinner (London: Penguin Classics, 1999), Book IV, p. 30.

23. Smith does not ascribe any value to 'capital'. This may have been deliberate or may simply have been due to circumstances: capital was not yet very important. The labour theory of value was only displaced when neoclassical economists introduced 'capital' as another 'factor of production', without any clear definition or measurement.

24. Smith, *The Wealth of Nations*, Introduction to Book IV.

25. The full quote is: 'The labour of some of the most respectable orders in the society is, like that of menial servants, unproductive of any value, and does not fix or realize itself in any permanent subject; or vendible commodity, which endures after that labour is past, and for which an equal quantity of labour could afterwards be procured. The sovereign, for example, with all the officers both of justice and war who serve under him, the whole army and navy, are unproductive labourers. They are the servants of the public, and are maintained by a part of the annual produce of the industry of other people. Their service, how honourable, how useful, or how necessary soever, produces nothing for which an equal quantity of service can afterwards be procured. The protection, security, and defence of the commonwealth, the effect of their labour this year, will not purchase its protection, security, and defence for the year to come. In the same class must be ranked, some both of the gravest and most important, and some of the most frivolous professions: churchmen, lawyers, physicians, men of letters of all kinds; players, buffoons, musicians, opera-singers, opera-dancers, etc. The labour of the meanest of these has a certain value, regulated by the very same principles which regulate that of every other sort of labour; and that of the noblest and most useful produces nothing which could afterwards purchase or procure an equal quantity of labour. Like the declamation of the actor, the harangue of the orator, or the tune of the musician, the work of all of them perishes in the very instant of its production.' Smith, *The Wealth of Nations*, Book II, pp. 430–31.

26. Ibid., p. 431.

27. Ibid., p. 447. The full quote is as follows: 'A man of fortune, for example, may either spend his revenue in a profuse and sumptuous table, and in maintaining a great number of menial servants, and a multitude of dogs and horses; or contenting himself with a frugal table and few attendants, he may lay out the greater part of it in adorning his house or his country villa, in useful or ornamental buildings, in useful or ornamental furniture, in collecting books, statues, pictures; or in things more frivolous, jewels, baubles, ingenious trinkets of different kinds; or, what is most trifling of all, in amassing a great wardrobe of fine clothes, like the favourite and minister of a great prince who died a few years ago.'

28. 'When the price of any commodity is neither more nor less than what is sufficient to pay the rent of the land, the wages of the labour, and the profits of the stock employed in raising, preparing, and bringing it to market, according to their natural rates, the commodity is then sold for what may be called its natural price' (Smith, *Wealth of Nations*, Book 1, p. 158). Moreover, in Smith there is also market price. 'The actual price at which any commodity is commonly sold is called its market price. It may either be above, or below, or exactly the same with its natural price. The market price of every particular commodity is regulated by the proportion between the quantity which is actually brought to market, and the demand of those who are willing to pay the natural price of the commodity, or the whole value of the rent, labour, and profit, which must be paid in order to bring it thither' (ibid., pp. 158–9). Finally, Smith affirms that there exists a process of gravitation of the market prices to natural prices: 'The natural price, therefore, is, as it were, the central price, to which the prices of all commodities are continually gravitating. Different accidents may sometimes keep them suspended a good deal above it, and sometimes force them down even somewhat below it. But whatever may be the obstacles which hinder them from settling in this centre of repose and continuance, they are constantly tending towards it [. . .] But though the market price of every particular commodity is in this manner continually gravitating, if one may say so, towards the natural price, yet sometimes particular accidents, sometimes natural causes, and sometimes particular regulations of police, may, in many commodities, keep up the market price, for a long time together, a good deal above the natural price' (ibid., pp. 160–61).

29. Ibid., p. 152.

30. C. Hill, *The Century of Revolution 1603–1714* (London: Nelson, 1980), pp. 25–6.

31. D. K. Foley, *Adam's Fallacy: A Guide to Economic Theology* (Cambridge, MA: Belknap Press, 2006).

32. J. A. Schumpeter, *History of Economic Analysis* (New York: Oxford University Press, 1954), p. 590.

33. 'In every society the price of every commodity finally resolves itself into some one or other, or all of those three parts; and in every improved society, all the three enter more or less, as component parts, into the price of the far greater part of commodities.' Smith, *The Wealth of Nations*, Book I, p. 153.

34. Foley, *Adam's Fallacy*, p. 28.

35. T. R. Malthus, *An Essay on the Principle of Population* (1798; 2nd edn 1803; 3rd edn 1821); critical edn ed. P. James, 2 vols (Cambridge: University Press, 1989).

36. D. Ricardo, *On the Principles of Political Economy and Taxation* (Cambridge: University Press, 1951), ch. 5.

37. In other words, Ricardo did not believe that there would be enough productivity increase in agriculture to keep the price of food down. History so far has not confirmed Ricardo's fear; there has been a lot of improvement in agricultural productivity (at least from the point of view of labour productivity), so food has not become a profit-choking part of production costs. See also Foley, *Adam's Fallacy*, for a concise and illustrative discussion of Ricardo's rent and population theory.

38. Ricardo, *Principles of Political Economy*, p. 71.

39. Another piece of Ricardian theory that has informed economics to the present day is his theory of comparative advantage to explain trade patterns.

40. M. Lavoie, *Introduction to Post-Keynesian Economics* (Basingstoke: Palgrave Macmillan, 2009), pp. 1–24.

41. J. M. Keynes, *The General Theory of Employment, Interest and Money* (London: Macmillan, 1936), ch. 24.

42. Ricardo, *Principles of Political Economy*, p. 150.

43. Ibid., p. 151 fn.

44. Ibid.

45. Ibid., p. 151.

46. This is the principle of primitive accumulation, the historical discussion of which is full of details of chilling violence and cruelty in Marx, *Capital: A Critique of Political Economy*, vol. 1 (London: Penguin Classics, 2004), Part VIII: Primitive Accumulation.

47. Already mentioned in K. Marx, *Economic and Philosophical Manuscripts of 1844* (Amherst, NY: Prometheus Books, 1988).

48. Marx, *Capital*, vol. 1, ch. 1.

49. Ibid., ch. 8, p. 317.

50. Marx, *Capital*, vol. 3 (London: Penguin Classics, 1992), chs 38 and 39.

51. In vol. 3 of *Das Kapital* Marx built a theory of crises of capitalism around the problem of a tendency of the average profit rate to fall as capitalism developed. This is because the composition of capital – variable and constant – tended to shift towards more constant capital relative to variable capital. But that implied that there would be less and less labour power to create the surplus value, so it would shrink relative to the investments necessary on the part of the capitalist, resulting in a falling rate of profit.

52. Ibid., ch. 10.

53. In Marx's time, 'transferring money' could involve transporting gold bullion from one country to another (Marx, *Capital*, vol. 3, ch. 19).

54. One of several passages to this effect in Marx (*Capital*, vol. 3, ch. 17) reads: 'Just as the labourer's unpaid labour directly creates surplus-value for productive capital, so the unpaid labour of the commercial wage-worker secures a share of this surplus-value for merchant's capital.' The difficulty lies here: 'Since the merchant's labour-time and labour do not create value, although they do secure for the merchant a share of already produced surplus-value, how does the matter stand with the variable capital that the merchant lays out in purchasing commercial labour-power?'

55. Marx, *Capital*, vol. 3, ch. 17.

56. Ibid.: 'To industrial capital the costs of circulation appear as unproductive expenses, and so they are. To the merchant they appear as a source of his profit, proportional, given the general rate of profit, to their size. The outlay to be made for these circulation costs is, therefore, a productive investment for mercantile capital. And for this reason, the commercial labour which it buys is likewise immediately productive for it.'

57. Marx (*Capital*, vol. 3, ch. 23): 'Money ... may be converted into capital on the basis of capitalist production, and may thereby be transformed from a given value to a self-expanding, or increasing, value. It produces profit, *i.e.*, it enables the capitalist to extract a certain quantity of unpaid labour, surplus-product and surplus-value from the labourers, and to appropriate it. In this way, aside from its use-value as money, it acquires an additional use-value, namely that of serving as capital. Its use-value then consists precisely in the profit it produces when converted into capital.'

58. Marx, *Capital*, vol. 3, chs 21–36.

59. Marx, *Capital*, vol. 3, ch. 17: 'All these [circulation] costs are not incurred in producing the use-value of commodities, but in realizing their value. They are pure costs of circulation. They do not enter into the immediate process of production, but since they are part of the process of circulation they are also part of the total process of reproduction.'

60. See I. I. Rubin, *Essays on Marx's Theory of Value* (1928; Detroit: Black and Red Press, 1972), ch. 19 for a detailed discussion of how labour is or is not productive depending on which function of capital it is employed by.

61. H. P. Minsky, 'The capital development of the economy and the structure of financial institutions' (1992), Hyman P. Minsky Archive, paper 179.

62. A. Barba and G. de Vivo, 'An "unproductive labour" view of finance', *Cambridge Journal of Economics* 36(6) (2012): http://doi.org/10.1093/cje/ber022; Duncan K. Foley, 'Rethinking financial capitalism and the "information" economy', *Review of Radical Political Economics*, 45(3) (2013), pp. 257–68: http://doi.org/10.1177/0486613413487154

2. VALUE IN THE EYE OF THE BEHOLDER:
THE RISE OF THE MARGINALISTS

1. J. B. Clark, *The Distribution of Wealth: A Theory of Wages, Interest and Profits* (New York: Macmillan, 1899), p. v.
2. A. Roncaglia, *The Wealth of Ideas: A History of Economic Thought* (Cambridge: University Press, 2005), ch. 4.
3. Léon Walras, *Elements of Theoretical Economics*, trans. and ed. by D. A. Walker and J. van Daal (1883; Cambridge: University Press, 2014), p. 5.
4. Roncaglia (*Wealth of Ideas*, p. 278) quoted Howey to say that Wicksteed and Wieser were the first to use 'marginal' in 1884, and that 'marginalism' was not introduced until 1914.
5. Jeremy Bentham, *A Fragment on Government* (London: 1776), Preface, p. ii. Niccolò Machiavelli, in his masterpiece *The Prince* (1513), expressed similar reasoning.
6. Jean-Baptiste Say, *Traité d'économie politique* (Paris: 1803); Roncaglia, *Wealth of Ideas*, p. 165.
7. 'By utility is meant that property in any object, whereby it tends to produce benefit, advantage, pleasure, good, or happiness (all this, in the present case, comes to the same thing), or (what comes again to the same thing) to prevent the happening of mischief, pain, evil, or unhappiness to the party whose interest is considered.' Bentham, *An Introduction to the Principles of Morals and Legislation* (1789), quoted in W. S. Jevons, *The Theory of Political Economy*, ed. R. D. Collison Black (Harmondsworth: Penguin Classics, 1970), ch. 3.
8. L. Robbins, *An Essay on the Nature and Significance of Economic Science* (London: Macmillan, 1932).
9. The classical economists were well aware that supply and demand changed prices – for example, Marx in Part 1 of vol. 3 of *Capital* – but saw this as fluctuations around the price determined by labour time.
10. P. Mirowski, 'Learning the meaning of a dollar: Conservation principles and the social theory of value in economic theory', *Social Research* 57(3) (1990), pp. 689–718.
11. Behavioural economics, which deploys psychology, sociology, neuroscience and other disciplines to look at how individuals really make choices, casts doubt on the simple assumptions of marginalism. See A. Tversky and D. Kahneman, 'Advances in prospect theory: Cumulative representation of uncertainty', *Journal of Risk and Uncertainty*, 5 (4) (1992), pp. 297–323; doi:10.1007/BF00122574

12. Robbins, *Essay on the Nature and Significance of Economic Science*, pp.73–4.
13. A term that Lerner actually picked up from Vilfredo Pareto, who first set the proposition in 1894. V. Pareto, 'Il massimo di utilità data dalla libera concorrenza', *Giornale degli Economisti* 9(2) (1894), pp. 48–66. This proposition was further refined by other economists, among whom we find Lerner, whilst nowadays the accepted proof is the one elaborated by Kenneth Arrow in 1951: 'An extension of the basic theorem of classical welfare economics', in *Proceedings of the Second Berkeley Symposium on Mathematical Statistics and Probability* (Berkeley and Los Angeles: University of California Press, 1951), pp. 507–32.
14. E. N. Wolff, *Growth, Accumulation, and Unproductive Activity: An Analysis of the Postwar U.S. Economy* (Cambridge: University Press, 1987).
15. T. Veblen, 'The Limitations of marginal utility', *Journal of Political Economy*, 17(9) (1909), pp. 620–36.
16. See Foley, 'Rethinking financial capitalism and the "information" economy' for further examples.
17. 'entrepreneur ne faisant ni bénéfice ni perte'; Walras quoted in J. A. Schumpeter, *History of Economic Analysis*, p. 860.

3. MEASURING THE WEALTH OF NATIONS

1. C. Busco, M. L. Frigo, P. Quattrone and A. Riccaboni, 'Redefining corporate accountability through integrated reporting: What happens when values and value creation meet?', *Strategic Finance*, 95(2) (2013), pp. 33–42.
2. P. Quattrone, 'Governing social orders, unfolding rationality, and Jesuit accounting practices: A procedural approach to institutional logics', *Administrative Science Quarterly*, 60(3) (2015), pp. 411–45.
3. Studenski, *Income of Nations*, p. 127.
4. Ibid., p. 121.
5. Ibid., p. 20; J. Kendrick, 'The historical development of national-income accounts', *History of Political Economy*, 2(2) (1970), p. 289.
6. A. Marshall and M. Marshall, *The Economics of Industry*, 4th edn (London: Macmillan, 1909), p. 52.
7. Studenski, *Income of Nations*, chs 7, 8, 9.
8. A. C. Pigou, *The Economics of Welfare* (London: Macmillan, 1926), Part 1, ch. 1, p. 5.

9. A. Vanoli, *A History of National Accounting* (Washington, DC: IOS Press, 2005), p. 280.

10. Ibid.; and E. J. Mishan, *The Costs of Economic Growth* (New York: Praeger, 1967).

11. S. Kuznets, *National Income: A Summary of Findings* (New York: National Bureau of Economic Research, 1946), p. 122.

12. United Nations, *A System of National Accounts and Supporting Tables*, Studies in Methods, series F, no. 2, rev. 1 (New York, 1953).

13. http://unstats.un.org/unsd/nationalaccount/docs/SNA2008.pdf

14. SNA 2008, p. 2.

15. Ibid.

16. P. S. Sunga, 'An alternative to the current treatment of interest as transfer in the United Nations and Canadian systems of national accounts', *Review of Income and Wealth*, 30(4) (1984), p. 385: http://doi.org/10.1111/j.1475-4991.1984.tb00487.x

17. B. R. Moulton, *The System of National Accounts for the New Economy: What Should Change?* (Washington DC: Bureau of Economic Analysis, US Dept. of Commerce, 2003), p. 17: http://www.bea.gov/about/pdf/sna_neweconomy_1003.pdf

18. The development of income and growth estimation is sometimes depicted as a purely empirical affair that is barely influenced by theory (R. Reich, *The Work of Nations: Preparing Ourselves for 21st-Century Capitalism* (New York: Knopf, 1991)). In fact, some histories of estimating growth tend to break off the link with theory that they acrimoniously depict up to Smith and Marx, and simply observe that a 'comprehensive measurement concept' prevailed in the capitalist world at the end of the nineteenth century (Studenski, *Income of Nations*; Kendrick, 'The historical development of national-income accounts'). Some individual estimators – such as Timothy Coughlan, an engineer in Australia who might not have been closely acquainted with economic theory – have seen themselves as neutral statisticians who simply compiled what was 'obviously' or 'common-sensically' value. However, these individuals – just like the politicians who demanded the statistics – were probably the 'slaves of some defunct economist', in this case the marginal economists, as the well-known quote by Keynes reminds us.

19. Source: Bureau of Economic Analysis (2016), NIPA Tables 1.1.5: GDP, 1.3.5: Gross Value Added by Sector, and 3.1: Government Current Receipts and Expenditures.

20. https://www.gov.uk/government/publications/independent-review-of-uk-economic-statistics-final-report

21. Ibid., p. 40.
22. Coyle, *GDP*, p. 14.
23. U. P. Reich and K. Horz, 'Dividing government product between intermediate and final uses', *Review of Income and Wealth*, 28(3) (1982), pp. 325–44.
24. SNA 2008, p. 583.
25. Ibid., p. 119.
26. B. R. Moulton, 'The Implementation of System of National Accounts 2008 in the US National Income and Product Accounts' (Eurostat Conference: The Accounts of Society, Luxembourg, 12–14 June 2014), p. 4.
27. The full quote reads: 'In studying the changes in the economic activity of an advanced industrial country it is unnecessary to impute an income to family services or to the services of household equipment and may even prove an embarrassment to do so, since, not only are there very little data in this field, but the principles on which such imputations should be made are obscure. On the other hand, if a comparison is to be made with a country in which subsistence and family production are important, problems of imputation will have to be faced squarely; indeed, for this purpose, it may be desirable to set up the system of accounts in a different way.' R. Stone, 'Definition of the national income and related totals', in Sub-committee on National Income Statistics, *Measurement of National Income and the Construction of Social Accounts* (Geneva: United Nations, 1947), p. 25.
28. SNA 2008, p. 99.
29. Ibid.
30. In the 1980s, a textbook on national income accounting boldly asserted that because roughly half the female adult population is working in the household, 'anything up to one-quarter of all production does not get recorded in the accounts'. G. Stuvel, *National Accounts Analysis* (Basingstoke: Macmillan, 1986), p. 29. Stuvel argued that household work is production and that something is missing. This raises a curious point that is redolent of Marx. If a single man employs a houseworker, her salary would, of course, be part of GDP (as long as it was paid legally). However, if he married her and she continued doing exactly the same work as before, but now as a married 'housewife', her work would no longer contribute to GDP.
31. SNA 2008, p. 99.
32. The recommended method for imputing rents is given thus: 'Households that own the dwellings they occupy are formally treated as owners of unincorporated enterprises that produce housing services consumed by those

same households. When well-organized markets for rented housing exist, the output of own-account housing services can be valued using the prices of the same kinds of services sold on the market in line with the general valuation rules adopted for goods or services produced on own account. In other words, the output of the housing services produced by owner occupiers is valued at the estimated rental that a tenant would pay for the same accommodation, taking into account factors such as location, neighborhood amenities, etc. as well as the size and quality of the dwelling itself. The same figure is recorded under household final consumption expenditures. In many instances, no well-organized markets exist and other means of estimating the value of housing services must be developed.' (SNA 2008, p. 109.)

33. For the US, this can be seen by comparing growth rates of GDP and of imputed rental of owner-occupied housing (Bureau of Economic Analysis, US Department of Commerce, 'Imputed rental of owner-occupied housing', table 7.12, line 154, last revised on 3 August 2016; accessed 13 March 2017).

34. SNA 2008, p. 48.

35. https://www.istat.it/it/files/2015/12/Economia-non-osservata.pdf?title=Eco nomia+non+osservata+-+04%2Fdic%2F2015+-+Testo+integrale+con+ nota+metodologica.pdf

36. S. Merler and P. Hüttl, 'Welcome to the dark side: GDP revision and the non-observed economy', Bruegel, 2 March 2015: http://bruegel.org/2015/ 03/welcome-to-the-dark-side-gdp-revision-and-the-non-observed-economy/

37. SNA 2008, p. 150.

38. Quoted in P. A. Samuelson and W. D. Nordhaus, *Economics*, 13th edn (New York: McGraw-Hill, 1989), p. 75.

4. FINANCE: A COLOSSUS IS BORN

1. R. Sahay, M. Cihak, P. N'Diaye, A. Barajas, R. Bi, D. Ayala, Y. Gao, A. Kyobe, L. Nguyen, C. Saborowski, K. Svirydzenka and S. Reza Yousefi, 'Rethinking financial deepening: Stability and growth in emerging markets', IMF Staff Discussion Note SDN/15/08 (May 2015): https://www.imf.org/external/pubs/ft/sdn/2015/sdn1508.pdf

2. C. W. Park and M. Pincus, 'Internal versus external equity funding sources and early response coefficients', *Review of Quantitative Finance and Accounting*, 16(1) (2001), pp. 33–52: https://doi.org/10.1023/ A:1008336323282; T. Hogan and E. Hutson, 'Capital structure in new technology-based firms: Evidence from the Irish software sector Centre',

Financial Markets Working Paper series WP-04-19 2004, University College Dublin School of Business, Centre for Financial Markets.

3. C. Furse, 'Taking the long view: How market-based finance can support stability', speech at Chartered Institute for Securities and Investment, 28 March 2014: http://www.bankofengland.co.uk/publications/Documents/speeches/2014/speech718.pdf ; Z. Moradi, M. Mirzaeenejad and G. Geraeenejad, 'Effect of bank-based or market-based financial systems on income distribution in selected countries', *Procedia Economics and Finance*, 36 (2016), pp. 510–21; B-S. Lee, 'Bank-based and market-based financial systems: Time-series evidence', *Pacific-Basin Finance Journal* , 20(2) (2012), pp. 173–97.

4. R. Bacon and W. Eltis, *Britain's Economic Problem Revisited* (Basingstoke: Macmillan, 1996), pp. 15–33.

5. H. Oliver Horne, *A History of Savings Banks* (Oxford: University Press, 1947), pp. 118–67.

6. M. da Rin and T. Hellmann, 'Banks as catalysts for industrialization', William Davidson Working Paper 443 (October 2001): https://deepblue.lib.umich.edu/bitstream/handle/2027.42/39827/wp443.pdf?sequence=3

7. J. Schumpeter, 'The theory of economic development', *Harvard Economic Studies*, 46 (1934); A. Gerschenkron, *Economic Backwardness in Historical Perspective* (Cambridge, MA: Belknap Press, 1962).

8. L. Akritidis, 'Improving the measurement of banking services in the UK national accounts', *Economic & Labour Market Review*, 1(5) (2007), pp. 29–37.

9. L. Fioramonti, *Gross Domestic Problem* (London: Zed Books, 2013), p. 111.

10. B. Sturgess, 'Are estimates of the economic contribution of financial services reliable?', *World Economics* 18(1) (2017), pp. 17–32.

11. The seller hopes that by the time he or she has to deliver the securities to the buyer the price will have fallen. The securities can then be bought at the new (lower) price and sold to the buyer at the contracted old (higher) price. The shorter pockets the difference between the two prices.

12. J. Allen and M. Pryke, 'Financialising household water: Thames Water, MEIF and "ring-fenced" politics', *Cambridge Journal of Regions, Economy & Society*, 6 (2013), pp. 419–39.

13. L. A. Stout, 'Why the law hates speculators: Regulation and private ordering in the market for OTC derivatives', *Duke Law Journal*, 48(4) (1999), pp. 701–86.

14. S. Strange, *International Monetary Relations* (Oxford: University Press, 1976), p. 180.

15. B. Eichengreen, *The European Economy since 1945: Coordinated Capitalism and Beyond* (Princeton, NJ: University Press, 2008), p. 76.

16. C. A. E. Goodhart, 'Competition and credit control', Financial Markets Group London School of Economics, special paper 229 (2014).

17. N. Ruggles and R. Ruggles, 'Household and enterprise saving and capital formation in the United States: A market transactions view', *Review of Income and Wealth*, 38(2) (June 1992), pp. 119–63.

18. M. McLeay, A. Radia and R. Thomas, 'Money creation in the modern economy', *Bank of England Quarterly Bulletin*, Q1 2014, pp. 1–14.

19. Competition Commission, 'The supply of banking services by clearing banks to small and medium-sized enterprises: A report on the supply of banking services by clearing banks to small and medium-sized enterprises within the UK' (2002), summary online at: http://webarchive. nationalarchives.gov.uk/20111202184328/http://www.competition-commission.org.uk/rep_pub/reports/2002/462banks.htm

20. B. Christophers, *Banking Across Boundaries* (Chichester: Wiley-Blackwell, 2013), p. 38.

21. Eichengreen, *The European Economy since 1945*.

22. J. M. Keynes, *The General Theory of Employment, Interest and Money* (London: Macmillan,1936), p. 59.

23. J. M. Keynes, 'Evidence to the Royal Commission on lotteries and betting' (1932), p. 400, quoted in Barba and de Vivo, 'An "unproductive labour" view of finance', p. 1492: http://doi.org/doi: 10.1093/cje/beso48

24. Ibid.

25. Keynes, *General Theory of Employment*, p. 159.

26. H. P. Minsky, 'The Financial instability hypothesis: An interpretation of Keynes and an alternative to "standard" theory" ', *Challenge*, 20(1) (1977), pp. 20–27.

27. L. Randall Wray and Y. Nersisyan, 'Understanding Money and Macroeconomic Policy', in M. Jacobs and M. Mazzucato (eds), *Rethinking Capitalism: Economics and Policy for Sustainable and Inclusive Growth* (Chichester: Wiley-Blackwell, 2016).

28. H. P. Minsky, *Stabilizing an Unstable Economy* (New Haven and London: Yale University Press, 1986), p. 369.

29. J. M. Keynes, 'Proposals for an International Clearing Union', April 1943, reprinted in J. K. Horsefield, *The International Monetary Fund 1945–1965: Twenty Years of International Monetary Cooperation* (Washington, DC: IMF, 1969), pp. 19–36.

30. A. Turner, *Economics After the Crisis: Objectives and Means* (Boston, MA: MIT Press, 2013), p. 18.

31. E. Fama, 'Efficient capital markets: A review of theory and empirical work', *Journal of Finance*, 25(2) (1970).

32. M. Mazzucato and A. Shipman, 'Accounting for productive investment and value creation', *Industrial and Corporate Change*, 23(4) (2014), pp. 1059–85: http://doi.org/10.1093/icc/dtto37

33. B. Cournède and O. Denk, 'Finance and economic growth in OECD and G20 countries', OECD Economics Department Working Papers no. 1223 (2015).

34. P. Hill, 'The Services of Financial Intermediaries, or FISIM Revisited', paper presented to the Joint UNECE/Eurostat/ OECD Meeting on National Accounts, Geneva, 30 April–3 May 1996: http://www.oecd.org/dataoecd/13/62/ 27900661.pdf

35. https://www.federalreserve.gov/boarddocs/speeches/2004/20040220/

36. Bank of England, *Financial Stability Report*, 30 (December 2011), p. 16; available at https:www.bankofengland.co.uk/media/boe/files/financial-stability-report/2011/december-2011

37. Ibid.

38. Lavoie, *Introduction to Post-Keynesian Economics*.

39. http://www.bbc.co.uk/news/uk-37873825

40. Using OECD data we can see that the budget surplus in the UK was 0.72 in 1990; 1.11 in 2000; and 0.39 in 2001. In the US it was 0 in 1999, 0.8 in 2000.

41. C. Borio, M. Drehmann and K. Tsatsaronis, 'Anchoring countercyclical capital buffers: The role of credit aggregates', BIS Working Paper no. 355 (November 2011).

42. See A. Glyn, *Capitalism Unleashed: Finance, Globalization and Welfare* (Oxford: University Press, 2006), p. 53; almost 80 per cent of the total increase in US demand from 1995 to 2000 is represented by household spending on consumption and residential investment.

43. A. Barba and M. Pivetti, 'Rising household debt: Its causes and macroeconomic implications – a long-period analysis', *Cambridge Journal of Economics*, 33(1) (2009), pp. 113–37.

44. Glyn, *Capitalism Unleashed*, p. 7.

45. T. Piketty, *Capital in the Twenty-First Century* (Cambridge, MA: Belknap Press, 2014), p. 438.

46. Source: A. Haldane, *Labour's Share* (London: TVC, 12 November 2015), p. 32, adapted from J. P. Pessoa and J. Van Reenen, 'The UK productivity and jobs puzzle: Does the answer lie in labour market

flexibility?', Centre for Economic Performance Special Paper 31 (2013), compared to 65–70 per cent during similar periods at the end of the 1960s and during the 1980s.

47. Source: author's elaboration from: piketty.pse.ens.fr/capital21c
48. https://www.oxfam.org/sites/www.oxfam.org/files/file_attachments/bp210-economy-one-percent-tax-havens-180116-summ-en_0.pdf
49. Source: author's elaboration on OECD data.
50. See A. Greenspan and J. Kennedy, *Estimates of Home Mortgage Originations, Repayments, and Debt on One-to-Four-Family Residences*, Finance and Economic Discussion Series 2005-41 (Washington, DC: Board of Governors of the Federal Reserve System, 2005). Greenspan and Kennedy (p. 5) define mortgage equity extraction as 'the extraction of equity on existing homes as the discretionary initiatives of home owners to convert equity in their homes into cash by borrowing in the home mortgage market'.
51. https://www.cbo.gov/sites/default/files/110th-congress-2007-2008/reports/01-05-housing.pdf
52. Source: adapted from Table 1 in Barba and Pivetti, 'Rising household debt'.
53. Source: Federal Reserve, *2004 Survey of Consumer Finances*.
54. C. Crouch, 'Privatised Keynesianism: An unacknowledged policy regime', *British Journal of Politics and International Relations*, 11(3) (August 2009), pp. 382–99.
55. Ibid., p. 390.

5. THE RISE OF CASINO CAPITALISM

1. H. Minsky, 'Reconstituting the United States' financial structure', Levy Economics Institute Working Paper no. 69 (1992).
2. http://www.economist.com/blogs/economist-explains/2016/02/economist-explains-0
3. R. Foroohar, *Makers and Takers* (New York: Crown, 2016), p. 7.
4. H. P. Minsky, 'Finance and stability: The limits of capitalism', Levy Economics Institute Working Paper no. 93 (1993).
5. F. Grigoli and A. Robles, 'Inequality overhang', IMF Working Paper 17/76, 28 March 2017; R. Wilkinson and H. Pickett, *The Spirit Level* (London: Penguin, 2009).
6. W. Churchill, 'WSC to Sir Otto Niemeyer, 22 February 1925', Churchill College, Cambridge, CHAR 18/12A-B.
7. Bank of England database, 'Three centuries of macroeconomic data': http://www.bankofengland.co.uk/research/Pages/onebank/threecenturies.aspx

8. Data in this sentence from House of Commons Library reports – Standard Note SN/EP/06193 (Gloria Tyler, 25.2.15) and Briefing Paper 01942 (Chris Rhodes, 6.8.15). The exact figures in Eurostat for Financial and Insurance Activities as a per cent of total value added are as follows: 1995: 6.3 per cent; 2000: 5.1 per cent; 2009: 9.1 per cent; 2015: 7.2 per cent. Or as percentage of GDP: 1995: 5.7 per cent; 2000: 4.6 per cent; 2009: 8.3 per cent; 2015: 6.5 per cent.

9. Source: (2009–13 data extended by author) P. Alessandri and A. Haldane, 'Banking on the State' (Bank of England, 2009): http://www.bankofengland.co.uk/archive/Documents/historicapubs/speeches/2009/speech409.pdf

10. Source: Bureau of Economic Analysis, Matthew Klein's calculations.

11. D. Tomaskovic-Devey and K. H. Lin, 'Income dynamics, economic rents, and the financialization of the U.S. economy', *American Sociological Review*, 76(4) (August 2011), pp. 538–59. The figure for 2014 is similar to what it was in 2009.

12. Source: Bureau of Economic Analysis, adapted from Tomaskovic-Devey and Lin, 'Income dynamics, ecnomic rents, and the financialization of the U.S. economy'.

13. https://www.ici.org/pdf/2015_factbook.pdf

14. *Asset Management in the UK*, The Investment Association Annual Survey: http://www.theinvestmentassociation.org/assets/files/research/2016/20160929-amsfullreport.pdf

15. http://www.bbc.co.uk/news/business-37640156

16. http://www.knightfrank.com/wealthreport

17. http://www.businessinsider.com/chart-stock-market-ownership-2013-3?IR=T

18. https://www.ons.gov.uk/economy/investmentspensionsandtrusts/bulletins/ownershipofukquotedshares/2015-09-02

19. https://www.ft.com/content/14cda94c-5163-11e5-b029-b9d50a74fd14

20. http://www.agefi.fr/sites/agefi.fr/files/fichiers/2016/07/bcg-doubling-down-on-data-july-2016_tcm80-2113701.pdf

21. http://uk.businessinsider.com/richest-hedge-fund-managers-in-the-world-2016-3

22. G. Morgenson, 'Challenging private equity fees tucked in footnotes', *New York Times*, 17 October 2015: https://www.nytimes.com/2015/10/18/business/challenging-private-equity-fees-tucked-in-footnotes.html

23. http://www.wsj.com/articles/kkr-to-earn-big-payout-from-walgreen-alliance-boots-deal-1420068404

24. B. Burrough and J Helyar, *Barbarians at the Gate: The Fall of RJR Nabisco*, rev. edn (New York: HarperCollins, 2008).

25. G. Moran, 'Urine lab flaunted piles of gold', *San Diego Union-Tribune*, 24 October 2015; J. Montgomery, 'Bankruptcy court must clarify Millennium Labs fraud release', *Law 360*, 20 March 2017.

26. Barba and de Vivo, 'An "unproductive labour" view of finance' p. 1491.

27. A. Hutton and E. Kent, *The Foreign Exchange and Over-the-counter Interest Rate Derivatives Market in the United Kingdom* (London: Bank of England, 2016), p. 225.

28. Bank for International Settlements, Basel III phase-in arrangements: http://www.bis.org/bcbs/basel3/basel3_phase_in_arrangements.pdf

29. Jordan Weissmann, 'How Wall Street devoured corporate America', *The Atlantic*, 5 March 2013: https://www.theatlantic.com/business/archove/2-13/03/how-wall-street-devoured-corporate-america/273732/

30. L. Randall Wray, *Modern Money Theory* (Basingstoke: Palgrave Macmillan, 2012), pp. 76–87.

31. Empirical groundwork in Lester Thurow, *Generating Inequality* (New York: Basic Books, 1975), ch. 6, pp. 129–54.

32. Source: Federal Reserve Bank of St Louis, author's elaboration: https://fred.stlouisfed.org/series/FBCOEPQ027S#o

33. Barba and de Vivo, 'An "unproductive labour" view of finance', pp. 1490–91.

34. Ibid., p. 1491.

35. Andy Verity, 'Libor: Bank of England implicated in secret recording', BBC, 10 April 2017: http://www.bbc.co.uk/news/business-39548313

36. Barba and de Vivo, 'An "unproductive labour" view of finance', p. 1489.

37. T. Philippon, 'Finance vs Wal-Mart: Why are financial services so expensive?', in A. Blinder, A. Lo and R. Solow (eds), *Rethinking the Financial Crisis* (New York: Russell Sage Foundation, 2012), p. 13: http://www.russellsage.org/sites/all/files/Rethinking-Finance/Philippon_v3.pdf

38. John C. Bogle, 'The arithmetic of "all-in" investment expenses', *Financial Analysts Journal*, 70(1) (2014), p. 18.

39. Ibid., p. 17.

40. John C. Bogle, *The Clash of the Cultures: Investment vs. Speculation* (Hoboken, NJ: John Wiley and Sons, 2012), p. 8.

41. Ibid., p. 2.

42. https://www.ft.com/content/ab1ce98e-c5da-11e6-9043-7e34c07b46ef

43. https://www.nytimes.com/2016/12/10/business/dealbook/just-how-much-do-the-top-private-equity-earners-make.html

44. A. Metrick and A. Yasuda, 'The economics of private equity', *Review of Financial Studies*, 23(6) (2011), pp. 2303–41: https://doi.org/10.1093/rfs/hhq020

45. If ratio of proceeds from PE investments to public investment is > 1, PE is considered superior. Source: *Journal of Finance*, 69 (5) (October 2014), p. 1860.

46. J. M. Hill, 'Alpha as a net zero-sum game: How serious a constraint?', *Journal of Portfolio Management*, 32(4) (2006), pp. 24–32; doi:10.3905/jpm.2006.644189

6. FINANCIALIZATION OF THE REAL ECONOMY

1. https://www.ft.com/content/294ff1f2-0f27-11de-ba10-0000779fd2ac

2. These figures give an approximate idea of the weight of large companies in the economy. On the one hand, some companies do not report their turnover, so total revenues are underestimated. On the other hand, the list includes the biggest banks.

3. G. Mukunda, 'The price of Wall Street's power', *Harvard Business Review*, June 2014.

4. E. Hadas, 'Seeing straight: Why buybacks should be banned', *Breakingviews*, 14 December 2014: https://www.breakingviews.com/features/why-buybacks-should-be-banned/

5. W. Lazonick, 'Profits without prosperity', *Harvard Business Review*, September 2014.

6. Ibid.

7. http://online.wsj.com/public/resources/documents/blackrockletter.pdf

8. Source: Adapted from Lazonick, 'Profits without prosperity'.

9. Jensen and Meckling, 'Theory of the firm', pp. 305–60.

10. Source: Bain & Co., *Global Private Equity Report* (2015), fig. 2, p. 43.

11. https://www.blackstone.com/the-firm/asset-management/private-equity

12. D. Burns, L. Cowie, J. Earles, P. Folkman, J. Froud, P. Hyde, S. Johal, I. Rees Jones, A. Killett and K. Williams, *Where Does the Money Go? Financialised Chains and the Crisis in Residential Care*, CRESC Public Interest Report, March 2015.

13. G. Ruddick, 'Four Seasons Health Care reports £264m annual loss', the *Guardian*, 27 April 2016.

14. K. Bayliss, 'Case study: The financialisation of water in England and Wales', FESSUD (Financialisation, Economy, Society and Sustainable Development), Working Paper series no. 52 (2014).

15. W. Lazonick, 'Innovative enterprise or sweatshop economics? In search of foundations of economic analysis', ISIGrowth Working Paper no. 17 (2016).

16. P. Aghion, J. Van Reenen and L. Zingales, 'Innovation and institutional ownership', *American Economic Review*, 103(1) (2013), pp. 277–304.

17. Bogle, *The Clash of the Cultures.*
18. J. M. Keynes, *The General Theory of Employment, Interest and Money* (London: Macmillan, 1936), p. 154.
19. Ibid., p. 155.
20. S. Patterson, *Dark Pools: The Rise of AI Trading Machines and the Looming Threat to Wall Street* (New York: Random House, 2012).
21. Amy Or, 'Average private equity hold times drop to 5.5 years', *Wall Street Journal*, 10 June 2015.
22. D. Barton and M. Wiseman, 'Focusing capital on the long term', *Harvard Business Review*, January–February 2014.
23. Ibid.
24. Keynes, *General Theory of Employment*, pp. 161–2.
25. Return on Invested Capital is a measure of profitability. It is calculated by dividing net (after tax) operating profits by invested capital (less cash and cash equivalents).
26. J. P. Morgan, 'Bridging the gap between interest rates and investments', JPM Corporate Finance Advisory, September 2014.
27. K. J. Murphy, 'Executive compensation: Where we are, and how we got there', in G. M. Constantinides, M. Harris and R. M. Stulz (eds), *Handbook of the Economics of Finance*, vol. 2 (Amsterdam: Elsevier, 2013), pp. 211–356.
28. L. Mishel and J. Schieder, *CEO Pay Remains High Relative to the Pay of Typical Workers and High-wage Earners* (Washington, DC: Economic Policy Institute, 2017).
29. The Conference Board, *CEO Succession Practices: 2017 Edition*, https://www.conference-board.org/publications/publicationdetail.cfm?publicationid=7537
30. Fig. 26 depicts data retrieved from the Bureau of Economic Analysis website.
31. J. Asker, J. Farre-Mensa and A. Ljungqvist, 'Comparing the investment behavior of public and private firms', *NBER Working Paper No. 17394* (September 2011).
32. Author's elaboration of data from the Bureau of Economic Analysis.
33. Author's elaboration of data from the Bureau of Economic Analysis.
34. Bogle, *The Clash of the Cultures*, pp. 22–3.
35. M. Friedman, *Capitalism and Freedom* (Chicago: University Press, 1962), p. 133.
36. R. E. Freeman, J. S. Harrison, A. C. Wicks, B. L. Parmar and S. de Colle, *Stakeholder Theory: The State of the Art* (Cambridge: University Press, 2010), p. 268.

37. https://www.kfw.de/KfW-Group/About-KfW/Identität/Geschichte-der-KfW/

38. C. Leggett, 'The Ford Pinto case: The valuation of life as it applies to the negligence-efficiency argument', *Law & Valuation*, Spring 1999.

39. C. Perez, *Technological Revolutions and Financial Capital: The Dynamics of Bubbles and Golden Ages* (Cheltenham: Edward Elgar, 2002).

40. C. Perez, 'The Double bubble at the turn of the century: Technological roots and structural implications', *Cambridge Journal of Economics* 33(4) (2009), p. 801.

7. EXTRACTING VALUE THROUGH THE INNOVATION ECONOMY

1. Peter Thiel, *Zero to One: Notes on Startups, or How to Build the Future* (New York, Crown, 2014).

2. https://www.netmarketshare.com/search-engine-market-share.aspx?qprid=4&qpcustomd=0

3. R. Solow, 'Technical change and the aggregate production function', *Review of Economics and Statistics*, 39 (3) (1957), pp. 312–20: JSTOR 1926047; R. R. Nelson and S. G. Winter, *An Evolutionary Theory of Economic Change* (Cambridge, MA: Harvard University Press, 2009).

4. D. J. Teece, 'Profiting from technological innovation', *Research Policy*, 15(6) (1986), pp. 285–305.

5. https://www.theatlantic.com/magazine/archive/2015/11/we-need-an-energy-miracle/407881/

6. https://www.washingtonpost.com/opinions/americas-miracle-machine-is-in-desperate-need-of-well-a-miracle/2017/05/05/daafbe6a-30e7-11e7-9534-00e4656c22aa_story.html?utm_term=.b38348fbc471

7. https://hbr.org/2014/05/why-germany-dominates-the-u-s-in-innovation

8. M. K. Block and F. Keller, 'Explaining the transformation in the US innovation system: The impact of a small government program', *Socioeconomic Review* 11(4) (2013), pp. 629–56: https://doi.org/10.1093/ser/mws021

9. S. W. Leslie, *The Cold War and American Science: The Military-Industrial-Academic Complex at MIT and Stanford* (New York: Columbia University Press, 1993).

10. See W. Lazonick, *Sustainable Prosperity in the New Economy? Business Organization and High-Tech Employment in the United States* (Kalamazoo, MI: W. E. Upjohn Institute for Employment Research, 2009), ch. 2: doi: https://doi.org/10.17848/9781441639851

11. *Business Week*, 1960, cited in H. Lazonick, *Sustainable Prosperity in the New Economy? Business Organization and High-tech Employment in the United States* (Kalamazoo, MI: Upjohn Press, 2009), p. 79.

12. W. Lazonick and M. Mazzucato, 'The risk–reward nexus in the innovation–inequality relationship: Who takes the risks? Who gets the rewards?', *Industrial and Corporate Change*, 22(4) (2013), pp. 1093–128: https://doi.org/10.17848/9781441639851 The structure of this market is particularly important in understanding where innovation risk truly lies. Liquidity is provided by market makers, who underwrite IPOs and ensure the instant sale and purchase of stock at close to market prices. In this way, investor risk is transferred to market makers. Market makers are backed by investment banks, which – as it turns out – are underwritten by the government (K. Ellis, R. Michaely and M. O'Hara, 'When the underwriter is the market maker: An examination of trading in the IPO aftermarket', *Journal of Finance*, 55(3) (1999), pp. 1039–74.

13. 'I have worked with investors for 60 years and I have yet to see anyone – not even when capital gains rates were 39.9 per cent in 1976–77 – shy away from a sensible investment because of the tax rate on the potential gain. People invest to make money, and potential taxes have never scared them off. And to those who argue that higher rates hurt job creation, I would note that a net of nearly 40 million jobs were added between 1980 and 2000. You know what's happened since then: lower tax rates and far lower job creation.', *The New York Times*, 14 August 2011: http://www.nytimes.com/2011/08/15/opinion/stop-coddling-the-super-rich.html?_r=2&hp

14. Lazonick and Mazzucato, 'The risk–reward nexus in the innovation–inequality relationship'.

15. N. Henderson and M. Schrage, 'The roots of biotechnology: Government R&D spawns a new industry', *Washington Post*, 16 December 1984: https://www.washingtonpost.com/archive/politics/1984/12/16/government-r38/cb580e3d-4ce2-4950-bf12-a717b4d3ca36/?utm_term=.27fd51946872. I am grateful to William Lazonick for pointing me to this article.

16. This section on the role of venture capital and the following section on executive pay draw heavily on Lazonick and Mazzucato, 'The risk–reward nexus in the innovation–inequality relationship'.

17. Ibid.

18. Ibid.

19. P. A. Gompers and J. Lerner, *The Venture Capital Cycle* (Cambridge, MA: MIT Press, 2002).

20. See S. Davidoff, 'Why I.P.O.s get underpriced', Dealbook, *New York Times*, 27 May 2011; J. Ritter, IPO data website, 2012: http://bear. warrington.ufl.edu/ritter/ipodata.htm ; M. Gimein, E. Dash, L. Munoz and J. Sung, 'You bought. They SOLD', *Fortune*, 146(4) (2002), pp. 64–8, 72, 74.

21. Gary P. Pisano, *Science Business: The Promise, the Reality, and the Future of Biotech* (Boston, MA: Harvard Business School Press, 2006).

22. W. Lazonick and Ö. Tulum, 'US biopharmaceutical finance and the sustainability of the US biotech business model', *Research Policy*, 40(9) (2011), pp. 1170–87.

23. R. Fontana, A. Nuvolari, H. Shimizu and A. Vezzulli, 'Reassessing patent propensity: Evidence from a dataset of R&D awards, 1977–2004', *Research Policy* 42(10) (2013), pp. 1780–92.

24. More formally, a patent holder is awarded a 'probabilistic' right to exclude others from using and commercializing an invention (M. A. Lemley and C. Shapiro, 'Probabilistic patents', *Journal of Economic Perspectives*, 19(2) (2005), pp. 75–98: doi: 10.1257/0895330054048650). The patentee must be willing and able to enforce its rights against infringement of the patent. The patentee can license others to use the invention in exchange for royalties.

25. The intensity of patenting activity and the importance of patents – both in relation to appropriability and disclosure – varies in importance across countries, sectors, technologies, and by firm size. Firms in pharmaceuticals, biotechnology and ICT, for example, tend to patent more than firms in other areas. Patents are the most important appropriability mechanism for pharmaceutical companies, for example, whereas in other sectors firms may rely more on secrecy, lead-times to production, trademarks and additional complementary assets to gain from their inventions. Similarly, patents play a far more important role in the diffusion of information for R&D labs in manufacturing firms in Japan compared with those in the US, where publication and informal information exchange is more important (W. M. Cohen, A. Goto, A. Nagata, R. R. Nelson and J. P. Walsh, 'R&D spillovers, patents and the incentives to innovate in Japan and the United States', *Research Policy*, 1(8–9) (2002), pp. 1349–67: doi: http://doi.org/10.1016/S0048-7333(02)00068-9

26. According to M. A. Lemley, in 'Software patents and the return of functional claiming', *Wisconsin Law Review*, 2013(4), pp. 905–64, the costs of software innovation are lower than innovation in the life sciences. Software is also protected by copyrights, which already provide for effective prevention of copying by others. Network effects may help

innovators to capture returns regardless of intellectual property protection (more on this later in this chapter). There is, in addition, the open-source community, which suggests that patents may not be a necessary condition for innovation in the sector. Finally, software patentability varies across regions and countries (for example, it is limited in Europe and India, and broad in the US), which also suggests that patent protection may reflect a policy choice.

27. Baumol, 'Entrepreneurship: Productive, unproductive, and destructive'.
28. R. Mazzoleni and R. R. Nelson, 'The benefits and costs of strong patent protection: A contribution to the current debate', *Research Policy*, 27(3) (1998), pp. 273–84.
29. M. Kenney and D. Patton, 'Reconsidering the Bayh–Dole Act and the current university invention ownership model', *Research Policy*, 38(9) (2009), pp. 1407–22.
30. http://www.nybooks.com/articles/2004/07/15/the-truth-about-the-drug-companies/
31. L. Burlamaqui and R. Kattel, 'Development as leapfrogging, not convergence, not catch-up: Towards Schumpeterian theories of finance and development', *Review of political Economy*, 28(2) (2016), pp. 270–88.
32. Mazzoleni and Nelson, 'The benefits and costs of strong patent protection'.
33. S. Haber and S. H. Werfel, 'Why do inventors sell to patent trolls? Experimental evidence for the asymmetry hypothesis', Stanford University Working Paper, 27 April 2015.
34. J. Bessen and M. J. Meurer, 'The Patent Litigation Explosion', *Loyola University Chicago Law Journal*, 45(2) (2013), pp. 401–40: http://lawecommons.luc.edu/luclj/vol45/iss2/5
35. J. E. Bessen et al., 'Trends in private patent costs and rents for publicly-traded United States firms'(March 2015). Boston University School of Law, Public Law Research Paper no. 13–24: SSRN: https://ssrn.com/abstract=2278255 or http://dx.doi.org/10.2139/ssrn.2278255
36. C. V. Chien, 'Startups and patent trolls', *Stanford Technology Law Review*, 17 (2014), pp. 461–506.
37. W. J. Baumol, *Entrepreneurship, Management and the Nature of Payoffs* (Cambridge, MA: MIT Press, 1993), ch. 2, p. 25; see also ch. 4.
38. Foley, 'Rethinking financial capitalism and the "information" economy'.
39. *The Economist*, 8 August 2015: http://www.economist.com/news/leaders/21660522-ideas-fuel-economy-todays-patent-systems-are-rotten-way-rewarding-them-time-fix

40. C. Forero-Pineda, 'The impact of stronger intellectual property rights on science and technology in developing countries', *Research Policy* 35(6) (2006), pp. 808–24.

41. E. M. F. t'Hoen, *The Global Politics of Pharmaceutical Monopoly Power: Drug Patents, Access, Innovation and the Application of the WTO Doha Declaration on TRIPS and Public Health* (Diemen: AMB, 2009).

42. M. Mazzucato, *The Entrepreneurial State: Debunking Private vs. Public Sector Myths* (London: Anthem Press, 2013).

43. Source: US Department of Health and Human Services: http://www.hhs.gov/opa/reproductive-health/stis/hepatitis-c and World Health Organization: http://www.euro.who.int/en/health-topics/communicable-diseases/hepatitis/data-and-statistics

44. Sovaldi is, however, more costly than Harvoni overall, because it needs to be taken in combination with other drugs.

45. The letter is available at http://www.finance.senate.gov/imo/media/doc/Wyden-Grassley%20Document%20Request%20to%20Gilead%207-11-141.pdf

46. A. Hill, S. Khoo, J. Fortunak, B. Simmons and N. Ford, 'Minimum costs for producing hepatitis C direct-acting antivirals for use in large-scale treatment access programs in developing countries', *Clinical Infectious Diseases*, 58(7) (2014), pp. 928–36: doi: 10.1093/cid/ciu012

47. M. Mazzucato, 'High cost of new drugs', *British Medical Journal*, 354: i4136 (2016): http://www.bmj.com/cgi/content/full/354/jul27 10/i4136

48. D. W. Light and J. R. Lexchin, 'Pharmaceutical research and development: What do we get for all that money?', *British Medical Journal* 345:e4348 (2012): http://dx.doi.org/10.1136/bmj.e4348

49. A. Swanson, 'Big pharmaceutical companies are spending far more on marketing than research', *Washington Post*, 11 February, 2015: http://www.washingtonpost.com/news/wonkblog/wp/2015/02/11/big-pharmaceutical-companies-are-spending-far-more-on-marketing-than-research/

50. Lazonick, 'Profits without prosperity'.

51. Mazzucato, *The Entrepreneurial State*.

52. H. Kantarjian and S. V. Rajkumar, 'Why are cancer drugs so expensive in the United States, and what are the solutions?', *Mayo Clinic Proceedings*, April 2015, report that 85 per cent of basic cancer research in the US is funded by the government.

53. J. Sachs, 'The drug that is bankrupting America', *Huffington Post*, 16 February 2015: http://www.huffingtonpost.com/jeffrey-sachs/the-drug-that-is-bankrupt_b_6692340.html

54. V. Roy and L. King, 'Betting on hepatitis C: How financial speculation in drug development influences access to medicines', *British Medical Journal*, 354:i3718 (2016).

55. P. Barrett and R. Langreth, 'Pharma execs don't know why anyone is upset by a $94,500 miracle cure', *Bloomberg Businessweek*, 3 June 2015: https://www.bloomberg.com/news/articles/2015-06-03/specialty-drug-costs-gilead-s-hepatitis-c-cures-spur-backlash

56. LaMattina's article on Forbes is available at: http://www.forbes.com/sites/johnlamattina/2014/08/04/politicians-shouldnt-question-drug-costs-but-rather-their-value-lessons-from-soliris-and-sovaldi/

57. R. Zirkelbach, 'The five essential truths about prescription drug spending', March 2015, available on PhRMA website at: http://catalyst.phrma.org/the-five-essential-truths-about-prescription-drug-spending

58. See for example Hilner and Smith, 'Efficacy does not necessarily translate to cost effectiveness'.

59. Peter Bach's interactive calculator can be accessed at www.drugabacus.org

60. According to the ranking compiled by Forbes for 2014, on average the ten largest pharmaceutical companies enjoy a 19 per cent net profit rate – the highest of all industries included in Forbes' worldwide analysis. Pfizer leads the group with a remarkable 41 per cent net profit margin. Only large banks, which are well known to enjoy rents because of their size and political influence, earn a profit rate comparable to that of large pharmaceutical companies, while for example the ten largest automobile companies – also one of the most profitable industries in the world – have on average a 6 per cent net profit rate.

61. P. David, 'Clio and the Economics of QWERTY', *American Economic Review*, 75(2), *Papers and Proceedings of the Ninety-Seventh Annual Meeting of the American Economic Association* (May 1985), pp. 332–7; G. Dosi, 'Sources, procedures, and microeconomic effects of innovation', *Journal of Economic Literature*, vol. 26 (1988), pp. 1120–71.

62. According to its own mission statement, for example, 'Facebook's mission is to give people the power to share and make the world more open and connected' (investor.fb.com/faq.cfm). Sergey Brin, one of Google's founders and President of its parent company Alphabet, has often talked about Google as trying to be against evil, and a 'force for good'. http://www.businessinsider.com.au/best-quotes-google-sergey-brin-2014-7#to-me-this-is-about-preserving-history-and-making-it-available-to-everyone-1

63. K. Kelly, 'The new socialism: Global collectivist society is coming online', *Wired* magazine, 17 June 2009.

64. E. Morozov, 'Silicon Valley likes to promise "digital socialism" – but it is selling a fairy tale', the *Guardian*, 28 February 2015.

65. Variously attributed. Common attribution is to Andrew Lewis, as blue_beetle on MetaFilter 2010, 'If you're not paying for it, you're not the customer; you're the product being sold': http://www.metafilter.com/95152/Userdriven-discontent#3256046

66. M. J. Sandel, *What Money Can't Buy: The Moral Limits of Markets* (London and New York: Allen Lane and Farrar, Straus and Giroux, 2013).

67. Evgeny Morozov, 'Don't believe the hype, the "sharing economy" masks a failing economy', the *Guardian*, 28 September 2014: http://www.theguardian.com/commentisfree/2014/sep/28/sharing-economy-internet-hype-benefits-overstated-evgeny-morozov; Evgeny Morozov, 'Cheap cab ride? You must have missed Uber's true cost', the *Guardian*, 31 January 2016: http://www.theguardian.com/commentisfree/2016/jan/31/cheap-cab-ride-uber-true-cost-google-wealth-taxation

68. Evgeny Morozov, 'Where Uber and Amazon rule: welcome to the world of the platform', the *Guardian*, 7 June 2015: http://www.theguardian.com/technology/2015/jun/07/facebook-uber-amazon-platform-economy

69. https://www.bloomberg.com/news/articles/2017-02-28/in-video-uber-ceo-argues-with-driver-over-falling-fares

70. http://fortune.com/2016/10/20/uber-app-riders/

71. A useful distinction can be made between direct and indirect network effects. When a higher number of participants increases the benefit to each individual member – as in the case of Facebook – the effect is direct. Where, instead, a higher number of members (for example, buyers) increases the convenience of using the platform, not for the members but for another group (for example, the sellers), we talk of indirect network effects.

72. Source: Statista database (www.statista.com), and http://uk.business insider.com/facebook-and-google-winners-of-digital-advertising-2016-6?r=US&IR=T

73. Morozov, 'Where Uber and Amazon rule'.

74. See note 70 for the distinction between direct and indirect network effects.

75. Mazzucato, *The Entrepreneurial State*.

76. Foley, 'Rethinking financial capitalism and the "information" economy'.

77. See ibid. for a rigorous but accessible explanation of the classical theory of surplus value and how it can be used to provide an alternative interpretation of the so-called 'new economy'.

78. https://www.theguardian.com/commentisfree/2016/dec/04/data-populists-must-seize-information-for-benefit-of-all-evgeny-morozov
79. H. A. Simon, 'Public administration in today's world of organizations and markets', *PS: Political Science and Politics*, December 2000, p. 756.
80. https://www.theguardian.com/technology/2016/jun/09/uber-suffers-legal-setbacks-in-france-and-germany https://www.theguardian.com/technology/2016/jun/08/berlin-ban-airbnb-short-term-rentals-upheld-city-court https://www.theguardian.com/media/2016/may/25/netflix-and-amazon-must-guarantee-20-of-content-is-european
81. For a discussion of the criteria and implementation issues behind mission-oriented policies see my recent report, M. Mazzucato, *Mission-oriented research & innovation in the European Union – A problem-solving approach to fuel innovation-led growth*, European Commission, 2018.
82. Such thinking is indeed what has inspired *Mission Innovation* (MI; http://mission-innovation.net), an alliance of twenty-two ministers and the European Union to combat climate change through national commitments (around $20 billion) to invest in clean energy innovation. The coalition was announced on 30 November 2015 during the COPS meeting in Paris. On the private-sector side the Breakthrough Coalition is committing an equal amount of money. Since 2014 I have been leading a project on the need for such mission-oriented thinking in innovation: http://marianamazzucato.com/projects/mission-oriented-innovation-policy/

8. UNDERVALUING THE PUBLIC SECTOR

1. https://www.gov.uk/government/speeches/mansion-house-2015-speech-by-the-chancellor-of-the-exchequer
2. 'The third industrial revolution', *The Economist*, 21 April 2012: http://www.economist.com/node/21553017
3. K. Polanyi, *The Great Transformation: The Political and Economic Origins of Our Time* (1944; Boston MA: Beacon Press, 2001), p. 144.
4. C. M. Reinhart and K. S. Rogoff, 'Growth in a time of debt', *American Economic Review*, 100(2) (2010), pp. 573–8.
5. Ibid., p. 573.
6. T. Herndon, M. Ash and R. Pollin, 'Does high public debt consistently stifle economic growth? A critique of Reinhart and Rogoff', *Cambridge Journal of Economics*, 38(2) (2014), pp. 257–79: http://doi.org/10.1093/cje/bet075, p. 5.
7. Ibid., pp. 7–8.

8. Reinhart and Rogoff: http://www.nytimes.com/2013/04/26/opinion/debt-growth-and-the-austerity-debate.html?_r=0 and Reinhard and Rogoff: http://www.nytimes.com/2013/04/26/opinion/reinhart-and-rogoff-responding-to-our-critics.html

9. http://www.focus-economics.com/countries/italy

10. https://www.theguardian.com/business/2014/oct/01/austerity-eurozone-disaster-joseph-stiglitz

11. Crowding out usually refers to the negative effect that government spending or investment may have on private investment, primarily because either government borrowing pushes up interest rates (making it harder for business to take out loans) or because government moves into activities that were in the private sector. Analyses on crowding out have been problematic due to the lack of proper analysis of what the private sector is willing to do.

12. A. Bergh and M. Henrekson, 'Government size and growth: A survey and interpretation of the evidence', *Journal of Economic Surveys*, 25(5) (2011), pp. 872–97: http://doi.org/10.1111/j.1467-6419.2011.00697.x

13. P. Steiner, 'Wealth and power: Quesnay's political economy of the "Agricultural Kingdom" ', *Journal of the History of Economic Thought*, 24(1) (2002), pp. 91–110.

14. The 'sterile class' comprised city dwellers or artisans. In Schumpeter's *History of Economic Analysis*, p. 239, the same word is used to describe the 'bourgeoisie'. 'Disposable class' is the name that Turgot gave to the class of landowners (classe propriétaire/souveraine/distributive).

15. Quesnay, quoted in Steiner, 'Wealth and power', p. 99.

16. Schumpeter, *History of Economic Analysis*, p. 230; Steiner, 'Wealth and Power', p. 100.

17. Smith, *The Wealth of Nations*, Book IV, Introduction.

18. Ibid., Book I, ch. 1.

19. Ibid., Book V, ch. 1.

20. Ibid.

21. David Ricardo, *The Works and Correspondence of David Ricardo*, ed. P. Sraffa with the collaboration of M. H. Dobb, vol. 1: *On the Principles of Political Economy and Taxation* (Cambridge: University Press, 1951), p. 150.

22. Ibid., p. 151.

23. Karl Marx and Friedrich Engels, *The Communist Manifesto* (1848; London: Penguin Classics, 2010), ch. 1.

24. A. Marshall, *Principles of Economics* (1890; London: Macmillan, 1920), Book I, ch. 4, para. 4.

25. Ibid.

26. B. Snowdon and H. Vane, *A Macroeconomics Reader* (London: Routledge, 1997), p. 3.

27. Keynes, *The General Theory of Employment, Interest and Money*, p. 249.

28. This and the following are from the Preface to the French edition of *The General Theory of Employment, Interest and Money*.

29. R. Reich, 'Economist John Maynard Keynes', *TIME* magazine, 29 March 1999.

30. McLeay, Radia and Thomas, 'Money creation in the modern economy', p. 14.

31. BEA, *Measuring the Economy: A Primer on GDP and the National Income and Product Accounts* (Washington, DC: Bureau of Economic Analysis, US Department of Commerce, 2014), pp. 9–4: http://www.bea.gov/national/pdf/nipa_primer.pdf

32. T. Atkinson, *Atkinson Review: Final Report. Measurement of Government Output and Productivity for the National Accounts* (Basingstoke and New York: Palgrave Macmillan, 2005).

33. M. G. Phelps, S. Kamarudeen, K. Mills and R. Wild, 'Total public service output, inputs and productivity', *Economic and Labour Market Review*, 4(10) (2010), pp. 89–112: http://doi.org/10.1057/elmr.2010.145

34. ONS (Office for National Statistics), *Public Service Productivity Estimates: Total Public Services, 2012* (2015): http://www.ons.gov.uk/ons/dcp171766_394117.pdf

35. The multiplier looks at how much total increase in GDP results from an initial increase in government spending. The calculation assumes a known marginal propensity to save and consume, i.e. how much of every pound or dollar earned a consumer will spend and how much he or she will save. If 80 per cent is consumed, then the GDP will increase by an amount of $1/(1-0.8)$ multiplied by the stimulus; so if the initial extra spending was £1 million, GDP will increase by £5 million.

36. 'Fiscal policy as a countercyclical tool', *World Economic Outlook*, ch. 5 (Washington DC: International Monetary Fund, October 2008); L. Cohen, J. Coval and C. Malloy, 'Do powerful politicians cause corporate downsizing?', *Journal of Political Economy*, 119(6) (2011), pp. 1015–60: doi:10.1086/664820; R. J. Barro and C. J. Redlick, 'Macroeconomic effects from government purchases and taxes', *Quarterly Journal of Economics* 126(1) (2011), pp. 51–102: doi: 10.1093/qje/qjq002

37. D. Leigh, P. Devries, C. Freedman, J. Guajardo, D. Laxton and A. Pescatori, 'Will it hurt? Macroeconomic effects of fiscal consolidation', IMF *World Economic Outlook* (Washington, DC: International Monetary Fund, 2010), pp. 93–124.

38. D. Leigh and O. J. Blanchard, 'Growth forecast errors and fiscal multipliers', Working Paper no. 13/1 (Washington, DC: International Monetary Fund, 2013).

39. A. O. Krueger, 'The political economy of the rent-seeking society', *The American Economic Review*, 64(3) (June 1974), pp. 291–303.

40. G. Tullock, A. Seldon and G. L. Brady, *Government Failure: A Primer in Public Choice* (Washington, DC: Cato Institute, 2002).

41. B. M. Friedman, 'Crowding out or crowding in? Economic consequences of financing government deficits', *Brookings Papers on Economic Activity*, 3 (1979), pp. 593–654.

42. J. M. Buchanan, 'Public choice: The origins and development of a research program', *Champions of Freedom*, 31 (2003), pp. 13–32.

43. J. E. Stiglitz, *Economics of the Public Sector* (New York: W. W. Norton, 3rd edn, 2000).

44. National Audit Office, 'Memorandum on managing government suppliers', 12 November 2013.

45. NHS, 'Principles and values that guide the NHS' (2018): http://www.nhs.uk/NHSEngland/thenhs/about/Pages/nhscoreprinciples.aspx#

46. WHO, 'The world health report 2000 – Health systems: improving performance' (2000): http://www.who.int/whr/2000/en/whr00_en.pdf?ua=1

47. E. C. Schneider, D. O. Sarnak, D. Squires, A. Shah and M. M. Doty (2017). *Mirror, Mirror 2017: International Comparison Reflects Flaws and Opportunities for Better U.S. Health Care*, The Commonwealth Fund.

48. OECD, 'Health expenditure and financing' (2017): http://stats.oecd.org/index.aspx?DataSetCode=HEALTH_STAT

49. YouGov, 'Nationalise energy and rail companies, say public' (2013): https://yougov.co.uk/news/2013/11/04/nationalise-energy-and-rail-companies-say-public/

50. J. Lethbridge, *Empty promises: The Impact of Outsourcing on NHS Services*, technical report, UNISON (London, 2012).

51. C. Crouch, 'The paradoxes of privatisation and public service outsourcing', in Jacobs and Mazzucato (eds), *Rethinking Capitalism*.

52. G. Kirkwood and A. M. Pollock, 'Patient choice and private provision decreased public provision and increased inequalities in Scotland: A case study of elective hip arthroplasty', *Journal of Public Health*, 39(3) (2017), pp. 593–60.

53. We Own It, 'We love our NHS – keep it public': https://weownit.org.uk/public-ownership/nhs

54. A. Pollock, 'This deadly debt spiral was meant to destroy the NHS: There is a way to stop it', the *Guardian*, 5 July 2016: https://www.the-

guardian.com/commentisfree/2016/jul/05/debt-spiral-destroy-nhs-health-social-care-act-bill

55. A. Pollock, 'The NHS is about care, not markets', the *Guardian*, 3 September 2009: https://www.theguardian.com/commentisfree/2009/sep/03/nhs-business-markets

56. J. Davis, J. Lister and D. Wringler, *NHS for Sale: Myths, Lies & Deception* (London: Merlin Press, 2015).

57. N. Chomsky, 'The state-corporate complex: A threat to freedom and survival', lecture given at the University of Toronto, 7 April 2011: https://chomsky.info/20110407-2/

58. L. MacFarlane, *Blueprint for a Scottish National Investment Bank* (New Economics Foundation, 2016): http://allofusfirst.org/tasks/render/file/?fileID=3B9725EA-E444-5C6C-D28A3B3E27195B57

59. Ibid.

60. C. Crouch, *The Knowledge Corrupters: Hidden Consequences of the Financial Takeover of Public Life* (Cambridge: Polity Press, 2016).

61. https://www.theguardian.com/society/2016/apr/15/g4s-fined-100-times-since-2010-prison-contracts

62. https://www.washingtonpost.com/news/wonk/wp/2013/07/16/meet-serco-the-private-firm-getting-1-2-billion-to-process-your-obamacare-application/?utm_term=.0ffc214237a8

63. United States Government Accountability Office, 'Contracting data analysis; Assessment of government-wide trends', March 2017: https://www.gao.gov/assets/690/683273.pdf.

64. As reported in J. A. Sekera, *The Public Economy in Crisis: A Call for a New Public Economics* (Springer International Publishing, 2016); J. Dilulio, *Bring Back the Bureaucrats: Why More Federal Workers Will Lead to Better (and Smaller!) Government* (West Conshohocken, PA: Templeton Press, 2014); and Paul R. Verkuil, (2007) *Outsourcing Sovereignty: Why Privatization of Government Functions Threatens Democracy and What We Can Do about It* (Cambridge: University Press, 2007), p. 128.

65. http://www.pogo.org/our-work/reports/2011/co-gp-20110913.html#Executive%20Summary

66. Crouch, *The Knowledge Corrupters*.

67. https://er.jsc.nasa.gov/seh/ricetalk.htm

68. R. Wood, 'Fallen Solyndra Won Bankruptcy Battle but Faces Tax War', *Forbes*, 11 June 2012.

69. G. Owen, *Industrial Policy in Europe since the Second World War: What Has Been Learnt?* ECIPE Occasional Paper no. 1 (Brussels: The

European Centre for International Political Economy, 2012): http:// eprints.lse.ac.uk/41902/

70. J. M. Poterba, 'Venture capital and capital gains taxation', in L. H. Summers (ed.), *Tax Policy and the Economy*, Vol. 3 (Cambridge, MA: MIT Press, 1989), pp. 47–68.

71. G. Akerlof, 'Comment' on the chapter by William J. Baumol in G. L. Perry and James Tobin (eds), *Economic Events, Ideas, and Policies: The 1960s and After* (Washington, DC: Brookings Institution Press, 2010).

72. Mazzucato, *The Entrepreneurial State*.

73. See https://www.project-syndicate.org/onpoint/growth-and-public-sector-investment-by-mariana-mazzucato-2017-12?barrier=accesspaylog

74. J. Gertner, *The Idea Factory: Bell Labs and the Great Age of American Innovation* (London and New York: Penguin, 2013).

9. THE ECONOMICS OF HOPE

1. Both Tony Blair, the former British Prime Minister, and Chuka Umunna, considered a rising star in the Labour Party, argued that the Labour Party needed to embrace business, calling them the wealth creators https://www.theguardian.com/commentisfree/2015/may/09/tony-blair-what-labour-must-do-next-election-ed-miliband and Chuka Umunna https://www.theguardian.com/commentisfree/2015/may/09/labours-first-step-to-regaining-power-is-to-recognise-the-mistakes-we-made

2. http://ec.europa.eu/eurostat/documents/118025/118123/Fitoussi+Commission+report

3. D. Elson, *Macroeconomics and Macroeconomic Policy from a Gender Perspective*, Public Hearing of Study Commission on Globalization of the World Economy-Challenges and Responses, Deutscher Bundestag, Berlin, 18 February 2002.

4. https://www.theguardian.com/us-news/2016/may/17/ceo-pay-ratio-average-worker-afl-cio

5. https://www.ifs.org.uk/publications/5362

6. P. Evans, *Embedded Autonomy: States and Industrial Transformation* (Princeton, NJ: University Press, 1995).

7. E. Morozov, 'Democracy, Technology and City', transcript of CCCB lecture, Barcelona, 2014.

8. C. Perez, 'Capitalism, technology and a green global golden age: The role of history in helping to shape the future', in M. Jacobs and M. Mazzucato (eds), *Rethinking Capitalism: Economics and Policy for Sustainable and Inclusive Growth* (Chichester: Wiley-Blackwell, 2016).

Index

Acorn computers 267
Advanced Research Projects
    Agency-Energy (ARPA-E) 195
agency theory 166, 171, 173
agriculture
    labour 44
    and Marx 52
    and physiocrats *see* physiocrats
    and production boundaries 29,
        29, 33, 78
    and Ricardo 41–3
Airbnb 190, 215–16, 225, 276
Akerlof, George 263
Alchemy Partners 169
Alitalia 259
Alliance Boots 145
Allianz Capital Partners 169
Alton, Gregg 209
Amalgamated Society of
    Engineers 58
Amazon 53, 190, 213, 215–16,
    218, 221
American Economic Review
    235–6
American Research and
    Development Corporation
    (ARD) 197
Amgen 201
AOL 218

Apple 190, 193, 199, 273
    and California 3
    intellectual property 3
    Irish subsidiaries 2–3
    share buy-back scheme 4
    value extraction 2–4
Apple Operations Europe 2–3
Apple Sales International (ASI)
    2–3
Aristotle 23, 230
ARM Holdings 267
asset/fund management 102,
    135–6, 141–5, 146, 149,
    153–60, 172–3
    fees 152–4, 155, 156–7, 159, 160
    hedge funds *see* hedge funds
    private equity *see* private
        equity (PE)
    and regulation 143, 159–60
    retail investment funds 135
    US mutual fund assets and
        charges 154
asset revaluation 149
AT&T 198, 266
Atkinson, Sir Anthony 246
auditors 173
austerity 169, 233, 234–8, 246,
    247, 277–8
    and GDP 234–5, 249

austerity – *cont.*
  and inequality 234–5
  and the magic of numbers 235–8
  and the 'new classicals' 249
  and unemployment 249

Bain Capital 145
Bank for International
  Settlements 128
Bank of England 116, 120
banks/banking
  bailouts 116, 118, 120, 152,
    233, 241
  'banking problem' 96, 104–10
  British-based banking
    families 138
  butterfly effect potentiality 120
  central banks 103, 116, 119,
    120, 132, 234, 244
  challenger banks 121, 148
  competitive instability 111
  and credit assessment 107
  customer funding gap 125
  and deregulation 97, 103,
    110–14, 121, 123–4, 127
  and economic growth 105
  and Enlightenment
    philosophers 117
  and the Eurodollar 112–13
  and financial crises 102,
    110–14, 115 *see also* financial
    crises
  and financial markets
    103–4, 149
  FISIM 107–9, 124, 147
  household lending 102, 127–8
    see also mortgages
  inter-bank lending rates 108
  intermediary role 106–7,
    115, 147

investment banks 15, 97, 105,
  110, 111, 114, 118, 119, 123–7,
  133, 149, 196, 256
licence restriction 115
and liquidity 107
loans not matched by deposits
  124–5
and maturity transformation
  106–7
money transfer services 53
monopoly/oligopoly power 110,
  111, 114, 116, 147–9, 150–51
and offshore currencies 112
and private/family debt 127–32,
  131, 132, 133, 151
privatization and division into
  'good' and 'bad' banks 259
'productivity' and value/money
  creation 96–7, 102, 106–10,
  115–16, 122–7, 133, 138–40,
  141
proprietary trading 148
public banks 160, 185, 196, 251,
  256, 265
regulation *see* regulation,
  financial
Russian banks 113
shadow banks 134, 135
speculative activities 5, 119,
  125, 133
'too big to fail' banks 74, 110,
  111, 120
US 111, 113, 115, 148
see also financial sector
Barbarians at the Gate 146
Baumol, William J. 121, 191, 206
Bayh–Dole Act 204
BBC 265, 267
  Microcomputer 267
BC Partners 145

Bean, Charles 87–8
Becker, Gary 71
Bell Labs 266
Bentham, Jeremy 61
Berg, Paul 199
Bernanke, Ben 124
Bessen, James 205–6
Bevan, Aneurin 253
BHS 1–2
big data 221, 225
big government 120, 229, 238
billionaires 143, 144, 189
Biogen 201
black economy 84, 90, 95–7
Black Wednesday 144
Blackrock 164
Blackstone Capital 145
Blankfein, Lloyd 12
Bogle, John 153–5, 175
Bolshevism 79
Braeburn Capital 3
Bray, John 58
Bretton Woods agreement
    111–12, 113
British Airways 251
British Gas 251
British Telecom 89–90, 251
Brown, Gordon 140
Buchanan, James 69, 249
budget deficits 234, 237, 238
Buffet, Warren 198
Bureau of Economic Analysis
    (BEA) 98

Cambridge Capital Critique 70
Canadian Pension Plan Investment
    Board 175
Cap Gemini 143
Capita 252, 256
capital gains 94

tax 3, 157, 198, 200–201, 273–4
capital types
    commercial 52, 54
    interest-bearing 53–4, 55
    patient 168, 171–4
    production/industrial 52–3,
        54, 117
    venture see venture capital (VC)
capitalism
    and the 2008 global financial
        crisis 270
    and asset management see asset/
        fund management
    capitalist society 49–50
    and entrepreneurship see
        entrepreneurs/entrepreneurship
    and financial markets 124
    industrial economies' difficulties
        seen as crisis of 113
    intellectual opposition by radical
        and socialist organizations 58
    lack of negotiation in Western
        capitalism 227–8
    and marginalism see marginalism
    and Marx 48–55, 58, 92, 117,
        192, 240–41
    'money manager capitalism'
        (Minsky) 136, 141
    platform 216–19
    'predatory' vs 'productive' 5
    regulatory 252
    and rent-seeking 4–5 see also
        rent: extraction/seeking
    and Ricardo 45, 47
    rise of casino capitalism 135–60
    and sources of profit 52–3
    and state's role as engine of
        growth 10–11
carbon tax 250
care homes (UK) 168–9, 183

Care Quality Commission 169
Carlyle Group 145
cash-hoarding 37, 128,
    227, 266
casino capitalism 135–60
Catholic Church 23, 61, 117
central banks 103, 116, 119, 120,
    132, 234, 244
    quantitative easing 120
CERN 194
challenger banks 121, 148
Chappell, Dominic 1–2
Charles I 39
Chartists 58
China 143, 238
Chinese Development Bank 196
choice 65, 73, 154, 164, 165,
    270–71, 277
    and entrepreneurship 271
    feeling deprived of 219
    and microeconomic theory 63
    patents and policy choices
    203
    and privatization 258
    Public Choice theory see Public
    Choice theory
Chomsky, Noam 255–6
Chrysler 233
Churchill, Winston 137, 138
civil servants 25, 26, 246, 257, 259,
    260, 273, 277
Civil War, England 39
Clark, John Bates 69–70
    epigraph 57
class struggle 51–2
classical economics/economists
    33–56, 73, 220–22
    eclipse of 57, 59–60 see also
    marginalism; neoclassical
    economics

new classicals 244, 248–9
    see also specific economists
climate change 193, 226, 266, 279
co-operativism 58, 160, 268
Commodity Exchange Act
    (CEA) 126
Commonwealth Foundation 253
competition 121
comprehensive boundary 77
computers 192–3, 267
conglomerates 169, 171–2
consumer preference, marginal
    utility theory see marginalism
consumption
    and feudalism 48–9
    and Ricardo 45–6
Coperform 255
Corn Laws 39, 44–5
corporate profits 110, 139,
    148, 221
corporate scandals 173
corporation governance 270
corruption, governmental 69, 232,
    249–50, 262, 265
    see also Public Choice theory
credit
    assessment 107
    availability 128, 133
    cards 116, 234
    Competition and Credit Control
    (UK) 114
    default swaps (CDSs) 125, 151–2
    and household debt 127–8,
        130–32, 131, 133, 151–2
    rating agencies 126, 173
    right to issue credit money 73
    shortage 114
    system 54–5
    see also mortgages
Cromwell, Oliver 26

Crouch, Colin 254
Cyprus 237

Dante Alighieri: *Inferno* 61
DARPA 194, 195, 266, 278
debt
  banks and family/private debt
    127–32, *131*, *132*, 133, 151
  deflation 110
  mortgage-related 127–8, 131,
    131, 151 *see also* mortgages
  and PE firms 157–8
  private 127–32, *131*, *132*, 151
  and 'privatized Keynesianism' 132
  public debt and the Maastricht
    Treaty 235–6, 237
  public debt as percentage of GDP
    235–6, 237, 278
  see also credit
DEC 197
Defense Advanced Research
  Projects Agency (DARPA)
  194, 195, 266, 278
depression, financial 75, 83,
  237, 245
  Great Depression 1, 80, 82, 89,
    111, 112, 118, 174, 242, 260
deregulation, financial 97, 103,
  110–14, 121, 123–4,
  127, 187
derivatives 112, 123, 124, 126, 127,
  150, 151
  concentration of US derivatives
    contracts *151*
  over-the-counter 126, 150
digital value 219–21
distribution
  curve 195
  Downsize and Distribute
    strategy 181

with an economics of hope 279
excessive profit distributions 164
financialization of distribution
  activities 160
inequalities 129–30
and Marx 117
national accounts and
  distribution of income 79, 84
Non-Profit Distributing (NPD)
  model 256
rent as income from
  redistributing value 55
Ricardo and the distribution of
  wages and income 41
Turgot and the distribution of
  wealth 32–3
and value creation 6, 9,
  14, 271
value redistribution 9, 30, 41, 55,
  231, 263
when value is determined by
  price 12–13
Dodd-Frank Act (2010) 133
Downsize and Distribute
  strategy 181
Draper, Gaither and Anderson 198
drugs industry *see* pharmaceuticals

earnings *see* wages/earnings
eBay 213
economic growth
  and the banks 105
  and government spending
    10–11, 82, 89, 160, 248,
    249, 278
  and household saving 128
  and innovation 225
  and policymaking 13–14
  state's role in value creation and
    10–11, 229–67 *see also* state

economic growth – *cont.*
  sustained through household
    borrowing 132
  unsustainable 132, 270
  and wages 114
economies of scale 52, 71,
  110, 217
Economist, The 207, 229
education 88, 241, 272
  subsidized 14
employee treatment 224–5,
  227, 269
energy
  nuclear 194
  prices 113–14
  renewable 110, 262, 279
  US government funding for
    advances 194
Engels, Friedrich 47, 58
Enron 173
entrepreneurs/entrepreneurship
  73–4, 149, 184, 271
  collectivity benefits 194, 271
  and 'creative destruction'
    189–90, 192
  dominant narrative of
    entrepreneurs as wealth
    creators 203
  'entrepreneurial state' 3,
    17, 264
  and innovation *see* innovation
  of Silicon Valley *see* Silicon
    Valley
  unproductive 190–91, 206–7
environmental pollution/damage
  90, 95, 231, 250, 267, 279
EPS (earnings per share) 163,
  178–9, 180
equilibria 63–4, 65, 66–71, 73–4,
  81–2

Eurodollar 112–13
European Central Bank (ECB)
  120, 234
European Commission 2–3,
  218, 234
European Exchange Rate
  Mechanism (ERM) 144
European Investment Bank 196
European Union
  debt/GDP ratio 236
Eurozone 236, 237–8
  crisis 236–8
exchange rates 15
  ERM 144
  management 27
exchange value 48
exploitation of workers 49, 192

Facebook 190, 197, 213, 214,
  215–16, 218–19, 221
Factory Acts (English) 34
Fama, Eugene 122
feudalism 48–9
finance, insurance and real estate
  (FIRE) 138, *140*
financial bubbles 118, 120,
  187–8
financial crises 102
  1929 Crash 112, 242
  1933 Wall Street Crash 111,
    118, 138
  2007–8 global crisis and 2008
    crash 102, 103, 110–14,
    121–2, 125, 133, 141, 175,
    233–4, 270, 277
  and the banks 102, 110–14,
    115
  and deficit-led recovery 243
  deregulation and seeds of 2008
    crash 110–14

Eurozone crisis 236–8
and governmental intervention
    120–21
financial intermediation 97, 106–9,
    147, 148, 152–3
    services, indirectly measured
    (FISIM) 107–9, 124, 147
financial sector 101–34
    asset management *see* asset/fund
        management
    banks *see* banks/banking
    Bretton Woods agreement
        111–12, 113
    competition 121, 148
    cross-border lending 103
    deregulation 97, 103, 110–14,
        121, 123–4, 127, 187
    diversification 141
    financial liberalization 103
    financial repression 103
    FIRE 138, *140*
    FISIM 107–9, 124, 147
    and GDP/national accounts 74,
        91, 96–7, 101, 103–4,
        106, 107–9, 118, 121, 122,
        139, 274
    government dependence on tax
        revenue from 133
    governmental rescues following
        2008 crash 233–4
    growth 136, 138–40
    hedge funds 125, 135, 137,
        144, 156
    and inequality 5, 127, 136–7
    interconnectedness 120
    Marx's locating of 117
    and private/family debt 127–32,
        131, 132, 133, 151
    and production boundaries 10,
        102, 105, 121–2, 138

and productivity 96–7, 102,
    106–10, 115–16, 122–7, 133,
    138–40, 141
and public-private partnerships
    276
regulation *see* regulation,
    financial
relating finance to the 'real'
    economy 117–22
relations between banks and
    financial markets 103–4, 149
scientists moving to 102
shadow banking 134, 135
share of employment and income
    139, *140*, 149–50, *150*
size of 14
speculation *see* speculation
transaction costs 146–7, 155–6,
    253, 255
and value extraction 110, 117,
    118–19, 120, 121, 133–4,
    136–7, 142, 146–59
wealth creation claims 12, 229
see also banks/banking:
    'productivity' and value/money
    creation
financial transaction (Tobin) tax
    155–6, 159–60
financialization 103–88
and agency theory 166,
    171, 173
and conglomerates 169,
    171–2
and corporate decision-making
    175–7
and governmental intervention
    187–8
and inequality 177–83, *177*,
    178–9, 180, 181–2, 183
and Marx 49

financialization – *cont.*
   MSV *see* maximizing
      shareholder value
   of real economy 161–88
   and retreat of 'patient' capital
      171–4
   and rise of casino capitalism
      135–60
   and share buy-backs 4, 162–5,
      164, 276
   short-termism and barriers
      to productive investment
      174–7, 178
   and stakeholder value
      184–6, 272
   and tenure of management
      178, *179*
   and value extraction 182–3, 187
Fink, Larry 164
first fundamental theorum (FFT)
   68–9
first mover advantages 191, 193,
   203, 213–19
Foley, Duncan 207
Food and Drug Administration
   (FDA), US 205
Forbes 210
Ford 162, 186
Four Seasons Health Care 169
fracking 194, 226, 232
France
   electricity industry 251
   Federation of the Socialist
      Workers 58
   government spending/GDP
      ratio 238
   national accounting 78–9
   physiocrats *see* physiocrats
free trade
   and Corn Law abolition 44–5

and mercantilists 39–40
negative effects 27
and Smith 36, 39, 40,
   268, 275
French Telecom 251
Friedman, Milton 119, 172, 184,
   185, 244
   and shareholder value 165–6
fund management *see* asset/fund
   management

G4S 252, 256–7
GAAP 179–80
Ganilh, Charles 79
Gates, Bill 194
GE Capital 162
Geithner, Tim 126
Genentech 196, 201
General Electric 184, 198
General Motors 233
Generally Agreed Accounting
   Principles 179–80
Genzyme 201
Germany
   budget surplus 277
   manufacturing 195
   Socialist Workers' Party 58
Gerschenkron, Alexander 105–6
Gilead 208, 209
Glass–Steagall Act 111, 112,
   114, 123
globalization 113
   and MSV 167
gold 23, 39–40, 113
   standard 112, 113
Goldman Sachs 12, 114, 124, 141,
   159, 169
Google 189, 190,
   204, 213, 215–16, 218,
   221, 272

government failure 69, 249–50,
   259, 264
government policies
   austerity *see* austerity
   fixing market failures 68–9,
      231, 264
   and inequality 114, 222,
      234–5
   mission-oriented 259–62
   see also state
government size 10–11, 238
government spending/public
   expenditure
   and austerity *see* austerity
   and economic growth 10–11, 82,
      89, 160, 248, 249, 278
   and final consumption
      88–90, 247
   and financial recovery 118
   as percentage of GDP 238
   public investment *see* public
      investment
   and public value 265–7
   and Ricardo 46
   as 'unproductive' 85, 264–5
   and value added 85–90,
      86, 245–7
government value *see* public/
   government value
GPS 194, 215, 226, 276
Gray, John 58
Great Depression 1, 80, 82,
   89, 111, 112, 118, 174,
   242, 260
Great Recession (from 2008) 96
Greece 237, 238
Green, Sir Philip 1–2
Green Investment Bank 110
green life 275, 278
Greenspan, Alan 126

gross domestic product (GDP) 11,
   13, 16, 75–100, 191, 271
   and austerity 234–5, 249
   and banks/financial sector
      74, 91, 96–7, 101, 103–4,
      106, 107–9, 118, 121, 122,
      139, 274
   and black economy 84, 90,
      95–7
   business investment as percentage
      of US GDP *180*
   calculation means 245
   debt/GDP ratio 235–6, 237, 278
   and expenditure 86, *86*, 89, 245
   and final consumption 81,
      88–90, 247
   finance as intermediate input
   government spending/GDP
      ratio 238
   government value added in
      85–90, *86*, 245–7
   and healthcare 253
   and income 75–6, 245
   and investment 91, 237
   and Keynes 82–3, 242, 245
   maximum growth 277
   and national accounts *see*
      national accounting
   patch-up attempts 98–9
   and pollution 90, 95
   and production 95, 245
   and production boundaries
      77–8, 92, 99, 274
   and profits vs rents 97–8
   and prostitution 94
   and R&D 91
   and the SNA *see* System of
      National Accounts
   and social convention 76–8
   US 93, 162, *180*, 236

gross domestic product – *cont.*
and value added 77–8, 83,
85–90, *86*, 95, 97, 106, 107–8,
110, 122, 124, 136, 138, *139*,
150, 180, 245–7
value of financial assets relative
to 162
and the value of housework and
house 84, 91–4
and value theory 77–82
guilds 36–7

Hands, Guy 169
Hanse 53
happiness 98–9, 271
Harvoni 208, 209, 212
Hatch–Waxman Act 205
Hayek, Friedrich 115
Haywood, Bill 1
healthcare 169, 277
Health and Social Care Act
(2012), UK 254
market-oriented 254–5 *see also*
private finance initiatives
(PFIs)
National Health Service and
Community Care Act (1990),
UK 254
NHS *see* National Health Service
(NHS), UK
NICE 211–13
privatization and outsourcing
253–6
see also care homes (UK)
hedge funds 125, 135, 137, 144,
156
Hegel, Georg Wilhelm 47
Herndon, Thomas 236
high-net-worth individuals
(HNWIs) 143, 144, 156, 189

Hill, Joanne 159
Hodgskin, Thomas 58
Hooper, Richard 258
household borrowing 102, 114,
127–8
household consumption
expenditure 128
housework 84, 91–3
housing market 94
and GDP 93–4
property prices 94, 128, 156, 272
human capital 14, 185, 263
hurdle rates 157, 176

IBM 179, 190, 192, 198, 221
ICT (information and
communications technology)
industry 114, 198, 276
see also Internet
import quotas 27
income
from charging interest 117
earnings-per share (EPS) 163,
178–9, 180
expenditure balanced with 24
and GDP 75–6, 245
and household debt 128–32,
131, *132*
inequalities 41, 114, 127,
128–30, *130*
just deserts 222, 263–4
and market competition 12
national accounts and
distribution of 79, 84
profits as earned income *see*
profits
Ricardo and the distribution of
wages and 41
tax 147
types (Ricardo) 43

types (Smith) 38–9
unearned 6, 9, 12, 56, 72, 74, 76,
    97 see also rent
wages see wages/earnings
when value is determined by
    price 12–13
individual utility 61
Industrial Revolution 57, 60
industrialization 207
inequality 4, 41, 100, 114, 127,
    128–30, 130
and austerity 234–5
in distribution 129–30
and the financial industry 5, 127,
    136–7
and financialization 177–83,
    177, 178–9, 180, 181–2, 183
government policies increasing
    114, 222, 234–5
and revolutions 187
and taxation 274
inflation 114, 141, 244
stagflation 113
infrastructure investment 160, 170,
    194, 221, 231, 235, 240, 241,
    246, 261, 266, 277, 278
and New Deal 260
outsourcing Scotland's
    infrastructure 256–8
vs PFI 254
initial public offerings (IPOs) 124,
    145, 199–202
product-less (PLIPOs) 201
innovation 17–18, 74,
    190, 241
and citizenship 225–6
collective 194–5, 222–3,
    226–7
and 'creative destruction'
    189–90, 192

cumulative 191–3, 196
and digital value 219–21
dynamics, and value creation/
    extraction 219–21
and economic growth 225
and employee treatment 224–5,
    227, 269
extracting value through
    innovation economy 189–228
and finance 195–202
financial returns for 195, 196
first mover advantages 191, 193,
    203, 213–19
high-risk public funding 195–6,
    197, 223, 241, 261
inclusive 225
investment 13, 14, 193, 195–7
and just deserts 222, 263–4
and monopolies 219–20, 227
network effects 191, 213–19
and patents see patents
and platforms 17–18
rate and direction 226
sharing risks and rewards 222–5
and timing 195–202
uncertain 193
and unproductive
    entrepreneurship 190–91,
    206–7
in VC industry 195–202
'waves' 192
Institute for Fiscal Studies
    234–5
intellectual property rights (IPR)
    3, 17, 190–91,
    221, 222
and patents 202, 203, 206–7,
    227 see also patents
interest-bearing capital 53–4
interest charging 61, 117

interest rates 106, 122, 149
  capping 103
  and FISIM 107–9, 124
  and investment 244
  rigging 150–51
Internal Rate of Return (IRR) 176
International Monetary Fund
    (IMF) 71, 103, 234, 236,
    249, 251
Internet 194, 219, 226, 232, 276
  monopolies 218–20, 221
  platforms 217–19, 220, 272 see
    also specific companies
investment
  banks/banking 15, 97, 105, 110,
    111, 114, 118, 119, 123–7, 133,
    149, 196, 256
  business investment as percentage
    of US GDP 180
  as capital 53
  in early-stage businesses 184,
    195–6, 197, 200, 223, 261
  and GDP 91, 237
  growth opportunities with
    active government investment
    193, 197–8, 201, 223,
    225, 244
  holding time average for equity
    investment 174–5
  in human capital 14
  hurdle rates 157, 176
  in infrastructure see
    infrastructure investment
  and innovation 13, 14, 193,
    195–7 see also innovation
  and interest rates 244
  in IT 198
  and job creation 195
  long-run investments 141–2,
    270

and long-term growth 160,
    187, 278
  management see asset/fund
    management
  mission-oriented 226, 277–9
  pension funds in risky
    investments 199
  and PFIs see private finance
    initiatives (PFIs)
  private-sector firm vs public firm
    rates 181–2, 181
  'prudent man' rule 143, 199
  in R&D 14, 78, 90, 91, 176,
    184, 187, 224
  reinvestment of profits 163, 168,
    187, 223, 227–8, 263
  retail investment funds 135
  short-termism and barriers to
    productive investment
    174–7, 178
  and Smith 38–9
  'socialization' of (Keynes) 160
  trusts 142
  US household 'investment'
    in consumption of durable
    goods 115
  VC see venture capital
  zero government return on
    245–6
iPhone 194
Ireland 237
IT see ICT (information and
    communications technology)
    industry
Italy
  black economy 96
  budget deficit 237
  primary budget surplus 237
  privatization of national
    airline 259

J. P. Morgan 124, 176
Japan 144, 207
Jensen, Michael 166, 185
Jesuit Order 76-7
Jevons, William Stanley 59-60
Jobs, Steve 193
John Lewis 269
just deserts 222, 263-4

Kahn, Richard 248
Kennedy, John F. 260, 261
Keynes, John Maynard 44,
    82, 118-19, 120, 248,
    259-60, 264
and counter-cyclical government
    241-4
and deficit-led recovery 243
The End of Laissez-Faire
    (epigraph) 229, 259-60
and GDP 82-3, 242, 245
The General Theory of
    Employment, Interest, and
    Money 82, 242
How to Pay for the War 82
macroeconomy theory 82,
    242-3
and the multiplier 248-9, 264
principle of effective demand 242
and short-termism 174-5
and the SNA 82-3
socialization of investment 160
Keynesianism 89, 244, 248
neo-Keynesians 250
'privatized' 132
King, Gregory 24, 25-6, 26, 27
Kirkwood, Graham 255
Kleiner Perkins 196
Kohlberg Kravis Roberts (KKR)
    145, 146
Korea, South 207

Kreditanstalt für Wiederaufbau
    (KfW) 185, 196
Kuznets, Simon 80-81, 89, 95

labour
exploitation 49, 192
laws 114
power 48, 49, 51, 52, 56
productivity and the division of
    35, 50, 191
productivity and wages 129
in services 61
theory of value 33-56, 57, 64,
    79, 92, 220-22
'unproductive' (Marx) 206
value in classical economics
    33-56, 220-22
working hours 227
Labour Party (UK) 58, 83, 271
Lagrange, Joseph Louis 78
LaMattina, John 210
landlords 9-10, 28, 30, 39,
    55, 59
and feudalism 48-9
and Ricardo 42-4, 47, 72
Lauderdale, James Maitland, 9th
    Earl of 59
Lazonick, William 163, 181
Lehman Brothers 119
Lerner, Abba 67-8
Libor 108, 150-51
life insurance 142, 172
Locke, John 117, 222
London 113, 114, 139, 140
Big Bang financial reforms 114
hedge funds 144
HNWIs 143
Mayfair 144
Stock Exchange 114
Louis XV 239

Maastricht Treaty 235–6, 237
Macquarie (bank) 109–10
macroeconomy, Keynes' theory of
    82, 242–3
Malthus, Thomas 42, 58–9
management tenure 178, *179*
manufacturing
    division of labour in 35
    German 195
    and globalization 113
    labour as source of value 36
    and mercantilism 25, 28
    output share giving way to
        finance 138
    and physiocrats 30, 31
    US 138
marginalism
    and equilibria 63–4, 65, 66–71,
        73–4, 81–2
    marginal productivity 63
    marginal utility theory 60, 62–3,
        65, 66–7, 68, 71, 72–3, 75, 76,
        79, 84, 97, 100, 122, 241, 247,
        250, 263
    and market failure 68–9
    and national accounting 80
    and prices 61, 62–3, 64, 65, 66
    production boundary 66–9,
        67, 77
    rise of the marginalists 57–74
market failures 231
    market failure theory 68–9
market forces/economy
    capitalism and financial
        markets 124
    efficiency 122, 127, 272
    instability of markets 242
    'invisible hand' of 36
    market-based value thinking
        7–8, 12, 271–3

markets as outcomes 274–7
    and the state 68–9, 120–21,
        231–2
    trust in market mechanisms 273
Marshall, Alfred 61–2, 63–4,
    66, 95
    The Economics of Industry 79
    national income estimates 79
    Principles of Economics 61–2,
        63–4, 79, 241
Marshall, Mary, née Paley 79
Marshall Library, Cambridge 62
Marx, Karl 28, 33, 34, 58, 63, 68,
    73, 206
    and agriculture 52
    Capital 34
    and capitalism 48–55, 58, 92,
        117, 192, 240–41
    and class struggle 51–2
    Communist Manifesto (with
        Engels) 47
    financial sector location 117
    and government value 240–41
    'monopoly' gain theory 54
    production boundary 50–51, *51*,
        54, 240
    on 'production' labour and
        value theory 47–56, 57, 64,
        79, 92, 117
    rent theory 54, 55
    and surplus value 48–53, *51*,
        54–5, 68, 73, 79, 92, 117, 192,
        206, 240, 275
    and technological change 192
Matthew, apostle 23
maturity transformation 106–7
maximizing shareholder value
    (MSV) 4, 17, 165–73, 174,
        177, 183–4, 268, 269, 272
    and EPS 178–9

and hurdle rates 176
and PE 167–70, *167*
and short-termism 176
McKinsey and Company 175
Meckling, William 166
Menger, Carl 60
mercantilists 22–7, 26
and free trade 39–40
and Smith 36, 39
Meurrer, Michael J. 205–6
Microsoft 190, 200, 221
Millennium Laboratories 146
Minsky, Hyman 56, 118, 119, 120,
   136, 141, 177
   epigraph 135
Mitterand, François 199
Mondragon 269
monetary policy 103
   and interest rates 244
   'monetarism' 115, 244
   quantitative easing 120
monopolies 9, 217–19
   and the banks 110, 111, 114,
      116, 147–9, 150–51
   and drug prices 212
   and innovation dynamics
      219–20, 227
   Internet and online platforms
      218–20, 221, 272
   listed companies' monopoly
      power 165–6
   Marx's theory of 'monopoly'
      gain 54
   monopoly rent-extraction
      104–5
   and regulation 219–20,
      252
   using monopoly power 109
Morozov, Evgeny 216, 218, 221,
   276–7

mortgage-backed securities (MBS)
   126, 151
mortgages 115–16, 123–4, 125, 126
   and debt 127–8, 131, *131*, 151
   subprime 125
Mun, Sir Thomas 23

Napoleon I 46, 79
NASA 278
NASDAQ 198, 201
national accounting 12–13, 15–16,
   24, 26, 75–100, 127
   and the banking problem 96,
      104–10
   GDP *see* gross domestic product
   government 245–9
   and happiness 98–9, 271
   history of 78–83
   and inequality 100
   inputs = outputs approach 88
   and multiplying value
      248–9, 264
   oddities of 84, 90–98, 121
   and R&D 84, 91
   and the SNA *see* System of
      National Accounts
national bailouts 237
   see also banks/banking: bailouts
National Health Service (NHS),
   UK 211–13, 246
   core principles 253
   hospitals 254, 255
   PFIs and outsourcing 253–6, 258
National Income and Product
   Account (NIPA) 182
National Institute for Health and
   Care Excellence (NICE)
   211–13
National Institutes of Health
   (NIH), US 194, 201, 209

National Venture Capital
Association (NVCA)
198–9
Navigation Act (England
1651) 23
neoclassical economics 57, 59–74,
241, 242, 243–4
and rent 68, 71–4
see also marginalism
Netflix 225
Netscape 204
networks 191, 213–19
externalities 214
and profits 215–16
New Deal 83, 260
New Economics Foundation 256
New York
City 114, 139
HNWIs 143
Stock Exchange 114 *see also*
Wall Street
New York Times 157, 236
Magazine 165
Nixon, Richard 113
non-conformism 59
Non-Profit Distribution (NPD)
model 256
Northern Rock 123
nuclear energy 194

Obamacare 257
Ofcom 89–90
Office for National Statistics,
UK 246
Office of National Statistics
(ONS), US 98
offshore currencies 112
oil price 113
OPEC 113
Openreach 89–90

Organization for Economic
Cooperation and Development
(OECD) 96, 129
Osborne, George 236
Ostrom, Elinor 267–8
outsourcing 251–8
over-the-counter (OTC) derivatives
126, 150
Owen, Robert 58
Oxfam reports
An Economy for the 1% 130
An Economy for the 99%
129–30

Palmisano, Samuel 179
Pareto-optimal markets 68
Pareto, Vilfredo 68
patents
appropriability function 203
Bayh–Dole Act 204
as gatekeepers to knowledge
base 204
and Hatch–Waxman Act 205
inhibiting economy 204–6
and IPR system 202,
203, 206–7, 227
see also intellectual
property rights
lobbying by companies over 268
patent-trolling 205–6
Patent Box policy in taxation
274
pharmaceuticals and the patent
system 205, 207–13, 276
strategic patenting 205
as tool to incentivize innovations
227
and unproductive
entrepreneurship 206–7
and value creation 203

and value extraction 190–91,
    202–13
patient capital 168, 171–4
Paulson, John 109, 156
Paulson and Co. 156
pay *see* wages/earnings
PE *see* private equity
pensions 85, 86–7, 88, 136,
    141–2, 144
  pension funds in risky
    investments 199
  private pensions industry 142
  Royal Mail Pension Plan 258–9
Perez, Carlota 187
Perkins, Tom 199
Personal Contract Plans
    (PCPs) 162
Petty, Sir William 24–5, 26, 26,
    27, 85
pharmaceuticals
  and the patent system 205,
    207–13, 276
  pricing 12, 14, 190,
    207–13, 224
  R&D 209–10, 224, 261, 276
  and risk 193
  US government investment 201
  and VC 201–2
Phoenicians 53
physiocrats 28–33, 30, 117, 239
  production boundary 29, 32–3
Pigou, Arthur Cecil 80
Piketty, Thomas: *Capital in the
    Twenty-First Century* 5
platform capitalism 216–19
platforms 17–18
  online 218–19, 221, 272
Polanyi, Karl 275–6
  The Great Transformation
    231–2, 268

political economy 34
Pollock, Allyson 255
pollution 90, 95, 231,
    250, 267
Portugal 237
poverty 13, 57
preferences 7, 8
  consumer preferences and
    marginal utility theory *see*
    marginalism
  maximization 71
price
  difference between value and
    140–41
  just price 61
  and marginalism 61, 62–3, 64,
    65, 66
  property 94, 128, 156, 272
  regarded as determiner of value
    7–8, 12–13, 271, 272
  and utility 61–3
  value-based pricing 12–13, 14,
    190, 210–13
private equity (PE) 135,
    143, 263
  and asset managers' demands on
    private corporation 173
  buyout funds performance
    158–9, *158*
  capital gains tax 157
  debt to equity ratio in companies
    owned by PE firms 145–6,
    157–8, 169–70
  effects on UK care and water
    industries 168–70, 183
  firms 125, 144–6, 157–9, *158*,
    167–70
  general partners (GPs) 145
  holding time average 175
  limited partners (LPs) 145–6

private equity (PE) – *cont.*
  and MSV 167–70, *167*
  and tax 157, 263
private finance initiatives (PFIs)
  252–8
  vs direct investment 254
privatization
  Chomsky on 'standard technique'
    of 255–6
  and efficiency 257–8
  healthcare 253–6
  and outsourcing 251–8
  'pseudo-privatization' 252
    see also private finance
    initiatives (PFIs)
  Public Choice theory and
    rationale for 249–59
  of rewards 191, 197–202, 220,
    222–5, 259
  of Royal Mail 258–9
  with sell-off of 'good company'
    and public retention of 'bad
    company' 258–9
production/productivity
  capital and labour as
    production's main inputs 69
  distinction between the
    productive and non-productive
    21–3, 26–7, *26*, 66 *see also*
    production boundary; value
    theory
  and division of labour 35,
    50, 191
  and economies of scale 52, 71,
    110, 217
  and the financial sector/banks
    96–7, 102, 106–10, 115–16,
    122–7, 133, 138–40, 141
  and GDP 95, 245
  informal production 96

marginal productivity 63, 66
  see also marginalism
material vs immaterial
  production 37, 40
and physiocrats *see* physiocrats
production enterprises 53
production function 232
and public value *see* public/
  government value
resilience of productive system 6
surplus 38, 46, 48–50
and usefulness 6 *see also*
  marginalism
and wages 129, *129*, 176
production boundary 8–11, *9*,
  15–16, 27, 240
  in the 1600s 24–6, *26*
  in the 1700s 29, 32–3, 78
  in the 1800s 37, *37*, 40, 46,
    50–51, *51*, 54
  and agriculture 29, *29*,
    33, 78
  and financial institutions 10,
    102, 105, 121–2, 138
  and GDP 77–8, 92, 99, 274
  and marginalism 66–9,
    67, 77
  and Marx 50–51, *51*, 54, 240
  and Smith 37, *37*, 40, 275
  and the SNA 84
profits
  Apple 2–3
  and the banks 15
  confused with rent
    272, 274
  of data-owning companies 190
  excessive profit distributions 164
  exploitation of workers for
    49, 192
  and marginalism 66, 69–71, 73

margins 180, 182, *182*,
212–13, 257
and Marx 49, 50, 52, 53–5
maximization 63, 64, 71,
72, 262
networking 215–16
non-financial sector public
company profitability 182, *182*
and patient health 209–13
and production boundaries *see*
production boundary
and Quesnay 32
reinvestment of 163, 168, 187,
223, 227–8, 263, 266
vs rents in GDP 97–8
returned to shareholders 182,
183, 269 *see also* maximizing
shareholder value (MSV)
and Ricardo 42, 43, 44, 45
and Robinson 70
and Senior 59
share price boosting with 3–4, 136
and Smith 39, 40, 41
sources of 52–3
surplus 54
and Turgot 32
and wages in equilibrium 66,
69–71
property income *see* rent
property management services 93–4
prostitution 94
protectionism, mercantilist *see*
mercantilists
public/government value 265–79
concept of 230–31
governing public value 267–9
government in national accounts
85–90, *86*, 245–9
government value added in GDP
85–90, *86*, 245–7

government value in history of
economic thought 239–41
Keynes and counter-cyclical
government 241–4
and Marx 240–41
from public goods to 264–7,
276–7
and Quesnay 239
reassessment for economics of
hope 270–79
and Ricardo 240
and Smith 239–40
undervaluing public sector 18,
229–67, 273
public-private partnerships 275,
276, 278
public banks 160, 185, 196, 251,
256, 265
Public Choice theory 69, 249–52,
259, 260, 273
and rationale for privatization
249–59
public expenditure *see* government
spending/public expenditure
public investment 160, 194, 235,
262, 266
ambition-driven 278
high-risk 220 *see also* risk-
taking: with public funds for
innovation
and PE *158*

quantitative easing (QE) 120
*Quarterly Journal of
Economics* 70
Quesnay, François 28–33, 66, 78
and government value 239
Tableau Économique 28, 30–32,
30, *31*, 239
QWERTY keyboard 214

railways 247
rating agencies 126, 173
RBS 259
Reagan, Ronald 37
rebalancing the economy 44
regulation, financial 5, 89, 105,
    110–12, 114, 115, 116, 120,
    121, 122, 127, 134
  and asset management 143,
    159–60
  light-touch 173
  on monopolies 219–20, 252
  self-regulation 127
  see also deregulation, financial
regulatory capitalism 252
Rehn, Olli 236
Reinhart, Carmen 235–6
renewable energy 110, 262, 279
rent
  as a capitalist necessity 186–7
  classical vs neoclassical
    concepts 73–4
  confused with profit
    272, 274
  extraction/seeking 4–5, 18, 39,
    40, 72, 104–5, 138, 142, 160,
    172–3, 262, 274
  housing, GDP and 93–4
  Marx's theory of 54, 55
  monopoly/oligopoly 150
  neoclassical concept of 68, 71–4
  as principal means of value
    extraction 72
  vs profits in GDP 97–8
  Ricardo's theory of 43–4, 55, 72
  and risk-taking with
    innovation 222
  and Smith 39
research and development (R&D)
  and drug prices 209–10

investment 14, 78, 90, 91, 176,
    184, 187, 224
  and national accounts 84, 91
  pharmaceutical 209–10, 224,
    261, 276
  public R&D agencies 195
  risk-taking in research 184, 187
  Small Business Innovation
    Research Programme 196
  tax credits 14, 224
retail investment funds 135
Retain and Invest strategy 181
Return on Invested Capital
    (ROIC) 176
revaluation, asset 149
Rheinische Zeitung 47
Ricardian socialists 58
Ricardo, David 33, 40–47, 48,
    68, 72
  and agriculture 41–3
  and capitalists 45, 47
  and consumption 45–6
  and government value 240
  growth and accumulation
    theory 42
  and landlords 42–4, 47, 72
  *On the Principles of Political
    Economy and Taxation*
    33–4, 41
  production boundary 46
  rent theory 43–4, 55, 72
  and Smith 41, 45
  and wages 34, 41–2
risk-taking 17, 106, 118, 122–7,
    133, 149, 226–7
  and first mover advantages 191,
    193, 203, 213–19
  and innovation returns 195
  with new technologies 184, 187,
    193, 241, 261

with public funds for innovation 195–6, 197, 223, 241, 261
by shareholders 183–4
sharing risks and rewards of innovation 222–5
socialization of risks 191, 222–5, 259, 264
see also speculation
RJR Nabisco 146
Robbins, Lionel 64, 67
Robinson, Joan 70
Roche 196
Rogoff, Kenneth 235–6
Roosevelt, Franklin D. 260
Royal Mail 258–9
Ryan, Paul 236

sales growth 180, 181, *181*
Samuelson, Paul 70, 243–4
savings 36, 108, 115, 135–6
investment trusts 142
pensions savings and taxation 142
post-war accumulation 141, 142–3
Say, Jean-Baptiste 65
Treatise on Political Economy 61
scarcity 7, 62, 64–5
Schmidt, Eric 194
Schumpeter, Joseph 105–6, 192
Scotland, infrastructure outsourcing 256–8
securitization 109–10, 123–4, 125–6, 128, 162
Senior, Nassau 59
Serco 252, 255, 256, 257
shadow banks 134, 135
share buy-backs 4, 162–5, 164, 176, 180, 276
share turnover, domestic 175
sharing economy 18, 220, 227

shipping Acts 23
short-selling 109
short-termism 174–7, 178
Shredded Wheat 146
Silicon Valley 189, 198–202, 215, 229, 232
silver 23
Simon, Herbert 222
SIRI 194
Small Business Innovation Research Programme 196
Small Business Investment Company 198
smartphone technology 194
Smith, Adam 8, 33, 34–40, 66, 68, 72, 117, 121, 191, 239–40
epigraph 21
and free trade/markets 36, 39, 40, 268, 275
and government value 239–40
on 'invisible hand' of market 36
and mercantilists 36, 39
national income estimates 79
production boundary 37, *37*, 40, 275
and Ricardo 41, 45
Theory of Moral Sentiments 40
value theory 34–40
The Wealth of Nations 33, 35–6, 38, 40, 41, 275
social dislocation 113
Social Enterprise UK 256
socialism 7–8, 47, 58, 64, 79–80
'digital' 215
Solow, Robert 70, 192, 263
Solyndra 223, 261
Soros, George 144
Sovaldi 208–9, 212
Soviet Union 79
US response to Sputnik launch 198

Spain 238
special purpose vehicles
  (SPVs) 126
speculation
  by banks 5, 119, 125, 133
  Keynes on 118–19
  speculative derivatives trading
    112, 123
  taxation of quick speculative
    trades 270
  value extraction *see* value
    extraction
Sports Direct 173
Sraffa, Piero 70
stagflation 113
stakeholder value/theory of business
  184–6, 268–9, 272
state
  agencies 265
  backlash in 1980s against
    government 18, 249
  big government 120, 229, 238
  'entrepreneurial state' 264
  government corruption 69, 232,
    249–50, 262, 265 *see also*
    Public Choice theory
  government failure 69, 249–50,
    259, 264
  government inefficiency
    narratives 231, 265
  government 'thinking big'
    259–60
  intervention in the economy
    120–21, 187–8, 232, 244
  and markets 68–9, 120–21,
    231–2
  and Marx 240–41
  mission-oriented government
    259–62
  policy *see* government policies

public spending *see* government
  spending/public expenditure
public value *see* public/
  government value
role in economic growth and
  value creation 10–11, 229–67
undervaluing public sector 18,
  229–67, 273
steel 27, 29, 97–8, 278
Stiglitz, Joseph 5, 238
stockbrokers 114
Stone, Sir Richard 92
supermarkets 147
supply and demand
  in equilibrium 65–6
  principle of effective demand
    242
syndication loans 146
System of National Accounts
  (SNA)
  1993 revision 107–8
  and black economy 95–7
  emergence of 83–5
  and FISIM 107–9, 147
  Keynes' influence on 82–3
  lack of value theory 98
  and profits vs rents 97–8
  and R&D 91

TA Associates 146
tariffs 27
taxation 10, 240, 241, 271,
  272, 276
  and Apple 2–3
  capital gains tax 3, 157, 198,
    200–201, 273–4
  carbon tax 250
  credits 14, 224
  financial transaction (Tobin) tax
    155–6, 159–60, 276

government dependence
   on revenue from financial
   sector 133
and government spending 46
havens 168
income tax 147
and inequality 274
and innovation 224
lobbying by companies over
   273–4
Patent Box policy 274
and PE 157, 263
and pensions savings 142
of quick speculative trades 270
rates on technology
   companies 220
and VC 224, 263
technology
   collective effort behind technical
      change 263–4
   computers 192–3
   economic theory and
      technological change 192
   governing 276–7
   government investment in 193,
      194, 241, 261
   Marx and technological
      change 192
   military 198
   and networks 191, 213–19
   and participatory democracy
      276–7
   risk-taking with 184, 187, 193,
      241, 261
   smartphone 194
   and social transformation 52
   tax on companies 220
Terra Firma 169
Tesla Motors 223, 261
Texas Instruments 198

Thames Water 109
Thatcher, Margaret 37, 254
Thiel, Peter 196–7
Thomas Aquinas 60–61
Thompson, William 58
Three Delta 169
Tobin, James 99, 155, 278
Tobin Tax 155–6, 159–60, 276
trade unions 58, 64, 114, 147,
   195, 227
training 14
transaction costs 146–7, 155–6,
   253, 255
Transamerica Corporation 172
Trident 11
Turgot, A. R. J. 32–3
Turner, Adair, Baron Turner of
   Ecchinswell 121–2
Twitter 213, 214, 218

Uber 190, 215–16, 217,
   225, 276
unemployment 110, 271
   and austerity 249
   and informal production 96
   Keynes and 'involuntary
      unemployment' 82, 242
   Marshall's state of 'equilibrium'
      and voluntary unemployment
      66–7
United Kingdom (UK)
   asset management 143, 144
   austerity 234–5
   Black Wednesday 144
   British-based banking families/
      trusts 138
   cash proportion of economy 116
   Competition and Credit
      Control 114
   Competition Commission 116

United Kingdom (UK) – *cont.*
customer funding gap 125
exchange control termination 114
financial sector 101, 137–8, 148
forced out of ERM 144
gross value added 1945–2013 *139*
Health and Social Care Act
(2012) 254
Heath government 114
household borrowing
escalation 127
household saving 128
income inequality 128–9, *130*
Labour Party 58, 83, 271
largest public companies 161
National Health Service and
Community Care Act
(1990) 254
NHS *see* National Health Service
(NHS), UK
Office for National Statistics
(ONS) 246
pensions savings and taxation
142
private equity effects on care and
water industries 168–70, 183
stock market 144
stockbrokers 114
Thatcher government 114
United Nations, SNA *see* System of
National Accounts
United States
ARPA-E 194, 195
asset management 143, 144
austerity 234
banking system 111, 113,
115, 148
Bayh–Dole Act 204
and Bretton Woods agreement
111–12, 113

Bureau of Economic Analysis
(BEA) 182
CEO-to-worker compensation
ratio *178*
CEO tenure *179*
concentration of derivatives
contracts *151*
Congressional Budget Office 131
DARPA 194, 195, 266, 278
debt/GDP ratio 236
debt deflation 110
Department of Energy 194,
223, 261
Dodd–Frank Act (2010) 133
Employee Retirement Security
Act (1974) 143
and the Eurodollar 113
FDA 205
Federal government
outsourcing 257
Federal Reserve 119, 120, 131–2
financial corporate profits as
share of domestic total
profits *139*
financial sector 101, 111, 113,
138–9, *139*
GDP 93, 162, *180*, 236
Glass–Steagall Act 111, 112,
114, 123
government spending
justification 89
government stake in Tesla 223
government value added and
expenditure as share of GDP
86, *86*, 89
Hatch–Waxman Act 205
hedge funds 144, 156
household 'investment' in
consumption of durable
goods 115

household saving 128
houses and GDP 93
income inequality 128–9, *130*
investment in pharmaceuticals
    201
investment in technologies 193,
    194, 261
largest public companies 161
manufacturing 138
median CEO pay *177*
mortgage-related debt 131, 151
mutual fund assets and
    charges *154*
National Institutes of Health
    (NIH) 194, 201, 209
New Deal 83, 260
Obamacare 257
patentability domain
    expansion 204
PE-backed companies as
    percentage of all US
    companies *167*
pension funds/savings
    142, 143
property prices 128, 156
response to USSR's Sputnik
    launch 198
share buy-backs 163, *164*
Small Business
    Administration 198
Small Business Innovation
    Research Programme 196
stagnant wages 129, *129*
taxation and pension
    savings 142
VC industry 197–202, 263
Veterans Administration 209
Wall Street *see* Wall Street
Works Progress Administration
    (WPA) 260

usury 61, 72, 96
utility
    individual 61
    and Jevons 60
    marginal utility theory of value
        see marginalism
    maximization 63, 64, 68,
        71, 72
    and Menger 60
    origin of utility theory
        61–2
    and prices 61–3

value
    added 77–8, 83, 85–90, *86*,
        95, 97, 102, 105, 106, 107–8,
        110, 122, 124, 136, 138,
        139, 150, 180, 245–7,
        249
    creation *see* value and wealth
        creation/creators
    defining 6–8, 14
    difference between price and
        140–41
    digital 219–21
    exchange value 48
    extraction *see* value extraction
    history of 21–56
    in labour 33–56, 57, 64, 79, 92,
        220–22
    and mercantilists 22–7, 26
    multiplying 248–9, 264
    and preferences *see* preferences
    price regarded as determiner of
        7–8, 12–13, 271, 272 *see also*
        value-based pricing
    public sector *see* public/
        government value
    reassessment for economics of
        hope 270–79

value – *cont.*
    redistribution 9, 30, 41, 55,
        231, 263
    and scarcity 7, 62, 64–5
    shareholder maximization *see*
        maximizing shareholder value
        (MSV)
    and spending 90
    stakeholder 184–6, 268–9, 272
    surplus 48–53, *51*, 54–5, 68, 73,
        79, 92, 117, 192, 206,
        240, 275
    theory *see* value theory
    and utility in marginalism *see*
        marginalism
    and utility in neoclassical
        economics 60
    wages as value of labour power
        52 *see also* wages/earnings
    and wealth terminology 6–7
value extraction 6
    Apple's 2–4
    common critiques 4–6
    digital value 219–21
    and financial bubbles 120
    and the financial sector 110, 117,
        118–19, 120, 121, 133–4,
        136–7, 142, 146–59
    from financialization 182–3, 187
    and innovation dynamics
        220–21
    and Keynes 118–19
    makers vs takers 1–8, 9–10
    MSV *see* maximizing
        shareholder value
    patented 190–91, 202–13
    rent as principal means of 72
    rent extraction/seeking 4–5,
        18, 39, 40, 72, 104–5, 138,
        142, 182–3

    through innovation economy
        189–228
    and transaction costs 146–7,
        155–6, 253, 255
    and unproductive
        entrepreneurship 190–91,
        206–7
    value creation confused with
        2, 4, 100, 121, 136–7, 138,
        271, 274
    through VC *see* venture capital
value theory 6–8, 270–71
    classical economics, and value in
        labour 33–56, 220–22
    and GDP 77–82
    importance of 11–15
    marginalist *see* marginalism
    Marx 47–56, 57, 64, 79, 117
    and national accounting 78–100
    neoclassical economics 57,
        59–74, 241
    and physiocrats 28–33, 29, 30
    and Ricardian socialists 58
    Ricardo 40–47
    rise of 27–33
    Smith 34–40
    subjective 7, 13
value and wealth creation/creators 6
    2007–8 global crisis and wealth
        creators 141, 270
    and the banks *see* banks/
        banking: 'productivity' and
        value/money creation
    collective nature of innovation
        and 184, 185, 194–5,
        222–3, 226–7, 263–4,
        274, 279
    confusion between value creation
        and extraction 2, 4, 100, 121,
        136–7, 138, 271, 274

and 'creative destruction'
    189–90, 192
digital value 219–21
dominant narrative of
    entrepreneurs as wealth
    creators 203
and hope 270–79
through innovation *see*
    innovation
link between structuring of
    activities and value creation
    13–15
makers vs takers 1–8, 9–10
narratives and myths about 12,
    17–18, 189–90, 268, 271–2
and patents 203 *see also* patents
and public value *see* public/
    government value
and risk taking *see* risk-taking
state's role in economic growth
    and value creation 10–11,
    229–67
value-based pricing 12, 15,
    190, 210–13
Vanguard 153
venture capital (VC) 14–15, 143,
    156–7, 263
    innovation and timing 195–202
    and IPOs 199–202
    NVCA 198–9
    public funds 195–6
    Silicon Valley VC industry
        198–202
    and tax 224, 263
viagra 191
Volkswagen, 'dieselgate' 173, 185–6
Voltaire 78

wages/earnings 39, 48
    CEO 177, 178, *178*

earnings margins 180
earnings per share (EPS) 163,
    178–9, 180
and economic growth 114
finance employee compensation
    share of national employment
    share 139, *140*, 149–50, *150*
and GAAP 179–80
just deserts and the socialization
    of rewards 222–5, 263–4
keeping executive pay in
    check 187
and marginalism 66, 69–71,
    72–3
median CEO pay in US *177*
and productivity 129, *129*, 176
and profits in equilibrium 66,
    69–71
and Ricardian socialists 58
and Ricardo 34, 41–2
and Smith 39, 41
stagnant 110, 129, *129*, 270–71
and trade unions 147
underestimation of purchasing
    power 82
US ratio of CEO-to-worker
    compensation *178*
as value of labour power 52
wage share 43, 51, 129
see also income
Wall Street 118, 167, 215
    Crash (1933) 111, 118, 138
Walras, Léon 59, 73–4
water companies (UK) 169–70,
    183
Water Services Regulation
    Authority (Ofwat) 170
Watson, Tom, Jr 179
wealth creation *see* value and
    wealth creation/creators

wealth extraction *see* value
    extraction
Welch, Jack 184
welfare maximization 68
working hours 227
World Bank 71, 251
World Federation of
    Exchanges 175
World Health Organization 253

WorldCom 173
Wyden, Ron 208

Xerox Parc 193, 198

Yahoo 218
Yozma 195–6

Zuckerberg, Mark 189

Stuart Robinson

Mariana Mazzucato is Professor in the Economics of Innovation and Public Value at University College London (UCL), where she is also Founder and Director of the Institute for Innovation and Public Purpose. Her widely published research focuses on the relationship between public policy, innovation, and economic growth and she advises policymakers around the world on how to steer innovation so that it produces growth that is more inclusive and sustainable. She is author of the highly acclaimed book *The Entrepreneurial State: Debunking Public vs. Private Sector Myths* and co-editor of *Rethinking Capitalism: Economics and Policy for Sustainable and Inclusive Growth*. She is winner of the 2014 *New Statesman* SPERI Prize in Political Economy, the 2015 Hans-Matthöfer-Preis and the 2018 Leontief Prize for Advancing the Frontiers of Economic Thought. She was named as one of the 'three most important thinkers about innovation' in *New Republic*.

PublicAffairs is a publishing house founded in 1997. It is a tribute to the standards, values, and flair of three persons who have served as mentors to countless reporters, writers, editors, and book people of all kinds, including me.

I. F. STONE, proprietor of *I. F. Stone's Weekly*, combined a commitment to the First Amendment with entrepreneurial zeal and reporting skill and became one of the great independent journalists in American history. At the age of eighty, Izzy published *The Trial of Socrates*, which was a national bestseller. He wrote the book after he taught himself ancient Greek.

BENJAMIN C. BRADLEE was for nearly thirty years the charismatic editorial leader of *The Washington Post*. It was Ben who gave the *Post* the range and courage to pursue such historic issues as Watergate. He supported his reporters with a tenacity that made them fearless and it is no accident that so many became authors of influential, best-selling books.

ROBERT L. BERNSTEIN, the chief executive of Random House for more than a quarter century, guided one of the nation's premier publishing houses. Bob was personally responsible for many books of political dissent and argument that challenged tyranny around the globe. He is also the founder and longtime chair of Human Rights Watch, one of the most respected human rights organizations in the world.

·　　·　　·

For fifty years, the banner of Public Affairs Press was carried by its owner Morris B. Schnapper, who published Gandhi, Nasser, Toynbee, Truman, and about 1,500 other authors. In 1983, Schnapper was described by *The Washington Post* as "a redoubtable gadfly." His legacy will endure in the books to come.

Peter Osnos, *Founder*

9 781541 758247